WOLVERINE
WEAPON X FILES

WOLVERINE
WEAPON X FILES

Front Cover Artist: FRANK MARTIN JR.

WOLVERINE: WEAPON X FILES

Head Writer/Coordinator
JEFF CHRISTIANSEN

Coordinating Assistants: STUART VANDAL,
MIKE O'SULLIVAN, SEAN MCQUAID
& MADISON CARTER

Art Refurbishment:
MIKE FICHERA & JASON LEWIS

Writers
RONALD BYRD, STUART VANDAL,
ERIC J. MOREELS, CHAD ANDERSON,
MICHAEL HOSKIN, MIKE FICHERA,
MARKUS RAYMOND, JEPH YORK,
JACOB ROUGEMONT & MADISON CARTER

Wolverine Gallery & Select Character Artwork
PACO DIAZ LUQUE

Art Reconstruction
POND SCUM & NELSON RIBEIRO

Select Coloring
TOM SMITH

WOLVERINE ENCYCLOPEDIA 1-2

Introduction
LARRY HAMA

Text Writers
PAUL BENJAMIN
PETER SANDERSON
DAVE RIOS
MARK ROBERT BOURNE

Design & Layout
DAN DANKO

Collection Editor
MARK D. BEAZLEY

Assistant Editors
JOHN DENNING & ALEX STARBUCK

Editor, Special Projects
JENNIFER GRÜNWALD

Senior Editor, Special Projects
JEFF YOUNGQUIST

Copy Editor
BRIAN OVERTON

Production
RYAN DEVALL

Book Designer
RODOLFO MURAGUCHI

Senior Vice President of Sales
DAVID GABRIEL

Editor in Chief
JOE QUESADA

Publisher
DAN BUCKLEY

Executive Producer
ALAN FINE

Special Thanks to JEPH YORK
and DERIC MARSHALL

Editors Note: Volume 3 of Wolverine
Encyclopedia was never printed.
As such, there are no entries for
sections S-Z.

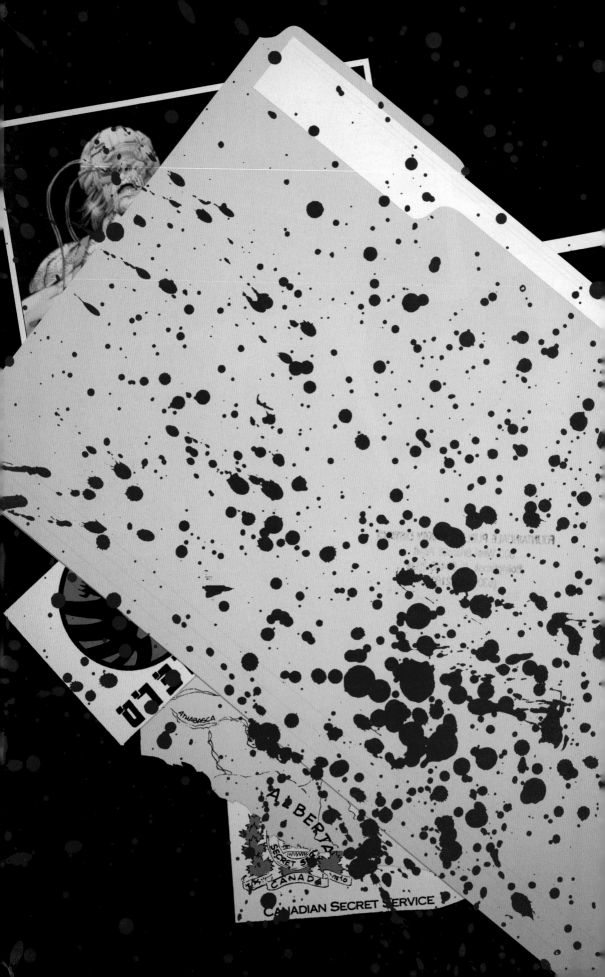

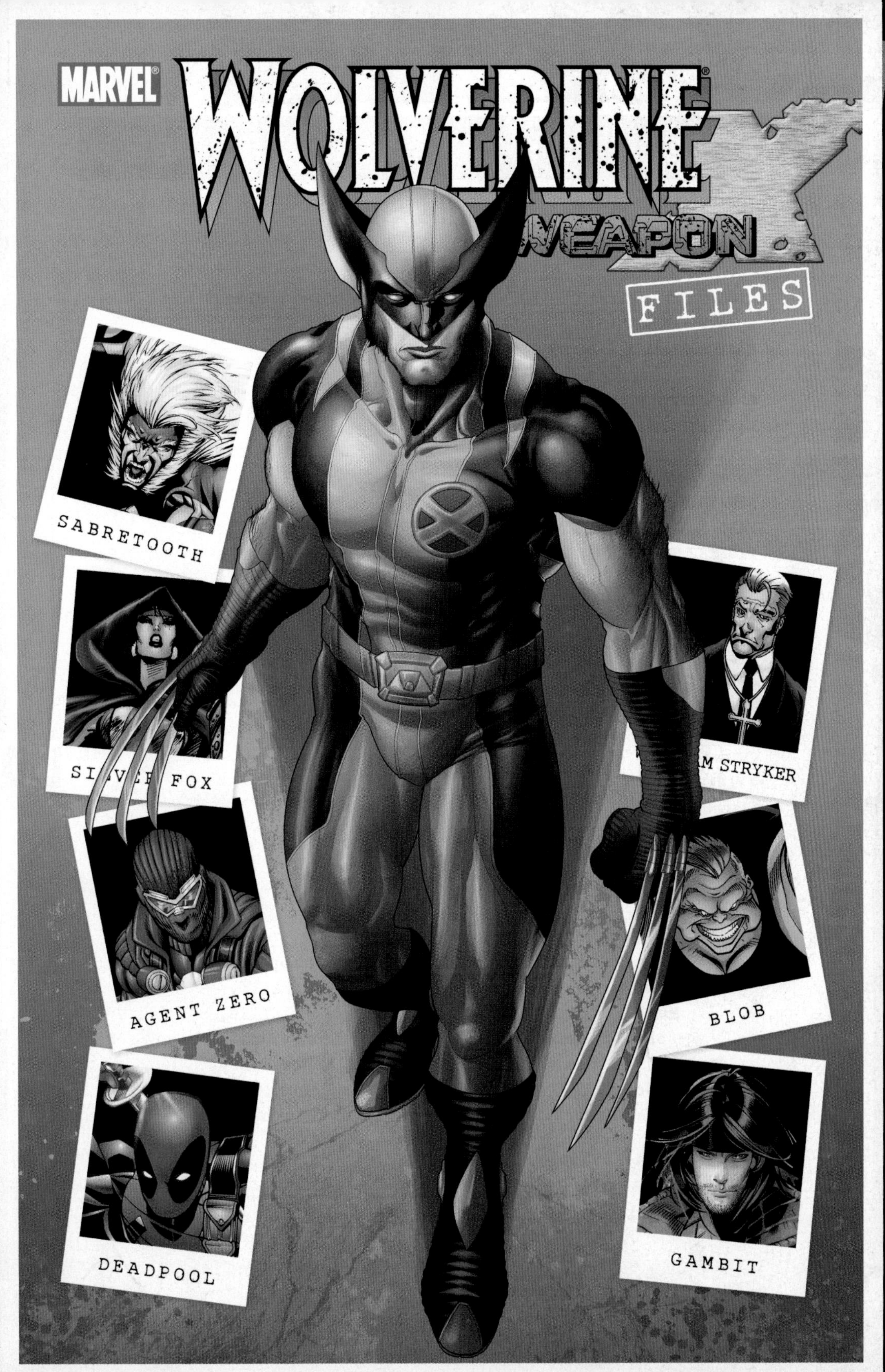

MARVEL
WOLVERINE
WEAPON X
FILES
SABRETOOTH
FOX
STRYKER
AGENT ZERO
BLOB
DEADPOOL
GAMBIT

WOLVERINE: WEAPON X FILES

Head Writer/Coordinator
JEFF CHRISTIANSEN

Coordination Assistants
STUART VANDAL, MIKE O'SULLIVAN,
SEAN MCQUAID & MADISON CARTER

Art Refurbishment
MIKE FICHERA & JASON LEWIS

Writers
RONALD BYRD, STUART VANDAL,
ERIC J. MOREELS, CHAD ANDERSON,
MICHAEL HOSKIN, MIKE FICHERA,
MARKUS RAYMOND, JEPH YORK, JACOB
ROUGEMONT & MADISON CARTER

Wolverine Gallery
& Select Character Artwork
PACO DIAZ LUQUE & THOMAS
MASON

Cover Artist
FRANK MARTIN JR.

Cover Design
RODOLFO MURAGUCHI

Art Reconstruction
POND SCUM & NELSON RIBEIRO

Select Coloring
TOM SMITH

Production
NELSON RIBEIRO & JERRON
QUALITY COLOR

Editor
JEFF YOUNGQUIST

Editors, Special Projects
MARK D. BEAZLEY & JENNIFER
GRÜNWALD

Assistant Editors
JOHN DENNING & CORY LEVINE

Editorial Assistant
ALEX STARBUCK

Copy Editor
BRIAN OVERTON

Senior Vice President of Sales
DAVID GABRIEL

Editor in Chief
JOE QUESADA

Publisher
DAN BUCKLEY

Executive Producer
ALAN FINE

Special thanks to
the guys at the Appendix (www.marvunapp.com),
www.g-mart.com, Tom Brevoort, Chris Allo,
Martin Allen, Thomas Coffman, Warren Ellis,
John Freeman, Marc Guggenheim, Larry Hama,
Clayton Henry, Christian Hinson, Bruce Jones,
Joe Kelly, Howard Mackie, Sean McQuaid,
John Ney Rieber, Fred Van Lente & Christopher Yost

The Official Handbook of the Marvel Universe Frequently Asked Questions page
— including data corrections and explanations, complete bibliographies, and Power
Grid legends: http://www.marvel.com/universe/OHOTMU

HISTORY: For millennia, Azrael has served as the Angel of Death. He has stalked the world since at least 200 BC, sending souls to the afterlife and slaying those who disrupt death's natural patterns, either by repeatedly surviving beyond their allotted time or regularly ending others' lives too soon. Opponents who killed Azrael's corporeal form won the right to battle Azrael in Purgatory if slain later, and to escape the afterlife if they prevailed again. Most of these victors would be trapped within their own rotting corpses, but those who could heal fatal wounds lived anew until they died again and repeated the cycle of challenge and rebirth.

On April 22, 1915, centuries since his last defeat, Azrael stalked Belgium's Ypres battlefield and confronted Canadian soldier Logan (James Howlett, later Wolverine), who possessed a healing factor and berserker nature. The pair battled, but Logan survived being impaled on Azrael's sword and used the blade against Azrael. Surprised at a mortal taking his weapon, Azrael was physically slain. Seconds later, Azrael's spirit told the shocked Logan they would meet again, then both apparition and corpse vanished. Gripped by ennui over the next few weeks, Logan ultimately attempted suicide. Sensing his intent, Azrael appeared and taunted Logan, angering him out of his depression. For decades Azrael would confront Logan each time he suffered a life-threatening injury. Logan continued to win, but with greater difficulty each time. Azrael's desire for vengeance grew, as did his anger that Logan had slain far more than his share of lives.

By the modern era, with Logan now Wolverine, another had drawn Azrael's attention and ire: Phaedra, who could resurrect the dead, but whose powers protected her from Azrael. Still unable to defeat Logan, Azrael bargained with Phaedra to have her kill Wolverine. To aid her, she resurrected the Logan-slain warrior Shingen Harada. Logan himself was slain by Gorgon, leader of the Hand organization, and Phaedra resurrected him as a Hand agent, controlling him by stealing a piece of his soul, which she placed inside the animated armor Shogun. Though Logan soon broke the Hand's control, he felt listless, unaware that part of him was missing, and over the next few months died repeatedly. Still needing to break Logan's will to live, Shogun killed Logan's lover Azir and then Logan himself, and this time Azrael won their bout. Logan's body healed, but his soul remained in Purgatory, until Sorcerer Supreme Dr.

REAL NAME: Apparently Azrael
ALIASES: Lazaer, Angel of Death, many others
IDENTITY: Existence as genuine angel of death widely believed a myth; (Lazaer) Secret
OCCUPATION: Angel of Death
CITIZENSHIP: Heaven
PLACE OF BIRTH: Unrevealed, possibly inapplicable
KNOWN RELATIVES: Undefined relationship to other angels
GROUP AFFILIATION: Heaven's Archangels
EDUCATION: Unrevealed
FIRST APPEARANCE: Wolverine #48 (2007)

Stephen Strange helped restore it to his body. Tracking down Phaedra, Logan learned of her arrangement with Azrael. Logan's split soul permitted Azrael to again fight Logan in the physical world, but Logan offered to kill Phaedra in return for Azrael making his soul whole again. Regarding Phaedra's resurrecting as a greater affront than Logan's ongoing survival, Azrael agreed, though he warned Logan that restoring his soul negated their previous arrangement, and the mutant's next death would be permanent.

NOTE: *It is unclear how or if Azrael may be related to the Angel of Death who empowered Dark Angel (Shevaun Haldane), or other death avatars such as John Kowalski. The sorceress Morgan Le Fay once invoked Azrael's name in relation to the Ebony Blade, but any prior association of Azrael with that sword remains unrevealed.*

HEIGHT: Variable   **EYES:** Variable
WEIGHT: Variable   **HAIR:** Variable

ABILITIES/ACCESSORIES: Azrael is immortal, neither aging nor vulnerable to mortal frailties such as disease. He can manifest anywhere either corporeally or as an immaterial apparition, allowing instantaneous travel across the universe. Though he can be defeated in combat and his corporeal form killed, he can re-manifest immediately, although he cannot challenge his victorious opponent again on the physical plane, and must battle them in Purgatory for the right to return to life if they subsequently die. He can also heal damaged souls. Azrael is seemingly aware of imminent death, and of those who break death's natural order, gaining an instant knowledge of their background and recent activities. An exceptionally skilled armed and unarmed fighter, he wields a sword able to cut through most substances with ease. He has no scent.

POWER GRID	1	2	3	4	5	6	7
INTELLIGENCE*							
STRENGTH							
SPEED**							
DURABILITY							
ENERGY PROJECTION							
FIGHTING SKILLS							

*AWARENESS OF THOSE BREAKING DEATH'S NATURAL ORDER
** AZRAEL IS A TELEPORTER

Art by Humberto Ramos with Howard Chaykin (inset)

BLOB

REAL NAME: Frederick "Fred" J. Dukes
ALIASES: "Freddie"
IDENTITY: Known to authorities
OCCUPATION: Actor; former criminal, terrorist, government agent, carnival performer
CITIZENSHIP: USA, with a criminal record
PLACE OF BIRTH: Lubbock, Texas
KNOWN RELATIVES: None
GROUP AFFILIATION: Formerly X-Corps, Brotherhood of Mutants, Freedom Force, Defenders impersonators, Brotherhood of Evil Mutants, Factor Three
EDUCATION: Unrevealed
FIRST APPEARANCE: X-Men #3 (1964)

HISTORY: Believing himself a freak after he developed an obese and super-massive body, Fred Dukes used his newfound mutant abilities as a carnival performer nicknamed "the Blob." Detecting Dukes' mutant status, telepath Charles Xavier sent his X-Men to invite Dukes to meet with him and Dukes accepted, mostly out of attraction to the beautiful young X-Man Jean Grey. At the X-Men's mansion, Xavier invited Dukes to join their team but he arrogantly refused, believing himself superior to them. Xavier decided to wipe the knowledge of the X-Men from Dukes' mind, but Dukes escaped back to the carnival, took it over, and led his fellow performers to attack the X-Men. They were defeated, and Xavier wiped their memories of the incident as well as the Blob's knowledge of the X-Men. Later, Magneto (Max Eisenhardt) offered Dukes membership in his terrorist Brotherhood of Evil Mutants. A blow to the head restored Dukes' lost memories and he accepted Magneto's offer, joining the Brotherhood in attacking the X-Men; however, during the battle, Magneto sent a barrage of torpedoes at the X-Men, not caring that Dukes was in the way. Uninjured but feeling betrayed, Dukes quit the Brotherhood

and rejoined the carnival. Dukes subsequently met fellow mutant Unus the Untouchable, and under subliminal commands from Xavier's enemy, Lucifer, the pair tried to frame the X-Men as thieves. The duo became fast friends and went on to join Factor Three, an organization that sought world conquest; but the X-Men soon convinced the Blob and his teammates that their leader, the Mutant Master, was merely using them, and the two groups joined forces to expose him as an extraterrestrial subversive before the defeated Mutant Master killed himself.

Soon after, the Blob was among those mutants captured by Larry Trask's giant robotic Sentinels, but was freed after the X-Men defeated them. Blob, Unus and Mastermind (Jason Wyngarde) re-formed the Brotherhood and were contacted by the power-dampening mutant Krueger, who had captured some X-Men and was hoping to sell them to the Brotherhood. Dukes had Mastermind create illusory money to fool Krueger, and sought revenge on the X-Men by trapping them in an illusory circus; however, the ruse collapsed after Krueger confronted the Brotherhood over their treachery, and the X-Men defeated the villains. Escaping custody, Blob's Brotherhood next tried to fool the Beast (Hank McCoy) into believing he had killed Iron Man (Tony Stark), thus manipulating McCoy into joining them. After realizing the truth, the Beast single-handedly defeated them. Dukes briefly re-formed Factor Three, and used information stolen from Xavier's computers to seek more mutant recruits. They kidnapped young mutant Sonny Baredo (the future Humus Sapien), though the Blob and others soon left him behind at Factor Three's Mount Charteris base with its caretaker, the Ogre (Brian Dunlap). Subsequently, Dukes, his mutant teammates and other mutants were captured by the subversive Secret Empire. They were ultimately freed by the combined efforts of the X-Men, Captain America (Steve Rogers) and the Falcon (Sam Wilson). Following Magneto's return, Dukes rejoined the Brotherhood and aided Magneto in an attempted world takeover using Magneto's creation, the powerful "Alpha, the Ultimate Mutant," but they were opposed by Xavier and the Defenders. Alpha ultimately turned on the Brotherhood, regressing them to infancy. Later restored to adulthood by the alien Shi'ar's Eric the Red (Davan Shakari), Dukes and the Brotherhood fought Los Angeles' Champions but were defeated.

Dukes then briefly joined a band of super-criminals posing as the Defenders during the heroes' "Defender for a Day" recruitment drive, but they were defeated by a Defenders team led by Hercules (Heracles). Later, Dukes was freed from prison by the shape-shifting mutant terrorist Mystique and joined her reorganized Brotherhood of Evil Mutants in an attempted assassination of presidential candidate Senator Robert Kelly, which the X-Men thwarted. Mystique's Brotherhood next attacked the Avengers, but again met with defeat. Dukes then joined Unus in battling the Hulk (Bruce Banner) and subsequently witnessed Unus' apparent death, which sent Blob on a grief-stricken rampage that was quelled by Spider-Man (Peter Parker) and the Black Cat. After Mystique had the US government pardon the Brotherhood for their crimes in exchange for becoming federal agents as Freedom Force, their first mission was to capture Magneto. Subsequent missions saw Freedom Force battling the X-Men, X-Factor, the Avengers, the New Mutants, Daredevil (Matt Murdock), the Grip, the Reavers, the Hulk and Firestar. During this time, Dukes also helped train replacement Captain America John Walker, who subsequently accompanied Freedom Force in fighting the Resistants.

After a disastrous Middle East clash with the Arab super-team Desert Sword, Dukes and his teammate Pyro were captured by Iraqi military forces and served for a time as the Iraqi commander's personal bodyguards until the Toad arranged for their release. Dukes and Pyro agreed to join the Toad's new Brotherhood. Following defeats at the hands of X-Force and X-Factor, Freedom Force's replacement as the government's sanctioned mutant team, the Brotherhood sought to capture the mutant Portal but were opposed by Darkhawk, Sleepwalker

AFTER WEIGHT LOSS

and Spider-Man. Overlooked for recruitment into Magneto's Acolytes, Dukes and the Brotherhood accompanied Pyro, who had contracted the deadly Legacy virus, to the island home of Jonathan Chambers, aka Empyrean, a mutant who drained the energy expended by those dying of the virus to ease their pain. Empyrean subsequently duped Dukes and the Brotherhood into stealing a time machine created by the X-Man Beast to allow Empyrean to travel back in time and release the Legacy virus earlier, but the X-Men intervened and Empyrean was instead sent back to a prehistoric age. The psionic monster Onslaught later augmented Blob's powers in exchange for his servitude. Teamed with the power-copying Mimic, Dukes battled the female members of the Cable-trained X-Force but was defeated by Meltdown (Tabitha Smith), who threatened to explode a plasma ball inside his body. After Onslaught was defeated, both Dukes and Mimic offered their services to the "favor trader" Sledge, who in turn granted them better control of their abilities.

After a clash with the mercenary Maverick (Christoph Nord), Dukes formed a new Brotherhood with Mimic, Post and Toad. On the run from the nanite-mutated computer Cerebro, Blob's Brotherhood broke Xavier out of a government facility so he could train them to better combat Cerebro. After helping the X-Men against Cerebro, Blob's Brotherhood was recruited by Mystique to recover the robotic Machine Man (X-51)'s head. After that failed mission, Dukes tried to hijack an armored car on his own, but Spider-Man defeated him. Mystique then assumed leadership of the Brotherhood and sent them to attempt another assassination of Kelly, but they again failed due to the intervention of the X-Men and a dying Pyro, who sacrificed himself to save Kelly. Blob subsequently joined the mutant army Magneto was amassing on the island nation of Genosha, but the X-Men defeated them. Later, Dukes and his former teammate Avalanche were among the mutant criminals forcibly recruited into Banshee's paramilitary X-Corps group, until it disbanded following infiltration by Mystique. After he was overlooked for a new Brotherhood formed by Magneto's former Acolyte Exodus, an aimless Dukes consulted psychologist Sean Garrison, who convinced him to be true to himself. Believing that "truth" lay in opposing the X-Men, Dukes went to the Xavier Institute only to find the X-Men absent. He attacked nonetheless, but was defeated by the school's students and taken into custody.

One of the many mutants depowered by the reality-warping Scarlet Witch, Dukes found he had lost his excess mass, but not the stretched skin which once covered it, resulting in tremendous folds hanging loosely off his frame. Distraught, Dukes attempted suicide by cutting his throat, but found the knife could not penetrate the excess skin. Overeating soon restored some of his weight, though not his powers. Elijah Cross recruited Dukes and other depowered mutants into the terrorist X-Cell, who clashed with X-Factor Investigations. Moving to Japan, Dukes shed his excess mass and became a media sensation as a weight-loss guru. He was then cast as the lead in amnesiac Eternal Kingo Sunen's latest movie, a science fiction epic filmed before the gigantic cosmic alien known as the Dreaming Celestial in San Francisco; however, this was part of a plot by the High Evolutionary to sample the Celestial's power. Dukes allied with the Evolutionary and Magneto as they embarked on the next phase of the Evolutionary's plan.

FREEDOM FORCE UNIFORM

HEIGHT: 5'10" EYES: Brown
WEIGHT: 182 lbs.; previously 510 lbs. HAIR: Brown

ABILITIES/ACCESSORIES: Dukes has recently gained some experience in marketing and acting. His former Blob powers related to the mass, strength, resilience and indestructibility of his then-obese body. Originally, he did not possess superhuman strength in proportion to his size; however, he underwent further mutation at various points in his life, greatly increasing his height and mass, and raising his strength to superhuman levels. In his later career, the Blob could lift 5 tons; while briefly enhanced by Onslaught, Blob may have achieved superhuman class 75 strength and could also shift his mass.

The Blob could become virtually immovable at will as long as he remained in contact with the ground, bonding himself to the ground beneath him by force of will, in effect creating a mono-directional increase of gravity extending about 5 feet in radius from his center of balance. His body's fat tissues could painlessly absorb and disperse kinetic energy, with large projectiles recoiling from his body while smaller ones embedded themselves in his fat; he could then expel these smaller objects by merely flexing his muscles. In addition, he could trap an opponent within the folds of his flesh. The Blob's skin could not be punctured, lacerated, frostbitten or ravaged by any skin disease, due in part to the skin's elasticity and toughness and in part to the highly accelerated rate at which his skin cells grew and replaced themselves. His skin was somewhat less resistant to burning, which also caused him far greater pain than impacts or other assaults. His eyes, ears, nose and mouth were not as resistant to injury as the rest of his body. He was somewhat limited in flexibility by his body's extreme volume.

Initially after losing his powers, the Blob possessed only the physical abilities of an unfit and obese man, though he could still use his mass and volume to some advantage against smaller opponents. While his X-Corps teammates used technology to replace their lost powers, there was no evidence of Blob doing so.

POWER GRID	1	2	3	4	5	6	7
INTELLIGENCE							
STRENGTH							
SPEED							
DURABILITY							
ENERGY PROJECTION							
FIGHTING SKILLS							

* BEFORE DEPOWERING

X-CORPS UNIFORM | ONSLAUGHT ENHANCED

CHIMERA

REAL NAME: Unrevealed
ALIASES: "Gaslight Frail"
IDENTITY: Known to authorities
OCCUPATION: Extradimensional terrorist
CITIZENSHIP: Unrevealed
PLACE OF BIRTH: Unrevealed
KNOWN RELATIVES: None
GROUP AFFILIATION: Sisterhood of Evil Mutants
EDUCATION: Unrevealed
FIRST APPEARANCE: Wolverine #97 (1996)

HISTORY: Having committed crimes across the multiverse for years, Chimera was hired by Genesis (Tyler Dayspring) on Earth-616 to free Cyber (Silas Burr) from his captivity by the extradimensional firm of Landau, Luckman, and Lake (LL&L), who use Warp Chamber doors to travel across the dimensions. Chimera freed Cyber, callously murdering his guards for fun, and escaped through a WC. LL&L equipped their teenage agent Emmett to pursue her, and he nicknamed her the "Gaslight Frail" as he chased her through different realities. Chimera began studying Earth mutant Wolverine (Logan/James Howlett) for Genesis, and soon clashed with him, but fled into another dimension after Wolverine put his claws through one of her hands. Chimera delivered the information on Wolverine to Genesis, then returned to her extradimensional crimes.

Chimera traveled to the Crunch at the End of Time and convinced several deadly Plasma Wraiths – bizarre, temporally-powered, leather-clad automatons with sharp claws – to serve her. Still purused by LL&L, Chimera learned the firm planned to recruit Wolverine. Seeking to stop this, Chimera set a trap for Wolverine by luring the parasitic Dirt Nap through a Warp Chamber. Things quickly got out of hand when Wolverine, Emmett, Dirt Nap, Donna Diego (the multi-colored human-symbiote later known as Scream) and a technologically advanced ship (a size-changing, symbiote-tracking vessel used by the extraterrestrial symbiote-devouring Phage which had followed Venom through the Warp Chamber), which had accidentally ensnared Earth youths Jerry and Rocky, passed back through the Warp Chamber in a bizarre battle. After taking the valuable Phage ship for herself, Chimera fled through the Warp Chamber to Earth and placed a Lepton Imploder on the WC, hoping the deadly technology would destroy the Warp Chamber and forever trap Wolverine and his allies, but the heroes survived using Emmett's Quark Emulation Disruptor. Chimera savagely ensnared Wolverine in barbed chains with her telekinesis, but he advanced on her, liberating the Phage Ship. Chimera soon activated another Imploder but fell through the dimensional walls with Dirt Nap and the Wraiths while the heroes escaped.

When Earth villains Emplate (Marius St. Croix) and DOA (George Baker) opened a WC door, they found Chimera and the others, who agreed to ally with Emplate in an attempt to increase his powers. Thinking the use of another Warp Chamber was too unreliable, Chimera used another Imploder to return them to Earth; there they fought young mutants Generation X while Emplate assimilated his sisters, Nicole and Claudette St. Croix, forming the deadly M-Plate. Chimera used her dragons to defend herself against the attacking mutants, but Emma Frost, Generation X's mentor, stunned Chimera with a telepathic blast. Chimera quickly recovered and escaped with M-Plate, who used his new powers to open a dimensional interface. M-Plate took them to the Universal Amalgamator and revealed his plan to join all sentient beings into a single, all-encompassing awareness. When Chimera balked at the plan, M-Plate seemingly incinerated her and was later defeated by Generation X. Chimera, exhibiting greater control of her dragons, was later seen operating as a hitman in Earth-616's Madripoor, where the enigmatic Red Queen recruited her into the Sisterhood of Evil Mutants. She aided the Sisterhood in recruiting Lady Deathstrike from Spiral's Body Shoppe and participated in a savage attack upon the X-Men.

HEIGHT: 6'1"   **EYES:** Blue
WEIGHT: 140 lbs.   **HAIR:** Blonde

ABILITIES/ACCESSORIES: Said to wield the wind between realities, Chimera can form deadly telekinetic "dragons," wearing them like sock puppets that she can extend from her hands; the dragons are composed of telekinetic energy which she can extend from her own form to ensnare opponents or pick up objects. Chimera possesses rudimentary telekinesis and has access to weapons from across the dimensions. Her mental stability is questionable.

POWER GRID	1	2	3	4	5	6	7
INTELLIGENCE							
STRENGTH							
SPEED							
DURABILITY							
ENERGY PROJECTION							
FIGHTING SKILLS							

HISTORY: Nguyen Ngoc Coy was a Vietnamese army general and a crimelord, secretly running the Saigon Black Market. When his nephew Tranh developed the mutant ability to possess minds, Coy employed him in his organization — but during a period of internal strife in Vietnam, Coy and Tranh fled to the USA with aid from the Kingpin (Wilson Fisk), one of Coy's international narcotics customers. Coy created a prosperous power base in New York City's underworld. Tranh's three siblings eventually escaped Vietnam as well, but Xi'an, who shared Tranh's abilities, refused a similar place in Coy's organization. When the terrorist Viper tried to assassinate Coy, Tranh stopped her and forced her into Coy's harem. Shortly thereafter, Coy kidnapped Xi'an's siblings Leong and Nga and demanded that Xi'an work for him. Desperate, Xi'an briefly possessed Spider-Man (Peter Parker), hoping to use him to free the twins. The Fantastic Four helped defeat Coy's henchmen, while Xi'an absorbed Tranh's essence. With Tranh's discorporation, all of Coy's slaves were freed, and he fled New York. Moving to San Francisco, Coy employed Deathstroke (Tani Uiruson) and his Terminators and the mercenary Flying Tiger, but Spider-Woman (Jessica Drew) foiled several of Coy's operations. When Coy met with the Kingpin, the Deterrence Research Corporation tried to assassinate both crimelords, hoping to spark a gang war, but Spider-Woman saved them.

Xi'an, now Karma, was later possessed by the Shadow King, and became the head of a Los Angeles Gladiatorial arena. "Karma" framed Coy when the police broke up the ring, and he relocated to Madripoor, where he employed superhuman muscle Roughouse and Bloodsport (later Bloodscream). When an unrevealed party kidnapped Leong and Nga, a desperate Karma rejoined Coy in exchange for using his underworld contacts to search for the twins. With the covert support of Madripoor's Prince Baran, Coy tried to dethrone reigning crimelord Tyger Tiger. Coy specialized in drugs and slaves, neither of which Tyger would touch, and he tried to hire Joe Fixit (the Hulk) to eliminate Tyger — but Wolverine (Logan/James Howlett) interceded as "Patch," forcing the two to share power. He also reminded Karma of her morals, and she began secretly working against her uncle. Coy later sold Roughouse to Geist, agent of drug-running Tierra Verde president Felix Caridad, who hoped to create a super-soldier using special cocaine tainted with remnants of the Deviant mutate Spore. After Wolverine defeated Spore, he destroyed Coy's drug sample. Stryfe later used Madripoor to develop the designer drug Sleet, and hired some of Coy's troops to battle the investigating New Mutants.

Still interested in super-soldiers, Coy brokered with Andover Enterprises, which brought him into the cyborg-creating Lazarus Project. When the renegade Captain Merrick slaughtered the island of Rumika's inhabitants to obtain the Project's Master Form with Coy's tacit approval, a horrified Karma helped Wolverine shut the Project down and left Coy's service. Later, Coy allied with the Yakuza to create a drug from an endangered monkey species' brains and dealt with Cyber, who offered a hallucinogenic drug for sale — but both times he was double-crossed. Coy contended

with new rivals Aardwolf and the Folding Circle, and betrayed supposed ally D.X. Hanrahan to his enemies Patricia Gambello and the Punisher (Frank Castle). Coy betrayed the Punisher as well, trying to kill all three at once, but the Punisher was prepared, and saved himself and Gambello. Genesis later had Coy and Baran frame Wolverine for several murders. The two sent their henchmen to kill Wolverine in his cell, but he escaped and chased them down. Coy, terrified, shot the Prince in the back of the head, seemingly killing him — but he was in turn shot by Tyger Tiger. Recovering, Coy traveled to New York and united several crimelords to assassinate rising mobster Vincente Fortunato; however, Fortunato survived and intimidated the crimelords into an uneasy alliance, and Coy returned to Madripoor. The heroic Scorpion (Carmilla Black) recently curtailed an arm of Coy's slave trade, but this was a drop in the bucket for Coy's sprawling, well-entrenched criminal operations.

REAL NAME: Nguyen Ngoc Coy
IDENTITY: No dual identity
OCCUPATION: Crimelord; former Vietnamese Army General
CITIZENSHIP: USA
PLACE OF BIRTH: Dong Nam Bo, Vietnam
KNOWN RELATIVES: Unidentified brother and sister-in-law (deceased), Xi'an Coy Manh (Karma, niece), Tranh Coy Manh (nephew, presumed deceased), Leong Coy Manh (Template, nephew), Nga Coy Manh (Template, niece)
EDUCATION: Vietnamese high school education and army training
FIRST APPEARANCE: Marvel Team-Up #100 (1980)

HEIGHT: 5'6"   **EYES:** Brown
WEIGHT: 155 lbs.   **HAIR:** Black

ABILITIES/ACCESSORIES: An expert military strategist, Coy is familiar with most military arms and vehicles. He speaks fluent English, French and Vietnamese.

POWER GRID	1	2	3	4	5	6	7
INTELLIGENCE							
STRENGTH							
SPEED							
DURABILITY							
ENERGY PROJECTION							
FIGHTING SKILLS							

REAL NAME: Akihiro
ALIASES: Wolverine, "Mongrel" (English translation of name); adoptive surname unrevealed
IDENTITY: (Daken) publicly known; (Wolverine) secret
OCCUPATION: Assassin
CITIZENSHIP: Originally Japan; currently unrevealed
PLACE OF BIRTH: Jasmine Falls, Japan
KNOWN RELATIVES: Logan/James Howlett (Wolverine, father), Itsu (mother, deceased), Akihira (adoptive father), Natsumi (adoptive mother), unidentified adoptive brother (deceased), extended family via Logan
GROUP AFFILIATION: Norman Osborn's Avengers; operative of Romulus
EDUCATION: Unrevealed
FIRST APPEARANCE: (Infant) Wolverine: Origins #5 (2006); (adult) Wolverine: Origins #10 (2007)

HISTORY: In 1946 in Jasmine Falls, Japan, Itsu — the pregnant, Japanese wife of Logan (James Howlett, later Wolverine) — was killed by the Winter Soldier (James Buchanan "Bucky" Barnes), a brainwashed KGB assassin acting at the behest of Romulus, the mysterious immortal and longtime manipulator of Logan. Unknown to Logan, his unborn baby had survived — likely due to his inherited mutant healing factor — and the infant was left (by the Winter Soldier or another operative) on the

AS BOY

doorstep of a wealthy young couple, Akihira and Natsumi. Childless for years, they adopted the baby and named him Akihiro; however, because of the boy's visibly mixed heritage, servants and others in Akihira's community dubbed him "Daken," or "Mongrel." Over the years, Akihira responded to the community's hostility by developing a cold, unfeeling personality toward everyone but his adoptive father, and the innate animal-like ferocity he had inherited from Logan enabled him to outfight and even secretly kill his tormentors during childhood.

In 1955, Akihira and Natsumi finally conceived a son, but a year later, Akihira killed the infant and boasted of the deed to Natsumi. Akihira's grieving adoptive parents disowned him and Natsumi attacked him with a sword, but he instinctively unleashed mutant claws, inadvertently killing her. Heartbroken, Akihira committed suicide. In the wake of these events, Romulus took custody of the boy and left Japan with unrevealed plans for Akihiro.

Four years later, the youth, who had discarded his adoptive name and taken "Daken" in its place, underwent training at Romulus' Canadian facility under Silas Burr, who had similarly trained Logan there years before; Daken became Burr's finest student. Nine months after Daken's arrival, Romulus decided the facility had outlived its usefulness and had Daken kill everyone there and burn it to the ground. Only Burr was allowed to live; Romulus eventually transformed Burr into the Adamantium-skinned Cyber.

Daken had believed his biological father long dead, but in 1977, after completing a murderous Afghanistan assignment, he was informed by Romulus that Logan, now the Department K operative Wolverine, still lived. Romulus further claimed Wolverine had slain Itsu hoping to prevent Daken's birth. With this lie, Romulus began instilling in Daken a deep hatred for Wolverine.

In recent years, despite decades of memory loss and manipulation by Romulus and others, Wolverine regained his memories of Itsu's death. Shortly after, mutant telepath Emma Frost revealed to Wolverine that his son was alive and full of hate for him. Preparing for the inevitable confrontation with Daken, Wolverine sought the only weapon that could negate his son's healing factor, the Carbonadium Synthesizer ("C-Synth"), held by the Black Widow (Natasha Romanoff). After a failed attempt to obtain the C-Synth in Brussels, Belgium, Wolverine was captured by SHIELD and imprisoned in a SHIELD facility in Berlin, Germany. Having been promised that he could someday confront his father on open ground, Daken infiltrated the SHIELD facility to finally meet Wolverine. Face-to-face with his helpless, captive father, Daken eviscerated him, but stopped short of killing him. He then facilitated Wolverine's escape, the better to battle him again later.

Still in Berlin, Daken returned to a student flat where he had been staying with an American girlfriend, whose emotions he had toyed with by allowing her to see him seemingly "seduce" an unidentified man, whom Daken later savagely killed for his passport. As Daken had anticipated, his distraught girlfriend sought solace in alcohol, which Daken had poisoned with sleeping pills. After further verbally tormenting the woman, Daken explained his actions to her, claiming he needed to kill her so that none of his acquaintances would be left alive after he departed. Daken then watched her die, having chosen such a sadistic method of murder purely for his own amusement.

Later, in Potsdam, Germany, Daken met an anonymous messenger, who reminded him of Romulus' displeasure at Daken neglecting his "ultimate goal" by instead shadowing Wolverine. After killing the messenger in reply, Daken traveled to Brussels, where a phone call from Cyber directed him to Wolverine's whereabouts. Daken observed as Wolverine broke into a bank vault to obtain the C-Synth, then confronted him in battle. After bloody combat, Daken defeated Wolverine. Cyber intervened,

Department K, a special weapons development branch of the Canadian government. Wilson became a test subject in Department K's branch of the joint US/Canadian superhuman enhancement project, Weapon X. His cancer was temporarily arrested via the implantation of a healing factor derived from another Department K agent, the mutant Wolverine (Logan/ James Howlett). Wilson was active in a covert field unit, possibly an early incarnation of Weapon PRIME (PRototype Induced Mutation Echelon), alongside the near-invulnerable Sluggo and the cyborgs Garrison Kane and Slayback. Wilson was reunited with Vanessa when, after manifesting mutant shape-shifting abilities, she joined the team as Copycat.

During one mission, Wilson seemingly killed Slayback for unrevealed reasons. When his healing factor ceased to function properly, Wilson's health worsened and, his body horribly scarred by cancer, he was sent to the Hospice, supposedly a government facility where failed superhuman operatives were treated or allowed to die with dignity; however, unknown to the Canadian government, the Hospice's patients served as experimental subjects for Dr. Emrys Killebrew and his sadistic assistant, the superhuman Attending, with the patients placing bets in a "deadpool" as to how long each subject would live. Killebrew subjected Wilson to various torturous experiments, both to learn why Wilson's healing factor had failed and for Killebrew's own deranged satisfaction. In the course of these experiments, Wilson reached the verge of death and was visited by the cosmic entity Death; able to perceive Death due to his unique status, he formed a semi-romantic relationship with her, and she regarded him as a kindred spirit.

Wilson's emotional strength during his trials earned him the respect of his fellow Hospice patients. The Attending, angered by Wilson's taunts and a perceived loss of respect from the patients, lobotomized one of Wilson's friends, cyborg Worm Cunningham. At Death's prompting, Wilson killed Cunningham to end his suffering. As the Attending well knew, under Killebrew's rules, any patient who killed another was to be executed, and Wilson, despite Killebrew's interest in his healing factor, proved no exception. The Attending tore out Wilson's heart and left him for dead, but Wilson's thirst for vengeance was so strong that it jump-started his healing factor, regenerating his heart, although not curing his scarred body. Wilson then attacked the Attending, leaving him for dead in turn, and was ready to die himself, but Death abandoned him. Taking the name Deadpool, he escaped from the Hospice with his fellow patients.

Deadpool has claimed he subsequently served as an enforcer alongside the surgically altered Maggia crime boss Hammerhead. He soon returned to freelance mercenary work, donning a costume in keeping with his new identity. At some point during this period, Deadpool was employed as an assassin by Wilson Fisk, the Kingpin of Crime. He also clashed with Wolverine, at that time a spy for Canada's Department H, neither man aware of the bond they shared via their healing factors. Also during these years, for reasons known only to himself, Deadpool abducted Blind Al and imprisoned her in his home, the "Deadhut." Al's escape attempts only resulted in Deadpool killing anyone whose help she sought, so she resigned herself to captivity and even developed an odd friendship with her captor.

Perhaps seeking compensation for the injuries inflicted by Killebrew, Deadpool returned to the Canadian government years later and was treated by Dr. Walter Langkowski, aka the bestial Sasquatch of Alpha Flight. Whatever his reasons, Deadpool soon deemed government work unsuited to his temperament, and he abandoned the endeavor. Hired by the criminal genius known as the Wizard (formerly Bentley Wittman), Deadpool at first went to the wrong address and received a job impersonating the criminal Hobgoblin. When again contacted by the Wizard, he joined fellow criminals the Taskmaster and the Constrictor in a short-lived version of the Frightful Four. When this plan also failed, Deadpool sought to reclaim his position as the Kingpin's assassin, only to be challenged by fellow assassin Bullseye.

Deadpool began frequenting the mercenary hangout called the Hellhouse, where the diminutive Patch issued assignments. There he clashed with T-Ray, a mystic assassin whom he disliked immediately. He subsequently found employment with the time-traveling arms merchant Tolliver (Tyler Dayspring), in whose service he was reunited with Sluggo and Copycat. Unknown to Deadpool, Tolliver subsequently sent Copycat to impersonate another mutant mercenary, Domino. Deadpool also recruited Weasel (Jack Hammer) as his weapon supplier, and the two became fast friends.

Tolliver eventually sent Deadpool to kill mutant soldier Cable, who was secretly Tolliver's father and in whose company Copycat was impersonating Domino; however, Deadpool was defeated by Cable and his new charges, the youthful New Mutants. When Cable reorganized this team as X-Force, Tolliver seemingly died in battle with them, setting off a search by his various mercenaries, including Deadpool, for the advanced technology he had left behind. Deadpool's search was interrupted by the surprising interference of Slayback, who had finally cybernetically reconstituted himself after his death at Deadpool's hands years ago and was eager for revenge. Copycat was gravely injured during the ensuing battle and Deadpool transferred part of his healing ability to her, saving her life.

Deadpool subsequently aided X-Force member Siryn against the unstoppable Juggernaut (Cain Marko) and her uncle Black Tom Cassidy, who had forced Killebrew into their service. Deadpool developed a strong attachment to Siryn, who only partially returned his feelings. Unsure of his worthiness, Deadpool sought out Copycat, only to find she was now dating fellow Department K alumnus Kane. Deadpool fought both Kane and Wolverine, who had been sent to check on Kane by a mutual friend, before exorcising his resentment. Information brokers seeking to cure the Legacy virus subsequently abducted Deadpool, but he was rescued by Wolverine and yet another mutant mercenary, Maverick (Christoph Nord).

Soon afterward, Deadpool was approached by Zoe Culloden of the rechristened Landau, Luckman and Lake, since she and some of her allies believed he was destined to be the Mithras, one who would help usher in a golden age for Earth. Skeptical at the notion of accomplishing anything worthwhile, Deadpool turned her away, only to be hit with a string of personal failures, including the alienation of Weasel and Blind Al, whom he later freed from imprisonment. Hoping to turn over a new leaf, he tried to give up killing but the ghosts of his fellow Weapon X patients spurred him to slay the Attending, now known as Ajax, who had murdered several of the patients themselves in the intervening years. Now eager to redeem himself, Deadpool accepted Culloden's offer, but was dismayed to learn that the Mithras' destined role was to kill Tiamat, a potential threat to an arriving "Messiah." Deadpool instead killed the Messiah itself when he learned it brought not true peace but only mindless bliss.

Having lost his optimism about bettering himself, Deadpool tried to return to his mercenary life. Troubled by recent events, he consulted deranged psychiatrist Dr. Bong, who advised him to work out his difficulties in a fight with Wolverine. The fight indeed cleared Deadpool's mind, but his psyche was dealt a stunning blow when T-Ray resurrected Mercedes Wilson, whom Deadpool still believed to be his wife. T-Ray also revealed himself as her husband, supposedly the true Wade Wilson. T-Ray hoped this would break his enemy's spirit, but Deadpool, robbed of the loving relationship with Mercedes that he had deemed his only saving grace, declared his situation ludicrous and vowed to cease contemplation of his past, the better to improve himself in the future. Swearing vengeance for another day, T-Ray departed with Mercedes Wilson.

Hired to assassinate author Duncan Vess, Deadpool again clashed with Wolverine, who was investigating Vess. After learning Vess was a relatively benign werewolf, Deadpool and Wolverine found themselves battling his more aggressive kin; despite their past differences, the two men parted on good terms. Weeks later, Deadpool sought medical treatment for his beloved Siryn, injured during an X-Force mission. Allying with the mysterious Watchtower group, Deadpool captured Wolverine in exchange for Siryn's treatment. Siryn was cured while Wolverine easily defeated his captors, though he still resented Deadpool's actions.

The feral mutant Sabretooth invited Deadpool to join a new Weapon X Program under US auspices. Impressed by Weapon X's upgrade of his healing factor, he agreed to join, but soon found the organization's anti-mutant methods to be too bloody even for him. After Copycat's death at Sabretooth's hands, a furious Deadpool confronted Weapon X's Director Malcolm Colcord, only to have his healing factor reversed to the point where he lost all physical cohesion and died.

The lingering effects of his upgrade unexpectedly resurrected Deadpool, but left him amnesiac. A chance encounter with Weasel restored his memory, and he discovered that four other individuals had claimed the Deadpool name. These imposters were aspects of his own personality given form by the Gemini Star device, wielded by his nemesis T-Ray, whom the intergalactic villain Thanos had hired; long enamored of Death, Thanos envied Deadpool's relationship with her. T-Ray intended to manifest and extinguish every aspect of Deadpool's personality, leaving him an empty shell, but Deadpool damaged the Gemini Star, causing his personality fragments to be absorbed into T-Ray, rendering him amnesiac in turn.

Following an assignment against the Four Winds crime family, Deadpool, believed to have killed the criminals, gained great status as a mercenary and formed DP, Inc. with business partner Sandi Brandenberg; however, fellow assassin Black Swan, who had actually slain the Four Winds himself, sought vengeance for Deadpool's wrongful claim. Both men were believed dead after an explosive confrontation, but the Swan's telepathic power caused the memories and skills of both himself and Deadpool to merge in the corpse of the Swan's underling, Nijo. Deadpool's healing factor resurrected Nijo, who, injured and amnesiac, found his way to Sandi's apartment. Sandi believed Nijo to be Deadpool and nursed him back to health. Choosing the name Alex Hayden, Nijo joined Sandi and the Taskmaster in a new mercenary endeavor, Agency X. The Black Swan soon resurfaced, with Deadpool in tow, intending to restore all three men to their previous states. During the transfer, the Swan betrayed both Deadpool and Nijo, absorbing all of their abilities and achieving great power. Aided by his friends, Nijo broke through the Swan's telepathic shield and defeated him, reversing the transfer. Himself once more, Deadpool declined an offer to join Agency X, returning to his solo career.

The One World Church hired Deadpool to steal the Facade Virus, with which the Church's leaders intended to transform the world's populace into blue-skinned beings like themselves. When Cable intervened, the virus de-powered both him and Deadpool, forcing Cable to use his teleportation technology to merge their deteriorating bodies into one and then separate them in healthy form. The process created a DNA link between the two, allowing Deadpool to tap into Cable's teleportation technology and accompany him in his activities — with the disadvantage of again merging the two every time the teleportation technology was used, requiring a painful separation. When Cable established the island community Providence as the first step of his long-term plan to change the world for the better, Deadpool became dedicated to his goals, siding with Cable against the X-Men, SHIELD and others, including Nijo as Agent X.

Estranged from Cable by their disagreement over the US Superhuman Registration Act, Deadpool joined the government-sanctioned Six Pack to discredit him, but the group's efforts only furthered Cable's goals. At loose ends following Providence's destruction and Cable's disappearance, Deadpool briefly joined Agency X alongside Weasel and the hapless Bob, Agent of Hydra, but soon set out on his own again. During the Skrulls' "Secret Invasion," Deadpool, under orders from Nick Fury, feigned cooperation with the aliens, who duplicated his healing factor in several Super-Skrulls, only for it to induce fatal cellular overload in the subjects. Deadpool acquired vital Skrull data, but it was intercepted by Norman Osborn, who subsequently led the Thunderbolts to be instrumental in the Skrulls' defeat. In response, Deadpool targeted Osborn and the Thunderbolts for vengeance.

NOTE: Hellhouse's Patch should not be mistaken for Patch, Wolverine's prefered alias in Madripoor.

HEIGHT: 6'2" EYES: Brown
WEIGHT: 210 lbs. HAIR: None (originally brown, then varied)

ABILITIES/ACCESSORIES: Deadpool's superhuman healing factor allows him to regenerate damaged or destroyed areas of his cellular structure at a rate far greater than that of an ordinary human, enabling him to regrow severed body parts in a matter of hours. The speed at which this ability functions is directly proportionate to an injury's severity and partially affected by Deadpool's mental state, working most efficiently when he is awake, alert and in good spirits. His healing factor also grants him virtual immunity to poisons and most drugs, as well as an extended life span and an enhanced resistance to diseases. Due to repeated brain injuries throughout his career, Deadpool's brain regenerates decaying brain cells at such a hyperaccelerated rate that his sanity and memories suffer regular damage. For a time, Deadpool could access Cable's bodysliding technology without use of machinery due to a mingling of the two men's DNA, but he no longer possesses this ability.

Deadpool is an extraordinary athlete and hand-to-hand combatant, skilled in multiple unarmed combat techniques. He is a master assassin, an excellent marksman, and an accomplished user of bladed weapons. He is fluent in Japanese, German and Spanish, among other languages. He employs any number of weapons depending on his current assignment or whim but is virtually never without a combination of guns and knives. He uses a teleportation device in his belt to whisk him out of (and occasionally into) danger, as well as a holographic image inducer to disguise his true appearance as necessary.

Art by Reilly Brown

CURRENT COSTUME

POWER GRID	1	2	3	4	5	6	7
INTELLIGENCE							
STRENGTH							
SPEED*							
DURABILITY							
ENERGY PROJECTION							
FIGHTING SKILLS							

*DEADPOOL IS A TELEPORTER

HISTORY: A body-stealing mutant, Dirt Nap absorbed Special Agent Daryll Smith of the NSA's Mutant Task Force when Smith sought to arrest him; shortly thereafter, Genesis (Tyler Dayspring) recruited Dirt Nap into his Dark Riders to help capture Wolverine (Logan/James Howlett). Believing the easiest way to achieve this was to absorb Wolverine, Dirt Nap stole the body of an innocent young boy, Algernon, using it to get close enough to strike. He consumed Wolverine, but his target's healing factor proved indigestible, forcing Dirt Nap to spit him back out, and Dirt Nap absorbed a rat to escape before Wolverine retaliated. Genesis captured Wolverine, then tried to brainwash Wolverine and bond Adamantium to his skeleton; however, the procedure failed, and Wolverine was instead regressed to a completely feral state. As Wolverine massacred his teammates, Dirt Nap fled.

Seeking to avoid Wolverine's wrath, Dirt Nap arranged to meet with the crazed mutant Chimera to secure passage to another dimension; however, Chimera viewed Dirt Nap as bait to capture Wolverine. After devouring Venom (Eddie Brock), Dirt Nap encountered Wolverine at a Landau, Luckman & Lake office. When Venom proved unable to be absorbed, Dirt Nap fled through a Warp Chamber, pursued by both Venom and Wolverine. Dirt Nap next devoured the female symbiote Donna Diego (later Scream) to oppose Venom while Chimera clashed with Wolverine, but Donna likewise escaped absorption, forcing Dirt Nap to expunge his past victims. Chimera then sought to destroy the heroes with a series of implosions; however, she and Dirt Nap were pulled into one of these implosions and seemingly died.

ABSORPTION MANIFESTATION

Art by Terry Dodson

Having survived the implosion, Dirt Nap and Chimera returned to Earth where Chimera allied with M-Plate — a merging of Claudette and Nicolette St. Croix and Emplate — to find the Universal Amalgamator in order to merge the universe into a single consciousness. In their eagerness, they left Dirt Nap behind; and after absorbing another rat, he was found by mutant students Generation X. Seeking to rejoin Chimera, Dirt Nap feigned

REAL NAME: Unrevealed
ALIASES: Impersonated Special Agent Daryll Smith, Wolverine, Eddie Brock, others
IDENTITY: Secret
OCCUPATION: Criminal
CITIZENSHIP: Unrevealed
PLACE OF BIRTH: Unrevealed
KNOWN RELATIVES: None
GROUP AFFILIATION: Formerly Dark Riders
EDUCATION: Unrevealed
FIRST APPEARANCE: Wolverine #95 (1995); (true form) Venom: Tooth and Claw #3 (1997)

helping Generation X recover their teammate Synch, whom M-Plate had captured. After they treated him with kindness for perhaps the first time in his life, and also saved him from a giant spider, Dirt Nap reconsidered his allegiances and turned on M-Plate, absorbing her; however, M-Plate's amalgamated form proved too much for Dirt Nap's molecular structure and he exploded, restoring M-Plate's constituent forms.

AS SMITH   AS ALGERNON

Art by Adam Kubert

AS RAT

HEIGHT: 5'8" (variable)   **EYES:** Brown (variable)
WEIGHT: 155 lbs. (variable)   **HAIR:** Balding (variable)

ABILITIES/ACCESSORIES: Dirt Nap could absorb others into his body by manifesting an enormous fanged mouth, occasionally with a clawed green hand for a tongue, and devouring them. This manifestation could apparently be of any size, depending on the size and mass of the intended victim. Upon devouring a victim, Dirt Nap could utilize their genetic imprint to take on their physical appearance and gain their abilities. He could also store the genetic imprints of his victims, allowing him to retrieve their identity for later use (and consequently allowing others to free them from Dirt Nap's form). Amalgamated forms, such as an alien symbiote and its host, proved difficult for Dirt Nap to absorb. After taking on another's appearance, Dirt Nap retained his own personality and voice, even if in animal form. Dirt Nap could be easily identified by a red smiling face symbol that appeared on any physical form he adopted.

POWER GRID	1	2	3	4	5	6	7
INTELLIGENCE							
STRENGTH							
SPEED							
DURABILITY							
ENERGY PROJECTION							
FIGHTING SKILLS							

* AFTER ABSORPTION

GAMBIT

REAL NAME: Remy Etienne LeBeau
ALIASES: Death, S. Templar, le Diable Blanc, Robert Lord
IDENTITY: Publicly known
OCCUPATION: Adventurer, thief; former terrorist
CITIZENSHIP: USA
PLACE OF BIRTH: New Orleans, Louisiana
KNOWN RELATIVES: Bella Donna Boudreaux (Belladonna, ex-wife), Jean-Luc LeBeau (adoptive father, deceased), Rochelle LeBeau (adoptive grandmother, deceased), Henri LeBeau (adoptive brother, deceased), Jacques LeBeau (adoptive grandfather, deceased), Mercy LeBeau (adoptive sister-in-law), Theoren Marceaux (adoptive cousin), Etienne Marceaux (adoptive cousin, deceased), Marius Boudreaux (father-in-law, deceased), Julien Boudreaux (brother-in-law, deceased)
GROUP AFFILIATION: Formerly Marauders, Horsemen of Apocalypse, X-Men, X-Treme Sanctions Executive, Unified Guilds (patriarch), Thieves Guild (patriarch)
EDUCATION: No formal education
FIRST APPEARANCE: Uncanny X-Men #266 (1990); (Death) X-Men #184 (2006)

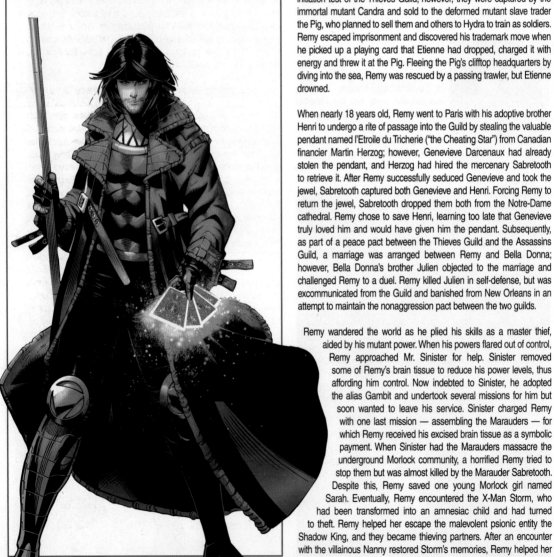

HISTORY: Gambit is allegedly a product of Black Womb, a black-ops government-funded project involved in the investigation and initiation of human mutation using recently acquired advanced extraterrestrial technology, under the guidance of geneticist Nathan Milbury (Mr. Sinister), Amanda Mueller and others. It is believed that Black Womb's experimentation upon a couple produced, either in their son or grandson, a mutant infant with burning red eyes whom they abandoned in a New Orleans hospital. Believing the child to be le diable blanc ("the white devil"), the one prophesied to restore the Old Kingdom, Thieves Guild patriarch Jean-Luc LeBeau followed the instructions of the Guild's prophet, the Antiquary, and kidnapped the infant from the hospital, placing him in the care of a gang of street thieves led by expatriate Guild member Fagan, who raised the child (now named Remy) and taught him the ways of thievery. When he was about 8 years old, Remy sought to save a young girl from being accosted by a group of thugs; however, the girl turned out to be Bella Donna Boudreaux, daughter of the Assassins Guild's patriarch and trained since birth in the killing arts. Remy and Bella Donna became best friends and eventually fell in love. When he was around 10 years old, Remy tried to pickpocket Jean-Luc, who took the boy in off the streets and adopted him. Remy's mutant abilities manifested at puberty, though he kept this secret. At age 15, Remy accompanied his cousin and best friend Etienne Marceaux on his "Tilling," the ritual initiation test of the Thieves Guild; however, they were captured by the immortal mutant Candra and sold to the deformed mutant slave trader the Pig, who planned to sell them and others to Hydra to train as soldiers. Remy escaped imprisonment and discovered his trademark move when he picked up a playing card that Etienne had dropped, charged it with energy and threw it at the Pig. Fleeing the Pig's clifftop headquarters by diving into the sea, Remy was rescued by a passing trawler, but Etienne drowned.

When nearly 18 years old, Remy went to Paris with his adoptive brother Henri to undergo a rite of passage into the Guild by stealing the valuable pendant named l'Etroile du Tricherie ("the Cheating Star") from Canadian financier Martin Herzog; however, Genevieve Darcenaux had already stolen the pendant, and Herzog had hired the mercenary Sabretooth to retrieve it. After Remy successfully seduced Genevieve and took the jewel, Sabretooth captured both Genevieve and Henri. Forcing Remy to return the jewel, Sabretooth dropped them both from the Notre-Dame cathedral. Remy chose to save Henri, learning too late that Genevieve truly loved him and would have given him the pendant. Subsequently, as part of a peace pact between the Thieves Guild and the Assassins Guild, a marriage was arranged between Remy and Bella Donna; however, Bella Donna's brother Julien objected to the marriage and challenged Remy to a duel. Remy killed Julien in self-defense, but was excommunicated from the Guild and banished from New Orleans in an attempt to maintain the nonaggression pact between the two guilds.

Remy wandered the world as he plied his skills as a master thief, aided by his mutant power. When his powers flared out of control, Remy approached Mr. Sinister for help. Sinister removed some of Remy's brain tissue to reduce his power levels, thus affording him control. Now indebted to Sinister, he adopted the alias Gambit and undertook several missions for him but soon wanted to leave his service. Sinister charged Remy with one last mission — assembling the Marauders — for which Remy received his excised brain tissue as a symbolic payment. When Sinister had the Marauders massacre the underground Morlock community, a horrified Remy tried to stop them but was almost killed by the Marauder Sabretooth. Despite this, Remy saved one young Morlock girl named Sarah. Eventually, Remy encountered the X-Man Storm, who had been transformed into an amnesiac child and had turned to theft. Remy helped her escape the malevolent psionic entity the Shadow King, and they became thieving partners. After an encounter with the villainous Nanny restored Storm's memories, Remy helped her

Art by Steve Skroce, Melvin Rubi & Jim Lee

SHI'AR SUIT

X-MEN TRAINING COSTUME

Art by Yanick Paquette

agreed to rejoin the team, mainly for his self-respect and for his love for Rogue; however, Mary began to threaten Remy and his friends if he didn't agree to stay with her forever. When the X-Men finally found out about Mary, the wraith fled with Remy to her old hometown, where she tried to force him to merge with her and become a new type of hybrid life form. While Remy struggled with her, Rogue charged in with a containment unit, which ultimately dispersed Mary. Later, during a trip back in time, Sinister restored Remy's powers to their maximum potential, and Gambit used them to return to the present. Soon after his return, Remy served for a time as the Thieves Guild's patriarch in his father's stead, as well as leading one of two X-Men teams. Gambit was also responsible for merging the Thieves and Assassins Guilds into the Unified Guild, serving briefly as its patriarch. Meanwhile, New Sun organized an assassination game for a cadre of super-powered mercenaries with Remy as the target. The attempt failed, and Remy discovered that New Sun was his Earth-9921 counterpart. In his own reality, New Sun's kinetic charging powers had flared out of control, burning the world and killing everyone but himself. As a result, New Sun hunted down and killed his counterparts in other realities so they would not repeat his mistakes. During their final battle, Remy burned through his enhanced powers to defeat New Sun, ending that threat and returning Gambit's powers to their normal level.

Mutant businessman Sebastian Shaw later framed Remy for the death of Australian crimelord Viceroy. Aided by Rogue, the X-Men and former Triad member Red Lotus, Gambit cleared his name. Soon after, Remy helped the X-Men oppose alien warlord Khan's attempted invasion of Earth. The invaders captured Gambit and used him to power a portal that would bring their full invasion fleet to Earth. Trying to rescue Remy, Rogue ended up trapped with him. The X-Men's enemy, the enhanced human Vargas, halted the process by plunging his sword through Rogue's back and into Remy's chest. Remy survived, but he and Rogue had lost their mutant abilities. The pair retired from the X-Men to live a normal life together, but soon became embroiled in the X-Men's fight against mutant predator Elias Bogan. After Bogan's defeat, the X-Man Sage (Tessa) reactivated Remy's mutant powers and he rejoined the team. Re-assigned by Cyclops onto Havok's X-Men squad, Remy accompanied them to China to investigate a mutant manifestation, but clashed with local superhumans the Eight Immortals; during their battle, one of Remy's charged cards blew up in his face, blinding him. As he recuperated, Remy seemingly developed the ability to foretell the future as he learned of an impending attack on the Institute by Exodus' Brotherhood of Mutants. With the young telepathic mutant student Mindee of the Stepford Cuckoos acting as his eyes, Remy helped repel the assault. After Sage restored his eyesight, Remy encountered Bella once more when her new boyfriend Bandit (Donyell Taylor) sought to usurp control of the Guilds. Aided by Detective Noreen Tanaka, who had sworn a vendetta against Remy, Bandit sought to kill Gambit; however, he was ultimately forced to ally with Remy and Bella against rebellious Guild members.

Art by Georges Jeanty

locate the missing X-Men. Storm then sponsored Remy's membership in that group, and he quickly became a valued team member. Remy soon became interested in his teammate Rogue, who absorbed the thoughts and abilities of others through skin-on-skin contact. The pair began dating, but their relationship became troubled after Bella Donna sought Gambit's help to defuse a war between the Guilds. Rogue was stunned to learn that Bella was Gambit's wife, but still joined her teammates in uncovering a Brood plot to conquer the world by controlling the Guilds' children. Accompanied by Rogue, Remy later returned to New Orleans to help save Bella's life by obtaining the Elixir of Life from Candra. Bella was saved, though her memories were gone after accidental contact with Rogue. When Bella later sought revenge on Rogue, Remy aided Rogue even though it meant opposing Bella.

When Legion diverged Earth-616's past into Reality-295 (the "Age of Apocalypse"), Rogue kissed Remy before the temporal wave struck. After Reality-616's timeline was restored, Rogue left Remy in a coma to follow up on a memory she had absorbed from him. When Remy awoke from his coma, he realized Rogue had absorbed his memory of his deal with Sinister, and he set off after her. Although she remained unaware of the truth, Rogue ultimately left both Remy and the X-Men. She later returned with Joseph, secretly a clone of Magneto, whom Remy quickly came to dislike. After aiding the interstellar Shi'ar Empire against the threat of the techno-organic alien Phalanx, Remy was captured and brought before a mock trial held by the true Magneto, then posing as Erik the Red. When the truth of his role in the Morlock massacre was revealed, Remy was summarily cast out of the X-Men and abandoned in Antarctica. Starving, Remy made his way back into Magneto's citadel where he encountered the psionic essence of dead mutant Mary Purcell. The wraith-like Mary bonded with him, allowing him to survive until he reached the Savage Land, a hidden jungle nestled in the icy wasteland. There, Remy struck a deal with the enigmatic New Sun. In exchange for passage back to America, Remy agreed to run errands for him.

On returning home, Remy encountered the X-Men again when he tried to steal the fabled Crimson Ruby of Cyttorak for his new employer. He

Following Apocalypse's return, Remy infiltrated the mutant conqueror's ranks by offering his willing service, unaware that Apocalypse's transformation procedure would also brainwash him, and he emerged as the newest Horseman Death. Alongside fellow new Horsemen War (Gazer), Famine (Sunfire) and Pestilence (Polaris), Remy attacked the X-Men, but Sunfire broke free of Apocalypse's control and fled, taking Gambit with him. Sunfire then used his flame powers to free Remy from his Horseman conditioning, and the pair returned to the Institute to do the same for Polaris but left empty-handed. Subsequently, Sinister recruited Gambit and Sunfire into a new incarnation of the Marauders, reversing Apocalypse's alterations to restore Remy's original appearance and powers. Foreseeing the birth of a mutant child who would shape mutantkind's future, Sinister had the Marauders slay precognitive mutants around the globe in an attempt to blind the X-Men to the event, then set the Marauders against the mutant heroes; during this conflict, Rogue was struck down by her estranged foster mother Mystique, one of Gambit's fellow Marauders, and captured. In the end, mutant cyborg Cable escaped into the timestream with the child, and Mystique apparently slew Sinister. Remy hoped to stay with a recovered Rogue, but she wanted solitude and departed, leaving Remy alone. After learning that the New

DEATH

Orleans Assassin's Guild had accepted a contract from Black Womb's Amanda Mueller to kill Sebastian Shaw, Cain Marko, Carter Ryking and Charles Xavier, Gambit followed and helped save Xavier's life. Attacked again by the assassins, Remy was saved by Shaw's arrival, though too late to prevent Xavier's capture. Following him to the abandoned Almagordo research facility, Gambit and Shaw helped oppose Mueller, destroying the Cronus device which had resurrected Sinister in Mueller's body, while Xavier defeated Sinister. Remy and Xavier then sought Rogue's whereabouts, finding her in Outback Australia where they aided her against the sentient Shi'ar tech Danger.

HEIGHT: 6'2" **EYES:** Black with red pupils
WEIGHT: 179 lbs. **HAIR:** Brown (briefly white)

ABILITIES/ACCESSORIES: Via direct physical contact, Gambit can transform the potential energy (stored energy and the energy of position — gravitational energy) contained within an inorganic object, converting it into kinetic (energy of motion) energy; specifically, this is biokinetic energy, kinetic energy generated by living beings. Once he has energized an object, Gambit can mentally cause it to explode with concussive force after a set time limit, though he usually allows such objects to detonate upon impact. By charging an object and keeping it close to his forehead, he can create a static interference that shields his mind from telepathic detection and intrusion by even the most powerful telepaths. Gambit cannot use this power to charge organic objects.

Gambit subconsciously taps into the potential energy surrounding him and channels that energy into himself, giving him peak human agility and dexterity. At their peak, his powers form an ambient biokinetic aura around his entire body. He also possesses a hypnotic charm granting him subtle influence over most sentient minds, compelling others to believe what he says and agree with anything he suggests. More powerful minds, however, can resist his charm.

Gambit is fluent in English and French, and can also throw small objects — including knives, throwing spikes and playing cards — with extraordinary accuracy. He is an extremely talented thief, adept at lock-picking and sleight of hand. He is an experienced combatant, utilizing both street fighting techniques and acrobatics, and he is highly skilled in the martial arts of bojutsu (staff technique) and savate (French kick-boxing).

Gambit's high-impact, lightweight, modularly aligned body armor is composed of high carbon, titanium steel alloy meshing. A layer of Freon gel constantly pumps through the armor's lining to mask his body's thermal signature. The suit's utility belt houses weaponry and devices such as ionized ferrous dust (which masks his presence on video cameras), talcum powder (used to view infrared beams), a mini-laser torch (used to cut glass), lockpicks and other devices. His

trench coat is made of a synthetic stretch fabric lined with Kevlar and a woven silica fiber cloth (Beta cloth) to provide protection against ballistic penetration up to .45 caliber as well as effective insulation against fire with a melting point of 650° celsius. Gambit often carries a few decks of playing cards upon his person, usually in a leather satchel or utility belt. He regularly wields a telescoping steel-alloy battle-staff (extending up to 10' in length) that can be broken down into two short clubs, which are strapped on each thigh. On occasion, Gambit has charged his staff and allowed it to discharge explosively against someone, yet the staff is not destroyed in the process as most of his charged objects usually are; how the composition of his staff allows this process is unrevealed.

When Gambit's powers were enhanced to their maximum potential, he could charge any object within his vicinity, including organic objects, without the need to physically touch it. Gambit could also manipulate the potency of an object's energy release, utilize stored kinetic energy to travel through time, and heal himself by tapping into his body's own kinetic energy. Following his climactic battle with the New Sun, Gambit lost this enhanced level of power.

As the Horseman Death, Gambit's hair was turned chalk white and his skin became onyx black. Gambit could manipulate the potential energy of objects within his vicinity and convert the materials into toxic substances, such as transforming oxygen into poisonous gas. Once converted, he could effectively project the gas at a range of up to 15 feet. Although he could project it beyond 15 feet, the gas gradually dissipated and lost its effectiveness.

POWER GRID	1	2	3	4	5	6	7
INTELLIGENCE							
STRENGTH							
SPEED							
DURABILITY							
ENERGY PROJECTION							
FIGHTING SKILLS							

HISTORY: Cameron Hodge roomed with Warren Worthington III in college. Though Warren believed Cameron to be his friend, Hodge deeply resented Warren's wealth and good looks, and grew to despise Worthington when he discovered him to be the winged mutant Angel. Hodge believed that mutants threatened normal humans and therefore had to be destroyed. After a successful advertising career and earning a certification to practice law, Hodge secretly founded the Right organization, conspiring with fellow mutant-haters to rid the world of mutants. Hodge helped design heavily armed armored suits for the Right's soldiers and liberated mad geneticist Dr. Frederick Animus from jail, employing him to find a way to stop all mutation. Calling himself the Ani-Mator, Animus began experimenting on animals on the isolated Paradise Island. Having studied the mutant phenomenon in depth, Hodge, still pretending to be Warren's friend, convinced Angel that mutants posing as human mutant-hunters could save endangered mutants, as they would be called in via a toll-free number by the very people who might otherwise harm mutants. Angel recruited his old X-Men teammates Beast (Hank McCoy), Cyclops (Scott Summers), Iceman (Bobby Drake) and Marvel Girl (Jean Grey) to join him in this venture, and Hodge heavily advertised their new X-Factor organization. Hodge regularly informed Angel and the others of the calls they received, but concealed reports of how X-Factor's "mutant-hunting" public image was actually turning the public more against mutants. When reporters such as Trish Tilby began investigating X-Factor, Hodge did

FIRST ROBOT BODY

Art by Jim Lee

his best to steer the media's coverage so as to serve his anti-mutant agenda; and when the radiation-poisoned mutants Bulk and Glowworm assaulted X-Factor's headquarters, Hodge posed as one of X-Factor's mutant hunters to help fool the media while driving off the attackers. Hodge later informed X-Factor that the Russian government was seeking their mutant-capturing secrets, and persuaded them to undertake a dangerous mission to aid ill-treated Russian mutants. After attending the funeral of young mutant Willie Evans Jr. with X-Factor, Hodge convinced the team to investigate whether Spider-Man (Peter Parker) was a mutant, causing a brief battle between the team and the vigilante.

Despite X-Factor's growing frustrations with him, Hodge continued representing the team publicly as their liaison with reporters and authorities. In time, known mutant Worthington was publicly exposed as X-Factor's financier, attracting more media attention. Hodge manipulated events in his favor, especially when Angel's wings were horribly damaged in a fight with the Marauders. Hodge arranged to have Angel's wings amputated, and had the courts declare Angel mentally incompetent so that the decision could not be changed. By that time, Hodge had also manipulated Angel into granting Hodge control of X-Factor's finances in case anything should happen to Warren. Hodge gained control of the

Art by Walter Simonson

funds when the wingless, despairing Angel seemingly died in a plane crash; though it looked like a suicide, Hodge had actually sabotaged Warren's plane. Hodge began exercising tighter control over X-Factor's funding while secretly siphoning much of Worthington's fortune into the Right, equipping their

THE RIGHT

REAL NAME: Cameron Hodge
ALIASES: Commander Hodge, the Commander
IDENTITY: No dual identity
OCCUPATION: Terrorist, leader of the Right; former public relations director, advertising specialist, lawyer
CITIZENSHIP: USA
PLACE OF BIRTH: Unrevealed
KNOWN RELATIVES: None
GROUP AFFILIATION: The Right; formerly X-Factor employee
EDUCATION: College graduate; J.D. in law from unspecified university
FIRST APPEARANCE: X-Factor #1 (1986)

armor with holographic technology and specially designing them to block the powers of X-Factor and their associates. With their primary base under the Arlington Interactive Museum of Science in Virginia, Hodge oversaw Right operations nationwide.

The Right captured and tortured Mexican mutant Rictor (Julio Richter), putting his vibratory powers under Hodge's control. Hodge manipulated X-Factor into trying to stop Rictor, supposedly an evil mutant threatening California, but they ended up saving him instead. Trying to push the emotionally fragile Cyclops over the edge, Hodge rigged X-Factor's computer to holographically taunt Cyclops with varying versions of Marvel Girl, the Phoenix Force entity which had once impersonated her, and her clone, Madelyne Pryor, all of whom Cyclops had been intimately involved

AS PHALANX

with, but Cyclops saw through the ruse and realized Hodge was behind it. On the day Angel's will was read, X-Factor, realizing some of Hodge's intentions, fired Hodge just before learning that Warren had left all his money to X-Factor and named Hodge as administrator of the funds. During news coverage of the will, Trish Tilby revealed Hodge's role in Angel's wing amputation and the X-Factor team tried to out themselves as mutants while condemning Hodge and his anti-mutant PR campaign; however, Hodge had the Right's armored soldiers open fire on the crowd outside X-Factor's headquarters, killing several and blaming the attack on mutants. More Right soldiers kidnapped X-Factor's young wards, Rusty Collins, Rictor, Artie Maddicks, Leech, Boom-Boom (Tabitha Smith) and Skids (Sally Blevins), taking them to the Arlington base. Hodge joined them there, gleefully itnforming the captives that the Right would torture them, experiment with their powers, and exploit their talents for the Right's benefit. X-Factor soon attacked, and the Right soldiers held them off as the kids escaped. Hodge sent a robot duplicate of himself into battle, but despite it wearing ruby quartz armor to ward off Cyclops' optic blasts, Cyclops destroyed it by cracking the armor and reflecting his optic blast inside.

When Angel's ex-girlfriend Candy Southern threatened to expose Hodge to the media, he captured her and began savagely experimenting on her until she was virtually brain-dead, kept alive only by machines. Hodge meanwhile learned that the Ani-Mator had been pursuing his own agenda, so he led several Right soldiers in stopping the Ani-Mator's operations, getting involved in a battle with the New Mutants, students affiliated with the X-Men. Hodge had the island destroyed, though his ship was pulled down into the water by a mutated octopus, and Hodge narrowly escaped to be rescued by a passing boat. Meanwhile, having survived Hodge's death trap and become the metal-winged Archangel, Warren was now looking for Southern, killing any Right soldiers he came across. Hodge used an ancient arcane ritual to make a pact with the demon N'astirh, offering his soul and the location of infant mutants the demon could use in sacrifices, in return for immortality and promised success for the Right. Archangel soon found Hodge and Southern, sparking a fierce battle. An armored Hodge tried to kill his former friend, but Archangel's razor wing decapitated Hodge; a freed Southern died moments later in Archangel's arms.

Kept alive by his demonic pact, Hodge's head was attached by the Right's cybernetic experts to a powerful robot body with a phase ability and extensive weaponry. Hodge struck a deal with the president of the mutant-enslaving nation Genosha, promising to help them get revenge on the X-Men, including X-Factor and the New Mutants. Granted authority over the Genoshan Magistrates and their enslaved mutates, Hodge sometimes wore a cardboard cutout of a suit and tie around his neck in a ludicrous attempt to appear more human. After wayward members of the Right, in new armored suits, battled X-Factor, the Genoshan Magistrates captured several X-Men, including their alien member Warlock of the Technarchy, whose transmode virus Hodge hoped to use to to upgrade himself. When Warlock sacrificed himself to free his friends, Hodge was furious and he made an example of the mutant Wolfsbane (Rahne Sinclair), submerging her identity via the Genoshan Mutate bonding process. When the rest of the X-Men arrived in Genosha, Hodge monitored their

RESURRECTED

ongoing battles with the Magistrates and saw many of the mutants captured. Hodge ripped off the metal arm of Cable (Nathan Summers) to showcase his power, and forced Archangel and Wolverine (Logan/James Howlett) to battle nearly to the death in an arena-style fight. The X-Men fought back, but Hodge nearly defeated over a dozen mutants single-handedly before Cyclops and Havok (Alex Summers) dislodged his head, which was ripped in half by Wolfsbane (who retained her original persona in her lupine form), and buried under a collapsing citadel by Rictor.

In time, the Phalanx, a group of humans who had been infected by the Technarch transmode virus, sought to assimilate and take over all life on Earth, hoping to turn the planet over to the Technarchy. The Phalanx found Hodge's still living head and brought him into the Phalanx movement, giving him a new body and new abilities. Hodge had Candy Southern's corpse unearthed and reanimated as a Phalanx; a facsimile of her consciousness regained control of her form, albeit with altered memories, and Hodge tied it directly into his own life force in an attempt to further torture Archangel; however, when Archangel injured Hodge during their next battle and Hodge drew on Southern's lifeforce to strengthen himself, Candy killed herself, and the sudden energy surge blew Hodge up. Re-forming, Hodge and Steven Lang, another Phalanx-reanimated X-Men foe, watched over the captive X-Men on Mt. Everest. Though Hodge suspected Lang was a traitor, he failed to act on his instincts before the X-Men got free and destroyed the base, leaving Hodge buried on the mountain under the collapsed citadel. The Phalanx were soon defeated. Sometime later, Bastion (a mechanical hybrid of the mutant-hunting robots Master Mold and Earth-811's Nimrod, enhanced by the transmode virus) plotted to resurrect several of the X-Men's greatest foes under his direct control. Bastion's Purifiers unearthed Hodge's head, had a new body created for him, and sent him to restart his Right organization. The Right obtained strains of the mutant-killing Legacy virus, though X-Force (X-Men strikeforce) soon destroyed one such strain.

HEIGHT: 5'10"		EYES: Blue	
WEIGHT: 180 lbs.		HAIR: Gray	

ABILITIES/ACCESSORIES: Cameron Hodge is a transmode-virus-enhanced human under Bastion's control. As Hodge was an undying head infected by the virus before his current infection, the extent of Bastion's control is unrevealed. Cameron Hodge's demon pact granted him virtual immortality, enabling him to survive even decapitation. Hodge was infected by the Phalanx's transmode virus, allowing him to form a body out of machinery, control machinery, drain life from organic beings, and share a collective consciousness with other techno-organic beings. Before this infection, Hodge had his undying head attached to a mechanical body, which weighed over 3000 lbs., was bulletproof, impervious to energy blasts, self-regenerating (through repair circuits), and equipped with long mechanical tendrils, phasing technology that allowed intangibility, a force field, shoulder spikes, lasers, bolo cords, molecular adhesives, mechanical saws, electric blasts, and super-strength (lifting 40 tons). Before his decapitation, Hodge utilized various armored suits equipped with offensive weaponry, including a ruby quartz suit, protecting him from Cyclops' optic blasts. He also had access to the Right robots and armor. Hodge was a trained lawyer, advertising executive, and public relations director, with some mechanical engineering experience.

POWER GRID	1	2	3	4	5	6	7
INTELLIGENCE							
STRENGTH							
SPEED							
DURABILITY							
ENERGY PROJECTION							
FIGHTING SKILLS							

HISTORY: Kimora ruled the extradimensional realm Kageumbra with an iron fist for many lifetimes. In the 1940s, Dr. Michael Carling invented a device that opened a portal between Earth and Kageumbra. He spent years there, met the native woman Jhet, fell in love, and fathered Rose. Carling continued his experiments but was eventually discovered and confronted by Kimora, who sought to use his technology to extend his reign to other dimensions. When Carling resisted, Kimora slew Jhet. Carling fled with Rose to Earth through a dimensional rift, and Kimora followed but was disoriented by the transit, enabling Carling's escape. Kimora pursued him for years, and Carling eventually sought protection with the research firm Landau, Luckman, and Lake (LLL). Kimora also at some point battled the warrior Logan (James Howlett, later Wolverine) in Kyoto, Japan. In the mid-1950s, Kimora captured Michael and Rose Carling, but Michael refused to give up his secrets, even when Kimora threatened Rose's life. Informed of this by LLL's Chang, Logan fought Kimora but was on the verge of defeat until Dr. Carling struck Kimora from behind and then decapitated him. Surviving even this, Kimora escaped through a pinhole rift, eventually returning to Kageumbra, where, due to fear, his despotic rule persisted despite his absence; upon his return, the natives wept. The rift allowed Kimora to travel between Earth and Kageumbra, but was too unstable for the large scale travel he desired for an invasion force.

Years later, Kimora recaptured Dr. Carling, taking him to Kageumbra. Kimora's agent Oracle took the knowledge of how to build the dimensional transporter from Carling's mind, and his agents began constructing a large rift to Earth. Chang recruited Logan to rescue Carling again. Having injured an opponent in a practice swordfight, Logan had recently had his sword taken away and replaced with a wooden blade. Upon arrival, Logan was assaulted by Kimora's agents, the lovers Shadow Walker (Mahog) and Shadow Dancer (Sydia), but was saved by Rose Carling, now possessing metamorphic powers, who slew Shadow Dancer. Still seeking Carling's moral surrender, Kimora continuously tortured him, whipping him with snakes even as the Oracle warned him that he could not foresee the outcome of the impending clash with Logan; Kimora was pleased, believing foreknowledge would dampen his enjoyment of the battle. Logan, Chang, and Rose entered Kimora's fortress via deception and force, but Shadow Walker pulled Rose through a shadow warp. Chang maintained the warp long enough for them to pass through it into Kimora's chambers. As Chang was then forced to use all of his psychic powers to prevent Oracle from incapacitating the others while Shadow Walker held a knife to Rose's throat, Kimora departed with the bound Dr. Carling. Enraged over the

REAL NAME: Kimora
ALIASES: Great One
IDENTITY: No dual identity; existence unknown to Earth's general populace
OCCUPATION: Warlord, ruler of his realm
CITIZENSHIP: Kageumbra
PLACE OF BIRTH: Kageumbra
KNOWN RELATIVES: None
GROUP AFFILIATION: Led Kageumbra's forces
EDUCATION: Unrevealed
FIRST APPEARANCE: Logan: Path of the Warlord #1 (1996)

threat to Rose, Logan entered a berserker state and took out Shadow Walker, then pursued Kimora; Rose and Chang agreed that if Logan endangered the mission they would have to kill him. Logan mowed a path through Kimora's warriors, but as he caught up with Kimora, the warlord slew Dr. Carling; Carling had refused to surrender to Kimora, and the warlord gave him the honor of a swift death. As Logan attacked Kimora savagely, the warlord mocked him, stating he could not die. Rose tossed Logan his wooden sword, helping him regain his focus and control. Logan then cast Kimora into the rift and destroyed the rift-creating device, leaving Kimora trapped between worlds.

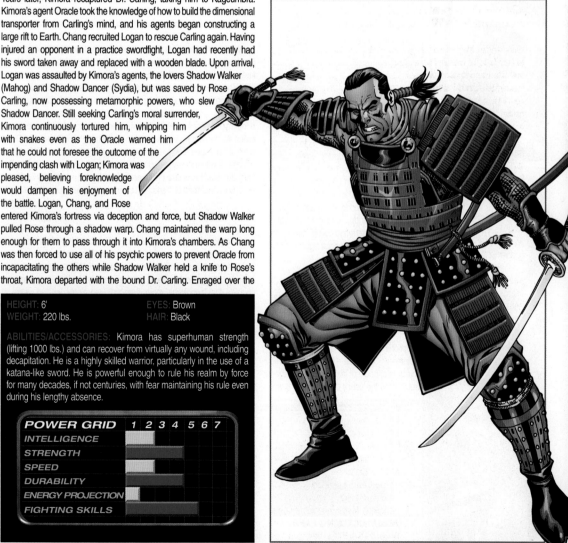

HEIGHT: 6'
WEIGHT: 220 lbs.
EYES: Brown
HAIR: Black

ABILITIES/ACCESSORIES: Kimora has superhuman strength (lifting 1000 lbs.) and can recover from virtually any wound, including decapitation. He is a highly skilled warrior, particularly in the use of a katana-like sword. He is powerful enough to rule his realm by force for many decades, if not centuries, with fear maintaining his rule even during his lengthy absence.

POWER GRID	1	2	3	4	5	6	7
INTELLIGENCE							
STRENGTH							
SPEED							
DURABILITY							
ENERGY PROJECTION							
FIGHTING SKILLS							

LANDAU, LUCKMAN & LAKE

CURRENT MEMBERS: (Principals) Lake, Landau, Luckman; (employees) Kel Blanchard, Goodson Coleman, Emmet, Wibo Epsg, Sarah Flowers, Herbert, Martin Lumley, Katrina Nance, Ngwn Richards, Daniel Roberts, Hiko Youngsoo, Neal Zeugridor; Black Out Troopers, Spin Doctors; many others

FORMER MEMBERS: Montgomery Burns, Dr. Michael Carling (deceased), Chang (deceased), Tomas Coolidge (deceased), Zoe Culloden, Deadpool ("Wade Wilson"), Doris (deceased), Noah DuBois (deceased), Hera Harding (deceased), Ms. Kierkegaard (deceased), Gerry LeQuare, Dixon Mason, Natikim Mikitan, Mr. Ramavishnu (deceased), Dietrich Woodrow (deceased), Rose Carling Wu (deceased)

BASE OF OPERATIONS: (Research and Development) A vast complex existing somewhere in outer space yet outside of time; (overall) at least 27 branch offices on Earth, including branches in Egypt, Hong Kong, Madripoor (closed), Morocco, Scotland, and the USA; branch offices in several unidentified dimensions

FIRST APPEARANCE: Wolverine #5 (1989)

HISTORY: Most commonly described as an intergalactic/interdimensional holding firm operating under a corporate charter, Landau, Luckman and Lake can allegedly buy and sell entire solar systems. Its employees frequently observe or predict events of potential cosmic significance and, if necessary, manipulate those involved to guarantee favorable outcomes. Each LL&L division is apparently managed by an "Overboss," who can control employees via a gem worn on his/her forehead. "Expediters" conduct field operations and supervise branch offices, acting as direct liaisons to high-maintenance clients when necessary. LL&L controls virtually all aspects of its employees' lives, going so far as to declare some of them LL&L property; emphasizing employee dismissal with property damage is not unheard of. All LL&L employees are implanted with neural kill-switches, enabling their superiors to render them unconscious as necessary. Landau, Luckman and Lake themselves — referred to collectively as the Principals — are mysterious figures rarely seen by most employees.

LL&L employs highly advanced technology, most notably teleportation throughout time and space via Warp Chambers; all LL&L offices are situated near "crossroads of destiny," evidently natural space/time disruptions that facilitate such travel. Other equipment includes bioelectrographic projectors capable of imposing 3-D images directly onto the user's optic nerves, quark emulation disruptor weapons, and advance thermal trace imaging devices to track individuals throughout multiple dimensions. LL&L has strict, albeit not always observed, regulations regarding such technology's field use. Employees act as consultants to corporations, governments and other influential bodies. In the Corporal Enhancement Division, aka Fleshwerks, various superhumans, most notably precognitives, are augmented or experimented upon to use their abilities on behalf of LL&L or its clients. The firm can acquire data from at least six non-Earth dimensions and three alternate timelines.

LL&L evidently gained their dimension-warping technology from Dr. Michael Carling, who joined their research firm in exchange for protection against the dimension Kageumbra's warlord, Kimora. In the 1950's, LL&L's psionic-powered Expediter Chang managed finances and business affairs for mutant mercenary Logan (James Howlett, later Wolverine). When Kimora abducted LL&L, Carling and his daughter Rose, Chang recruited Logan to accompany him to Kageumbra. The pair rescued Rose, although Kimora slew Dr. Carling, and Logan trapped Kimora in a dimensional rift. Eventually, Rose Carling became Expediter/Head of LL&L's Hong Kong branch, while Chang rescued a young girl from an inhumane Romanian orphanage; named "Zoe Culloden," she became Chang's protégé at LL&L. At some point, Gerry LeQuare, apparently an Earth-born superhuman and friend to future Sorcerer Supreme Dr. Stephen Strange, became fourth Principal to the firm, thus renamed Landau, Luckman, Lake and LeQuare. LeQuare's bailiwick included supervision of Zoe and her peers Noah DuBois and Dixon Mason.

Early in her career, Zoe worked with Noah, Dixon and precognitive Montgomery Burns to prepare for an alien "Messiah," whom Burns foresaw would visit Earth in less than 20 years to initiate a galaxywide era of peace and prosperity; his predictions also indicated, however, the Messiah would be slain by a monstrous destroyer, Tiamat, unless protected by a superhuman champion, the Mithras. They scanned many people's probable futures, and Burns eventually proclaimed a mercenary called Wade Wilson was destined to be Mithras; while Noah and Dixon were unconvinced, Zoe made surveillance and preparation of Wilson her pet project within the larger operation, dubbed the Mithras Directive. The four attempted to conceal the Directive from LeQuare until they had more facts, but he learned of it and kept them under covert surveillance.

Some five years after Burns' initial prediction, his research revealed Wilson's destiny had grown uncertain, and Dixon, now an Overboss, recommended Zoe find a new candidate. Zoe, believing Wilson's success integral to her success at LLL&L, infiltrated Wilson's life by befriending his girlfriend Vanessa Carlysle; Zoe learned Wilson had contracted cancer, making his long-term survival unlikely, and she regretted the couple's lost happiness more than her seemingly wasted years of championing Wilson as Mithras. Soon afterward, LeQuare disappeared on an extradimensional safari and was believed dead, causing the firm to revert to its earlier name. He actually went into hiding on Earth after LL&L employees made an attempt on his life for unrevealed reasons. Having followed the Mithras Directive's progress from the beginning, LeQuare continued to do so, manipulating Wilson, Zoe and others from afar. Eventually, Wilson became the superhuman Deadpool, and Zoe again sponsored him for the Mithras Directive.

In recent years, Logan, now the X-Man Wolverine, renewed his LL&L contacts when Rose aided him following an attack by the Reavers; by then, she had apparently married and taken the last name Wu. Months later, while protecting Wolverine's ally Tyger Tiger, Chang, now Expediter of Madripoor, was slain by General Nguyen Ngoc Coy's enforcers Bloodscream and Roughhouse. Rose eventually retired from LL&L, using her corporate annuity to buy Madripoor's Princess Bar, while Noah DuBois, following unrevealed orders, infiltrated Senator Robert Kelly's presidential campaign staff. Zoe Culloden, now an Expeditor with some of Rose's responsibilities, first met Wolverine while investigating Cyber's

LANDAU, LUCKMAN & LAKE
DEADPOOL #25 (1999)

attempt to abscond with Wolverine's LL&L-held funds in Scotland. Initially suspecting Wolverine of Chang's murder, Zoe soon learned otherwise and assisted Wolverine and his Excalibur allies in battling Cyber.

Aware Wolverine, then divested of the Adamantium formerly bonded to his skeleton, would soon be abducted by Genesis (Tyler Dayspring), both Zoe and Noah kept him under surveillance. When Juggernaut (Cain Marko) renewed his longtime feud with the X-Men, the pair teleported Wolverine away. Despite Zoe's reservations, LL&L arranged for Genesis' underling Dirt Nap to battle the increasingly bestial Wolverine, whom LL&L believed would follow Dirt Nap to his master. The ploy failed, but Wolverine and his teammate Jean Grey again encountered LL&L employees when they battled interdimensional criminal Chimera, whose activities threatened LL&L's extradimensional resources.

Soon afterward, Rose Wu and several other Wolverine allies were, in a presumably unrelated incident, murdered by General Coy and others to frame Wolverine. Zoe escorted Wolverine to Akkaba, Egypt, where Genesis captured him, intending to transform him into Death, Horseman of Apocalypse (En Sabah Nur). Per LL&L's interests, Zoe prevented Wolverine's teammate Cannonball (Sam Guthrie) from intervening until Genesis had replaced Wolverine's lost Adamantium. Weeks later, Wolverine, evidently unaware of Zoe's role in his transformation, visited LL&L's Manhattan office, where Chimera arranged for Dirt Nap to again battle their common foe. LL&L office boy Emmet assisted Wolverine in battle, as did human/symbiote hybrid Venom (Eddie Brock) and others drawn into the encounter. LL&L later entrusted Wolverine with an artifact containing his evil ex-mentor Ogun's spirit, who escaped but was defeated by the X-Men.

Meanwhile, the Messiah's arrival approached, and Zoe and Noah shifted attention to Deadpool, unaware he had befriended Gerry LeQuare, who kept his true nature secret. Zoe and Noah manipulated Deadpool into preventing a gamma core meltdown in Antarctica to steer him toward heroic endeavors, but he was skeptical of such a future, even more so when he learned the stakes of the predicted Messiah/Tiamat encounter. When Burns' latest premonition indicated Tiamat would slay Deadpool, Dixon, dubious of Deadpool from the start, concluded Captain America (Steve Rogers) would better fill the Mithras role despite Zoe's continued confidence in Deadpool.

Dixon sent Black Out Troops across the world to prevent anyone else from detecting the Messiah's arrival, but at the SETI Radio Telescope in Puerto Rico, Tiamat slew them. With regret, Dixon, truly convinced of his actions' rightness, sent Noah and a team of operatives to investigate, knowing they too would perish. As he anticipated, Deadpool, having befriended Noah, fought Tiamat prior to the foreseen timetable, enabling Dixon to record Tiamat's capabilities to better prepare Captain America. A defeated Deadpool, followed by Zoe, fled to his home base; Dixon bombed it, intending to kill both loose ends, but LeQuare rescued them. Having bested Captain America in Egypt, Tiamat prepared to attack the arriving Messiah, but Deadpool defeated him; learning the Messiah (an alien named S'met'kth) brought not true peace but only mindless bliss, Deadpool killed the alien, saving the world. Unable to accept the Messiah's true nature, Dixon suffered a nervous breakdown and was personally institutionalized by Landau, Luckman and Lake, while Zoe was promoted to Overboss in his place

Burns, having befriended Deadpool, accompanied him to a new base in Bolivia but was injured by mystic mercenary T-Ray weeks later. Deadpool brought the precognitive back to LL&L, where Zoe initially planned to detain both men as LL&L property, but she ultimately resigned as Overboss and accompanied Burns to parts unknown. Months later, the couple resurfaced at Deadpool's apparent funeral, but Landau, Luckman and Lake's subsequent activities remain unrevealed.

KEL BLANCHARD
Security Chief
Deadpool #31 (1999)

MONTGOMERY BURNS
Precognitive
Deadpool Minus-One (1997)

CHANG
Expediter, Madripoor
Wolverine #5 (1989)

TOMAS COOLIDGE
Field Operative
Deadpool #22 (1998)

ZOE CULLODEN
Expediter, Overboss
Wolverine #79 (1994)

DEADPOOL
Field Operative, "Mithras"
New Mutants #98 (1991)

DORIS
Research Subject
Deadpool #15 (1998)

NOAH DUBOIS
Field Operative
Uncanny X-Men #299 (1993)

EMMET
Office Boy
Wolverine #97 (1996)

WIBO EPSG
Receptionist
Deadpool #15 (1998)

SARAH FLOWERS
Biophysicist
Deadpool #21 (1998)

HERA HARDING
Field Operative
Deadpool #22 (1998)

HERBERT
Living Database
Deadpool #15 (1998)

GERRY LEQUARE
Firm Principal
Deadpool #1 (1997)

MARTIN LUMLEY
Research Scientist
Deadpool #15 (1998)

DIXON MASON
Overboss
Deadpool Minus-One (1997)

KATRINA NANCE
Receptionist
Deadpool #15 (1998)

DANIEL ROBERTS
Personnel Director
Deadpool #16 (1998)

DIETRICH WOODROW
Field Operative
Deadpool #22 (1998)

ROSE CARLING WU
Expediter, Hong Kong
Uncanny X-Men #257 (1990)

HIKO YOUNGSOO
Administrator
Deadpool #23 (1998)

STEVEN LANG

REAL NAME: Steven Lang
ALIASES: None
IDENTITY: No dual identity
OCCUPATION: US Department of Defense advisor; former Phalanx leader, rogue scientist
CITIZENSHIP: USA
PLACE OF BIRTH: Grand Forks, North Dakota
KNOWN RELATIVES: None
GROUP AFFILIATION: Formerly Phalanx, Project: Armageddon; ally of the Council of the Chosen
EDUCATION: Ph.D. in engineering
FIRST APPEARANCE: X-Men #96 (1975)

HISTORY: Department of Defense special advisor Steven Lang was strongly influenced by the anti-mutant rhetoric of Bolivar Trask, inventor of the mutant-hunting robot Sentinels. Lang eventually launched Project: Armageddon, a government program investigating mutants' potential threat. Lang's project developed a new line of Sentinels (Mark III) funded by the Council of the Chosen, a Hellfire Club conclave headed by Edward Buckman. Lang and Buckman claimed that their research would enable the Hellfire Club to control the "x-factor" gene which caused mutations, but secretly they planned to massacre all mutants. Lang appropriated the SHIELD Orbital Platform as his Sentinels' base and designed his own Master Mold robot based on Trask's, as well as a band of human-sized "X-Sentinels" designed to mimic the powers and appearances of the heroic mutant X-Men.

Lang's Sentinels abducted the X-Men's Marvel Girl (Jean Grey), Banshee, Professor X and Wolverine (Logan/James Howlett), holding

CONSCIENCE

Art by Ron Lim

them on the orbital platform; however, Lang's Sentinels were less powerful than the earlier Trask models, and the remaining X-Men soon freed their captured comrades. The X-Men escaped Lang and left him for dead, though radiation exposure during their escape led to Jean being replaced by Phoenix. Using a cybernetic helmet, Lang tried to awaken his Master Mold, but this imprinted Lang's mind upon the robot, leaving his body comatose. Believing itself to be Lang, the Master Mold tried to continue his work by capturing the mutants Angel (Warren Worthington) and Iceman, but when the Hulk (Bruce Banner) interfered, Master Mold learned that Lang was alive in a psychiatric hospital. Eventually, Master Mold cast Lang's mind from its body and into a robot named Conscience to serve as an advisor. Conscience aided Master Mold in a scheme to design a "Retribution Virus" to eliminate mutants, but when Conscience learned that the virus would target humans as well, he turned against Master Mold and was destroyed halting the virus' launch.

Friends of Humanity agents later removed the real Lang from his hospital and enlisted him into the Phalanx project, utilizing the techno-organic being Warlock's remains to design an army of similar creatures to combat mutants. By joining the Phalanx group mind, Lang became a techno-organic being but was allowed to retain his individuality so he could facilitate interactions with humans. Working alongside Cameron Hodge, Lang had the Phalanx attack the X-Men and brought most of them to their base on Mount Everest so they could analyze their genes and determine why mutants resisted the techno-organic process; however, Lang foresaw that Hodge would eventually try to replace humanity with the Phalanx, a threat worse than mutants, and secretly helped the X-Men destroy the Phalanx base. Lang intended to restart the Phalanx under his sole authority, but Hodge dragged him into their base as it was destroyed. Years later, Lang was retrieved by the Purifiers, an anti-mutant cult allied with Bastion. Using the Magus (Warlock's father), Bastion spread the Technarch's transmode virus into Lang and other anti-mutant zealots. Lang rejoined the Department of Defense.

AS PHALANX

Art by Andy Kubert

HEIGHT: 5'11"   EYES: Blue
WEIGHT: 166 lbs.   HAIR: Blond

ABILITIES/ACCESSORIES: As a human, Lang was a brilliant inventor in cybernetics and robotics and had access to sophisticated weapons such as his one-man flying gunship and Sentinels. As a techno-organic Phalanx, Lang could reshape himself into any form, share in the Phalanx's group mind, temporarily transfer his consciousness into the body of another Phalanx and infect other humans with the techno-organic virus. With the infusion of the Technarch virus into his techno-organic body Lang's current powers are unrevealed, but he remains able to assume a human-like appearance.

RESURRECTED

POWER GRID	1	2	3	4	5	6	7
INTELLIGENCE							
STRENGTH							
SPEED							
DURABILITY							
ENERGY PROJECTION							
FIGHTING SKILLS							

HISTORY: During Tigon Liger's early career as a British Army colonel, he was on attachment to US Special Forces in Antarctica and South America, prior to his transference to British Intelligence Shadow Section. While tracking Madripoor armament sales, Liger encountered Wolverine (Logan/James Howlett) who tried to deliver a cryptic message. They fought, and Liger awoke days later with his face scarred. Soon after, his brother Lynx recruited him into Mys-Tech as an advisor before disappearing through a wormhole in Antarctica. Liger became one of Mys-Tech's dimension-hopping Warheads, hoping to track Lynx down. Surviving a number of jumps, including one where an advanced reptilian race wiped out his troop, Liger acquired a château in France's Bordeaux region. As Kether Troop's leader, Liger confided in Psi-Scout, Misha and their Master Key (Alfred J. Swinburne). Other regular team members included his lover Cale, hit-man Gregory, empathic medic Perez, and Stacy Arnheim, responsible for troop defense. He discovered another "companion," a voice operated gun from the city Numeropolis, on planet Septimus Primo III in the Magellanic Clouds. Liger named the gun Clementine, and it became his main weapon. During a jump into the past, Kether Troop stumbled upon Wolverine in the Australian Outback. Liger realized this was what Wolverine had tried to warn him about in Madripoor, but was unable to prevent him from killing three team members, including Cale.

After returning from a shadow realm that turned fears into reality, some of Liger's teammates were injured by Nick Fury's agent Bad Hand (Thomas Pyke). While they recovered, Liger was unaware when Fury switched one of their temporary replacements, technician Grierson, with Iron Man (Tony Stark). Reunited with his regular troopers, Liger opposed a corrupt warlike civilization by destroying their control room. Then, a wormhole trap led Kether Troop to the magical domain of the witch Aeish, where they encountered Cable's X-Force. Cable's recognition of the French lilt to Liger's voice suggests an unrevealed connection between them. On other missions, Kether Troop liberated a magical box from the planet Karnos, and encountered Spider-Man (Peter Parker) and the Knights of Pendragon on the planet Arakne, inhabited by the spider-like Araknoids. While on the world of Genghis, Wizard Majestrix,

REAL NAME: Tigon Liger
ALIASES: Ephesus
IDENTITY: No dual identity
OCCUPATION: Warheads Strike Troop leader; formerly British Army colonel, Mys-Tech advisor
CITIZENSHIP: UK
PLACE OF BIRTH: Horsham, Sussex, Britain
KNOWN RELATIVES: Lynx Liger (brother)
GROUP AFFILIATION: Dark Guard, Warheads Kether Troop; formerly British Army, British Intelligence Shadow Section, Mys-Tech
EDUCATION: Degree in engineering gained in British Army
FIRST APPEARANCE: Overkill #1 (1992)

---

the cybernetic mercenary Death's Head (Minion) and his partner Tuck arrived to repossess Clementine, but ultimately stole the wizard's power source, the Sapphire Lotus, instead. Trying to return home, Kether Troop's journey bizarrely led them through dreamscapes belonging to Wolverine and Psylocke. The demon Blackheart secretly manipulated Kether Troop for some time before using them in a failed attempt to assassinate his father Mephisto. Liger also opposed the Mys-Tech board's efforts with the reality-altering Un-Earth device, though this was forgotten when several of Earth's heroes used the device to undo events.

Liger later encountered a civilization in suspended animation on the 26th century planet Moana, the scientist Ashmael with his genetically augmented dinosaur army, and the reptilian race that had slain his earlier troop. However, when the ghosts of former Warheads revealed that Mys-Tech had made them dependent on wormhole travel to survive, Kether Troop went rogue, using Misha's powers and the ghosts' knowledge to open their own wormholes. Liger finally located Lynx, now a vampire on Earth-7931, but was unable to help him. The Time Guardian then recruited Liger into Dark Guard to fight Mys-Tech.

ABILITIES/ACCESSORIES: Liger has peak human agility and reflexes, and athletic stamina, speed and strength. Mys-Tech's alterations make him dependent on regular wormhole travel to survive. He is trained in the use of personal weapons, field guns and tanks, and is a master of ninjitsu. He is a skilled strategist and helicopter pilot. Liger and his Warheads can form a septagram, an extremely dangerous maneuver that generates a vast psychic blast. Liger generally wears mystically enhanced battle armor, including anti-gravs and a personal force shield. He has assorted personal weaponry, but his main weapon is Clementine, a voice-activated gun with several weapons systems. Clementine's effects range from "disable" (stun) to "obliterate," including computer virus placement, eldritch forces, gravitic particle generation, laser scattershot, Shakaran hellfire, and much more. Diagnostic systems continuously update Clementine's programming and can assimilate new effects, including magic. Clementine can also tap into external power sources such as the Sapphire Lotus.

POWER GRID	1	2	3	4	5	6	7
INTELLIGENCE							
STRENGTH							
SPEED							
DURABILITY							
ENERGY PROJECTION							
FIGHTING SKILLS							

Art by Simon Coleby

MANA

REAL NAME: Mana Yanowa
ALIASES: None
IDENTITY: No dual identity
OCCUPATION: High priestess, warrior
CITIZENSHIP: Japan
PLACE OF BIRTH: Kyoto, Japan
KNOWN RELATIVES: Hana (sister, deceased), numerous unidentified high priestesses (ancestors, deceased)
GROUP AFFILIATION: The Shosei Order
EDUCATION: Mystic tutelage by Shosei Order
FIRST APPEARANCE: (Mentioned, pictured) Wolverine: Soultaker #1 (2005); (full) Wolverine: Soultaker #2 (2005)

HISTORY: Mana is the latest in a line of Miko priestesses of the Shosei Order, mystic guardians protecting Japan from demons, curses and magical threats for 800 years. As each priestess died, her blood was drawn and added to a case holding the Blade of Blood, the Shosei's powerful ceremonial weapon, adding within it a part of the deceased's soul to all who had served before her. Mana and her twin sister Hana were born to the Miko priestess lineage, destined to clash over this role. As they aged, they became bitter rivals, with Mana eventually winning leadership and Hana turning her back on the Order. In 1864 AD, Hana returned, having studied dark and forbidden mystic arts and seeking to take over the Order. As Mana and Hana battled, Hana loosed the ancient demon Ryuki from Ashurado, the fourth level of Hell. Ryuki possessed Hana, intending to have his undead minions slay innocents and usurp their souls for power, then to open a gateway at the Bridge of Six Realms and cross over into Earth in his own body. With no other timely options, Mana trapped Ryuki's, Hana's and her own soul within her necklace, the Mark of Mana. For decades the Shosei Order protected Mana and Hana's bodies and the Mark of Mana, fruitlessly seeking a spell to release the sisters without freeing Ryuki. One night, an Ashurado cult stole Hana's body and the Mark of Mana, but the Shosei kept hidden Mana's body, without which the cult could not release Ryuki.

In recent years, the thief Yukio stole the Mark of Mana from the Ashurado cult. Hearing evil whispers from the Mark, she brought it to Wolverine (Logan/James Howlett), who located Mana via the Mark's guidance, though the cult slew many remaining Shosei in the process. Upon touching the Mark to Mana, Wolverine revived her, but also unleashed Ryuki/Hana. Mana mystically blessed Wolverine to allow him to oppose Ryuki's reanimated minions while she summoned Oinari (aka Inari), the silver-haired fox god of rice and food, messenger of the Heavens, to learn Ryuki's weakness to gold, indebting herself to him in the process. Ryuki/Hana offered to end their struggle if Mana brought the Blade of Blood to the Bridge of Six Realms at the next sunset. While Mana knew Ryuki wished to use the Blade's souls' power to open a gateway to Ashurado, she gave Logan the Blade, telling him he would wield it against Hana/Ryuki at the Bridge, as this would be their chance to end Hana's threat and send Ryuki's spirit back to Ashurado.

Wolverine and Mana met them as planned, but Ryuki/Hana had taken Wolverine's foster daughter Amiko Kobayashi and Yukio hostage, so Wolverine surrendered the Blade of Blood. Mana battled Hana/Ryuki, then got Yukio and Amiko to safety while Wolverine impaled Hana/Ryuki with his claws, which Mana had coated in gold, banishing Ryuki from Earth. After slaying the corrupted Hana, Mana began training Amiko, who proved to be a descendant of the Shosei Order, as her successor.

HEIGHT: 5'2"	EYES: Brown
WEIGHT: 100 lbs.	HAIR: Black

ABILITIES/ACCESSORIES: Mana can form magical shields, project mystic bolts, and cast a variety of spells (including freezing other objects and beings). She can mystically bless objects and beings, granting them a Shosei purification aura that allows them to better combat dark mystical threats. She is aware of anything that happens or is stated around the Mark of Mana, and she has bound her own and other spirits within the Mark, her body remaining unchanged over centuries despite this separation. She also is the holder of the mystically powerful Blade of Blood, able to at least deflect or disrupt magic and open dimensional portals. The Blade only responds to the Shosei Order's high priestess, unless she willingly gives it to and commands the souls to respond to another. Additionally, she wields and is proficient in combat with an unidentified blade and dagger.

POWER GRID	1	2	3	4	5	6	7
INTELLIGENCE							
STRENGTH							
SPEED							
DURABILITY							
ENERGY PROJECTION							
FIGHTING SKILLS							

HISTORY: In Reality-3071's mid-21st century, unidentified researchers sought to re-engineer flesh-eating bacteria to naturally decompose the toxic materials poisoning Earth's ever-deteriorating ecosystem. Seemingly succeeding in 2047 AD, they synthesized an organic orb-like containment unit in which to store and transport the bacteria. They then learned that their mutations had granted it sentience, while containment within the orb-core concentrated the sentience into a brain, and it soon began to form bodies from materials around them. This first Mandate, later known as the Primogenitor, conceived new orb-cores and created new bodies for new Mandates; however, the offspring did not inherit the ability to procreate. Their flesh-eating properties — clearly still intact, now combined with their toxic decomposition abilities — enabled the Mandate to wipe out their city of creation within days. The Mandate continued to multiply, rapidly taking over much of the world unchecked before humanity had any idea of what was going on. Even the Anti-Mandate Armored Corps, developed specifically to combat the Mandate, stood no chance against these ever-evolving warriors who eventually wiped out most of humanity. A small band of human survivors relocated to an underground Compound in Japan, protected from the Mandate because it was composed of the one substance the Mandate could not penetrate: Adamantium. Among this Underground group was the Colonel, sole survivor of the Anti-Mandate Armored Corps, who wore Adamantium armor and used a gun firing Adamantium bullets. The survivors lost almost all technical knowledge and data over the years, as well as any kind of labs or raw materials. They had a limited supply of the Adamantium bullets required to destroy the Mandate's orb-cores and were unable to produce more. While the Primogenitor continued to produce orb-cores and build massive

colonies of Mandate warriors, the human survivors were unable to produce the weapons and ammunition that they needed to combat them. There was another group of survivors in a base like the Compound, but those in the Compound eventually lost contact with them.

In 2058 AD, the Underground's Fusa had a vision of Wolverine (Logan/James Howlett) and realized he was the only person who could save her world. Using her unique time/space/dimension transport ability, Fusa confronted Wolverine in Earth-616's modern era and brought him with her to her world; suspicious of her, Wolverine let go in mid-transfer and emerged at a point distant from the Compound, where Fusa arrived. The Underground's Yaa, a pair of telepathic albinos, located Wolverine, and the Colonel saved him from attacking Mandate and explained their weakness. Fusa brought them back to the Compound, but the Underground's Takeo was infected with micro-nucleate Mandate parasites and transformed into a Mandate that terrorized the Compound before Wolverine destroyed it. Wolverine joined the Underground's warriors in assaulting a Mandate

colony to destroy the Primogenitor, but the Primogenitor turned out to be the entire colony base itself. After all other warriors had perished in the effort, the Colonel sacrificed himself exposing the Primogenitor's orb-core, and Wolverine destroyed it. With the Primogenitor dead, the rest of the Mandate literally fell apart. Fusa invited Wolverine to stay with her people but returned him home after he declined, hoping to never see them again.

KNOWN MEMBERS: The Primogenitor; others unidentified
BASE OF OPERATIONS: Formerly numerous nests across Earth-3071
FIRST APPEARANCE: Wolverine: Snikt #1 (2003)

TRAITS: The Mandate are sentient bacterial colonies contained within a protective "orb-core," which can only be destroyed by Adamantium. Each Mandate's orb-core uses an enzyme-soluble synthetic process to create and maintain its cybernetic body. As long as its orb-core continues to function, it can regenerate itself and any of its appendages. The Mandate can adapt their form to anything they want, depending on the situation's requirements. Some of them can develop wings to fly, while others arm themselves with any type of weapon imaginable. They can destroy flesh, plastics and other synthetics, and possibly metal. They can also teleport, though not into structures surrounded with Adamantium. Only the Primogenitor, larger and much more powerful than the others, could generate new Mandate. Under unspecified circumstances, however, Mandate can transform into micronucleate parasites, which could infect humans and take over their bodies, transforming them into new Mandate.

MASTERMIND

REAL NAME: Jason Wyngarde
ALIASES: Nikos; impersonated Nabatone Yokuse, Cyclops (Scott Summers), Captain Britain (Brian Braddock), others
IDENTITY: Secret
OCCUPATION: Former criminal, subversive, terrorist, carnival mentalist
CITIZENSHIP: USA
PLACE OF BIRTH: Unrevealed
KNOWN RELATIVES: Martinique Jason (Mastermind, daughter), Regan Wyngarde (Lady Mastermind, daughter)
GROUP AFFILIATION: Formerly Hellfire Club (rejected Inner Circle applicant), Factor Three, Brotherhood of Evil Mutants
EDUCATION: Unrevealed
FIRST APPEARANCE: X-Men #4 (1964)

HISTORY: Mutant illusionist Jason Wyngarde fathered two daughters during two different failed relationships and worked as a carnival mentalist before Magneto (Max Eisenhardt) recruited him into the subversive Brotherhood of Evil Mutants. As Mastermind, Wyngarde helped Magneto usurp control of the tiny nation Santo Marco, creating an illusory army to frighten the populace into submission, but the X-Men opposed them. Wyngarde delayed the X-Men with an illusory flame river while Magneto armed a nuclear bomb to destroy the country before

escaping, though morally conflicted Brotherhood member Quicksilver defused the bomb. While with the Brotherhood, Wyngarde lusted after his teammate the Scarlet Witch, quarreled with her brother Quicksilver, and showed contempt for another teammate, the Toad (Mortimer Toynbee). The Brotherhood sought revenge on the X-Men, using Toad as bait to draw the X-Men out and capturing Angel (Warren Worthington), but the X-Men followed Toad back to the Brotherhood's orbiting Asteroid M base, freed Angel and again defeated the Brotherhood. Following Magneto's failed attempts to recruit Namor the Sub-Mariner and the Asgardian god Thor into the Brotherhood, Wyngarde aided Magneto's recruitment of the Blob (Fred Dukes), which was short-lived after Magneto betrayed the Blob in another clash with the X-Men. When Magneto sought to ally with the enigmatic alien Stranger, Wyngarde was turned to living stone after angering the Stranger, who also trapped Magneto and Toad on an alien world.

The Stranger's transformation eventually wore off, and Wyngarde subsequently joined Factor Three's efforts to dominate humanity. Opposed by the X-Men, Wyngarde and his allies were ultimately betrayed by Factor Three's leader, the Mutant Master, who was revealed to be an alien planning to conquer Earth. Wyngarde was then among several mutants captured by the Sentinels, but the X-Men freed them. Wyngarde subsequently joined a new Brotherhood formed by the Blob. After the mutant Krueger captured the X-Men and offered to sell them to the Brotherhood, Wyngarde created illusory money that they used to "buy" the captured heroes; however, their attempt to exact revenge on the X-Men failed after Krueger confronted them over their deception, allowing the X-Men to escape Wyngarde's illusory trap. Wyngarde then assumed leadership of the Brotherhood and recruited an amnesiac Beast (Hank McCoy) after fooling him into believing he had killed Iron Man (Tony Stark). Wyngarde had the Beast steal the world's largest gem, the Rahmur Diamond, but the Beast's memory returned and he single-handedly defeated the Brotherhood. Wyngarde's sanity briefly frayed as a result of the defeat; however, he soon recovered his faculties and joined the Blob's new incarnation of Factor Three, helping them steal information from Xavier's computers to use in recruiting more mutants such as young Sonny Baredo (later called Humus Sapien).

Wyngarde was later among those mutants briefly captured by the Secret Empire until their defeat by the X-Men, Captain America (Steve Rogers) and the Falcon (Sam Wilson). The militant General then hired Wyngarde to manipulate the General's nemesis the Sentry (Robert Reynolds) by creating the illusion that Reynolds was unaware of both his super-powered personas, the Sentry and the Void. In turn, Reynolds' own untapped psionic powers strengthened Wyngarde's illusion and broadcasted it to everyone in existence, making it seem as if the Sentry and the Void had never been. Reynolds' subconscious mind tried to fight Wyngarde's suggestions, planting vague impressions of the Sentry and the Void in the minds of certain comic book creators, making their stories a potential clue to his true nature whenever fragments of his memories resurfaced in the ensuing years.

EXPANDED CONSCIOUSNESS

Art by Ron Lim

ILLUSORY FORM

After Magneto returned to Earth, he reclaimed leadership of the Brotherhood and created Alpha, whom he dubbed "the Ultimate Mutant." During a clash with the Defenders, Alpha turned on the Brotherhood and reverted them to infancy. Later restored to adulthood by the alien Shi'ar Eric the Red (Davan Shakari), Wyngarde declined to rejoin the Brotherhood. Subsequently, Wyngarde was invited to apply for admission to the Inner Circle of the Hellfire Club's New York chapter. To prove his worth, Wyngarde sought to psionically alter the personality of the X-Man Jean Grey. The Inner Circle hoped she would willingly become their new Black Queen, but they were unaware that Wyngarde's victim was not the real Jean Grey but the cosmic Phoenix Force, which had duplicated Grey's form and personality. Wyngarde initially posed as Greek youth Nikos and romanced the faux Grey, then manipulated her by using a mind-tap mechanism created by the Hellfire Club's White Queen (Emma Frost) that allowed him to project his illusions directly into the faux Grey's mind, causing her to believe she was time-shifting to inhabit the body of her own ancestor, an aristocrat married to Wyngarde. While at the Club, Wyngarde also sought to pit his psionic powers against those of Frost by playing a game of psychic chess which ended in a draw, though the effort left him physically and mentally exhausted. Wyngarde eventually turned Phoenix against the X-Men, but when her lover Cyclops (Scott Summers) failed in an attempt to free her by duelling Wyngarde on the astral plane, his psychic "death" snapped her out of Wyngarde's control. Enraged by Wyngarde's actions, the Phoenix Force responded by expanding his mind to encompass all of reality. Unable to cope with the resultant flood of cosmic imagery, Wyngarde was driven mad. Fleeing from paranoid delusions of the Avengers, Magneto, the Brotherhood and others, Wyngarde was picked up by the police and taken to the psychiatric ward of Bellevue Hospital. His Inner Circle application was, unsurprisingly, rejected.

Eventually regaining his sanity, Wyngarde remembered the cosmic glory he had perceived and felt tormented that he could no longer experience it. Desiring revenge on the X-Men, he manipulated Wolverine's lover Mariko Yashida into calling off their wedding by impersonating the Grand Oyabun of the Yakuza, Nabatone Yokuse, and fooled the X-Men into believing that Cyclops' new lover, Madelyne Pryor, was the Phoenix; however, Cyclops uncovered Wyngarde's deception, and despite Wyngarde's attempt to make the X-Men believe Cyclops was the Phoenix and thus attack him, Wyngarde was defeated. Later, Wyngarde sought to again experience the connection to the universe that the Phoenix Force gave him and located its new host, Rachel Summers, impersonating her Excalibur teammate Captain Britain (Brian Braddock) and creating an illusion of the adult Franklin Richards from her own reality (Earth-811) in order to gain her trust enough that she would psi-link with him. Creating illusions to keep the rest of Excalibur at bay, Wyngarde successfully restored his consciousness' universal connection, though this proved to be brief after Kitty Pryde realized his involvement and convinced Rachel of same. Angered at his contempt for her feelings, Rachel lashed out with the Phoenix Force's power, severing Wyngarde's cosmic connection while placing an illusion in his own mind that the connection remained. Wyngarde was then placed in the hospital wing of the Muir Island research facility.

Ultimately, Wyngarde contracted the Legacy virus, and as he lay dying he contacted Jean Grey to make amends for his past, unaware that she wasn't the Phoenix. Arriving at Muir Island to honor the dying man's request, Jean and her fellow X-Men Iceman and Bishop were unwittingly trapped when Wyngarde's powers flared out of control as a result of the virus, creating an illusory world wherein mutants were respected and beloved; however, he had inadvertently imperiled their lives, for if he died, they would too. Meanwhile, the other X-Men fought the vigilante X-Cutioner (Carl Denti) when he sought to assassinate Wyngarde. After Jean pierced Mastermind's illusory world, Wyngarde apologized to her for his actions as he had only sought to give them a glimpse of a better world. As the virus took hold of his body, Jean sought to remain with Wyngarde as long as possible, sending her teammates back to reality. As his last act, Wyngarde sent Jean back to reality as well, thus dying a happy man.

Wyngarde is survived by his two daughters, both mutants who inherited his illusion-casting ability and who compete against each other for the right to use the name "Mastermind." They have reluctantly joined forces as part of the Red Queen's sisterhood, in return for her promise to resurrect their father.

DEATH FROM LEGACY VIRUS

HEIGHT: 5'10"; (illusory) 6'2"
WEIGHT: 140 lbs.; (illusory) 190 lbs.
EYES: Brown; (illusory) gray
HAIR: Gray; (illusory) brown

ABILITIES/ACCESSORIES: Mastermind could create convincing psionic visual, auditory, tactile, olfactory and gustatory illusions, causing others within his vicinity to see, hear, touch, smell and/or taste things that do not actually exist. He could also cause those within his vicinity to see, hear, touch, smell and/or taste real things in ways that they would not do naturally. For example, he often cast an illusion to make himself look and sound like a younger, more masculine man or used his power to make others oblivious to his presence as though he were invisible. His power affected the minds of others so strongly that even if they knew they were being subjected to an illusion, they would still react to it as if it were reality unless they could rid themselves of all doubts about its true nature. Invariably, Mastermind's illusions were so realistic that most of his victims believed his illusions were real, at least subconsciously. His power had a greater effect on those with stronger minds, especially those who believed they could not be fooled by mere illusions.

Without artificial aids, Mastermind could not cause only one individual among many present to see his illusions; everyone within his vicinity would see them. During his psionic enthrallment of the Phoenix entity, Mastermind used a miniature mind-tap device designed by Emma Frost that enabled him to project illusions directly into the entity's mind and monitor its thoughts, even over great distances. On occasion, Mastermind wielded a small conventional pistol.

POWER GRID	1	2	3	4	5	6	7
INTELLIGENCE							
STRENGTH							
SPEED							
DURABILITY							
ENERGY PROJECTION							
FIGHTING SKILLS							

REAL NAME: Christoph "Christopher" Nord
ALIASES: Agent Zero, David North
IDENTITY: Secret, known to certain officials in US, Canadian, and German governments
OCCUPATION: Former mercenary, government operative, freedom fighter
CITIZENSHIP: German
PLACE OF BIRTH: Unrevealed location in former East Germany
KNOWN RELATIVES: Unidentified parents (deceased), Andreas Nord (brother, deceased), Ginetta Lucia Barsalini (wife, deceased), unnamed child (deceased)
GROUP AFFILIATION: Formerly Weapon X, Team X, Cell Six, former bodyguard of Psi-Borg, former agent of Major Barrington
EDUCATION: Unrevealed
FIRST APPEARANCE: X-Men #5 (1992); (Agent Zero) Weapon X: The Draft — Agent Zero #1 (2002)

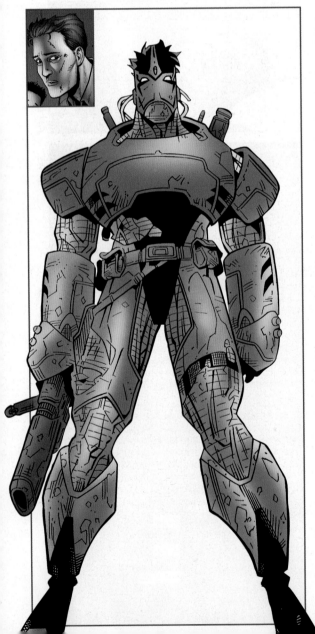

HISTORY: Born in the former East Germany, Christoph Nord was an idealist who fought against the communist regime as a freedom fighter for the West German Cell Six. Nord's brother Andreas fought for the East Germans, and when the two met in battle Nord was forced to kill his brother. Later, after an encounter in Italy with the assassin the Confessor, Nord was recovering in a German hospital where he fell in love with nurse Ginetta Barsalini. The two married, and she soon became pregnant, but he later learned that she was a double agent and was forced to kill her after she attacked him. Guilt and pain drove him further into his mercenary work, and he eventually accepted an offer to join the CIA's Weapon X Program. Nord joined the Program's covert operations unit Team X, changed his name to David North, and took the codename Maverick.

In recent years, Japanese crimelord Matsu'o Tsurayaba and his allies, including former Weapon X scientist Dr. Cornelius, resurrected the Russian super-soldier Omega Red. In order to stabilize his mutant power, Omega Red required the Carbonadium Synthesizer, a device stolen from him by Team X decades earlier. Omega Red captured Maverick's former Team X teammate Wolverine, who had the location of the C-Synthesizer buried in his memory, and several of Wolverine's teammates in the X-Men. Maverick was hired by former Team X liaison Major Arthur Barrington to prevent Omega Red from obtaining the device, and he tracked another former Team X member, Sabretooth, to Omega Red's location. With Maverick's help, the X-Men were able to defeat the villains, and he subsequently killed Cornelius in an act of revenge. Barrington later sent Maverick to recover documents known as the Xavier Files, after the father of the X-Men's telepathic founder, Professor Charles Xavier. The files were in the possession of a former colleague of Xavier's father, Dr. Alexander Ryking, who was under the protection of the superhuman mercenary Warhawk. During the ensuing clash, Warhawk exploded, killing Ryking and seemingly destroying the files.

Maverick was then assigned by the US Government to protect Aldo Ferro, a former Weapon X ally. Maverick's former Team X alumni sought Ferro after one of their number, Mastodon, died when his age suppression factor was seemingly reversed. Unbeknownst to Team X, Ferro was responsible for secretly implanting them all with false memories during their time with Weapon X. After Ferro betrayed Maverick, he sided with his former teammates against Ferro who was seemingly killed in the subsequent battle.

Maverick next sought to hunt down Sabretooth to make him pay for his numerous crimes, and joined forces with the X-Men in capturing him. Maverick subsequently learned that he had contracted the deadly mutant-killing Legacy virus. He asked Wolverine to kill him in order to avoid prolonged suffering, but Wolverine refused and Maverick came to form a sibling-like bond with another Virus sufferer, Chris Bradley. During the final stages of his infection, Maverick encountered the Russian mutant telepath Elena Ivanova who was hunting Sabretooth to avenge his murder of her mother. The Virus claimed Maverick's life, but Ivanova managed to use her powers to coax him back to life. As a result, Maverick's Legacy virus went into full remission and his powers further mutated. Maverick was then captured by Russian crimelord Ivan Pushkin, whose scientists implanted false memories into Maverick's mind to make him believe that Barrington had been responsible for his wife's betrayal. Pushkin intended for Maverick to kill Barrington to prevent him from providing testimony that threatened Pushkin's financial interests. Maverick located Barrington's safehouse but was opposed by members of the Canadian super-team Alpha Flight. Maverick overcame Pushkin's mental manipulation, however it was too late to save Barrington from Pushkin's agents, Hammer (Boris Lubov) and Sickle (Nickolai Vronsky).

In a later encounter with Hammer and Sickle, Maverick's left eye was gouged out by Sickle, and he was left to die in the Swiss Alps. Forced to cauterize the wound to stop from bleeding to death, Maverick survived and later resurfaced to aid Wolverine against a revived Weapon X Program. This new Program sent Sabretooth to recruit both Maverick and fellow Team X alumnus John Wraith. Neither accepted the offer, and so Sabretooth killed Wraith and critically injured Maverick. Brought to the Program with only minutes to live, Maverick reluctantly joined in order to survive and was genetically modified to become Agent Zero. Although an efficient operative, Zero hated what he had become and frequently considered suicide. On his first assignment as Zero, he was sent to assassinate Wolverine in an attempt by the Director, Malcolm Colcord, to further break his spirit. Deliberately missing his target, Zero was punished with an electric shock. Later, Zero recaptured Sabretooth after his betrayal of the Program and would have killed him had the Director not shocked him again. After a change in leadership of the Program, Zero was assigned to track the anti-human terrorist group Gene Nation that had been revived by former Weapon X operative Marrow. Confronting her, Zero learned that her latest recruit, a man using his former identity of Maverick, had been sent to attack New York's Grand Central Station. Confronting the impostor, Zero inflicted a fatal wound upon him only to learn that it was his friend, Chris. Zero then set about the task of wiping out Gene Nation with new zeal, although he declined to make Marrow a martyr. Returning to an abandoned Weapon X facility, Zero's investigations led him to join Wolverine and the enigmatic mercenary Fantomex in opposing the Project's original founder, John Sublime.

Later, Nord was among those mutants depowered on "M-Day" and came to join a clinic for ex-mutants run by fellow depowered mutant Jubilee (Jubilation Lee). He was contacted by Wolverine who was seeking the whereabouts of the C-Synthesizer in order to use it against his son, Daken. However, Wolverine had been followed by Omega Red who was also seeking the C-Synthesizer. Nord was wounded in the ensuing clash by Omega Red but survived.

AGENT ZERO

HEIGHT: 6'3"	EYES: Blue
WEIGHT: 230 lbs.	HAIR: Black (formerly Brown)

ABILITIES/ACCESSORIES: Nord is a deadly hand-to-hand combatant, a precision marksman skilled in the use of almost any firearm, and an expert in covert operations and demolitions. He also has vast experience with computers and communications equipment.

Nord's mutant powers allowed him to absorb the kinetic energy of impacts within certain limits without injury to himself. He could survive falls from great heights, direct hits from energy blasts, and being struck by superhumanly strong foes without harm. As Maverick, he could release that energy as localized heat or as concussive force blasts. Like other members of the Weapon X Program, Maverick's DNA contains an age suppression factor that greatly retards his aging process. Subsequent modification by the Program removed all discernable scent from his body; recent evidence indicates that Nord again has a scent, but it is unclear whether his age suppression continues post M-Day. As Agent Zero, Maverick's powers were modified so that he channeled his stored energy as blasts of concussive-corrosive energy via an acidic enzyme secreted from his fingertips. This enzyme was specifically designed by the Weapon X Program to counteract an opponent's self-healing abilities by reversing the process so that the more an opponent attempted to heal an enzyme-inflicted wound, the worse it became. Zero could also channel absorbed energy into raw strength, allowing him to deliver blows ten times stronger than normal.

As Maverick, Nord wore full body armor that contained airtight seals and a mask containing a limited oxygen supply, and he used various firearms. As Zero, Nord wore body armor woven from the rare metal Vibranium that rendered him completely silent as he moved. The armor also refracted light, which in total darkness rendered him nearly invisible to detection. He wielded an array of weapons including wrist-mounted plasma blasters, pistols that fired Adamantium bullets, an Adamantium-coated knife, and a sniper rifle loaded with bullets forged of Adamantium-piercing "anti-metal."

POWER GRID	1	2	3	4	5	6	7
INTELLIGENCE							
STRENGTH							
SPEED							
DURABILITY							
ENERGY PROJECTION							
FIGHTING SKILLS							

*RED BARS INDICATE RATINGS BEFORE DEPOWERING

REAL NAME: Muramasa
ALIASES: None
IDENTITY: No dual identity
OCCUPATION: Swordsmith
CITIZENSHIP: Presumably Japan
PLACE OF BIRTH: Presumably Japan
KNOWN RELATIVES: None
GROUP AFFILIATION: None
EDUCATION: Unrevealed
FIRST APPEARANCE: (Black Blade) Wolverine #1 (1988); (Muramasa mentioned) Wolverine #3 (1989); (full) Wolverine #40 (2006)

HISTORY: Muramasa is a master swordsmith dating back to, at least, Japan's birth in the 17th century when he forged the legendary Black Blade, imbuing the metal with a piece of his soul to create a sentient, bloodthirsty weapon. Based atop a mountain outside Jasmine Falls, Muramasa continued to harvest men's souls to create greater and more terrible weapons, capable of only destruction. The Black Blade developed a cult who executed human sacrifices at dawn to mirror the sword's creation in spring, the beginning of the Japanese year. The Cult had a major resurgence in the 1920s during the pre-war rise of Japanese militarism. US General MacArthur's counter-intelligence crew supposedly eliminated them during the post-war occupation of Japan. Around this same time, the mutant Logan trained for four years to relearn inner peace under master Bando Suboro in Jasmine Falls. An explosion from Muramasa's mountain caused Logan to unleash his claws, wounding another of Suboro's students. Logan judged himself unworthy of his pregnant lover, Itsu, and planned to leave her but instead found her murdered (at the hands of the Winter Soldier, under Romulus' direction, though Logan did not know this at the time). Having lost everything he

held dear, Logan reverted to savagery and scaled Muramasa's mountain, mistakenly blaming Muramasa for the murder. Having waited for Logan to come to him as he truly was, Muramasa then took Logan's fury and purified it, making it stronger and harder, and forged it into a mighty blade, his masterwork: the Muramasa Sword. A month later, Muramasa released the completely incapacitated Logan, who lost his memories of these events.

Decades later, Clan Yashida head Mariko had the Black Blade transported from America to Madripoor into the hands of detectives Lindsay McCabe and Jessica Drew. While the Cult tried to reclaim the Blade, it bonded to Drew, and then to Logan (now Wolverine) when he tried to free Drew from its influence. The Black Blade-possessed Logan tried to sacrifice Drew via the Cult's ritual to forge a permanent bond, but Logan cast off the Blade's influence and hurled it away. It was claimed by the Silver Samurai, which it chose as its fated master, its own sentience fading to better serve the Samurai.

In recent years, having regained his memories, Logan traveled to Muramasa's mountain. When Logan admitted he sought vengeance, Muramasa gave him the Muramasa Sword he had forged from Logan's savage spirit and told him to wield it like an angry god. Armed with this sword, Logan traveled to Washington DC for answers and destroyed Weapon X's powerful Shiva robot. Logan subsequently used the sword to cripple government agent Nuke (Frank Simpson) and defeat Captain America (Steve Rogers) before turning it over to his teammate Cyclops (Scott Summers) so it could be used to stop Logan if he ever again went rogue. Logan reclaimed the Sword one last time to decapitate his old enemy Sabretooth. Seeking to create the perfect weapon through Daken, Romulus sent him to obtain the Muramasa Sword. The X-Men were duped into using the sword against Daken, who did steal it, but it shattered against Armor (Hisako Ichiki), with Daken escaping with only part of it.

| HEIGHT: 5'10" | EYES: Brown |
| WEIGHT: 180 lbs. | HAIR: Black |

ABILITIES/ACCESSORIES: A master swordsman, Muramasa can forge portions of the spirit and emotions into powerful swords. He is allegedly immortal, can apparently somehow incapacitate others and likely has other, unrevealed, abilities. He is served by armored samurai-like warriors.

The Black Blade is virtually indestructible. Save for the warrior chosen by fate to be the Blade's master, those who wielded it were possessed, consumed by an unquenchable bloodlust, and granted superhuman strength and durability. Once a bond was forged via a mystic ceremony involving human sacrifice, that bond could only be broken by the host's death. Prior to the formal bonding, the Blade itself could choose a new host if a more suitable one presented itself, and those of sufficient will could forcibly sever the possession. Those possessed by the Black Blade were instantly transformed in garb and behavior, with the Blade speaking through them. The Blade can directly speak to others.

The Muramasa Sword is similarly virtually indestructible. It may enhance its user's fighting prowess, but any other supernatural abilities are unrevealed.

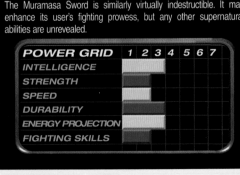

POWER GRID	1	2	3	4	5	6	7
INTELLIGENCE							
STRENGTH							
SPEED							
DURABILITY							
ENERGY PROJECTION							
FIGHTING SKILLS							

HISTORY: Centuries ago, a group of humans in the Ural Mountains (part of modern Russia) broke off their ties with the rest of humanity in order to cultivate a closer connection to Gaea, the goddess of the Earth. Through meditation, the group began to unlock the secrets of life. Now called the Neuri, they moved ever further from their neighbors into the mountains, possessing control over their forms so that their bodies would adapt to changes in the environment. Secluded from humanity, the Neuri spent their time in meditation, accessing a plane of existence called the Alshra, from which they could gather mystical energy. The Neuri also learned how to link their minds into a group consciousness that could expand from Earth and explore the universe.

However, as industrialization took hold, the Neuri's primordial connection to the Earth began to affect their group mind. Roughly seventy years ago one Neuri came out of hiding to assist a gypsy family, only to become their prisoner. The family exploited the captive Neuri's powers for decades, but greed gradually caused them to turn on each other. Eventually only two gypsy brothers remained, using the Neuri to prolong their lives. Meanwhile, as divisions entered their ranks, some Neuri attempted reconciliation with humans. Taking up human disguises, these Neuri settled around Winzeldorf, Germany; however, the young mystic Stefan Szardos sensed that the creatures were not what they appeared to be. Suffering a bout of madness, Stefan tried to murder a Neuri child named Helmut but was prevented by his mutant foster brother Kurt Wagner, who killed Stefan during the struggle. Kurt's flight from Stefan's death eventually led to him becoming Nightcrawler of the X-Men.

Industrialization's continued pollution of the Earth finally drove several of the Neuri into a bloodlust. Fleeing the Neuri refuge of Siberia, they ventured into Alaska and headed toward the Yukon Territory, killing whatever humans they encountered. Along the way, the Neuri met Wolverine (Logan/James Howlett), a mutant whose inner struggle with savagery mirrored the clash within the group mind. The Neuri who maintained their sanity explained their plight to him and received his aid in tracking the last of the savage Neuri, a female calling herself Saskia. Although Wolverine was nearly overcome by Saskia's telepathic bloodlust, he ultimately slew her. The remaining Neuri returned to Siberia.

Later, heroes Phoenix (Rachel Summers) and Meggan of Excalibur came to Germany searching for Meggan's lost family, following rumors of a magical creature hidden in a gypsy caravan, which they believed referred to Meggan's formerly hiding in her parents' caravan. Instead they discovered the Neuri prisoner held by the elderly gypsy brothers, and Phoenix and Meggan rescued him from their grasp. The Neuri revealed Meggan's true appearance to her by allowing her to access the Alshra, but his own life force was spent and he died soon afterward.

Soon after, Nightcrawler was summoned back to Winzeldorf by members of the circus der Jahrmarkt who were seeking the destruction of the local Neuri. Wolverine also arrived to investigate and met with Helmut, who tried to convince Nightcrawler that his people were pacifists and wished only to find peace with humanity; however, der Jahrmarkt arranged Helmut's death. When Nightcrawler and Wolverine located the rest of the Winzeldorf Neuri they realized that Helmut had been telling the truth, but der Jahrmarkt spurred an angry mob into torching the Neuri's homes. The Neuri refused to fight back and were all apparently slain in the fires.

KNOWN MEMBERS: Helmut, Rutger, Saskia
BASE OF OPERATIONS: Various including Yukon, Canada; Winzeldorf, Germany; Siberia, Russia; Alaska, USA
FIRST APPEARANCE: Wolverine Annual #2 (1990)

TRAITS: Neuri can tap into the mystical energy of the mystic Alshra plane for various effects, including the ability to cast illusions, heal wounds with their touch, form telepathic links (including a group mind collective of all Neuri that can expand their consciousness to other worlds), summon bolts of eldritch energy and conjure energy shields. The Neuri can draw other beings into the Alshra; within the Alshra, all beings appear as they truly are. Neuri who have dwelt in the northern part of the Earth adapted to exist in a sub-zero environment; they typically appear as fur-covered creatures with fangs and claws. The Neuri who dwelt in Winzeldorf possessed pointed ears and fangs, and their veins were visible under their skin. When Neuri die, their bodies crumble into dust.

WEIGHT: 235 lbs
HEIGHT: 7'
EYES: Various
SKIN: (Winzeldorf) yellow; (northern) brown

ALSHRA

WINZELDORF NEURI

SASKIA

HELMUT

RUTGER

REAL NAME: Peter (last name unrevealed)
ALIASES: None
IDENTITY: Secret
OCCUPATION: Warrior
CITIZENSHIP: Unrevealed
PLACE OF BIRTH: Unrevealed
KNOWN RELATIVES: None
GROUP AFFILIATION: Agent of Nanny
EDUCATION: Taught by Nanny
FIRST APPEARANCE: X-Factor #31 (1988); (identified) X-Factor #33 (1988)

HISTORY: Peter was allegedly a mutant held by mad geneticist Mr. Sinister who initially sought to exploit his abilities, then planned to destroy him when Peter proved uncontrollable. The cyborg mutant Nanny rescued Peter, encasing him in armor to better control him, and enlisted him into her crusade to gather young mutants as her own "salvation army," protected from the world's dangers. Since Peter was to kill the young mutants' parents during his abductions, Nanny called him Orphan-Maker, though he failed to apprehend young mutant Johnny Gallo (later Ricochet) after killing his mother. Orphan-Maker swiftly grew jealous of the children they gathered, worrying that Nanny would favor them more. After Nanny's enemies, the anti-mutant Right organization, provided lists of young mutants to demons for sacrifice, Nanny increased her efforts; she accompanied Peter and her Lost Boys (and Girls) – Big Top, Bonzo, Monitor, Shatter-Box and Speed-Freak

– to liberate a floor of mutant children from a Nebraska orphanage, where Mr. Sinister had gathered them as future experimental subjects. X-Factor's Cyclops (Scott Summers) and Marvel Girl (Jean Grey) opposed Nanny's forces, but when the demons arrived and began stealing babies, Nanny fled with her children. Orphan-Maker was sent to kidnap young Franklin Benjamin, unaware the boy was really Franklin Richards, son of the Fantastic Four's Mr. Fantastic and Invisible Woman, who were living incognito to give Franklin a more normal childhood. Orphan-Maker successfully snatched Franklin, but failed to slay the parents when Invisible Woman's force field blocked his kill shot. He lied to Nanny about this, but when she discovered Franklin's true identity and exposed Peter's lie, a furious Nanny disciplined Peter with an electric prod. Nanny encased Franklin in armor and placed his mind under her control just before his parents attacked along with the Captain (Steve Rogers) and the Eternal Gilgamesh. When Orphan-Maker found himself outmatched, Nanny sent Franklin against his parents, but she willingly surrendered him when Mr. Fantastic threatened Peter. Orphan-Maker and Nanny fled, teleporting out when the Invisible Woman held their ship with a force field. Later attacking X-Factor to save the orphanage babies, Orphan-Maker panicked when Nanny was injured, telling the mutants about his past and giving up their ship before teleporting Nanny to safety. Nanny subsequently tried to apprehend the X-Men in Australia and the heroes drove her off, though not before Nanny ensnared X-Men member Storm using technology to revert Storm's age to that of a pre-teen. When Storm escaped, Orphan-Maker tried hiding Storm's location from Nanny, not wanting a rival for Nanny's attention, but Nanny scolded him. They pursued Storm to Cairo, Illinois, but she evaded them again with the aid of her new ally, Gambit.

In time, Nanny sent Peter to kill Cartier St. Croix, a father of mutant children, but Peter's powers changed and his armor began sloughing off. Panicking, he rushed back to Nanny, who comforted him and made new armor to contain his powers. When Elliot, a young boy refused a school place because his disfigured appearance made others wrongly assume he was a mutant, took a class hostage, Orphan-Maker tried to "rescue" him, but mutant students Generation X drove him off. The next Christmas, Orphan-Maker again fought Generation X while trying to recruit new mutant Matthew, but a visit by Santa Claus stopped the fight. Orphan-Maker later briefly captured the now-grown Ricochet, but he easily escaped. Nanny subsequently sent Orphan-Maker to recruit young Trance (Hope Abbott), but a battle with Trance and Wolverine (Logan/James Howlett) left Peter severely wounded.

HEIGHT: 7'6" (in armor)	EYES: Unrevealed
WEIGHT: Unrevealed	HAIR: Unrevealed

ABILITIES/ACCESSORIES: Orphan-Maker is a mutant of unrevealed abilities. He has worn two sets of armor with varying capabilities, including force-blast guns, repulsor fields, a jet pack, a screening unit (which disrupts the powers of others), "clouds of glory" dust (which freeze targets), and bone-shattering bullets. Both armors enhanced strength and were reinforced, capable of reflecting Cyclops' optic blasts and screened against telepathic attacks. Orphan-Maker has also carried guns that fire energy blasts. Orphan-Maker flies a specially equipped ship and uses a teleporting unit. Orphan-Maker often throws "Pixie Dust," a chemical that renders its target more susceptible to Nanny's telepathy.

POWER GRID	1	2	3	4	5	6	7
INTELLIGENCE							
STRENGTH							
SPEED '							
DURABILITY							
ENERGY PROJECTION							
FIGHTING SKILLS							

'ORPHAN-MAKER IS A TELEPORTER

HISTORY: Anton Pierce took over the wealthy Randall House in Boston, Massachusetts in 1876. Wealthy from trading in cotton, gin and slaves, Pierce was recruited into the prominent Hellfire Club the same year and into its sinister Inner Circle two years later. Positions in the Club were held by Pierce's descendants over the following generations, eventually passing on to Donald Pierce in the modern day. Donald sought power and position at an early age. Years ago, he tried taking over Albania and was defeated by the time-traveling mutant Cable (Nathan Summers) and Iron Man (Tony Stark). Severely wounded in this battle, Pierce received his first cybernetic enhancements as a result, blaming Cable for this and vowing revenge. Sebastian Shaw recruited Pierce into the Hellfire Club's new Inner Circle as its White Bishop, the only non-mutant in the group. Pierce was largely an observer while Mastermind (Jason Wyngarde) sought to earn Inner Circle membership by corrupting the X-Man Jean Grey (secretly the cosmic Phoenix Force posing as Grey) and bringing her power under Inner Circle control, and the Inner Circle's White Queen (Emma Frost) tried to recruit emerging mutants Kitty Pryde and Alison Blaire (Dazzler). Pierce took a more active role when the X-Men invaded the Club's mansion after learning of the Club's part in their recent woes. He helped subdue the X-Men, but when "Grey" overcame Mastermind's control and freed the heroes, the Inner Circle retreated, though not before Colossus (Peter Rasputin) ripped off one of Pierce's bionic arms. Pierce remade Club guards Angelo Macon, Murray Reese and Wade Cole into cyborgs after Wolverine (Logan/James Howlett) severely wounded them, and the trio became loyal to Pierce.

Seeking personal power and no longer able to hide his growing hatred of mutants, Pierce sought to manipulate a new generation of mutants into working for him. His operatives recruited Samuel Guthrie (later Cannonball) from Kentucky; attacked Roberto DaCosta (later Sunspot) in Brazil, inadvertently killing DaCosta's girlfriend Juliana Sandoval; and attacked Danielle Moonstar (later Psyche) in the southwest, killing her grandfather, Black Eagle. Pierce also captured the X-Men's Professor X (Charles Xavier) and Shaw's aide Tessa (later Sage). Xavier's recruits Da Costa, Moonstar, Xi'an Coy Manh (later Karma) and Rahne Sinclair (later Wolfsbane) attacked, turned Guthrie against Pierce and freed Xavier, who telepathically subdued Pierce. On Tessa's suggestion, Pierce was handed over to the Club for punishment, and remained their captive for months, during which time, he presumably manipulated his way into the White King position to avoid harsher sanctions.

Backed by Cole, Macon and Reese, Pierce took control of the Reavers, cybernetic criminals whose ranks had been decimated by the X-Men; the three remaining original Reavers, Bonebreaker, Skullbuster and Pretty Boy, accepted Pierce's leadership in return for further cybernetic enhancements and the promise of retaking their Australian base, which the X-Men had appropriated. Lady Deathstrike (Yuriko Oyama), a cyborg foe of the X-Man Wolverine (Logan/James Howlett), joined the group as well; Pierce found her fascinating, but despite his frequent flirtations, Deathstrike never returned his affections. The Reavers staked out the base for days until they captured Wolverine, crucifying him and beating him repeatedly. The other X-Men, forewarned by premonition, escaped through the mystical Siege Perilous portal, and Pierce destroyed the portal's generating crystal in an effort to cause Wolverine despair by thinking his teammates forever lost. When Wolverine escaped, Pierce designed three mechanical dingoes to track him, but Wolverine and his ally Jubilee (Jubilation Lee) evaded them. While retaking the base, the Reavers had recaptured the mutant Gateway, able to create teleportation portals. Pierce led the Reavers to attack Muir Island, where mutants

REAL NAME: Donald Pierce
ALIASES: White Bishop, White King
IDENTITY: (White Bishop/King) Secret
OCCUPATION: Criminal; former CEO and principal shareholder of Pierce-Consolidated Mining
CITIZENSHIP: USA
PLACE OF BIRTH: Philadelphia, Pennsylvania
KNOWN RELATIVES: Anton Pierce (ancestor, deceased), Justin Pierce (nephew)
GROUP AFFILIATION: Formerly Cleaning Crew, Reavers, Inner Circle of the Hellfire Club
EDUCATION: Unrevealed
FIRST APPEARANCE: X-Men #129 (1980)

allied to the X-Men lived. During their incursion the Reavers slew the Morlock Sunder, and Pierce personally killed Stonewall (Louis Hamilton) of the government-sponsored Freedom Force, but the cyborgs fled after Skullbuster was destroyed and Muir's defenders nearly overwhelmed them. Pierce recruited the crippled pilot Cylla Markham from a hospital to replace Skullbuster, and subsequently sent some of the Reavers to attack the vigilante Punisher (Frank Castle) after Castle's ally Microchip hacked the Reavers' computers. Pierce built killer androids Albert and Elsie-Dee to slay Wolverine, but they broke their programming to become Wolverine's allies instead. When the telepathic Gamesmaster formed the Upstarts, who competed to kill various targets to get "points," he made the Hellfire Club's Inner Circle his targets. Upstart Trevor

Fitzroy targeted Pierce, sending giant robotic Sentinels to attack his Australian base. As the other Reavers fell, Pierce ordered Gateway to take him to the perpetrator, appearing before the X-Men, who were battling Fitzroy, and wrongly concluding it was the heroes who had sent the Sentinels. The Sentinels followed Pierce through the portal and seemingly incinerated him, though Fitzroy later salvaged Pierce's remains.

An unidentified benefactor later revived Pierce, implanting a directive to make new cyborgs. Pierce rebuilt Skullbuster and recruited fellow Reavers survivor Lady Deathstrike, and together they kidnapped genius Milo Thurman. Milo's ex-lover Domino (Neena Thurman) was also taken to the Reavers' Arctic base but escaped and defeated all three villains, rescuing Milo. Before the base exploded, Pierce transferred his intelligence electronically into another body. Returning to Randall House, Pierce was invited back to the Inner Circle by Shaw, despite his former betrayal and Fitzroy now being an integral member. Pierce was put in charge of the "Tomorrow Agenda" and he began relocating arms to Switzerland at Shaw's orders, without knowing the full plan as Shaw was unwilling to trust him with details. Pierce ordered the killings of reporter Irene Merryweather, who had been investigating Shaw, and his old foe Cable, but both escaped. Knowing Pierce wanted a personal showdown, Cable faked a sighting in Algeria, luring Pierce away while he invaded Randall House to access Pierce's records. He succeeded, incidentally destroying the house while battling its remaining defenders. Pursued by Cable, Pierce traveled with Shaw to a Hellfire residence in London where he met Ch'vayre, a giant from Cable's future (Earth-4935), and learned that Shaw planned to exploit the ancient mutant Apocalypse (En Sabah Nur)'s hidden technology. They released the entombed Harbinger of Apocalypse, then fled while the Harbinger fought Cable. Pierce, Shaw and Ch'vayre penetrated Apocalypse's hidden Swiss base, but before they could use its technology, Cable attacked and shattered Pierce's hand with a telekinetic blast. The building collapsed around them and Pierce followed the fleeing Shaw, but when he tried to climb into Shaw's hovering escape helicopter, Shaw cut the ladder loose, proclaiming Pierce a failure. Pierce eventually found his way to Cable's safehouse in the Alps, took control of its cyber sentries and found caches of Adamantium, using it to enhance his systems. When Wolverine and Jubilee arrived, Pierce battled them until the enigmatic cyborg Khyber arrived; claiming Pierce's Adamantium was his, Khyber ripped Pierce's arm off and beat Pierce severely before teleporting away.

A rebuilt Pierce later recruited new, human Reavers in New York City, including Josh Foley, who was unaware he was himself a mutant. Taking hostage Walter Barrett, the father of Xavier's student Sofia Mantega (later Wind Dancer), they set a trap for any mutants that might come to his rescue; however, a group of Xavier's students defeated the Reavers, and Pierce was left nearly dead due to the lethal touch of young Kevin Ford (later Wither). Without flesh over his metallic bones, Pierce was incarcerated in the Cage until his nephew, FBI Agent Justin Pierce, offered him a chance to testify against Ford. Pierce escaped from the airport, gathered the Reavers and attacked Xavier's school, but they were swiftly defeated. Pierce soon created new cyborg warriors, the Cleaning Crew, and launched an attack on both the Hellfire Club's new Inner Circle and the X-Men. During a savage battle, Shaw dislodged Pierce's

head and left him for dead. Revived again, Pierce was controlled by the Shadow King into leading his old team of Reavers, nearly all rebuilt, in attacking some X-Men, but Rogue defeated them almost single-handedly. Pierce was soon taken against his will by the mutant-hating Purifiers, led by Bastion, and forcibly infected with the transmode virus, putting him under Bastion's control. Several other anti-mutant bigots were similarly infected, including Cameron Hodge, the Leper Queen, Graydon Creed, Steven Lang, Bolivar Trask and William Stryker.

Plotting to manipulate former X-Men students into killing other mutants, Pierce used an image inducer to pose as Cyclops (Scott Summers), recruiting Ink (Eric Gitter), Rockslide (Santo Vacarro), Dust (Sooraya Qadir), Wolf Cub (Nicholas Gleason) and Blindfold (Ruth Aldine) and trained them to kill for weeks before sending them against Cannonball, Sunspot, Moonstar, and Magma (Amara Aquilla). The battle soon led back to Pierce, who was exposed by Jonas Graymalkin (apparently a long-buried ancestor of Charles Xavier), but Pierce killed Wolf Cub before being defeated. Held captive by the X-Men, Pierce continued manipulating Dust, who strangely chose Pierce as a confidant. After coercing Dust into setting him free, Pierce was severely beaten by Rockslide for the murder of Wolf Cub, and recaptured by the X-Men.

| HEIGHT: 6'2" | EYES: Blue |
| WEIGHT: 220 lbs. | HAIR: Blond |

ABILITIES/ACCESSORIES: Donald Pierce is currently a transmode-virus enhanced human under at least partial control by Bastion. Though Pierce seems to have retained his cyborg enhancements, the extent of his free will and control over his own form is unknown, such as whether he can infect other organic beings with the transmode virus or whether he can still regenerate from major or minor injuries (or even total destruction). Previously, Pierce was strictly a cyborg, his body mostly comprised of cybernetic enhancements. Upon physical death, Pierce downloaded his consciousness into electronic components and uploaded it into a newly prepared body, so it is likely that little of his later systems were biological, though this has not been confirmed. Pierce is an electronics genius, able to create deadly robots with distinct personalities and offensive weaponry, and to cybernetically enhance biological entities with electronic components. In addition, Pierce has upgraded his own systems with various additions, including hydraulic jumps, super strength (Class 10), energy weapons, Tantalus webs (temporarily binding and paralyzing targets), missiles, combat nanites (which can infect biological systems and overwrite healing processes), laser claws, electric shocks, psychic shielding and an image inducer.

POWER GRID	1	2	3	4	5	6	7
INTELLIGENCE							
STRENGTH							
SPEED							
DURABILITY							
ENERGY PROJECTION							
FIGHTING SKILLS							

HISTORY: During her first year at Cuba's University of Havana, Cecilia Cardinale fell in love with a man named Vassily, part of the Russian Embassy's military attaché. When their affair resulted in Cecilia's pregnancy, however, Vassily, possibly under coercion from his superiors, denounced her as a prostitute seeking political favors. Imprisoned under unsanitary and inhumane conditions, Cecilia contracted a debilitating disease. Deported to the US as an "undesirable," she gave birth to her son Carlos in a Florida refugee camp, her illness worsening considerably. She was near death when the extradimensional semi-tangible warrior Ylandris, stranded in the Earth dimension and at risk of dispersing into Earth's atmosphere, offered to merge with Cecilia and save both their lives. Although believing Ylandris, whose name meant "poison," to be a demon, Cecilia agreed, and Ylandris' life force eventually restored her to health. She and Carlos moved to Miami, where she became a hotel chambermaid and, empowered by Ylandris' alien energies, the vigilante Poison. Hunting any who harmed the vulnerable, her battle thirst was driven partly by Ylandris and partly by her own determination to never again be victimized.

Poison spent years as a sporadic crimefighter. After Carlos reached school age, the High Evolutionary sent his Purifiers and Eliminators to Florida to, among other things, hunt people potentially infected by the Nexus of All Realities within the Man-Thing's Citrusville, Florida swamp. Poison fought the Evolutionary's forces, briefly encountering Spider-Man (Peter Parker) in the process, and Ylandris departed the Earth dimensions via the Nexus. Retaining her superhuman powers, Poison continued her war against criminals, particularly Miami's drug trade.

Whether by coincidence or otherwise, another of Ylandris' race, Mrinhä, arrived in Miami and formed a quasi-symbiotic relationship with now-homeless ex-executive Joe Trinity, who had been betrayed by those he trusted. As the Mop Man, Trinity maimed or killed many criminals with Mrinhä's power. Targeted by Miami druglord Slug (Ulysses Lugman), Mop Man and Mrinhä defeated two hired killers, attracting Poison's interest. The injured Mop Man merged directly with Mrinhä, who healed his wounds and fueled his rage, as Ylandris had Poison's. Poison forced Mrinhä from his body, then resisted Mrinhä's attempt to possess her instead.

Months later, representatives of Trenton Lipton III offered Poison a contract as a player in the Great Game, where wealthy sponsors pitted superhuman combatants against each other. Intrigued, Poison relocated to Manhattan with Carlos, but they had barely moved into an apartment when Game player Toro Negro, jealous of Poison's contract offer, set the building ablaze. Spider-Man (Ben Reilly) rescued Carlos, who was rushed to medical treatment before Poison escaped the flames. When

REAL NAME: Cecilia Cardinale
ALIASES: None
IDENTITY: Secret
OCCUPATION: Hydra operative; former vigilante, cleaning woman, hotel chambermaid
CITIZENSHIP: Cuba, US immigrant
PLACE OF BIRTH: Unrevealed, possibly unidentified location in Cuba
KNOWN RELATIVES: Carlos Cardinale (son)
GROUP AFFILIATION: Hydra
EDUCATION: College (first-year, unfinished)
FIRST APPEARANCE: Web of Spider-Man Annual #4 (1988)

Toro Negro abducted Carlos, Poison refused Lipton's offer but was forced to fight Spider-Man when he intervened. Pretending to incinerate Spider-Man, she teleported him yards away to knock out Toro Negro. Whether Poison and Carlos remained in New York or returned to Florida is unrevealed.

When Hydra and the Hand joined forces to kill, resurrect and brainwash superhumans into their service, Poison became one of the few heroes subjected to the process. She joined Northstar, SHOC (Neil Aiken) and over two hundred super-villains in a mass assault on the SHIELD Helicarrier. Poison was among the first raiders killed by Wolverine (Logan/James Howlett), but despite the efforts of Wolverine and SHIELD, the Helicarrier was brought down over Arkansas, apparently incinerating most of the invading force; however, at least one such invader, the Spot, later resurfaced, evidently alive and uncontrolled, and it may be that Poison will as well.

YLANDRIS

AS HYDRA OPERATIVE

COSTUME PROVIDED BY GREAT GAME

HEIGHT: 5'6"
WEIGHT: 115 lbs.
EYES: Brown
HAIR: Brown

ABILITIES/ACCESSORIES: Poison possessed at least Class 10 superhuman strength. She could levitate, transform her body to the consistency of hardened steel, and psionically mold the flesh of others. She possessed exceptional athletic ability and enhanced hearing. She could teleport at least one person at a time over distances of several yards, although she found the process exceptionally draining. When occupied by Ylandris, she benefited from the alien's counsel and apparent telepathic knowledge of others.

POWER GRID	1	2	3	4	5	6	7
INTELLIGENCE							
STRENGTH							
SPEED							
DURABILITY							
ENERGY PROJECTION							
FIGHTING SKILLS							

CURRENT MEMBERS: Jack Abrams, Dr. Ramsey, William Stryker, Daniel, Gabriel, Jacob, Joseph, Mary, Michael, Paul, Phillip, Rocco
FORMER MEMBERS: Anne, Eli Bard, Rev. Craig (deceased), Jeremy Latcham (deceased), "Joaquin 'Jake' Murrieta" (Rictor alias), Matthew Risman (deceased), Taylor
BASE OF OPERATIONS: Various bases throughout the USA
FIRST APPEARANCE: Marvel Graphic Novel #5 (1982)

HISTORY: When US army Sgt. William Stryker rolled his car in the desert, his pregnant wife Marcy went into premature labor and gave birth to a hideous mutant. Horrified, he killed his wife and child, then set alight the leaking gas, hoping to kill himself. Miraculously surviving the resulting explosion, which hid the evidence of his crimes, Stryker lived aimlessly through alcohol and fighting until the military discharged him. Eventually, he read an article about mutants and became convinced they were Satan's creations, and that God had spared him so that he could destroy them. Stryker reinvented himself as a televangelist, soon becoming very successful and wealthy preaching an anti-mutant doctrine. From his growing following he gathered individuals with military backgrounds and other useful skills to become his Purifiers, and he began gathering information on the world's mutants, concluding the X-Men's leader Charles Xavier was the Antichrist. The Purifiers began killing mutants, leaving their bodies publicly displayed adorned with "Mutie" signs for the media to discover; this also drew the interest of mutant supremacist Magneto (Max Eisenhardt).

Considering the X-Men the Purifiers' greatest foes, Stryker studied them and had covert monitoring devices hidden in Xavier's School's grounds. While Stryker engaged in a televised national debate against Xavier, who was not publicly known as a mutant at the time, the Purifiers, shielded by psi-screens, prepared an ambush. As Xavier and the X-Men Cyclops (Scott Summers) and Storm (Ororo Munroe) drove home, their car was intercepted and blown up; having narrowly evacuated the vehicle in time, the mutant trio was tranquilized by the Purifiers, who let the world believe them dead. Suspecting their friends' "deaths" were not accidental, X-Men

Colossus (Peter Rasputin), Nightcrawler (Kurt Wagner) and Wolverine (Logan/James Howlett) investigated, soon spotting and confronting a Purifier surveillance team monitoring them. Caught off guard by armored Purifiers, the X-Men were unexpectedly assisted by Magneto, who easily defeated the Purifiers and tortured the bigots for information.

Meanwhile, Purifiers Rocco and Anne, Stryker's confidant and second-in-command, captured young mutants Illyana Rasputin and Kitty Pryde, who had discovered the monitoring equipment at the School, while Stryker and Phillip brainwashed Xavier with drugs, sensory deprivation, electrodes and mindwash procedures, planning on amplifying his psi-powers to kill mutants worldwide. When Kitty escaped, the Purifiers pursued her until the X-Men and Magneto rescued her. Stryker took the brainwashed Xavier to a televised Madison Square Garden sermon, then ordered him to kill the mutants while Stryker preached. As Xavier's attack visibly marked affected mutants via nasal and aural bleeding, Magneto arrived in the stadium, but was downed when Stryker had Xavier concentrate his power on the newcomer. After inciting the crowd to riot against Magneto, Stryker realized that Anne, bleeding from her ears, was a latent mutant, and Stryker was caught on camera pushing her off the high stage to her death as she begged for mercy. The X-Men knocked Xavier out, ending the psi-assault, then publicly decried Stryker's murder of innocents; when Stryker pulled a gun and threatened to shoot the teenaged Kitty, a human policeman shot Stryker. The wounded Stryker was arrested, though he claimed religious persecution.

With Stryker imprisoned, the Purifiers became less publicly active, though they continued to recruit new members. Eventually Stryker was broken out by Lady Deathstrike (Yuriko Oyama) and sent Purifiers against the X-Men again. He and Deathstrike investigated the mutant stronghold of Mount Haven, where Stryker seemingly sacrificed himself, sealing himself in a containment pod to prevent the spread of nannites designed by an artificial intelligence to spread through Earth's computers and slay normal humans. Freed months later by an earthquake, Stryker encountered Nimrod, a powerful mutant-hunting Sentinel from Reality-

811 ("Days of Future Past")'s future. Nimrod's databanks linked up with present day computers to both contain information on the past and accurately predict information on the future, but as its computers noted the data flux as a chronal error, Nimrod's active systems shut down. Stryker's agents accessed Nimrod's databanks, gaining foreknowledge of events such as the approaching "M-Day," when most of the world's mutants would lose their powers. Nimrod's records of obituaries facilitated Styker's reorganization of the Purifiers as he gained a loyal core of skilled agents such as surgeon Dr. Jack Abrams and assassin Matthew Risman by saving them from imminent deaths. Forewarned of the birth of the first mutant child after M-Day, Stryker employed the Facility – a group of proficient scientists for hire – to create a race of beings able to track and devour mutants, so these beings would hunt down and kill the newborn mutant. The database

guided Stryker in a series of other plots, though sometimes the records were vague, such as information on forming a powerful army via the wings of a mutant.

Appearing publicly, Stryker increased his following via accurately predicting events such as earthquakes; several anti-mutant speeches predicting God's imminent plans for mutants preceded M-Day, after which he exhorted the world to finish what had been started. Via knowledge of Icarus (Jay Guthrie)'s lover Julia Cabot's death, Stryker approached the grieving winged mutant Icarus and earned his confidence, ultimately convincing him that by allowing his wings to be severed he could be reunited with Julia. Stryker further convinced Icarus to give him updates on the Xavier Institutes plans, enabling Purifiers to blow up a bus carrying dozens of depowered mutants, former Xavier School students now being sent home, the biggest tragedy to ever strike the school. The Purifiers next targeted mutant students Wallflower (Laurie Collins) and Dust (Sooraya Qadir), who Nimrod's database identified as severe threats to their plans. The Purifiers slew Wallflower, but Dust survived the assassination attempt due to her teammate suspecting a trap and impersonating her. Seeking freedom from Stryker, the partially reactivated and severely power-depleted Nimrod falsified his databanks to make it appear Stryker's forces would now slay the young mutants, when instead his records showed Stryker would perish in the attempt. After Stryker fatally shot Icarus, he donned Nimrod's gauntlet and led the Purifiers in attacking the mansion. Student Quill (Max Jordan) was killed before the Purifiers were defeated, and mutant Elixir (Josh Foley) slew Stryker. Nimrod subsequently escaped, uploaded itself into a new body and was sent into the past, where he battled the X-Men before being incorporated into Steven Lang's Master Mold Sentinel, which subsequently evolved into the being Bastion.

Risman, whose face had badly been scarred by Dust, took control of the Purifiers and continued with many of Stryker's plans. As the Facility determined that Icarus' wings were useless to him, Risman resolved that the Angel (Warren Worthington)'s wings were the ones they needed and initiated plans to get them. Risman also completed Stryker's arrangement with the Facility, who used the mutant Mercury (Cessily Kincaid)'s metallic bodily material to coat the surface of and finalize three Predator X creatures – deadly, continuously evolving mutant-hunting beasts. Two of the Predators inflicted some casualties before eventually getting killed, while the third attacked mutants across the USA.

Via information previously gathered from Nimrod's database, Risman predicted a new mutant would be born in Cooperstown, Alaska. The Purifiers razed Cooperstown on the day of the baby's birth, slaying the town's children, but were confronted by the villainous mutant Marauders and suffered heavy casualties. Using government and media connections, the Purifiers initially kept the massacre quiet, but it was eventually reported publicly by another X-Men enemy, Simon Trask.

Art by Brent Eric Anderson

While other mutants affiliated with the X-Men sought to beat various anti-mutant groups to the baby, who had been rescued by Cable (Nathan Summers), the depowered mutant Rictor posed as mutant hater Joaquin "Jake" Murrieta, and infiltrated the Purifiers; meanwhile, the New X-Men, schoolmates of the bus massacre victims, attacked the Purifiers' Washington DC base, easily overpowering the Purifiers, then escaped with Rictor's help. Risman then hired Lady Deathstrike and the cyborg Reavers to find the mutant baby, a goal prevented by X-Force (X-Men strikeforce), the infant taken into the future for safekeeping by Cable. Taylor, the Purifier who had recruited "Murrieta," was expelled, and subsequently hired the assassin Arcade in a failed revenge attempt against Rictor before committing suicide.

New Purifier Eli Bard (secretly a vampiric being) guided Risman to Bastion's head held by SHIELD in North Dakota, and they grafted it onto Nimrod's original body, hoping to regain their visions of the future, but Bastion quickly announced his intentions to wipe out mutantkind his own way. Despite Risman's reservations, Bastion had the Purifiers retrieve the techno-organic body of the Technarch Magus and used it to reanimate and/or take over several X-Men enemies — including Stryker, Cameron Hodge, Stephen Lang, Donald Pierce, the Leper Queen, Graydon Creed, and Bolivar Trask — putting them directly under Bastion's control.

Risman, meanwhile, having recruited the Reverend Craig into the Purifiers, captured Craig's former ward Wolfsbane (Rahne Sinclair). Craig helped brainwash her into retrieving Angel's wings, which she savagely ripped from his body and delivered to the Purifiers. Material from these wings, created by Apocalypse (En Sabah Nur), was implanted into Purifiers to grant them their own wings as the Choir. X-Force, meanwhile, waged war on the Purifiers, killing dozens of them across the USA, seeking to kill Risman and take the Purifiers down once and for all. Realizing Bastion's plans did not mesh with those of the Purifiers, Risman planned a coup on Bastion, hoping to kill him before Stryker's apparent resurrection was revealed to the Purifiers and Bastion gained complete control of the organization. Risman had the Choir attack Bastion and those with him, but X-Force intervened at the same time. A massive battle broke out, and Bard was revealed as a vampiric traitor when he drained the Magus' life. X-23 slew Risman while Angel, who had grown new, metallic wings, savagely killed most of the Choir. Bastion escaped with his techno-organic charges and put Stryker back in charge of the remaining Purifiers, uniting them against all remaining mutants.

Art by Clayton Crain

Art by Clayton Crain

SABRETOOTH

REAL NAME: Victor Creed

ALIASES: Der Schlächter ("the Butcher" in German), Slasher, el Tigre, others

IDENTITY: Secret; known to various government officials

OCCUPATION: Mercenary; former terrorist, government agent, possibly others

PLACE OF BIRTH: Unrevealed

CITIZENSHIP: Unrevealed, numerous international criminal records

KNOWN RELATIVES: Graydon Creed (Tribune, son, deceased), Zebadiah Creed (father, presumed deceased), unidentified mother (presumed deceased)

GROUP AFFILIATION: Agent of Romulus, Lupine; formerly X-Men, Weapon X, Brotherhood of Mutants, Hound Program, Marauders, X-Factor, Team X; former agent of Tribune, Foreigner, Montenegro and others; former partner of Constrictor

EDUCATION: Unrevealed

FIRST APPEARANCE: Iron Fist #14 (1977)

Art by Mark Bright

HISTORY: Allegedly descended from a variant wolf-like strain of mankind's evolution known as the Lupine, Victor Creed apparently suffered an abusive childhood, frequently beaten and chained up in the basement by his father. Taking the name Sabretooth as an adult, Creed intimidated a small Canadian frontier community in the early 20th century. One of the few who did not fear him was a young man named Logan (James Howlett), apparently a fellow Lupine descendant. Hating the love that existed between Logan and young Native American girl Silver Fox, Creed brutally assaulted her, raping her and leaving her for dead. The enraged Logan then attacked Creed but was defeated, unaware that Silver Fox had survived the attack. Sabretooth was later found by the Lupine Romulus, who gave Creed's life purpose. In the early 1960s, under Romulus' direction, Creed joined Team X, a special intelligence unit run by the CIA for the subversive Weapon X Program. In Team X, Creed was reunited with both Logan, now known as Wolverine, and Silver Fox; however, none of them recalled their past experiences due to false memory implants provided by Weapon X's ally Psi-Borg (Aldo Ferro). Creed had a falling out with Wolverine during a mission in East Berlin in Germany, exacerbating the animosity between the two. Creed remained with Team X until its disbandment, then became a solo hired assassin, earning a worldwide reputation. At some point in the subsequent decades, he studied under the enigmatic master assassin Foreigner. For reasons of her own, mutant shape-shifter Mystique manipulated Creed and seduced him to become pregnant with his child; however, the resultant son had no mutant potential and Mystique abandoned him. Despising his parents, the boy grew up to become anti-mutant activist Graydon Creed. Sabretooth also annually stalked Wolverine on the day Wolverine believed to be his birthday.

In recent years, Creed abducted noted attorney Jeryn Hogarth who was rescued by his client, the martial artist Iron Fist (Daniel Rand). Later, Creed partnered with the mercenary Constrictor on an assignment for the crimelord Montenegro; however, driven by his hunger for violence, a disguised Creed slew several people in New York City, with the press dubbing him the "Slasher." When Creed was exposed as the perpetrator, he and the Constrictor were opposed by Iron Fist and his allies Power Man (Luke Cage), Misty Knight and el Aguila (Alejandro Montoya). Forced to retreat, Creed and the Constrictor later sought revenge on Knight, but were again defeated by Power Man and Iron Fist. Later, trying to prove himself to the Foreigner, Creed tracked down the Black Cat (Felicia Hardy) and clashed with both her and Spider-Man (Peter Parker), which resulted in Creed being hospitalized under guard. Escaping, he was recruited by Gambit to join the Marauders, a team of assassins serving depraved geneticist Mr. Sinister. Sent to slaughter the underground mutant community of Morlocks, the Marauders clashed with the Morlocks' allies, the X-Men, including Wolverine. Creed and Wolverine fought several times during the so-called "Mutant Massacre," with Creed ultimately meeting defeat.

As his bloodlust increased, Sabretooth hired the telepathic Birdy to help keep his urges in check; however, Birdy was murdered by Graydon, who, disguised as the armored Tribune, had hired Sabretooth to assassinate Mystique. Sabretooth then slipped into a killing spree, but was captured by his former Team X colleague Maverick (Christoph Nord) and the X-Men. The X-Men's telepathic founder Professor Charles Xavier tried to help Sabretooth overcome his bloodthirsty impulses. Sabretooth played along, but he escaped from his holding cell at the first opportunity. Confronted by Wolverine, the two fought savagely until Wolverine thrust one of his claws into Creed's brain, nearly lobotomizing him. Following this attack, Creed seemed unusually passive, and young mutant Tabitha Smith took pity on him and sought to help him reform; however, Creed soon regained his true personality and turned against Smith and the X-Men, almost killing the X-Man Psylocke during his escape. Not long after, the US government's Hound Program recruited Creed to pursue their

AS CHILD

malfunctioning mutant tracker. To that end, Creed was made a member of the government-sponsored X-Factor team, much to the chagrin of X-Factor's leader Forge, who was unaware that Creed was under orders to kill X-Factor should they be deemed uncontrollable. Creed was forced to wear an inhibitor collar that severely shocked his nervous system if he became overly aggressive towards any of his teammates or if he tried to remove it. After joining his teammate Mystique in opposing the terrorist organizations Hydra and AIM, Creed obtained pills to help him overcome the pain and, after removing the collar, he savagely attacked X-Factor before escaping. Rejecting the government's authority, Creed killed several potential members of the Hound Program, setting back the government's efforts to control mutants. Creed also clashed with the Russian super-soldier Omega Red who sought to capture him and bring him to the Russian telepath Elena Ivanova, whose mother Creed had killed years earlier.

Under unrevealed circumstances, Creed had Adamantium bonded to his skeleton and claws and then attacked Wolverine during his wedding to Viper (the former Madame Hydra) in Madripoor, only to be forced into cooperating with Wolverine to repel the Hand and Hydra's attempted invasion of Madripoor. In a later encounter, Creed and Wolverine were set against each other by the immortal mutant Apocalypse (En Sabah Nur), who intended to transform the winner into a Horseman. Wolverine defeated Creed, tearing out his heart, and Apocalypse removed Creed's Adamantium and bonded it to Wolverine's skeleton instead. Left for dead, Creed was found by mutant thief Gambit and the mutant shapeshifter Courier (Jacob Gavin). The trio broke into one of Sinister's bases, and, after some haggling, Creed received a treatment to kick start his healing factor. Gambit subsequently secured enough Adamantium from the Constrictor to keep Creed alive.

Restored to his former self, Creed joined Mystique's restructured Brotherhood of Mutants in seeking to release a virus that would infect normal humans, but the X-Men's Bishop defeated Creed during an assault on the Muir Island research base. Subsequently captured by the revived Weapon X Program, Creed again had Adamantium bonded to his skeleton. The program's key operative, Creed was responsible for bringing other former members back into the fold and successfully recruited the mercenary Deadpool, but failed to recover Maverick and John Wraith. Creed soon betrayed Weapon X by stealing its data on the world's known mutants, which he used as a lure to recruit fellow Wolverine foes Omega Red and the cyborg Lady Deathstrike in attacking Wolverine's friends and family, capturing Wolverine's young ward Amiko. Creed quickly betrayed these allies in turn, teleporting himself and Wolverine to the original and long abandoned Weapon X facility. Using command codes stolen from the Weapon X project's Director, Creed used a device that stripped Wolverine of his mutant powers, then challenged him to a supposed final battle during which Creed's mutant abilities were negated by the same device. Both mutants nearly died of wounds sustained in the ensuing fight, but revived once their powers reactivated.

Weapon X ultimately recaptured Creed, but he escaped again with Sinister's clandestine help. Returning to his mercenary ways, Creed was hired by a Weapon X offshoot to track down their escaped test subject the Native. Outfought by the Native, Creed manipulated Wolverine into tracking her for him, but his employers betrayed him as they recaptured their quarry. Seeking vengeance, he allied with Wolverine to raid the facility holding the Native. After killing his employers and watching Wolverine and the Native escape, Creed swore to finish the job he started. Following clashes with Sasquatch (Walter Langkowski) and the Wendigo in Canada, Creed joined Exodus' new Brotherhood of Mutants against the X-Men, but was yet again defeated by Wolverine. Creed was later hired to kill a team of scientists in Peru, one of whom revealed that their project involved a group of hyper-evolved humans called Niños de la Camara (the Children of the Vault). Creed attacked them on their flying tanker,

the Conquistador, but found himself outmatched after they nullified his healing factor, forcing him to flee to the X-Men, who reluctantly granted him sanctuary. After the Children sent Northstar and Aurora against the X-Men, Rogue pressed Creed into joining the X-Men to oppose the Children, injecting him with Nano-Sentinels to control him. After defeating the Children, Creed was imprisoned on the Conquistador, which Rogue's X-Men had commandeered, allowing his healing factor time to eradicate the Nano-Sentinels. After opposing rogue geneticist Pandemic, Creed escaped his imprisonment while the X-Men battled the Shi'ar's Hecatomb weapon on Cable's Providence island. Hijacking the Conquistador, Creed refused to aid the team, so Cable caused the Conquistador to crash into the Hecatomb. Surviving, Creed hid out on Providence until Cable began evacuating the island. Creed then killed Cable's ally Black Box (Garabed Bashur) and held his friend Irene Merryweather hostage; when Deadpool rescued her, Cable telekinetically hurled Creed into the ocean.

Returning to the X-Men's mansion, Creed was confronted by Wolverine, intending to settle things between them once and for all. Their battle took them to Wakanda where they were informed of their alleged Lupine ancestry. Imprisoned by Wakanda's ruler the Black Panther (T'Challa), Creed was liberated by Romulus' agent Wild Child and returned to the former Weapon X facility where Romulus devolved him into a more feral state. After Wolverine and others also of supposedly Lupine descent tracked Creed to Weapon X, Creed broke free and killed the depowered Feral (Maria Callasantos) before Wolverine decapitated Sabretooth using the Muramasa Blade, a sword that blocked their healing factors.

TEAM X UNIFORM

Art by Steve Epting

HEIGHT: 6'6"
WEIGHT: 275 lbs.
EYES: Amber
HAIR: Blond

ABILITIES/ACCESSORIES: Sabretooth possessed superhumanly acute animal-like senses of sight, hearing, smell and taste, allowing him to track prey with unerring accuracy. His night vision was preternaturally sensitive, extending into the infrared spectrum. Sabretooth could also regenerate his cellular structure at a rapid rate, making him virtually immune to poisons and most drugs, as well as rapidly healing his injuries, enhancing his endurance and slowing his aging. He had claws on his hands and animal-like canine teeth that were strong enough to rend through bone. Sabretooth was a formidable hand-to-hand combatant, having been trained by the CIA, the Foreigner and others. Sabretooth was also an extraordinary hunter and tracker even without his heightened senses.

POWER GRID	1	2	3	4	5	6	7
INTELLIGENCE							
STRENGTH							
SPEED							
DURABILITY							
ENERGY PROJECTION							
FIGHTING SKILLS							

SERAPH

REAL NAME: Unrevealed
ALIASES: Unrevealed, but likely several
IDENTITY: Secret
OCCUPATION: Spy, assassin, adventurer, bar owner/hostess; former dancer
CITIZENSHIP: Unrevealed
PLACE OF BIRTH: Unrevealed
KNOWN RELATIVES: None
GROUP AFFILIATION: Operative of Romulus
EDUCATION: Unrevealed
FIRST APPEARANCE: Uncanny X-Men #268 (1990)

HISTORY: Early in the 20th century, Seraph was instrumental in building a bar/nightclub in Madripoor, which she eventually purchased and named "Seraph's." Despite her diminutive size, she commanded respect and power in the island nation. At some point she became an operative of the mysterious immortal Romulus, apparently brokering an alliance between Romulus' organization and the ninja Hand. In the late 1900s or early 1910s, the mutant Logan (James Howlett), then in his late teens, met and romanced Seraph during his first visit to Madripoor, unaware his trip had been manipulated by Romulus precisely to establish their relationship. By his own analysis decades later, Logan was at this time "all instincts and muscles," acting with "no mercy and less brains"; from Seraph, he learned to better appreciate the world and to understand his actions' morality and consequences. Seraph and Logan parted ways by 1914, when World War I began.

By 1932, Logan had returned to Madripoor and renewed his affair with Seraph, who taught him to be a more effective and controlled assassin, restraining his berserker nature as a secret weapon and killing whomever she targeted. Seraph genuinely returned Logan's love, and she regretted her role in manipulating him for Romulus. Logan later described Seraph as a "fallen angel," but the context of this remark is unrevealed. During World War II, Seraph acted as Logan's handler in Madripoor and prepared him for missions undertaken for Romulus, whose identity was unknown to Logan, while fellow operative Cyber directed Logan in the field. In the summer of 1941, under Seraph's direction, Logan worked with Captain America (Steve Rogers) and others to seemingly sabotage an alliance between the ninja cult Hand and Baron Strucker, then in the early stages of forming his Hydra organization; Seraph's true goal, however, was the assassination of the Hand's Jonin (leader), assigned to young Natasha Romanoff (later the Black Widow) but ultimately performed by Logan, who acted as Natasha's mentor much as Seraph had served as his. Later that year, Seraph assigned Logan to work with Captain America and his partner Bucky (James Barnes) in Tunisia, with orders to recruit Cap and learn how to duplicate the Super-Soldier serum that empowered him, or kill him. Logan again clashed with Strucker in the process, and in mid-mission Seraph, informing him their forces were now allies of Strucker's, ordered him to kill Cap and Bucky. Logan arranged Strucker's escape but declined to kill the American heroes, possibly creating a rift with Seraph. Following the war Seraph and Logan apparently had no further contact for decades. Eventually she mentored another young mercenary, Viper (later Madame Hydra).

In recent years, shortly after Logan became Department H operative Wolverine, Seraph recruited him and Viper for an unrevealed mission that brought them into conflict with Sabretooth, suggesting her mission, self-imposed or not, was contrary to Romulus' interests, perhaps even to his direct orders. Although the mission was a success, Sabretooth mortally wounded Seraph, who died after she and her two protégés returned to Madripoor. As a dying wish, Seraph extracted from Wolverine a vow to grant Viper a request, no matter the cost, at some future date. She also bequeathed him part-ownership of Seraph's, later renamed the Princess Bar. Years later, Viper reminded Wolverine of his promise, and he married her to help cement her power in Madripoor. Wolverine regained his suppressed memories a few years later and, realizing Seraph had left a message for him in her coffin, exhumed her body to recover it and finally learned the name of their shared master, Romulus.

Art by Kaare Andrews

HEIGHT: 3'3"
WEIGHT: 68 lbs.
EYES: Blue
HAIR: White

ABILITIES/ACCESSORIES: Seraph was an accomplished and ruthless spy and assassin, able to dispatch opponents over twice her size. She had access to the resources of Romulus' worldwide organization.

POWER GRID	1	2	3	4	5	6	7
INTELLIGENCE							
STRENGTH							
SPEED							
DURABILITY							
ENERGY PROJECTION							
FIGHTING SKILLS							

HISTORY: Several decades ago, young Blackfoot woman Silver Fox fell in love with mutant adventurer Logan (James Howlett), who had retreated from a life of manipulation and murder. In a cabin near a Canadian frontier community, the couple lived together happily for months. On Logan's birthday, Sabretooth, possibly under orders from immortal mastermind Romulus, attacked Silver Fox in Logan's absence, raping her and leaving her for dead. Enraged and grief-stricken, Logan fought Sabretooth, who soundly defeated him. Believing the nearby townspeople shared responsibility for the attack, Logan, possibly under Romulus' influence, killed several and departed. Logan's presumption of Silver Fox's death, however, may have stemmed from either grief or deliberate memory alteration by Romulus, since she survived.

Circa the early 1960s, Silver Fox joined the Weapon X Project and its field unit, Team X, alongside Logan (now called Wolverine), Sabretooth and others. Like Romulus, Weapon X subjected some operatives to memory alterations, both through staged events and via Aldo Ferro's psionic powers, making it unclear whether or not the three fully remembered their shared past. In 1963, Silver Fox, perhaps erroneously believing Wolverine had known she was still alive when he departed decades before, betrayed Team X during a Cuban mission in retaliation for the supposed wrong. Later, joining a terrorist cell with unrevealed goals, she again clashed with her former teammates in Canada. By 1972, some years after Team X's disbandment, she had joined Hydra, which had a history of allying with Romulus, and Weapon X lost track of her.

Years later, following inhumane experimentation by Weapon X, Wolverine consulted Adamantium expert Myron MacLain, and Silver Fox and her Hydra agents observed while Wolverine and his allies fought Sabretooth, sent to kill him by Romulus or other parties. Following Sabretooth's defeat, Silver Fox contemplated killing Wolverine but ultimately let him live, thinking him likely to oppose Hydra's rivals.

In recent years, Wolverine, now an X-Man and still under surveillance by Silver Fox, sought information on Weapon X. When one of its surviving scientists, Truett Hudson, aka "Prof. Thornton," plotted against him, Silver Fox murdered Hudson. Soon afterward, she allied with Matsuo Tsurayaba's Hand faction and hired Japanese assassin Reiko to poison Wolverine's beloved, Mariko Yashida, member of the Hand's rival Yashida Clan. Weeks later, Aldo Ferro, now Psi-Borg, reversed former Team X member Mastodon's longevity factor, inducing rapid aging and death. As Psi-Borg suspected, other Team X survivors, including Silver Fox and Wolverine, traced the deed to him; although Silver Fox remained hostile to Wolverine, she came to doubt her grudge against him. At Psi-Borg's

REAL NAME: Silver Fox (apparently)
ALIASES: Zora de Plata, numerous others
IDENTITY: No dual identity
OCCUPATION: Terrorist, former government operative
CITIZENSHIP: Canada
PLACE OF BIRTH: Presumably an unidentified community in the Canadian Rockies
KNOWN RELATIVES: None
GROUP AFFILIATION: Hydra; formerly unidentified terrorist cell, Team X, Weapon X (multinational)
EDUCATION: Unrevealed
FIRST APPEARANCE: Wolverine #10 (1989)

island fortress, where he hoped to experiment upon Team X to reverse his own aging, Psi-Borg telepathically directed Sabretooth to kill Silver Fox during battle. Psi-Borg and Sabretooth escaped, and Wolverine, locating the cabin he and Silver Fox once shared, buried her adjacent to the site of their long-ago happiness. Years later, however, Wolverine, now possessing his full memories, seemed doubtful the woman beside whom he fought Psi-Borg was in fact Silver Fox.

HEIGHT: 5'7"	EYES: Blue
WEIGHT: 121 lbs.	HAIR: Black

ABILITIES/ACCESSORIES: Although Silver Fox was, like other Team X members, presumably a mutant, her powers were never specified. She possessed a healing factor developed from Wolverine's but not as powerful. She aged very slowly due to either Team X age suppression treatments or some other factor. She was an exceptional markswoman and a trained hand-to-hand combatant; her rise through Hydra's ranks indicates strong leadership skills. She used handguns and other weapons, both conventional and otherwise, as a Team X operative, terrorist and Hydra agent.

POWER GRID	1	2	3	4	5	6	7
INTELLIGENCE							
STRENGTH							
SPEED							
DURABILITY							
ENERGY PROJECTION							
FIGHTING SKILLS							

SPORE

REAL NAME: Spore
ALIASES: None
IDENTITY: No dual identity
OCCUPATION: Warrior
CITIZENSHIP: None
PLACE OF CREATION: Unrevealed
KNOWN RELATIVES: None
GROUP AFFILIATION: None
EDUCATION: No formal education
FIRST APPEARANCE: (Behind the scenes) Wolverine #17 (1989); (full) Wolverine #21 (1990)

HISTORY: The Deviants, a deformed subspecies of humanity, created Spore from a human template to be the ultimate weapon against their enemies, the Eternals. Spore quickly took to its task, becoming virtually indestructible by consuming the Eternals' unique genetics. As it grew in size and power, the consumption of Eternals proved insufficient to satiate Spore's hunger, and it soon turned on its Deviant creators. During the time of the Celestials' Second Host in 18,000 BC, Spore was deemed too dangerous to exist and the Celestials themselves incinerated the creature, reducing it to the slime from which it was created on what was later known as el Jardin del Rey mountain in the South American nation Tierra Verde. Over time, Spore's remnants became incorporated into el Jardin del Rey's soil.

In recent years, Spore's residue was absorbed into Tierra Verde's cocaine crop. Spore's life force survived within each dose, and sought release within each user. The tainted cocaine gave drug-addicted former boxer Hammer Cody superhuman strength and durability, but sent him on a rampage, battling Daredevil (Matt Murdock) and the New York Police Department. Unable to survive Spore's energy growing inside him, Cody died, but his rampage sparked interest in the tainted drug. Tierra Verde President Felix Caridad, after hearing of the crop's effects, commissioned the scientist Nikolaus Geist to create a superhuman agent for him. Geist traveled to Madripoor, where the Spore-tainted cocaine had been impounded by Madripoor's Prince Baran. Geist then purchased and injected the enforcer Roughouse with the cocaine, sending him into a rampage. The mutant Wolverine (Logan/James Howlett), having tracked the cocaine's shipment to Madripoor, battled Roughouse until Geist tranquilized them both. He delivered the cocaine-addled Roughouse to President Caridad, who coerced his estranged wife, now the nun Sister Salvation, to use her healing power to calm Roughouse in exchange for seeing their

son, Palo. Joined by local heroine la Bandera, Wolverine freed Roughouse and Salvation. As they escaped into the jungles, Geist shot Wolverine with multiple doses of the Spore-tainted cocaine.

Despite Salvation boosting Wolverine's innate healing factor, Spore tried to control Wolverine, explaining its origins in the process. Eventually, Wolverine's healing factor expelled Spore's particles from his body, and he, Salvation and Roughouse were recaptured. Caridad planned to make a willing Palo his Spore-powered super-agent, with Salvation's powers controlling the inherent rages. When Caridad shot tainted cocaine darts at Palo, Wolverine freed himself and deflected all but one of the darts into the president himself, who was driven mad by the drug. As Sister Salvation used her healing abilities to purge the cocaine from Palo's body, the crazed president injected himself with his entire supply, which allowed Spore to consume Caridad's body and re-form its own. Spore quickly engulfed Wolverine and the surrounding local rebels, growing in size and power until Wolverine tore his way out of the creature, briefly causing its collapse. It immediately began re-forming itself anew, but Sister Salvation's healing touch incinerated the creature much like the Celestials' fire, severely burning it until nothing remained.

HEIGHT: Variable	EYES: Red
WEIGHT: Variable	HAIR: None

ABILITIES/ACCESSORIES: Spore was composed of an amorphous material and was resistant to physical harm and virtually immortal. Spore could engulf and consume living matter, growing in size and power. It could regenerate even from near-total molecular dispersal, provided enough of its surviving particles were in close vicinity to one another to re-form itself. If its particles entered living creatures, Spore could influence them, transforming them into superhumanly strong and durable savages.

POWER GRID	1	2	3	4	5	6	7
INTELLIGENCE							
STRENGTH							
SPEED							
DURABILITY							
ENERGY PROJECTION							
FIGHTING SKILLS							

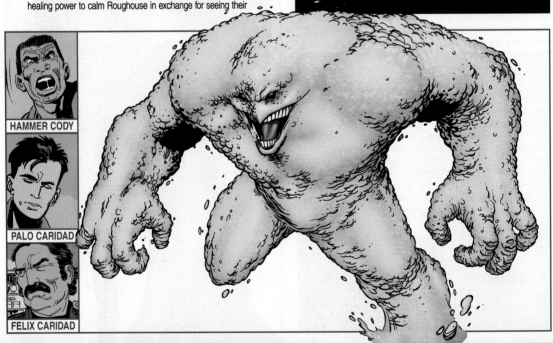

HAMMER CODY

PALO CARIDAD

FELIX CARIDAD

Art by Paco Diaz Luque with John Byrne (insets)

HISTORY: A devoted sergeant in the US Army Rangers, William Stryker had a car accident during which his pregnant wife, Marcy, was shocked into labor. When their newborn child had mutant features, William deemed this an abomination; he cruelly killed his child with a knife and murdered his wife by breaking her neck. Despairing, William blew up their car by setting fire to the gas leak, but he survived the explosion. Stryker turned to alcohol for a time until he learned of the world's growing mutant population. Feeling enlightened, William became religious and focused his spiritual mission on eradicating the world's mutant population, which he believed was Satan's most insidious tool on Earth. Over the following quarter century, Stryker gathered other like-minded individuals and developed a strong following as he posed as a reverend and a televangelist. Growing wealthy, Stryker formed the Stryker Crusade and established an armored force of Purifiers, intended to kill mutants. Through an FBI agent follower, Stryker eventually learned of the X-Men, who used their headquarters as a school for mutants. Stryker regarded X-Men leader Charles Xavier as the Antichrist, and the X-Men as the epitome of the mutant outbreak. In time, Stryker, who quoted scripture to support his ideals, ordered his Purifiers to act, beginning with slaughtering two young mutant children in Connecticut. After a televised debate with Xavier about the mutant issue, Stryker, equipped with psi-screens to block Xavier's telepathy, had Xavier kidnapped along with two of Xavier's students, Cyclops (Scott Summers) and Storm. Stryker tried to brainwash Xavier into using a complex machine to massacre many mutants telepathically, but Stryker's plot unraveled when the Purifiers fought several X-Men and Magneto (Max Eisenhardt), a deadly magnetic mutant. The battle came to Stryker's feet and ended abruptly when Stryker threatened young X-Man Kitty Pryde and was shot by a policeman.

Surviving, Stryker spent years in prison, ministering to various inmates and gaining certain privileges due to believers among the prisoners and guards. He continued his organization's work through sleeper cells that his believers maintained. When Stryker learned that an artificial intelligence called Reverend Paul had seized a town, killed its human residents and used nanites to transform the minds of the town's mutants into cybernetic computers to protect them, he kidnapped Kitty Pryde and attempted to use her power to disrupt electronics to destroy Paul. When this failed, Paul responded by attempting to transfer his consciousness into a global network. To prevent this, Stryker merged with Paul, sacrificing himself as a containment unit to imprison Paul, though Stryker was freed from this fate soon after. Feeling destitute and forsaken, Stryker contemplated suicide before the future-mutant-hunting machine Nimrod appeared before him. Thinking this a sign from God, Stryker's faith was renewed. Stryker considered it his mission to bring about Nimrod's future, where mutants were hunted and killed or placed in concentration camps — using Nimrod's databanks to gain foreknowledge, Stryker learned of "M-Day," where most of Earth's mutants were depowered, and through

REAL NAME: William Stryker
ALIASES: None
IDENTITY: Publicly known
OCCUPATION: Former reverend, leader of Stryker Crusade, U.S. Army Ranger
CITIZENSHIP: USA
PLACE OF BIRTH: Phoenix, Arizona
KNOWN RELATIVES: Marcy (wife, deceased), unnamed child (deceased)
GROUP AFFILIATION: Leader of Stryker Crusade; Purifiers
EDUCATION: Unrevealed
FIRST APPEARANCE: Marvel Graphic Novel #5 (1982)

obituaries, Stryker saved and then recruited followers who would have otherwise died, engendering their loyalty. Stryker then focused on killing several who were destined to bring about Nimrod's destruction. Needing a spy inside Xavier's new school, Stryker deceived young winged Icarus into serving him, and amputated Icarus' wings. Stryker blew up a bus full of former mutants and had one student, Wallflower, assassinated. After Dust, another student, was believed killed, Stryker shot Icarus and donned a Nimrod Gauntlet, attacking the school with a troop of Purifiers. The healing mutant Elixir grabbed Stryker's face and reversed his healing power, killing Stryker. Stryker was recently revived as a techno-organic being by Bastion. Controlled by Bastion, Stryker is leading the Purifiers toward the destruction of mutants once again.

HEIGHT: 5'11"
WEIGHT: 170 lbs.
EYES: Brown
HAIR: White

ABILITIES/ACCESSORIES: William Stryker is now a techno-organic being under Bastion's control. The full extent of his powers remains unrevealed. William Stryker had military training and access to his worldwide followers' technology, including several squads of Purifiers, Mandroid armor, and a deadly Nimrod Gauntlet. Nimrod's records granted him knowledge of the future.

POWER GRID	1	2	3	4	5	6	7
INTELLIGENCE							
STRENGTH							
SPEED							
DURABILITY							
ENERGY PROJECTION							
FIGHTING SKILLS							

REAL NAME: S'ym
ALIASES: Duke Bleys
IDENTITY: No dual identity; Earth's general populace is unaware of S'ym's existence
OCCUPATION: Servant of Magik (Illyana Rasputin); former servant of Belasco, ruler of limbo
CITIZENSHIP: Limbo/Otherplace
PLACE OF BIRTH: Limbo/Otherplace
KNOWN RELATIVES: None
GROUP AFFILIATION: Limbo's demons
EDUCATION: Unrevealed
FIRST APPEARANCE: Uncanny X-Men #160 (1982)

Art by Steve Skroce

HISTORY: Spawned in the pits of limbo (aka Otherplace, center of the hellish Splinter Realms and allegedly part of the Nexus of all Realities; not to be confused with the Immortus-ruled timeless Limbo), the demon S'ym became one of his realm's most feared inhabitants, and chief enforcer for limbo's ruler Belasco. S'ym relished punishing any who displeased his master, including disciplining Belasco's human disciple, 15th century girl Maire O'Connell. Some time after Belasco exiled Maire back to Earth for becoming too arrogant, he chose a new disciple, seven-year-old mutant Illyana Rasputin, luring her from Earth-8280 through one of limbo's teleportational "stepping discs." Her brother, Peter (the X-Man Colossus) and his teammates Storm (Ororo Munroe), Sprite (Kitty Pryde),

Nightcrawler (Kurt Wagner) and Wolverine (Logan/James Howlett) pursued, and were trapped in turn. When Illyana tried to flee, S'ym captured her, but was prevented from slaying her by demon mage N'astirh, whose precognitive magic had shown him she would one day be useful to him. Before Belasco could corrupt Illyana, she was rescued by the New Mutants (of Earth-616), the X-Men's junior counterparts who had traveled back in time. Belasco settled instead for spending decades corrupting the X-Men. S'ym eventually slew Wolverine and feasted on his heart, and later killed Colossus too, crushing his chest and pinning his corpse to a wall after Colossus tried to prevent Belasco from corrupting Kitty, turning her into the feral Cat.

Due to limbo's unstable temporal nature, though from S'ym and Belasco's perspective Illyana was only kidnapped once, two divergent reality's events took place within the same realm, and Reality-616's Illyana and the X-Men subsequently arrived there. Though S'ym hoped to slay both Colossus and Wolverine anew, Storm-8280 assisted the newer group's escape, but Illyana-616 was trapped instead. Despite the efforts of the elder Storm and Cat-8280, Illyana-616 became Belasco's new apprentice; S'ym punished her for imagined transgressions whenever he could. After several years Illyana rebelled, and after learning to control the stepping discs, creating a powerful Soulsword and giving in to her corrupted "Darkchilde" side, the 15-year-old Illyana confronted Belasco with a view to slaying him; when S'ym tried to attack her, she easily gutted him with her blade, incapacitating him. Defeating Belasco too, Illyana spared him, rejected her Darkchilde, and returned to Earth.

Belasco soon departed limbo too and with his master gone, S'ym found his way to Earth and tracked Illyana to Charles Xavier's school, intending to take her back to limbo. Attacking the school, he easily overpowered Illyana's fellow students, the New Mutants (younger versions of the group who had rescued Earth-8280's Illyana), but surrendered in terror when Illyana threatened him with the Soulsword. He informed her of Belasco's departure and swore fealty to her as limbo's new mistress. Now code-named Magik, Illyana gradually became comfortable using limbo both as a refuge from enemies such as the White Queen (Emma Frost) or the Shadow King, and a temporary jail, complacently trusting S'ym to guard and intimidate prisoners, including the Asgardian Enchantress (Amora), jobs S'ym undertook with gusto. S'ym also delighted in informing her shocked teammate, the Technarch alien Warlock, that Illyana had slain Cat and Storm during her apprenticeship to Belasco. When Warlock's malevolent father Magus pursued the New Mutants into limbo, demons trying to defend Magik were transformed by Magus' transmode virus into techno-organic beings like him and Warlock, then drained of their life energy. When the New Mutants fled again, Magus struck a deal with S'ym; he changed the demon into a techno-organic being, granting him power enough to claim limbo's throne, in return for S'ym blocking the New Mutants from transiting limbo again, preventing them fleeing their next encounter with Magus. S'ym began spreading the virus, weakening Magik's control over the realm with each new convert. When the New Mutants returned, S'ym attacked them; Magik soon learned that while her Soulsword could no longer permanently harm S'ym, it could halt the transmode virus' spread so long as she sheathed it in limbo's soil. Even though Magus was soon defeated, Magik's attempts to destroy S'ym failed, and though S'ym proved vulnerable to her teacher Magneto (Max Eisenhardt)'s powers, she rejected Magneto's offer to destroy S'ym for her, insisting it was her responsibility. Every time circumstances forced Magik to use the Soulsword in battle, removing it from limbo, S'ym's power grew, and when she returned accompanied by Belasco's other apprentice, Maire, S'ym mortally wounded the older girl.

Noticing that Magik's use of wild magic was weakening limbo's boundaries so that demons began slipping through to Earth, S'ym stepped down his campaign, letting Magik think she was gaining the upper hand, while he secretly planned to conquer Earth when the barriers completely failed; however, S'ym was unaware that his old rival N'astirh was plotting against him, protected from transmode infection by his spells. When her teammate Cypher (Doug Ramsey) was murdered, Magik, increasingly influenced by her demonic Darkchilde, callously teleported those she held responsible, the anti-mutant Right's armored soldiers, into S'ym's clutches; he swiftly infected them, adding them to his army. Soon after this, Colossus helped Magik defeat S'ym in battle. Wrongly believing her dominance in limbo confirmed, Magik and the New Mutants returned to using it as a way station on their travels. Meanwhile, S'ym entered the dreams of Madelyne Pryor, the X-Man Cyclops (Scott Summers)'s abandoned wife, offering her power to avenge herself and beginning her transformation into the Goblin Queen.

Intending to trick Magik into opening a breach between Earth and limbo, then to magically lock that rift open, and knowing N'astirh's sorcery permitted access to Earth even while the barriers were intact, S'ym forcefully ordered his rival to go there and prepare the way. N'astirh feigned compliance, and per S'ym's instructions, N'astirh's lackeys kidnapped 13 babies of power to place at the points of an inverted pentagram, focusing mystical energies ready to open a portal over Manhattan; the infants were then to be sacrificed to keep the breach open. Meanwhile, N'astirh's spells further weakened the interdimensional barriers, beginning Manhattan's transformation into a demonic realm; realizing he could not cast all his incantations in the time available, N'astirh forced the machinery-manipulating mutant Wiz Kid (Takeshi Matsuya) to create and operate a computer to cast the required spells simultaneously. Needing the Darkchilde to use the Soulsword to complete the process, S'ym took the blade from Magik in battle; N'astirh, seemingly assisting Magik against S'ym, told her that S'ym had only been able to do so because she was rejecting her true nature. Accepting her dark side, Magik transformed into the Darkchilde and reclaimed her weapon, but when she returned to Earth with the New Mutants, her stepping disc completed N'astirh's spell, and demons flooded through from limbo to Earth. Disagreeing over whether or not to slay the Darkchilde, S'ym and N'astirh fought, but while they were distracted, the New Mutants worked with the X-Terminators (Wiz Kid's team) to rescue the babies and disrupt the pentagram so the portal would close. Losing the fight, N'astirh allowed S'ym to transform him, but when S'ym attempted to drain the now techno-organic N'astirh's life energy, N'astirh instead leeched S'ym's; however, when N'astirh merged with the spell computer seeking greater power, Wiz Kid blew it up, closing the portal in the process. Though no new demons could come through, Manhattan remained infested. Wrongly believing his rival dead, S'ym sought to slay Illyana, but the newly arrived Colossus intervened. While S'ym was locked in battle with him, Illyana opened a new disc to limbo, sacrificing herself to generate an eldritch fire pillar that sucked most of the demons out of Manhattan, S'ym included. Having avoided this fate, N'astirh soon tried to have the Goblin Queen create a new portal between realms, but was defeated by the X-Men and X-Factor.

Dr. Doom (Victor von Doom) subsequently sought to collapse limbo in on itself to create a supply of magical Promethium using the Soulsword, now in Shadowcat (Kitty

Pryde)'s possession. S'ym tried to take the sword for himself, but was swallowed whole by fellow limbo resident Darkoth (Desmond Pitt), who instead used the blade to cleanse limbo for a time. Escaping, S'ym next tried to expand the Nexus of All Realities to engulf Earth, but a returned Belasco recruited mutant cyborg Cable to stop him; the unique combination of Cable being Madelyne Pryor's son, formerly one of N'astirh's 13 sacrificial infants, and infected with the techno-organic virus, made him toxic to S'ym, who crumbled to dust at his touch. Belasco reclaimed limbo, with a humbled S'ym once again serving him; however, sorceress Margali Szardos soon deposed Belasco. Her daughter, Amanda Sefton, claimed Illyana's Magik title and became limbo's new ruler. Contacted by the Archenemy, which planned to conquer the Splinter Realms, S'ym agreed to serve it in return for ruling limbo; as Duke Bleys, he became one of Amanda's advisors, encouraging her to unify the Splinter Realms against the Archenemy, so that they would gather their forces into a single, easy target; however, Amanda's ally Nightcrawler exposed this deception, and Amanda imprisoned S'ym; the Archenemy was subsequently defeated. Belasco later returned and drove Amanda out, reclaiming limbo; he purged S'ym of the techno-organic virus and reinstated him. Trying to resurrect Illyana, Belasco recreated her Darkchilde body, but not her soul; she soon deposed him, aided by the X-Men's newest students. S'ym switched his loyalties to the Darkchilde, but Belasco's daughter Witchfire soon challenged the Darkchilde for her father's crown, seized control of limbo, and tortured S'ym for opposing her.

BLEYS

HEIGHT: 7'5"; formerly variable   EYES: Red; formerly variable
WEIGHT: 1500 lbs.; formerly variable   HAIR: Gray; formerly variable

ABILITIES/ACCESSORIES: Immensely strong (lifting over 90 tons) and durable, Sy'm has skin tough enough to resist molten magma and penetration even from Adamantium blades; magical weapons however, can pierce his skin with comparative ease. He is also resistant to psionic attacks, and has sharp claws and fangs. While infected with the transmode virus, his body was composed of malleable living circuitry, making him invulnerable to conventional injury as he could reconstitute his body if destroyed, so long as a single molecule remained; however, he was vulnerable to those able to psionically manipulate metal or machinery, as well as to Cable's unique touch. He could shape-shift to any form he could imagine, allowing him to disguise himself, grow to immense size, or mimic the function of any machine. He could infect others with the transmode virus by touch, though Colossus' metal form proved immune, and some magic could also prevent the infection; S'ym could drain the life energy of other techno-organic beings, so long as his will was stronger than theirs.

POWER GRID	1	2	3	4	5	6	7
INTELLIGENCE							
STRENGTH							
SPEED							
DURABILITY							
ENERGY PROJECTION							
FIGHTING SKILLS							

* WHILE TECHNO-ORGANIC

TECHNO-ORGANIC FORM

TYGER TIGER

REAL NAME: Jessan Hoan
ALIASES: Tyger, "Tiger"
IDENTITY: Secret
OCCUPATION: Monarch; former crimelord, bank executive
CITIZENSHIP: Madripoor, Singapore
PLACE OF BIRTH: Singapore
KNOWN RELATIVES: Mr. Hoan (uncle, deceased), several unidentified family members (all deceased)
GROUP AFFILIATION: Former leader of her own criminal organization
EDUCATION: Harvard Business School
FIRST APPEARANCE: Uncanny X-Men #229 (1988); (Tyger) Marvel Comics Presents #6 (1988); (Tyger Tiger) Wolverine #6 (1989)

HISTORY: After graduating from Harvard, Jessan Hoan worked for her family's bank, the Hoan International Bank, in Singapore. She quickly became a successful young executive and helped the bank become a rival to Asia's largest bank, the Meridian Bank. After failing to subvert the Hoan Bank's success through legal means, the Meridian Bank's heads paid the Madripoorian crimelord Roche to deal with the problem. Roche, in turn, hired the cyborg mercenary Reavers to attack the Hoan Bank. They looted the vault and murdered almost all of the bank's staff, leaving Jessan as the sole survivor. Despite efforts to resist them that earned her the nickname "tiger" from the Reavers, they kidnapped her and took her back to their base in the Australian outback. There, the Reaver Pretty Boy tried to reprogram Jessan's mind, replacing her moral standards with an amorality more appropriate to a Reaver and endowing her with enhanced fighting skills; however, he was interrupted by the arrival of the X-Men, leaving Jessan's reprogramming incomplete. Though she no longer had her original personality, she was not completely amoral either. After the Reavers were defeated, the X-Men's ally Roma returned Jessan to the place and moment from which she was abducted.

Jessan learned that the Reavers' attack had crippled the Hoan Bank's operations, forcing it out of business. It had also made her an outcast, as being the massacre's only survivor left her suspected of being in league with the Reavers. Learning that Roche was behind the Reavers, Jessan moved to Madripoor and set herself up as a rival crimelord, calling herself "Tyger." Roche hired super-powered enforcers such as Razor-Fist (Douglas Scott) to help defeat Tyger, and in turn she enlisted the help of Wolverine (Logan/James Howlett). When Roche mistook the Princess Bar's proprietor O'Donnell for the Tyger and had him kidnapped, the true Tyger and Wolverine stole into Roche's villa to rescue him. While Wolverine dealt with Razor-Fist, Tyger beheaded Roche. Tyger then petitioned Madripoor's Prince Baran for the right to take over Roche's criminal empire, and set about dismantling Roche's drug trafficking and slave rings; however, this left a void that was soon filled by General Nguyen Ngoc Coy, leading to a gang war that was resolved only after both sides agreed not to interfere with each other's operations.

Tyger later faced rival criminals Cyber, Aardwolf, the Folding Circle and Abdul Alhazred, but overcame them all. When Baran and Coy framed Wolverine for murder, Tyger helped clear his name, after which Coy shot and apparently killed Baran in an act of self-preservation but was himself shot by Tyger. She was later among those women in Wolverine's life who were co-opted by the nihilist Viper (the former Madame Hydra) to capture Wolverine and force him to honor an old vow that saw Wolverine and Viper married, paving the way for Viper to become Madripoor's new ruler. Tyger was soon forced underground after Viper marked her for death. Increasingly unhappy with Viper's rule, which saw Madripoor turned into a haven for the terrorist Hydra organization, Tyger agreed to the help offered by SHIELD Director Tony Stark in overthrowing Viper. After Stark tricked Viper into publicly declaring her intent for Hydra to control Madripoor,

Tyger incited the people to openly rebel against her rule. As Iron Man, Stark defeated Viper's bodyguards and destroyed Hydra's latest doomsday weapon while Tyger's rebellion advanced on the palace. As a result, Viper was forced to flee, and Tyger was crowned interim ruler. She established a free election process to allow the Madripoorian people to elect their new ruler, after which she resumed control of the criminal underworld.

AS REBEL

Art by Harvey Tolibao

HEIGHT: 5'10"   **EYES:** Brown
WEIGHT: 135 lbs.   **HAIR:** Black

ABILITIES/ACCESSORIES: Tyger Tiger is a highly formidable hand-to-hand combatant and has great skill with firearms and knives. She once briefly wore a suit of flexible yet seemingly indestructible armor that was loaned to her by Landau, Luckman & Lake. A talented financial executive, Tyger is also a skilled negotiator and cunning strategist, making her a fearsome business rival.

POWER GRID	1	2	3	4	5	6	7
INTELLIGENCE							
STRENGTH							
SPEED							
DURABILITY							
ENERGY PROJECTION							
FIGHTING SKILLS							

JESSAN HOAN

IN ARMOR

Art by John Buscema with Marc Silvestri (Jessan Hoan inset)

REAL NAME: James Howlett
ALIASES: Logan; formerly Death, Mai'keth, Mutate #9601, Weapon Ten, Peter Richards, Jim Logan, Patch, Canucklehead, Wildboy, Agent Ten, Weapon Chi, Weapon X, Experiment X, Emilio Garra, Canada, "Little Uncle," Amazing Immortal Man, Wild Man, many others
IDENTITY: Secret, known to certain government agencies
OCCUPATION: Adventurer; former instructor, spy, government operative, mercenary, bartender, bouncer, criminal, soldier, sailor, miner, many others
CITIZENSHIP: Canada, possible dual citizenship in Japan and/or Madripoor
PLACE OF BIRTH: Alberta, Canada
KNOWN RELATIVES: Itsu (wife, deceased), Viper (Madame Hydra, ex-wife), Daken, Erista (sons), unborn child by Native (presumed deceased), Amiko Kobayashi (foster daughter), John Howlett Sr. (presumed father, deceased), Elizabeth Hudson Howlett (mother, deceased), John Howlett Jr. (brother, deceased), Howlett (grandfather, surname unrevealed, deceased), Elias Hudson, Frederick Hudson (uncles, deceased), two unidentified aunts (presumed deceased), Frederick Hudson II (cousin, deceased), Truett Hudson (cousin once removed, deceased), Victor Hudson (cousin once removed), James Hudson (Guardian, cousin once removed, deceased), Heather Hudson (cousin once removed by marriage), Hudson (unidentified cousin twice removed, surname unrevealed), Shogun (soul fragment)
GROUP AFFILIATION: X-Force, Avengers, X-Men; formerly Horsemen of Apocalypse, Fantastic Four, Secret Defenders, Clan Yashida, Department H, the Flight, Department K, Team X, Weapon X, Devil's Brigade (World War II), Maximillian Ernesto Seville Circus, Mystique's Kansas City gang, Romulus' organization, Devil's Brigade (World War I), likely others
EDUCATION: Privately tutored as a child
FIRST APPEARANCE: Incredible Hulk #180 (1974); (Patch) Marvel Comics Presents #1 (1988); (Death) Astonishing X-Men #1 (1999)

HISTORY: The second son of wealthy John and Elizabeth Howlett in Alberta, Canada, James Howlett, a frail boy of poor health, was largely neglected by his mother Elizabeth, who had been institutionalized for a time following the death of her first son, John Jr., in 1897. James befriended a young girl named Rose and a youth known as Dog, son of groundskeeper Thomas Logan. Dog grew obsessed with Rose and assaulted her, prompting James' father to evict the Logans. Thomas and Dog returned to convince Elizabeth Howlett, with whom Thomas was having an affair, to accompany them, and Thomas shot and killed John. The shock of his father's murder triggered James' mutant abilities, with bone claws unexpectedly jutting from his hands, and unleashed a berserker fury during which he slew Thomas and slashed Dog's face. Completely unhinged, Elizabeth drove James away.

To avoid scandal, James' grandfather ordered James and Rose to flee by train. James' healing factor drove the trauma from his memories, leaving him partially amnesiac. The two found refuge at a stone quarry, where Rose, claiming James was her cousin, gave his name as "Logan." Within months, the rough environment provoked dramatic changes in Logan, who developed into a healthier, more violent youth displaying enhanced agility and strength, and possessing animal-like heightened senses that rivaled an animal's. After many months at the quarry, a teenage Logan was estranged from Rose when she became engaged to camp foreman Smitty. Logan worked off frustrations in cage fights, where his prowess earned him the nickname "the Wolverine." Logan later fought Smitty but allowed him to win, hoping to reconcile with Smitty and Rose, but Dog, dispatched by the elder Howlett to retrieve his grandson, arrived intending to slay Logan instead. During the ensuing fight, Logan accidentally impaled Rose on his claws, killing her. Stricken with grief and guilt for the death of his first love, Logan fled into the nearby woods and lived in a feral state for months, if not years. Romulus, immortal mastermind and ruler of the wolflike Lupine, had taken interest in the Hudson line, Logan's mother's family, and over coming decades he, whether directly or through proxies, altered or erased Logan's memories to suit him.

Apparently under Romulus' guidance, Logan next surfaced as a mercenary in Madripoor. At some point he met Chang, a businessman employed by mysterious firm Landau, Luckman and Lake. Logan also met and romanced Seraph, a diminutive but formidable woman already employed by Romulus, who had instructed Seraph to cultivate such a relationship; over the years, Logan realized Seraph and various others of his acquaintance answered to a single authority, but he neither knew nor cared who it was. During what may have been his first trip to Japan, Logan encountered members of the Hand ninja sect, who extorted him into fighting Sabretooth (Victor Creed), another Romulus operative who was, for whatever reason, murdering women in Tokyo. Logan defeated

AS WEAPON X
EXPERIMENT

ORIGINAL DEPT. H
COSTUME

Sabretooth and left him for dead, not realizing Sabretooth's healing factor was as strong as his own. At some point in subsequent years, Sabretooth sought Logan out and found him living a peaceful, loving life with a young Blackfoot Indian woman, Silver Fox. On Logan's birthday, Sabretooth, possibly under Romulus' orders, brutally attacked Silver Fox, raping her and leaving her for dead. Grief-stricken, Logan fought Sabretooth but was nearly killed; Sabretooth then manipulated the distraught Logan into believing the people of a nearby town had ordered Silver Fox's death, prompting Logan to murder the town's inhabitants. When World War I began in 1914, Logan joined the Devil's Brigade, a special Canadian military unit sometimes used by Romulus. Logan was trained by mutant Silas Burr, yet another Romulus operative, and per Burr's manipulation, fell in love with female operative Janet. Logan and other soldiers were soon sent to Europe, and in April 1915, he encountered Lazaer, alleged Angel of Death. Lazaer impaled Logan in combat, but Logan's will to live overcame even death, enabling him to remove Lazaer's sword and turn it against the angel; as a result, over the coming decades, whenever Logan was wounded severely enough to tax even his healing factor, he recovered by defeating Lazaer in an astral arena. When Logan was restationed in Canada, Burr, under orders from Romulus' proxy, murdered Janet as a lesson that whenever Logan overcame his inner bestial nature to care for someone, that person would die. Logan sought vengeance against Burr, who severely beat him and gouged out his left eye. Descending to a near-feral state as his healing factor again obscured traumatic memories, Logan fled Canada to travel abroad, as Romulus intended.

Logan surfaced in Shanghai, China, where he intervened in a conflict between locals and Ogun, a Japanese soldier, samurai and sorcerer. Impressed by Logan's courage, Ogun offered to train him in the martial arts, but Logan declined. By 1921, Logan was in Mexico, about to be executed as a horse thief. Before being shot, he met the mutant shape-shifter Mystique, a female adventurer similarly sentenced to death. Both escaped their captors, and Logan accompanied Mystique to Kansas, where she led a group of misfit criminals. Logan joined her group but tipped off the police about a planned bank robbery. Mystique evaded capture and, despite Logan's protests, her associates were killed by the police. Logan continued his own criminal activities for a few years, smuggling bootleg alcohol during Prohibition of the mid-1920s.

By 1932, Logan was back in Madripoor, where Seraph taught him to be a more effective assassin. During these years, if not before, Logan sometimes used the alias "Patch." Logan remembered Ogun's offer and sought him in Japan to better learn self-discipline. He spent years under Ogun's tutelage, eventually regarding him as a surrogate father. Circa the mid-1930s, Logan formed a partnership with Raven Darkhölme and Irene Adler, two mutant adventurers and lovers; perhaps due to memory alteration, Logan may have been unaware the apparently male Raven

was truly Mystique. Soon afterward, Logan saw action in Spain during its Civil War. In 1937, Logan, apparently under Romulus' orders, spent two years learning espionage from Taras Romanov; Logan in turn gave hand-to-hand combat lessons to Taras' ward Natasha Romanoff. When Taras instructed Natasha to kill Logan, Logan completed his assignment by slaying Taras but allowed Natasha to depart.

When World War II began in 1939, Logan returned to the Devil's Brigade, still under Burr's command, although Logan's memories of Burr's crimes were mostly purged. Seraph acted as Logan's handler in Madripoor and prepared him for more covert missions for Romulus. In the summer of 1941, Logan and Seraph worked with US Super-Soldier Captain America (Steve Rogers) and others to sabotage an alliance between the Hand and Baron Strucker, luring the Hand's Jonin (leader) out of hiding. Natasha Romanoff, now herself a Romulus operative, intended to kill the Jonin, but Logan, regretting his role in grooming her to be an assassin, killed the Jonin himself. Later that year, Logan, under orders to recruit or kill Captain America, worked with Cap and his partner Bucky (James Barnes) in Tunisia, where Logan first befriended Sgt. Nick Fury. Ultimately, Logan refused to kill Cap, possibly creating a rift between Seraph and himself.

By 1942, Logan was a prisoner in Sobibor Death Camp, his healing factor confounding the Nazis' every attempt to execute him. A year later, he surfaced in Newell, California, where he oversaw inhumane experimentation on Japanese POWs; although Logan had been a hardened killer for years, his activities during this period were atypically cruel, suggesting his personality had been altered by Romulus. In 1945, the Japanese captured Logan, but he escaped and romanced a woman named Atsuko the day before the atomic bombing of Hiroshima.

At the war's end, Logan sought redemption in Jasmine Falls, Japan, where he studied with Bando Suboro in hope of leaving his warrior nature behind. At peace for the first time since Silver Fox's supposed death, Logan married local woman Itsu and conceived a child with her. Tragically, in 1946, Bucky Barnes, now the brainwashed Winter Soldier, murdered Itsu while Logan was absent; although ostensibly serving the USSR after the war, Barnes acted under Romulus' orders in this instance. Believing their child dead as well, Logan erroneously blamed a local samurai, Muramasa, who captured and tortured Logan. When Muramasa's underlings prepared to dispose of Logan, Romulus, or his operative, killed them. Unknown to Logan, his son was safely born and adopted by a Japanese couple. Named Akahiro, he eventually took the name "Daken," meaning "Mongrel." Falling under Romulus' influence nine years later, Daken was told lies about being despised and abandoned by his father, filling him with hatred.

IN CIVILIAN CLOTHES

IN IMPERIAL GUARDSMAN
FANG'S UNIFORM

Logan next resurfaced as a mercenary, and whether he retained his memories of Itsu remains unclear. His friend Chang arranged for Landau, Luckman and Lake to handle Logan's business affairs and find assignments in exchange for Logan's occasional services. Operating mostly from Ottawa and Calgary, with occasional forays into South America and Madripoor, Logan frequently worked for government agencies, becoming one of the intelligence field's deadliest free agents. Logan still occasionally indulged in brutal missions per Romulus' command, as when he subjected young Frank Simpson to the trauma of his parents' deaths in 1953, inevitably regaining his true, more troubled persona afterward. While guarding scientist Michael Carling for LL&L, Logan fought Kimora, who sought Carling's expertise in establishing large-scale transportation between Earth and his home dimension, Kageumbra. Kimora defeated Logan and derided him as "a beast in a man's clothing," but Chang seemingly decapitated the despot. Logan retired from action and was next heard from back in Jasmine Falls, where he spent years seeking his lost tranquility until Chang sought his help in preventing Kimora from conquering Earth via Carling's technology. Logan and Chang traveled to Kageumbra, and Logan relied upon both meditative training and berserker rage in battle, allowing him to hurl Kimora into a dimension-traveling device, then destroy it. Back on Earth, Chang offered Logan a position with Landau, Luckman and Lake, but Logan declined.

Circa 1961, Logan, code-named Wolverine, joined the Weapon X Project, part of the Weapon Plus Program, formed to create super-agents to fight the supposed "mutant menace." At this stage, however, Weapon X merely employed mutants as superhuman operatives on international assignment. Logan's teammates included Sabretooth and Silver Fox, although to what extent, if any, the three remembered their past history at this point is unrevealed; other Team X members included Maverick (Christoph Nord, aka Wildcat), John Wraith, and Mastodon. During these years, Logan and his teammates received memory implants via several methods, including elaborately staged scenarios, telepathic manipulation by Weapon X ally Aldo Ferro (aka Vole), and technology provided by outside parties. Weapon X also duplicated Wolverine's healing factor and instilled a version of it in the rest of Team X, slowing their aging processes. In 1963, Silver Fox, for her own reasons, betrayed Wolverine and Sabretooth to enemy soldiers and fled Weapon X.

In early 1968, Wolverine was shot with Carbonadium bullets, which slowed his healing factor, apparently so Weapon X and/or Romulus could determine how to kill him if necessary. After the bullets' removal, Wolverine awoke earlier than expected and, his memories not yet altered, apparently regained his full memories for the first time in years. Trying to keep this secret, Logan rendezvoused with Team X at their next assignment in Berlin, East Germany. Team X retrieved experimental Carbonadium technology and double agent Janice Hollenbeck, but Sabretooth, apparently aware Wolverine had regained his memories,

killed Janice to reinforce Wolverine's conditioning about innocents dying when he overstepped Romulus' boundaries. Wolverine quit Team X but apparently fell back under Romulus' influence, for he again turned to atypically sadistic activities. In late 1968, while in Vietnam as a Russian advisor, he tortured and brainwashed Frank Simpson, now a soldier, into becoming a murderous madman later known as Nuke.

Circa 1972, Wolverine, evidently again his normal self, joined Department K, a secret Canadian Defense Ministry branch with ties to Weapon X. Again based in Ottawa, he partnered with fellow mutant Neil Langram and also frequently worked with Nick Fury, now a high-ranking CIA agent, as well as spies Richard and Mary Parker. Many years after Wolverine joined Department K, Langram was sought as an operative by the Hellfire Club, then slain by hired mercenary Sabretooth when he refused. Wolverine joined young US spy Carol Danvers to investigate and confronted Sabretooth at the Club's Canadian facility. From Sabretooth, Wolverine learned details of the Club's intent to guide a "war" between mutants and normal humans. Although Sabretooth bombed the facility, he, Wolverine and Danvers survived. Troubled by Sabretooth's revelations, Wolverine turned to drugs and alcohol. He was dismissed from Department K after accidentally shooting a fellow agent and, disgusted with himself, planned to lose himself in the Yukon.

Before leaving Canada, however, Wolverine was abducted by the Weapon X Project for experimentation, possibly under Romulus' orders. The near-indestructible metal Adamantium was bonded to Wolverine's skeleton and claws, and his personality buried beneath the most intense brainwashing he had ever undergone. Reduced to a near-mindless state, he was forced by Weapon X to slaughter every inhabitant of the small town Roanoke as a test. Wolverine eventually broke free of Weapon X's programming and fell into a berserker fury, slaying almost everyone at the facility before fleeing into the nearby woods. Wolverine's healing factor may have been nearly exhausted by his ordeal, since over the next few years he healed more slowly than ever before in his long life.

Inhabiting the woods for months, Wolverine eventually encountered young honeymooners James and Heather Hudson, whom he attacked, only to be shot by Hudson, whom neither knew was Wolverine's cousin from his maternal Hudson line. While recuperating, Wolverine regained enough of his human persona to be horrified at his claws, incorrectly believing them to be artificial implants. Recovering his mental faculties with the Hudsons' help, Wolverine joined Department H, the superhuman-oriented government agency James Hudson founded. Soon afterward, Wolverine consulted Adamantium expert Dr. Myron MacLain and, in the process, was targeted by both Sabretooth and, under Silver Fox's leadership, Hydra. Wolverine was aided against his assailants by former allies Nick Fury, Carol Danvers and Natasha Romanoff, now Russian super-spy Black Widow. Although Wolverine and his allies triumphed, his full

AS PATCH

MADRIPOOR COSTUME

X-MEN TRAINING COSTUME

memories remained unrestored, and he recognized neither former friends nor enemies. Under Department H's treatment, Wolverine eventually regained memories of Burr, Seraph, Cap and many other parts of his life, but Weapon X's lingering influences, as well as his healing factor's effects, left certain areas blank, including his life with Itsu and much of his Team X service. He underwent ongoing intense psychotherapy to help him control his berserker rages. As an H operative, he returned to espionage and served primarily in Siberia and the Western Pacific, notably Asia's Pacific Rim and its adjacent islands, including Japan. He accepted deadly, brutal assignments no other agent would touch, rising to the rank of Captain in the Canadian Armed Forces. Eventually Romulus or his proxies reestablished contact with Wolverine, who periodically received secret orders to facilitate Romulus' interests even while on Department H missions.

Following the Fantastic Four's debut, Hudson steered Department H's resources to form a government-sponsored super-team. He nominated Wolverine for leadership of this team, which, in early development, was called the Flight. Contemplating the wisdom of this move, Wolverine took temporary leave and returned to Madripoor to reunite with Seraph. He helped Seraph and her new student, the mercenary Viper (later Madame Hydra), against Sabretooth, possibly a case of infighting in Romulus' forces. Seraph sacrificed her life to save Wolverine, but before dying, she exacted a promise from him to help Viper in the future. Seraph's heroism seemingly influenced Wolverine to agree to Hudson's proposal; although agreeing to train the Flight and eventually become its leader, he also continued espionage missions abroad.

When D'Von Kray, a 40th century time-traveler hunting fellow time-traveler Cable, invaded Canada, Wolverine captured Kray and turned him over to Department H. Although Hudson hoped Kray's science could empower super-agents, Kray quickly escaped and resumed tracking Cable, pursued by Wolverine. Wolverine and Cable defeated Kray, and the newly arrived Cable eventually became a mercenary whom Wolverine encountered during select missions. Soon after Cray's defeat, Wolverine worked with CIA agent Rick Stoner to retrieve one of Hudson's prototype empowered-armor suits, stolen by Hydra. Meanwhile, Hudson subjected convicted murder William Nowlan to experimental procedures to manifest any latent superhuman powers. Wolverine, perhaps subconsciously remembering his Weapon X experimentation, warned Hudson his test subject, code-named Bedlam, might prove uncontrollable. His prediction proved accurate, and Wolverine assisted Hudson in placing the violently insane Bedlam in suspended animation. Some months after the Avengers' debut, Wolverine recruited Canadian Detective Sean Bernard for the Flight. As Groundhog, Bernard was assigned use of Hudson's Guardian armor. Weeks later, criminal genius Egghead led superhuman mercenaries to extort funds from Canada via threat of a nuclear warhead. Wolverine led Flight trainees against Egghead's forces, but although the mission succeeded, trainee Saint Elmo died, Groundhog resigned, and

other trainees proved unsuited for such missions. Hudson eventually divided the Flight into three divisions of increasing proficiency: Gamma Flight, Beta Flight, and Alpha Flight.

Later, Wolverine's espionage work took him to Vladivostok, Russia, where he worked with longtime ally Nick Fury prior to the latter's appointment to directorship of SHIELD. As Alpha Flight's preparation continued, Wolverine traveled to Japan to seek Ogun's advice but was shocked to learn Ogun had surrendered himself to dark magic and become an assassin, a role into which he intended to enslave Wolverine. Escaping this fate and deeply disturbed by the encounter, Wolverine vowed to never return to Japan.

As Wolverine prepared to publicly debut as a super hero, he was abducted by the mutated genius Leader (Samuel Sterns), as were the Olympian demigod Hercules (Heracles) and the Deviant Karkas, all of whom the Leader intended to use against the Hulk (Bruce Banner). Wolverine and his fellow prisoners escaped, but by coincidence, the Hulk himself arrived in Canada shortly before Wolverine's return. The Canadian military mobilized to oppose the Hulk, but Wolverine received instructions from Romulus to attract an unidentified party's attention by battling the Hulk. Wolverine fought both Hulk and a Wendigo (Paul Cartier), ultimately failing to defeat either. Still slated to take leadership of Alpha Flight, Wolverine spent some weeks completing his last few espionage missions, although various factors made him increasingly troubled by his Department H service.

When the sentient island Krakoa captured the American mutant X-Men, their founder, Professor X (Charles Xavier), sought other mutants to aid in their rescue. Wolverine's Hulk battle had attracted Xavier's attention as Romulus expected, so Xavier approached Logan and Wolverine resigned from Department H to join Xavier's new team of X-Men, helping rescue their predecessors from Krakoa. Wolverine tried to assassinate Xavier per Romulus' instructions, but Xavier broke Romulus' hold on Wolverine by blocking the effects of Romulus' programming, although neither man knew their enemy's identity at the

"SECRET WAR" COSTUME

IN FERAL STATE

AS DEATH

time. Following the Krakoa incident, most of the X-Men's early members resigned from active service, leaving Wolverine and his fellow recruits to continue their mission. Aside from Xavier, the only remaining founding member was team leader Cyclops (Scott Summers), with whom Logan regularly quarreled; however, Wolverine was immediately attracted to Scott's girlfriend, telekinetic telepath Jean Grey, who soon rejoined the group. Despite decades of hard-earned cynicism, Wolverine grew to admire the X-Men's determination and goals, and he and fellow recruit Nightcrawler (Kurt Wagner) became close friends.

After being captured by mutant terrorist Magneto (Max Eisenhardt), Wolverine and the X-Men escaped to the prehistoric Savage Land in Antarctica. From there they traveled to Japan, Wolverine's first visit since breaking with Ogun. Wolverine met young Mariko Yashida, cousin of former X-Man Sunfire (Shiro Yoshida). Initially frightened, Mariko was soon set at ease by Wolverine, who was attracted to her gentle demeanor, and the two eventually fell in love. The X-Men departed but were diverted to Canada, where James Hudson, now Vindicator, led Alpha Flight in trying to arrest their former would-be leader. Wolverine surrendered to spare the X-Men further conflict but quickly escaped. Soon afterward, Wolverine, accompanied by Nightcrawler, returned to Canada and made peace with Alpha Flight, helping them against a Wendigo (Georges Baptiste) in the process.

Later, Wolverine learned Mariko's father, crimelord Shingen Harada, had forced her to marry his criminal associate Noburo Hideki. Shingen manipulated Wolverine to drive a further wedge between him and Mariko, but when Wolverine was forced to slay Shingen in savage combat, Mariko, shamed by her father's actions, declared Wolverine her champion. The couple became engaged, but Mariko called off the wedding while controlled by illusionist Mastermind (Jason Wyngarde), who forced her to strengthen ties between Clan Yashida and the Japanese underworld. After escaping Mastermind's control, Mariko felt honor-bound to extract her family from criminal alliances and vowed to prove her own worth by doing so without Wolverine's help. Wolverine, respecting her wishes, agreed to postpone their marriage. Weeks later, when the X-Men were teleported to Japan, they assisted during an attack by a giant dragon. Unable to save a dying woman, Wolverine vowed to protect her daughter Amiko Kobayashi, who, initially left in Mariko's care, became

X-FORCE COSTUME

his foster daughter. Soon afterward, Ogun mentally controlled Wolverine's teammate Kitty Pryde, transforming her body and soul as he had originally intended to do to Wolverine. Wolverine helped Pryde overcome Ogun's control, then killed Ogun, although his spirit survived.

Eventually, Wolverine began spending more time away from the X-Men, returning to Madripoor for perhaps the first time since Seraph's death. In memory of Seraph, Wolverine re-established his reputation as "Patch," keeping peace between Madripoor's criminal factions. Increasingly troubled by his fragmented memories, Wolverine investigated the abandoned Weapon X facility where he had been transformed years before, inadvertently activating the artificial intelligence Shiva, programmed to kill rogue Team X members. Later, Wolverine returned to Japan, where Clan Yashida was besieged by both internal dispute and attacking Hand ninjas. Silver Fox, still with Hydra, observed the proceedings and cooperated with Hand leader Matsuo Tsurayaba to poison Mariko. Faced with a slow, painful demise, Mariko asked Wolverine to grant her a quicker, merciful death, which he reluctantly did. After Team X alumnus Mastodon died from reversal of his age suppression factor, Wolverine investigated alongside other Team X survivors, including Sabretooth and, to Wolverine's shock, Silver Fox. Tracing Mastodon's death to Aldo Ferro, now called Psi-Borg, the Team X members were overwhelmed by his illusions, and Sabretooth, under Psi-Borg's control, killed Silver Fox.

Soon after these tragedies, Wolverine and the X-Men attacked Magneto, who forcefully removed the Adamantium from Wolverine's body, initially overloading his healing factor. Ultimately recovering, Wolverine rediscovered his forgotten bone claws. The Adamantium's loss jump-started both Wolverine's healing factor, restoring it to wartime levels, and his berserker nature. Time-traveler Genesis (Tyler Dayspring), hoping to transform Wolverine into a Horseman of Apocalypse (En Sabah Nur), abducted Wolverine, attempting but failing to re-bond him to Adamantium. Wolverine instead reverted to a more animalistic state but eventually reclaimed his humanity with help from ninja Elektra Natchios. Months later, Viper invoked Wolverine's promise to Seraph years before, and Wolverine married Viper, giving her the necessary status to become ruler of Madripoor. Soon afterward, Apocalypse captured Wolverine and succeeded where Genesis had failed, re-bonding Adamantium to Wolverine's skeleton and transforming the mutant into the Horseman Death. Meanwhile, one of a Skrull faction allied with Apocalypse impersonated Wolverine in the X-Men and was, ironically, slain by Wolverine/Death himself, who soon broke Apocalypse's conditioning and returned to the X-Men.

At Viper's request, Wolverine returned to Madripoor to battle against Ogun, active as a possessing spirit, and Viper agreed to divorce Wolverine, freeing him from her debt. Malcolm Colcord, a rare survivor of Wolverine's Weapon X rampage years before, felt the X-Man owed him a debt as well, and Colcord revived Weapon X and Wolverine's

ties to it, remote-controlling him as an assassin. Escaping Colcord's control, Wolverine, with Cyclops and fellow Weapon Plus experimentee Fantomex, penetrated the so-called World, Weapon Plus' mysterious base. To his horror, Wolverine learned how he had been used in the Roanoke slaughter years before, along with other Weapon Plus secrets.

Wolverine was later controlled by the Hand, but one of their mystics, Phaedra, retained a fragment of Wolverine's soul, which became the warrior Shogun. Escaping, Wolverine helped SHIELD defeat both the Hand and their allies in Hydra. Following the House of M crisis, during which Scarlet Witch altered Earth's reality and then restored it, Wolverine regained all of his memories. US government officials, possibly under Romulus' command, sent both a Shiva robot and Nuke to kill Wolverine, but he survived. X-Men telepath Emma Frost learned Wolverine's son by Itsu, Daken, had survived and been manipulated into hating Wolverine, and Wolverine swore to locate him.

Working with Atlanteans in the wake of the Stamford, Connecticut disaster, Wolverine fell in love with Atlantean woman Amir, but when Scimitar terrorists killed her and attacked Wolverine, Lazaer defeated him on the astral plane, leaving him brain-dead. Recovering with help from Sorcerer Supreme Dr. Stephen Strange, Wolverine confronted Scimitar

members Phaedra and Shogun, who resurrected Shingen Harada to fight him. Defeating Shingen, Wolverine apparently slew Shogun and Phaedra, and Lazaer, resenting the pair's machinations, returned the stolen soul fragment but warned Wolverine he could never again escape death by defeating him in astral combat. Soon afterward, Wolverine became leader of X-Force, a special covert unit of the X-Men.

Eventually, Romulus made himself known by sending his ancient memories into Wolverine's psyche and inserting himself into Wolverine's pre-existing memories. Now aware of the true manipulator of himself, his son, and countless others, Wolverine arranged for Daken to be shot with Carbonadium bullets, slowing his healing factor so Wolverine could capture him in hope of removing Romulus' influence. Sebastian Shaw abducted Daken, however, intending to brainwash him into servitude, setting Wolverine against Shaw's Hellfire Club rivals in the process. Blocked by a psychic booby trap in Daken's mind, Shaw manipulated Prof. X into triggering the trap and absorbing most of the damage, restoring Daken's memories. Wolverine and Daken then defeated Shaw and resolved to seek vengeance on Romulus together, but the two again parted ways when Daken joined Norman Osborn's Avengers.

HEIGHT: 5'3" EYES: Blue
WEIGHT: 300 lbs.; (without Adamantium) 195 lbs. HAIR: Black

ABILITIES/ACCESSORIES: Wolverine can regenerate damaged or destroyed areas of his cellular structure far more rapidly than ordinary humans. The speed of this healing factor varies in direct proportion with an injury's severity. He is virtually immune to poisons, most drugs, and most diseases; it is nearly impossible for him to become intoxicated by alcohol. He is partially immune to fatigue poisons generated by physical exertion and thus has greater endurance than ordinary humans. His agility and reflexes are similarly enhanced. Wolverine's healing factor slows the effects of aging; although over a century old, he is as healthy and fit as a man in his prime.

Wolverine possesses superhumanly acute senses, enabling him to see and hear things at distances far greater than those of ordinary humans. His sense of smell is even more magnified, enabling him to recognize people and objects by scent alone; as a result, Wolverine is one of the world's foremost trackers. His skeleton includes six retractable, slightly curved, foot-long bone claws, three in each arm, beneath his forearms' skin and muscle. He can, at will, release these claws through his skin beneath his knuckles. The claws are naturally sharp and tougher than normal human bone, allowing them to, even unaugmented, penetrate most types of flesh and natural materials. Wolverine's entire skeletal structure, including his claws, is bonded to the nearly indestructible metal Adamantium, rendering his bones virtually unbreakable and his claws capable of penetrating almost any substance, depending on

its thickness and the amount of force he can exert. His healing factor prevents the Adamantium from interfering with normal bone generation of blood corpuscles, and his reinforced skeleton enables him to withstand high levels of physical pressure, giving his muscles sufficient force to briefly lift over 800 pounds.

Wolverine is an exceptional hand-to-hand combatant, having mastered virtually every fighting style on Earth, as well as a trained expert in multiple weapons, vehicles, computer systems, explosives and assassination techniques. He is fluent in many languages, including Japanese, Russian, Chinese, Cheyenne, Lakota and Spanish, with some knowledge of French, Thai and Vietnamese. Throughout his life, Wolverine has used various bladed weapons, most frequently daggers and, at times, swords. He has also wielded many different types of firearms as a soldier, mercenary and spy.

POWER GRID	1	2	3	4	5	6	7
INTELLIGENCE							
STRENGTH							
SPEED							
DURABILITY							
ENERGY PROJECTION							
FIGHTING SKILLS							

HISTORY: The mutant most commonly known as "John Wraith" was a CIA agent by the 1960s, when he joined the Weapon X Project's field unit, Team X, alongside Mastodon, Maverick (Christoph Nord), Sabretooth, Silver Fox and Wolverine (Logan/James Howlett). Like his teammates, Wraith received false memory implants from telepath Aldo Ferro (aka Vole), the better to manipulate them when necessary. Team X conducted missions in Southeast Asia, Cuba, Canada and elsewhere, and Wraith's willingness to avoid harming innocents when possible earned him the bloodthirsty Sabretooth's dislike. Wraith kept some of his capabilities secret even from his teammates, and when Team X stole Russia's Carbonadium Synthesizer, which Soviet super-agent Omega Red needed to stabilize his powers, Wraith delayed Omega Red's pursuit, then teleported away, a feat only Wolverine witnessed. Following Team X's disbandment Wraith dropped out of sight. At some point, whether with assistance or not, he learned to distinguish implanted memories from true ones. He resurfaced to serve with another clandestine government agency, Mutant Special Forces, where some fellow agents, such as the regenerative Poppa, considered him a near-legendary figure. At times he clashed with Omega Red, seeking the Carbonadium Synthesizer. Eventually Wraith, in supposed retirement, took up residence in South Central Los Angeles, California, where he lived next door to Mr. and Mrs. Higgenbotham and their son Ornette.

In recent years, Wraith was apparently sought out by Mastodon, who was rapidly aging because his age suppression factor had been deactivated by Aldo Ferro, now Psi-Borg. Concerned he and other Team X members might suffer a similar fate, Wraith tracked down Sabretooth, helping him defeat a Weapon X Shiva robot, and used espionage contacts to summon Wolverine and Silver Fox, who were present when Mastodon withered and perished. With Ornette's help in searching databases, they located Psi-Borg's island fortress, where they recruited Maverick, now Psi-Borg's bodyguard, to help them. Team X ultimately failed to defeat Psi-Borg, Silver Fox dying in battle; they learned, however, that Psi-Borg had deliberately induced Mastodon's breakdown and thus their own age suppression factors were unlikely to fail. Wraith used his influence to find Silver Fox's former home in order for Wolverine to bury her there. Weeks later, learning Omega Red, still seeking the Carbonadium Synthesizer, was pursuing Maverick, Wraith kept Maverick under surveillance. Maverick, then infected with the Legacy virus, fled Omega Red with Russian telepath Elena Ivanova's help, and Wraith joined the pair to lead their enemy to an abandoned Weapon X facility. With Omega Red trapped within, the Canadian military, whom

REAL NAME: Unrevealed
ALIASES: Carlisle, Expediter, Halcon, Kestrel, Wraith-Man, others
IDENTITY: Secret
OCCUPATION: Government operative
CITIZENSHIP: Unrevealed
PLACE OF BIRTH: Unrevealed
KNOWN RELATIVES: Unidentified sister
GROUP AFFILIATION: Weapon X (USA); formerly Mutant Special Forces, Team X, Weapon X Project (multinational), CIA
EDUCATION: Unrevealed
FIRST APPEARANCE: (Illusion) Wolverine #48 (1991); (full) Wolverine #60 (1992)

Wraith had manipulated into following him, strafed the facility. Leaving Elena to care for the weary Maverick, Wraith returned to his solitary life.

Years later, Wraith was approached by a new Weapon X, organized by mutant-hating Malcolm Colcord, aka Director. Feigning a dedication to government work but actually in fear for his life, Wraith joined, as did Sabretooth. Both Team X alumni arranged to meet a third, Maverick, at a hotel, where Sabretooth intended to kill Maverick if he refused Wraith's recruitment. Maverick used Wraith as a human shield, blasting through him to strike down Sabretooth. Leaving Wraith to bleed, Maverick fought Sabretooth on the hotel's roof, then escaped. Following Maverick's escape, Sabretooth apparently strangled Wraith to death, then reported to Weapon X that Maverick had killed Wraith.

HEIGHT: 6'
WEIGHT: 195 lbs.
EYES: Brown
HAIR: Black, later shaved

ABILITIES/ACCESSORIES: John Wraith could teleport by establishing an energy field between his present location and a remote location, then shifting through space from one point to another. He aged very slowly as a result of treatments undergone in Team X. He customarily carried two .45 automatic Colt pistols loaded with copper-jacketed bullets containing depleted uranium cores; he frequently used shaped charges, explosives designed to focus an explosion's energy into a specific region. His government clearance and contacts gave him access to an array of military equipment.

POWER GRID	1	2	3	4	5	6	7
INTELLIGENCE							
STRENGTH							
SPEED *							
DURABILITY							
ENERGY PROJECTION							
FIGHTING SKILLS							

*JOHN WRAITH IS A TELEPORTER

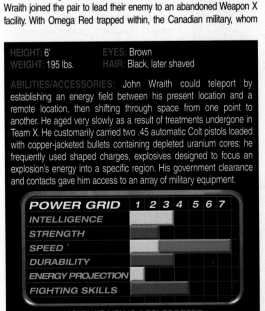

CURRENT MEMBERS: Archangel/Angel (Warren Worthington III), Domino (Neena Thurman), Elixir (Josh Foley), Vanisher (Telford Porter), Warpath (James Proudstar), Wolfsbane (Rahne Sinclair), Wolverine (Logan/James Howlett), X-23 (Laura Kinney)
FORMER MEMBERS: Caliban, Hepzibah
BASE OF OPERATIONS: The Aerie, Colorado
FIRST APPEARANCE: Uncanny X-Men #493 (2008)

ARCHANGEL

DOMINO

ELIXIR

HEPZIBAH

CALIBAN

VANISHER

HISTORY: After "M-Day," when most of the world's mutants were depowered, X-Men leader Cyclops (Scott Summers) sought ways to protect his species at any cost. When a new mutant baby was born in Cooperstown, Alaska, the mutant-hating Purifiers killed the town's children in an attempt to eliminate the mutant, and the baby was kidnapped (by former X-Man cyborg Cable, unknown to all others at the time). Cyclops assembled X-Force, a group of trackers and fighters, led by Wolverine, to find the kidnapper and rescue the baby by any means necessary. Wolverine led Caliban, Hepzibah, Warpath, Wolfsbane and X-23 to Alaska, and they soon determined Cable had the child. After tracking Cable across the Canadian wilderness, X-Force protected him from the cyborg Reavers, led by Lady Deathstrike, who had been hired by the Purifiers to kill the child, but Caliban was killed during the subsequent battle, causing Warpath to blame the Purifiers for his death. X-Force continued working to protect the child, who was targeted for assassination by another former ally, Lucas Bishop, in order to change the future. They tracked Bishop first to Texas, then to Muir Island, from where Cable took the child into the future for protection.

Soon after, Cyclops secretly reinstated X-Force with Wolverine, Warpath and X-23 as members, and sent them to hunt down and kill the Purifiers before they could strike again, concealing this from the X-Men proper as the team disapproved of killing. As X-Force attacked Purifier bases across the US, killing all those they found, Wolfsbane, whom Wolverine resisted joining X-Force, undertook her own investigation and discovered her bigoted father, Reverend Craig, was working with the Purifiers; Craig captured and brainwashed her, then left her behind for X-Force to find. X-Force, now based at Angel's Aerie in Colorado, helped Wolfsbane recover, but she attacked Angel savagely, fulfilling her brainwashing by tearing off his wings and delivering them to the Purifiers; however, Angel's metallic wings, genetically implanted by Apocalypse (En Sabah Nur) years before, regrew, and Worthington attacked the Purifiers' headquarters as Archanel, finding Purifier leader Matthew Risman in a leadership struggle with recently revived X-Man foe Bastion. Risman led the Choir, Purifiers who had wings created from the DNA of Archangel's wings attached to their bodies, but Archangel viciously assaulted the Choir while the rest of X-Force attacked. Risman was killed, while the vampiric Purifier Eli Bard fled promising future revenge. Wolfsbane, meanwhile, saw Craig standing in front of a pair of wings and her programming kicked in, causing her to attack and consume him, though she later had no memory of this. Bastion escaped along with revived versions of many of mutantkind's greatest foes, including Cameron Hodge, the Leper Queen, Donald Pierce, Stephen Lang, Graydon Creed, William Stryker and Bolivar Trask.

WARPATH, X-23, WOLVERINE, WOLFSBANE

-Crain-

The team has since faced multiple threats, including the Skrull invasion in California; the Demon Bear, which had stolen and resurrected the corpses of Caliban and Warpath's deceased tribe in a plot created by Eli Bard to gain the affection of his former lover, the ages-old Selene; and a group of deadly clones of the Marauders and Hodge's Right soldiers to stop the spread of the deadly mutant-killing Legacy virus. After the Vanisher (Telford Porter) was recruited against his will, Wolfsbane went AWOL alongside the Asgardian wolf-boy Hrimhari, her former romantic interest. The team then battled the Leper Queen, and subsequently traveled to the future of Reality-80521 to save the mutant baby, now a young girl named Hope, from the threats of Bishop, Stryfe (Cable's clone), and Apocalypse.

REAL NAME: Aria
ALIASES: None
IDENTITY: No dual identity
OCCUPATION: Former prisoner
CITIZENSHIP: Zenna

PLACE OF BIRTH: Zenna
KNOWN RELATIVES: None
GROUP AFFILIATION: None
EDUCATION: Unrevealed
FIRST APPEARANCE: Wolverine #133 (1999)

HISTORY: An inmate on a Prison World run by the Elder of the Universe known as the Collector (Tanaleer Tivan), Aria sought a means to free her fellow prisoners. Hearing of the legendary X-Men, she escaped imprisonment by faking her death then possessing the guard who came to check on her. Stealing a ship, Aria headed for Earth where she possessed the X-Man Wolverine (Logan/James Howlett). To ensure her mission's success, she tested his abilities against Warbird (Carol Danvers), Vision (Victor Shade), Firestar, Justice (Vance Astrovik), Moon Knight (Marc Spector), USAgent, Falcon (Sam Wilson), Black Widow (Natasha Romanoff), Solo (James Bourne), Cardiac, Black Cat (Felicia Hardy), Human Torch (Johnny Storm), and others by making Wolverine appear as a threat. Satisfied with his performance, Aria then convinced him to help her. Arriving on Prison World in her stolen ship, Aria possessed another guard to help Wolverine free the inmates, but they faced staunch opposition and Aria was recaptured. Forced back into her own body, she was fitted with an inhibitor to suppress her power. Freed by Wolverine, she had him shut down Prison World's security systems, unaware that this made the planet visible to the world devourer Galactus. Learning that the Collector had created the planet to protect its inhabitants from Galactus, Aria sought to make amends by possessing the world devourer; however, Galactus quickly shook off her possession and discorporated her spirit. Her physical form then sustained mortal wounds during Galactus' consumption of Prison World.

| **HEIGHT:** 5'9" | **WEIGHT:** 132 lbs. | **EYES:** White (no visible iris) | **HAIR:** Purple |

ABILITIES/ACCESSORIES: Like all members of the Zennan race, Aria could detach her spirit from her corporeal form and possess others, controlling their actions, communicating with them telepathically, and having access to their thoughts.

INTELLIGENCE: 2 STRENGTH: 2 SPEED: 2 DURABILITY: 2
ENERGY PROJECTION: 3 FIGHTING SKILLS: 3

Art by Jeff Matsuda

REAL NAME: Unrevealed
ALIASES: Mr. Big
IDENTITY: Secret
OCCUPATION: Terrorist, scientist, warrior
CITIZENSHIP: Unrevealed

PLACE OF BIRTH: Unrevealed
KNOWN RELATIVES: Known
GROUP AFFILIATION: Hydra
EDUCATION: Unrevealed
FIRST APPEARANCE: Wolverine: Inner Fury (1992)

HISTORY: Hydra agent Big worked with the cyborg Whale to develop a nanotechnology weapon for Baron Strucker under agent Daniel Braniff's supervision. After the Whale went rogue and escaped with his nanotech, Big investigated and slew agent George Leon to prevent his informing Strucker. Seeking to regain the nanotech and punish the Whale, Big obtained a prototype of the nanotech virus from the Whale's reject pile, then lured Wolverine (Logan/James Howlett) into battle with cyborgs who infected him with the virus. Big then posed as a mercenary hired to fight Hydra, revealed Wolverine's infection and joined him in tracking down the Whale to find a cure. Wolverine progressively weakened as his healing factor exhausted itself against the virus, which was extruding his skeleton's Adamantium content. Confronting the Whale, Wolverine recognized Big's scent on his equipment. As Big attacked Wolverine, the weakened mutant stabbed his own brain (the Adamantium having departed his skull sufficiently to allow this), which essentially rebooted his nervous system and healing factor, allowing it to eliminate the virus and restore his status quo. Assuming Wolverine had killed himself, Big decided to dispose of his body so that the X-Men would not link him to the death and seek vengeance. As Big's chainsaw scraped against Wolverine's re-Adamantiumized shoulder, it broke apart, and the kickback hurled him against a hanging hook which pierced his chest, apparently killing him.

| **HEIGHT:** 3'6" | **WEIGHT:** 98 lbs. | **EYES:** White (no visible pupil) | **HAIR:** Dark brown |

ABILITIES/ACCESSORIES: A fierce fighter skilled with various weapons, Big was fast enough to avoid simultaneous attacks from multiple sources. Crafty and manipulative, he was smart enough to understand the Whale's nanotechnology designs. He flew via personal rocket craft, which had a powerful light and a pair of servo arms. Often wielding various firearms and a large chainsaw, Big wore a monocle, either due to unilateral vision deficit or for appearance. He enjoyed describing everything in terms of size.

INTELLIGENCE: 4 STRENGTH: 3 SPEED: 2/3* DURABILITY: 2
ENERGY PROJECTION: 1 FIGHTING SKILLS: 4
* IN ROCKET CRAFT

Art by Bill Sienkiewicz

BRASS

REAL NAME: Sean Watanabe
ALIASES: None
IDENTITY: Publicly known
OCCUPATION: Vigilante; former Navy SEAL
CITIZENSHIP: USA
PLACE OF BIRTH: New York City, New York

KNOWN RELATIVES: Emmaline Brigitte Watanabe (sister), Yuji Watanabe (father)
GROUP AFFILIATION: Formerly US Navy
EDUCATION: Extensive military and martial arts training
FIRST APPEARANCE: Marvel Comics Presents #65 (1990)

HISTORY: Trained by his father in martial arts since he could walk, Sean discovered during competitions that he could telepathically predict his opponent's next move. He joined the Navy SEALs and gained the nickname Brass for taking on jobs nobody else wanted. During this time, he met the love of his life, Theresa, but while out on a date she saw the Mandarin attacking the Avengers, panicked and was run over by a car. Learning that the Mandarin's attack was part of the "Acts of Vengeance" conspiracy, Sean vowed to kill everyone involved, starting by attacking Mandarin's Chinatown operations. Hoping to win the Mandarin's favor, Deathwatch's brother-in-law, Langley, plotted to kill Brass and Wolverine (Logan/James Howlett). He sent Deathwatch's ninjas to kidnap Brass' sister Emmaline, but Ghost Rider (Dan Ketch/Noble Kale) and Wolverine rescued her. Langley had Emmaline kidnapped again along with Ketch's friend Jack D'Auria. Brass, his father, Ghost Rider and Wolverine battled ninjas and Deathwatch's agents, the Triad Brothers, to get to Langley. Discovering the unwanted attention Langley's unauthorized actions had drawn, Deathwatch killed Langley, and the heroes and kidnapped friends barely escaped. Brass added Deathwatch to his revenge list and continued his crusade. Scarlet Witch's "M-Day" reality warp depowered Brass, and his energy signature became part of the Collective. Despite Being depowered, Tony Stark considered him a potential Initiative recruit due to his fighting skills and military background.

HEIGHT: 5'6"	WEIGHT: 194 lbs.	EYES: Brown	HAIR: Black

ABILITIES/ACCESSORIES: Brass is a martial arts expert and trained Navy SEAL, in peak physical and mental condition. An exceptional team player and an expert in explosives, SCUBA diving and land-warfare, he is specially trained for tactical ambushes, sniper assaults, close-quarters combat, underwater demolition, combat-swimming attacks, close air support, naval gunfire support, raids and hydrographic reconnaissance. Before M-Day, he was a low-level telepath, automatically reading others' thoughts to anticipate their next move.

INTELLIGENCE: 3 STRENGTH: 2 SPEED: 2 DURABILITY: 2
ENERGY PROJECTION: 1 FIGHTING SKILLS: 6

Art by Mark Texeira

BRECKER

REAL NAME: Edward Brecker
ALIASES: None
IDENTITY: No dual identity
OCCUPATION: Terrorist and bio-weapons manufacturer; former SHIELD research scientist
CITIZENSHIP: USA

PLACE OF BIRTH: Unrevealed
KNOWN RELATIVES: Unidentified mother (deceased)
GROUP AFFILIATION: Rogue SHIELD faction; formerly SHIELD
EDUCATION: At least one unspecified doctorate, probably more
FIRST APPEARANCE: Spider-Man/Wolverine #4 (2003)

HISTORY: Roughly 50 years ago, young Edward Brecker watched horror-stricken as his mother was slain by debris created by dragon-like creatures battling Thor (Odinson) above Manhattan. Nursing an intense hatred of superhumans, Brecker, as an adult scientist, joined SHIELD and developed Project: Stuff of Legends, using superhuman DNA — taken, despite SHIELD Director Nick Fury's opposition, from Wolverine (Logan/James Howlett), Spider-Man (Peter Parker), and presumably others — to design biological weapons to use against superhumans if necessary. Although Stuff of Legends received strong government support, Brecker, unwilling to wait for an excuse to implement his work, went rogue, as did several like-minded SHIELD agents. Funded by corrupt Japanese businessman Takeshi Kishimoto, a longtime enemy of Wolverine, Brecker created a serum imitating Wolverine's healing factor, intending to sell it, along with his bio-weapons, on the international black market. Kishimoto abducted and tortured Wolverine on a private island, using Brecker's work to disable Wolverine's healing factor; he also filmed Wolverine's torture via satellite as an advertisement of Brecker's work. Unable to intervene directly due to international law, Nick Fury recruited Spider-Man to rescue Wolverine, who then killed Kishimoto. Wolverine and Spider-Man traced Kishimoto's satellite transmission to France, but Brecker's accomplices destroyed any evidence. After learning Brecker's plans from Fury, Wolverine and Spider-Man penetrated Brecker's Switzerland base; although Brecker had custom-designed toxins to kill both men, the two changed costumes, enabling Spider-Man to survive attacks intended for Wolverine and vice versa. Brecker was knocked unconscious and taken into custody; although Brecker's base was destroyed, his government connections may have prevented his imprisonment.

HEIGHT: 5'8"	WEIGHT: 170 lbs.	EYES: Green	HAIR: White (originally red)

ABILITIES/ACCESSORIES: Edward Brecker is a brilliant geneticist who used superhuman DNA to develop biological weapons, an artificial healing factor, and probably other discoveries.

INTELLIGENCE: 5 STRENGTH: 2 SPEED: 2 DURABILITY: 2
ENERGY PROJECTION: 1 FIGHTING SKILLS: 2

Art by Vatche Mavlian

CHARLEMAGNE

REAL NAME: Unrevealed
ALIASES: Charlie, others
IDENTITY: Secret
OCCUPATION: Mercenary
CITIZENSHIP: Unrevealed

PLACE OF BIRTH: Unrevealed
KNOWN RELATIVES: None
GROUP AFFILIATION: None
EDUCATION: Unrevealed
FIRST APPEARANCE: Spider-Man vs. Wolverine #1 (1987)

HISTORY: A mercenary since her youth, Charlemagne romanced the mutant Logan many years ago, when both were, by her description, "young." In recent years, Charlemagne acquired sensitive information during an undisclosed assignment from covert European factions, causing her employers to target her for death. Logan, now Department H operative Wolverine, came to her rescue, and the pair killed many enemy agents, including several who abandoned years-old undercover identities to pursue Charlemagne. Wolverine joined the X-Men shortly thereafter and lost touch with Charlemagne, who became a legend in espionage circles, some doubting her very existence. Years later, she resurfaced to kill former clients and co-workers whom she felt had betrayed her years before, earning renewed enmity from many espionage agencies. Wolverine arranged to meet Charlemagne in Berlin, Germany, where Spider-Man, as photographer Peter Parker, was investigating Charlemagne's spree; Wolverine unsuccessfully tried to persuade him to leave Europe. Later, Charlemagne, having slain her targets, renewed her romance with Wolverine. Rather than let her enemies kill her slowly and painfully, she wanted Wolverine to provide a quick death, but Spider-Man intervened. As enemy operatives closed in, Charlemagne approached Spider-Man from behind, tricking him into striking her thinking that she was Wolverine. Although Wolverine would have survived Spider-Man's super-strength, Charlemagne did not. She died in Wolverine's arms, causing the operatives' withdrawal. Spider-Man was haunted by his inadvertent role in Charlemagne's death, while Wolverine mourned his longtime friend and lover's death.

HEIGHT: 5'7"   **WEIGHT:** 132 lbs.   **EYES:** Green   **HAIR:** Auburn-red

ABILITIES/ACCESSORIES: Charlemagne was an exceptional spy, assassin, and both armed and unarmed combatant. Her tracking skills rivaled Wolverine's, and she could evade even him due to her intimate knowledge of his abilities. Customarily carrying a 9mm handgun of European design, she was experienced in using firearms, knives, and other weapons. Depending on how long she and Wolverine had known each other, she may have had a slowed aging factor.

INTELLIGENCE: 3 STRENGTH: 2 SPEED: 2 DURABILITY: 2
ENERGY PROJECTION: 1 FIGHTING SKILLS: 6

Art by Paco Diaz Luque

AVERY CONNOR

REAL NAME: Avery Connor
ALIASES: Various cover identities (unrevealed)
IDENTITY: Secret (uses cover identities)
OCCUPATION: Presumably student
CITIZENSHIP: Canada
PLACE OF BIRTH: Tignish, Prince Edward Island, Canada

KNOWN RELATIVES: Daniel Connor (father, deceased), Veronica Connor (mother)
GROUP AFFILIATION: None
EDUCATION: High school student
FIRST APPEARANCE: Elektra & Wolverine: The Redeemer #1 (2002)

HISTORY: Daniel and Veronica Connor extracted DNA from Logan (James Howlett; later Wolverine) while he was having his Adamantium implanted. Working under the direction of Kiefer and his shadowy organization, the Connors implanted the DNA within a child, Avery, grown in Veronica's womb, such that Avery's powers would be triggered at a certain age. Kiefer regularly visited and monitored Avery as she grew, acting as if her third parent and ignoring her dislike for him. When Avery was 14, her parents, having grown to love her, feigned separation, and Daniel brought Avery to Manhattan while they planned to flee Kiefer's detection and start life anew. Realizing this, Kiefer hired Elektra to assassinate Daniel, which Avery witnessed, but also manipulated Wolverine into recovering Avery, allegedly to save her from Elektra. Elektra fought off Wolverine and fled with Avery, with whom she swiftly bonded as Avery's abilities surfaced. Avery took naturally to Elektra' combat training, but Kiefer, having secretly implanted a chemical signature in Avery during the initial experiments, led his agents and Wolverine to them. After some struggle, Wolverine realized Kiefer's manipulation and joined Elektra in protecting Avery. Kiefer took Veronica hostage to force Avery's compliance, but Wolverine rescued Veronica, and Elektra slew Kiefer. Wolverine and Elektra then arranged and Elektra bankrolled — using the money she earned for killing Daniel Connor — a lifetime of new identities and hidden locations from which Veronica and Avery could continue their lives in peace.

HEIGHT: 5'2"   **WEIGHT:** 101 lbs.   **EYES:** Blue   **HAIR:** Black

ABILITIES/ACCESSORIES: Avery has enhanced human strength, speed, agility, reflexes, durability and healing (recovering from a bullet to the chest in minutes). She was designed so that at maturity her abilities would exceed Wolverine's. Avery exudes a certain chemical marker which can be tracked across great distances by specially designed equipment. She takes a drug to inhibit excretion of this chemical. Avery has a natural affinity for hand-to-hand combat.

INTELLIGENCE: 2 STRENGTH: 4 SPEED: 3
DURABILITY: 4 ENERGY PROJECTION: 1 FIGHTING SKILLS: 4

Art by Yoshitaka Amano

DOGMA

REAL NAME: Unrevealed
ALIASES: The Bishop of Assassins, the Enlightened Soul
IDENTITY: Secret
OCCUPATION: Shadow Pulpit operative
CITIZENSHIP: Vatican City (presumably)

PLACE OF BIRTH: Unrevealed
KNOWN RELATIVES: None
GROUP AFFILIATION: The Shadow Pulpit
EDUCATION: Unrevealed
FIRST APPEARANCE: Wolverine #177 (2002)

HISTORY: Apparently an energy-bodied superhuman operative of the Roman Catholic Church — others include the invocation-empowered Stigmata and a mysterious Black Knight who once attacked Wakanda — Dogma is more specifically employed by the Shadow Pulpit, a brutal power-seeking faction within the Vatican. Cardinal Panzer, the Pulpit's "Shadow Pope," planted a device emitting Extra Low-frequency Vibration Emanations (ELVEs) on the Brooklyn Bridge, seeking to brainwash Manhattan to support him in replacing the true pope. Panzer's ex-protégé, monster-hunter Father Thomas Braun, learned his plans and sought help from mutant adventurer Wolverine (Logan/James Howlett), whom Braun had previously encountered in battle with a monster mutated by the alien Plodex. Dogma attacked the pair while Panzer's ninja-like soldiers observed from rooftops. Dogma soon wounded Wolverine, but Braun distracted Dogma, and Wolverine rallied his strength to drive him off. Tracking the ELVEs to their source, Wolverine again fought Dogma while Braun destroyed the device. Abducted to Vatican City, Braun was tortured by Panzer's associate Sister Inquisitor, while Wolverine penetrated Panzer's headquarters to battle Dogma a third time, literally tearing Dogma's suit in half and leaving him to dissipate. Too late to prevent Braun's murder, Wolverine departed with Braun's body when Panzer's superior, Cardinal Parente, intervened. Although skeptical, Wolverine failed to realize Parente was also a Shadow Pulpit member.

Art by Dan Fraga

HEIGHT: Variable	**EYES:** None
WEIGHT: Unrevealed, possibly negligible	**HAIR:** None

ABILITIES/ACCESSORIES: Apparently sentient vapor-like energy, Dogma maintains humanoid form via a containment suit that he can manipulate to re-shape himself to a limited degree; the suit can seal most damage and ensnare opponents. While so contained, Dogma possesses sufficient superhuman strength (enhanced human), speed and fighting ability to overpower an accomplished combatant like Wolverine. He can spew blinding acid, possibly part of his suit's capabilities. His shining sword can conduct intense heat.

INTELLIGENCE: 2 **STRENGTH:** 3 **SPEED:** 3 **DURABILITY:** 7
ENERGY PROJECTION: 3 **FIGHTING SKILLS:** 4

DOOMBRINGER

REAL NAME: Unrevealed
ALIASES: None
IDENTITY: Secret
OCCUPATION: Chaos-bringer
CITIZENSHIP: Unidentified dimension

PLACE OF BIRTH: Unidentified dimension
KNOWN RELATIVES: Presumably other members of his race
GROUP AFFILIATION: Doombringers
EDUCATION: Unrevealed
FIRST APPEARANCE: Wolverine: Doombringer (1997)

HISTORY: Over 1000 years ago, extradimensional "Messengers in Black" influenced the cultists of Tangkor Marat (in what would become Thailand), feeding secret knowledge of certain arts to chosen mystics, perhaps to facilitate an invasion. The cultists concluded that the world's end was predestined, but while the southern sect wished to hasten this doom so they could pass on to the next world, the northern sect sought to prevent this. As the two factions warred, the southern sect opened a portal to summon the Doombringer, but the northern sect halted time, freezing all cultists and the emerging Doombringer. One thousand years later, an earthquake disrupted the spell, awakening a southern cultist, who sought out Japan's Mariko Yashida, head of the Yashida Clan who had descended from one of the sects. The cultists convinced twenty of the Silver Samurai (Mariko's half-brother)'s men to help disrupt the spell, and Mariko had her beloved Wolverine (Logan/James Howlett) join the Silver Samurai in stopping them. The twenty renegades played a recording of the reverse of the sonic vibrations used in the time spell, disrupting it. Wolverine shattered the crystal that maintained the portal, severing the Doombringer's hand as it closed, but a Doombringer had already emerged, slaying cultists and renegades alike, while all other cultists perished from rapid aging. Working together, Wolverine and Silver Samurai killed the Doombringer with their blades. Wolverine lied to Mariko, telling her Clan Yashida was descended from the northern sect, but she realized the truth.

Art by Michael Dutkiewicz

HEIGHT: 10'	**EYES:** Unrevealed
WEIGHT: 1400 lbs.	**HAIR:** None

ABILITIES/ACCESSORIES: The Doombringer was super-strong (enhanced human). Its thick, scaly hide shrugged off normal arrows, but was easily pierced by Wolverine's Adamantium claws and the Silver Samurai's tachyon-field-coated blade. Its brethren (and presumably it) could also be hurt by the closure of an interdimensional portal while it was in mid-passage. It had razor sharp claws and was covered sporadically by gleaming crystals. It did not speak, and it is unclear whether it was anything more than a rampaging, murderous beast.

INTELLIGENCE: 1 **STRENGTH:** 4 **SPEED:** 3 **DURABILITY:** 3
ENERGY PROJECTION: 1 **FIGHTING SKILLS:** 4

REAL NAME: Unrevealed
ALIASES: None
IDENTITY: Secret
OCCUPATION: Thief, extortionist
CITIZENSHIP: Unrevealed

PLACE OF BIRTH: Unrevealed
KNOWN RELATIVES: None
GROUP AFFILIATION: None
EDUCATION: Unrevealed
FIRST APPEARANCE: X-Men Annual #11 (1987)

HISTORY: Horde described himself as a powerful mutant who sought conquest rather than "the betterment of humanity"; this may mean he comes from Earth, although "humanity" may refer to sentient beings in general. In any event, he conquered several planets, destroying those whose inhabitants refused to cater to his whims, and stole many treasures throughout the universe, including a gem that sustained him throughout lifetimes of wanton cruelty and self-indulgence; he frequently forced others to steal for him rather than unnecessarily exert himself. He recruited the X-Men (along with Captain Britain/Brian Braddock and Meggan) to acquire a powerful crystal from the Citadel of Light and Shadow, guarded by immobile past seekers. Within the Citadel, all the X-Men except Wolverine (Logan/James Howlett) succumbed to illusions of their hearts' desire. When Wolverine reached the crystal, Horde, smugly assuming the Citadel's defenses penetrated, tore out Wolverine's heart, but the hero's blood struck the crystal, which amplified Wolverine's healing factor to re-create him from a single drop. Granted cosmic power in the process, Wolverine removed Horde's gem, crumbling his enemy into dust. Wolverine rejected his new power and destroyed the crystal, unaware that his actions had proved humanity's worthiness, whereas if he had retained the power, he would have been condemned to immobile life as a Citadel guardian, with humanity's evolution forever halted. The Citadel then teleported the X-Men home and restored the crystal to await a new seeker.

HEIGHT: 14'   **WEIGHT:** 2500 lbs.   **EYES:** Blue   **HAIR:** Orange

ABILITIES/ACCESSORIES: Superhumanly strong, Horde could punch through stone walls and lift at least 50 tons, and was immune to most forms of physical or psionic injury. He could emit blinding light, teleport himself and others across galaxywide distances, levitate people and objects, perceive events from afar, and instantaneously transform the clothing of and restore the health of several people simultaneously. Inasmuch as he destroyed several planets, he presumably possessed additional powers. He carried a harpoon and wore a gem on his forehead that sustained his health and youth for centuries or more; it is unclear how it might have contributed to his other powers.

INTELLIGENCE: 4 STRENGTH: 6 SPEED: 3/7(teleporter) DURABILITY: 6
ENERGY PROJECTION: 6 FIGHTING SKILLS: 2

Art by Alan Davis

REAL NAME: Unrevealed
ALIASES: Entity, Misery's Maitre D', Chef of Starvation, Waiter to the Waifs of the World, Hash-Slinger to the Homeless, Pestilence, Desolation
IDENTITY: Secret
OCCUPATION: Psychic scavenger
CITIZENSHIP: Unrevealed

PLACE OF BIRTH: Unrevealed
KNOWN RELATIVES: None
GROUP AFFILIATION: None
EDUCATION: Unrevealed
FIRST APPEARANCE: Heroes for Hope Starring the X-Men #1 (1985)

HISTORY: Originally appearing in ancient Africa, the being calling itself Hungry may be either a demonic entity or a primal mutant from the dawn of humanity. It warred with local tribes before being imprisoned in a temple created to appease it. Over centuries, its power radiated beyond the temple again — strengthened by the growing hopelessness of a starvation epidemic — and targeted the powerful X-Men, possibly due to its connection to their member Storm, whose ancestors were among those who once battled it. Its psychic attacks left several of the X-Men temporarily hospitalized — though Wolverine (Logan/James Howlett) overcame Hungry's assault — and the team soon traveled to Africa to confront it. There, Rogue (Anna Marie) stole her teammates' powers to battle the creature, but it possessed her instead. The X-Men, led by Storm, who inherited genetic memories about her ancestors' confrontations with Hungry, rallied against the possessed Rogue. Phoenix (Rachel Summers) tore Hungry's psychic essence from Rogue, sending it into retreat. Though the battle was won, the X-Men realized Hungry still existed and vowed to do what they could to keep fighting it.

TEMPLE FORM

HEIGHT: Variable   **WEIGHT:** Variable   **EYES:** Variable   **HAIR:** Variable

ABILITIES/ACCESSORIES: Hungry feeds on the emotions of other beings, notably hopelessness and despair. Its psychic powers are strong enough to engage against Phoenix and can possess others and alter reality to a limited extent. For a time, Hungry utilized the physical form of a giant reptilian creature, though it is unrevealed if this was its true form or just another possessed being.

INTELLIGENCE: 4 STRENGTH: 3 SPEED: 2/7 (teleporter)
DURABILITY: 7 ENERGY PROJECTION: 6 FIGHTING SKILLS: 4

Art by Jim Starlin with Paul Gulacy (inset)

AMIKO KOBAYASHI

REAL NAME: Amiko Kobayashi
ALIASES: Akiko, Aki, Kiko
IDENTITY: No dual identity
OCCUPATION: Student
CITIZENSHIP: Japan
PLACE OF BIRTH: Tokyo, Japan

KNOWN RELATIVES: Unidentified mother (deceased), Logan/James Howlett (Wolverine, foster father), Mariko Yashida (foster mother, deceased), unidentified foster parents
GROUP AFFILIATION: None
EDUCATION: High school student
FIRST APPEARANCE: Uncanny X-Men #181 (1984)

HISTORY: When Amiko was a child, her mother was fatally wounded by falling debris during a rampage in Tokyo by an extraterrestrial dragon (later named "Puff"). As the mother died, the X-Man Wolverine (Logan/James Howlett) promised to take care of Amiko. Serving as Amiko's foster father, Wolverine placed her with Mariko Yashida, head of the powerful Yashida Clan. Amiko lived happily with her until the Hand slew Mariko. Wolverine provided money for Amiko to be cared for by new foster parents, but they squandered the money on themselves and mistreated Amiko. Learning of this, Wolverine removed Amiko and gave her to mercenary assassin Yukio, with financial support for her upbringing from Mariko's half-brother the Silver Samurai. Amiko was once kidnapped by the Hand, who brainwashed her to serve them, intending to use her against Wolverine. The brainwashed Amiko betrayed Yukio and Elektra to the Hand before her mind was evidently restored to normal. Although Amiko had grown up admiring Wolverine as her protector, she began to resent his lengthy absences. Yukio gradually taught Amiko how to fight, inadvertently making her a would-be brawler. Amiko was threatened again when the Kaishek clan targeted Wolverine, but in the end she used her newfound fighting skills to aid Wolverine. Amiko was also briefly kidnapped by Maximillian Zaran and then by Sabretooth. Later, Amiko and Yukio were abducted by the Ashurado Clan, a mystical group dedicated to bringing hell on Earth and led by Hana, who was possessed by the demon Ryuki. Hana's sister Mana of the Shosei Order joined with Wolverine to defeat Hana and rescue Amiko and Yukio. Afterward, Mana discovered that Amiko's mother had been a member of the Shosei Order, granting Amiko a spiritual connection to their forces. Amiko agreed to undergo training as Mana's eventual successor.

Art by Steve Skroce

HEIGHT: 4'4"	WEIGHT: 88 lbs.	EYES: Brown	HAIR: Black

ABILITIES/ACCESSORIES: Amiko has limited training in the martial arts. Owing to her lineage, she has the potential to develop mystical abilities.

INTELLIGENCE: 2 STRENGTH: 2 SPEED: 2 DURABILITY: 2
ENERGY PROJECTION: 1 FIGHTING SKILLS: 3

SAINT CYRUS LEVITICUS

REAL NAME: Unrevealed
ALIASES: None
IDENTITY: Secret
OCCUPATION: Would-be world conqueror
CITIZENSHIP: Unrevealed

PLACE OF BIRTH: Unrevealed
KNOWN RELATIVES: None
GROUP AFFILIATION: Partnered with Ezra Asher
EDUCATION: Unrevealed
FIRST APPEARANCE: Wolverine: Black Rio (1998)

HISTORY: According to St. Cyrus, an alien traveled to Earth from across the cosmos (light years away) 1000 years ago, symbiotically bonding with a man and forming the being who became St. Cyrus Leviticus. The man ceased aging, but in return the alien demanded to be fed the psionic turbulence of thousands of dying souls, thus allowing him to claim his destiny, which allegedly larger than the known universe. St. Cyrus became allied and romantically involved with the vampire Ezra Asher. They plotted a mass slaughter at the Carnaval celebration in Rio de Janeiro, which would grant Cyrus the energy he needed while allowing Asher to feast on blood. Ezra's slaughters were investigated by local detective Antonio Vargas, coincidentally Ezra's ex-husband before she had disappeared after being vampirized years before. This in turn drew the attention of Vargas' visiting friend Wolverine (Logan/James Howlett), and Ezra and St. Cyrus ambushed the two after a night of partying, knocking out Wolverine and slaying Vargas. Seeking vengeance, Wolverine allowed himself to be captured by St. Cyrus, and Ezra fed on Wolverine repeatedly. St. Cyrus failed to convince Wolverine that their immortality placed them above humanity and then left him to Ezra, but Wolverine broke free and drove her off. Wolverine then slaughtered St. Cyrus' agents and confronted him as he stood above the crowds awaiting his destiny. St. Cyrus battered Wolverine until the mutant exposed and skewered Cyrus' symbiote, then stabbed the maddened St. Cyrus' heart seconds later.

Art by Paco Diaz Luque

HEIGHT: 6'	WEIGHT: 180 lbs.	EYES: Pale yellow	HAIR: White

ABILITIES/ACCESSORIES: Via his alien symbiote, St. Cyrus had enhanced longevity (and possible immunity to aging and disease), plus superhuman strength (Class 10), and possibly speed. He apparently fed on the energy released by violent death and could apparently revive people slain under certain conditions as "decaying children" under his command; these servants retained the power of speech and had more independent thought than true zombies. The alien advised St. Cyrus telepathically on how to behave.

INTELLIGENCE: 2 STRENGTH: 4 SPEED: 2
DURABILITY: 3 ENERGY PROJECTION: 4 FIGHTING SKILLS: 2

LORD DARK WIND

REAL NAME: Kenji Oyama
ALIASES: Dark Wind
IDENTITY: Publicly known
OCCUPATION: Warrior, inventor, soldier, pilot
CITIZENSHIP: Japan
PLACE OF BIRTH: Yokosuka, Japan

KNOWN RELATIVES: Yuriko Oyama (Lady Deathstrike, daughter), two unidentified sons (deceased)
GROUP AFFILIATION: Led samurai warrior army; formerly the Japanese Army
EDUCATION: Unrevealed
FIRST APPEARANCE: Daredevil #196 (1983)

Art by Luke McDonnell

HISTORY: In 1945, famous war hero Oyama flew a kamikaze plane into a US aircraft, but his bombs failed to detonate. Shamed and scarred, Oyama became a prisoner of war. After Japan's surrender, a hooded Oyama vowed to hide his face until he had restored Japan's tarnished honor and old values. Profiting from a war experiences book, Oyama bought an island off Hokkaido's coast, married and had three children whose faces he branded as a sign of superiority. His code attracting devotees, Oyama financed reactionary political activity, and his sons died trying to assassinate Japan's prime minister. Oyama renamed himself Dark Wind, symbolizing a wind from the past that would sweep away the land's shame, and began his quest for the ultimate warrior. He invented a process for bonding the near-indestructible metal Adamantium to bone, but his notes were stolen and eventually used on the mutant Logan (James Howlett, later Wolverine); it took him decades to reinvent the process. Tomo Yoshida later sent Sunfire (Shiro Yoshida), Mystique, Rogue (Anna Raven) and Blindspot to steal Oyama's formula from his Yokohama facility, but Dark Wind escaped with his hard drives. Dark Wind subsequently enhanced the crippled assassin Bullseye via the Adamantium-bonding process, despite the interference of Daredevil (Matt Murdock) and Wolverine. As Daredevil tracked Bullseye, joining forces with Dark Wind's daughter, Yuriko, Dark Wind sent the fully restored Bullseye to assassinate Japan's trade minister, though Bullseye ungratefully abandoned this quest upon departing. Daredevil became trapped under debris during an earthquake while fighting Dark Wind's men. Dark Wind prepared to execute the helpless hero, but Yuriko struck down her father with a sword, and they left him for dead.

HEIGHT: 5'11" **WEIGHT:** 170 lbs. **EYES:** Unrevealed **HAIR:** Unrevealed

ABILITIES/ACCESSORIES: A scientific genius and a skilled swordsman, Dark Wind employed ninja, and numerous samurai armed with swords and bows and arrows.

INTELLIGENCE: 5 STRENGTH: 2 SPEED: 2 DURABILITY: 2
ENERGY PROJECTION: 1 FIGHTING SKILLS: 4

LORD SHINGEN

REAL NAME: Shingen Harada
ALIASES: Shingen Yashida
IDENTITY: No dual identity
OCCUPATION: Clan Yashida leader, professional criminal
CITIZENSHIP: Japan
PLACE OF BIRTH: Presumably the Yashida ancestral stronghold near Agarashima, Japan
KNOWN RELATIVES: Mariko Yashida (daughter, deceased), Kenuichio

Harada (Silver Samurai, son), Noburo-Hideki (son-in-law, deceased), Shiro Yoshida (Sunfire, nephew), Saburo and Tomo Yoshida (nephews, deceased), Leyu Yoshida (Sunpyre, niece, deceased)
GROUP AFFILIATION: Clan Yashida, Yakuza
EDUCATION: Unrevealed
FIRST APPEARANCE: (Mentioned, unidentified) Daredevil #111 (1974); (full) Wolverine #1 (1982)

HISTORY: Shingen was head of Japan's Clan Yashida, which he felt had a claim to Japan's throne. At some point incurring a debt of honor to the criminal Mandrill, Shingen disappeared during his daughter Mariko's childhood and was believed dead. He later resurfaced, reclaimed control of his clan, and used it to run his criminal empire. To repay another debt, Shingen had Mariko marry Noburo-Hideki despite her love for Wolverine (Logan/James Howlett). When, Logan sneaked into the Yashida Clan's stronghold and learned of Mariko's abusive marriage, Shingen's men drugged him. To prove Logan unworthy to Mariko, Shingen challenged him to a duel. As Shingen struck several paralyzing blows, Logan recognized Shingen's intent and unsheathed his claws, appearing to dishonor the duel in Mariko's eyes. Shingen easily defeated the drugged and humiliated Logan and cast him to the streets. Shingen then sent the mercenary Yukio to befriend Logan and protect him from Hand attacks. Yukio manipulated Logan into helping her assassinate Shingen's chief rival, Katsuyori. Logan's usefulness now ended, Shingen ordered Yukio to slay him, then sent Hand agents after them when she hesitated to do so, having fallen in love with Logan. After Yukio slew Logan's friend Asano Kimura (mistaking him for another Hand agent), she fled Logan and tried to kill Shingen to redeem herself, but he easily defeated her. Meanwhile, Logan hindered Shingen's operations, humiliating him before fighting him anew. Though Shingen delivered better strikes, Logan's Adamantium protected him until he stabbed Shingen's neck, killing him. Mariko realized her father's deceptions and Logan's true honor. Shingen's spirit once apparently attacked Logan's in a purgatory-like realm. He was later resurrected by Phaedra, becoming her lover and battling Wolverine for her until Logan slew him again.

Art by Howard Chaykin

HEIGHT: 5'10" **WEIGHT:** 185 lbs. **EYES:** Brown **HAIR:** Bald (formerly black)

ABILITIES/ACCESSORIES: Shingen was a master swordsman and combatant.

INTELLIGENCE: 3 STRENGTH: 3 SPEED: 2 DURABILITY: 2
ENERGY PROJECTION: 1 FIGHTING SKILLS: 5

MELTDOWN

REAL NAME: Unrevealed
ALIASES: General Meltdown
IDENTITY: Secret
OCCUPATION: Megalomaniac; former general
CITIZENSHIP: Presumably Russia
PLACE OF BIRTH: Presumably Russia

KNOWN RELATIVES: None
GROUP AFFILIATION: Partner of Dr. Neutron and Quark (aka Scarlett McKenzie)
EDUCATION: Unrevealed
FIRST APPEARANCE: (Voice, caricature) Havok and Wolverine: Meltdown #1 (1988); (full) Havok and Wolverine: Meltdown #2 (1988)

HISTORY: Meltdown apparently served in the Russian army as a general, but he was stripped of his rank at some point. He allied with the genius Dr. Neutron to engineer the explosion of a Russian nuclear power plant to jumpstart Meltdown's own radiation powers. While successful, the radiation released was dispersed too widely for direct absorption. Many people died and/or developed radiation sickness, while Meltdown and Neutron were placed in a Siberian asylum, which they soon gained control of. They identified Havok (Alex Summers)'s ability to absorb radiation and release it in a concentrated form as the means to better "jumpstart" Meltdown. Two years after their first effort, they allied with Quark who helped Neutron's agents' capture Havok and infect his ally Wolverine (Logan/James Howlett) with bubonic plague. As nurse Scarlett McKenzie, Quark manipulated Havok into falling in love with her as she guided him across the world in pursuing Wolverine's seeming killers. Recovering, Wolverine tracked the pair but was captured and brainwashed into attacking Havok. Suspecting treachery, Havok pretended to fatally injure Wolverine, then accompanied Scarlett to India's Tarapur nuclear reactor, which Meltdown had destabilized. Having fallen in love with Havok as well, Scarlett tried to warn Havok, but Meltdown incinerated her. As planned, the enraged Havok drew on the reactor's radiation and blasted Meltdown with all his power, jumpstarting Meltdown's powers. Both Havok and the arriving Wolverine were powerless against Meltdown until Wolverine impaled him with a series of boron control rods. Apparently having been converted into pure energy, Meltdown weakened and then dissipated. Havok stabilized the reactor, and Wolverine allowed him to believe Scarlett had been innocent.

| HEIGHT: 5'3" | WEIGHT: 220 lbs. | EYES: No visible iris | HAIR: Unrevealed |

ABILITIES/ACCESSORIES: Meltdown could absorb radiation and release it as destructive blasts. He could only absorb radiation in a highly concentrated form, and he could not generate his own radiation unless given a "jumpstart" by absorbing a large amount of pre-existing radiation. When sufficiently charged, Meltdown had superhuman healing. Boron rods dampened his powers.

INTELLIGENCE: 2 STRENGTH: 2 SPEED: 2 DURABILITY: 4
ENERGY PROJECTION: 5 FIGHTING SKILLS: 2

PHAEDRA

REAL NAME: Unrevealed
ALIASES: None
IDENTITY: Secret
OCCUPATION: Former High Priestess
CITIZENSHIP: Unrevealed
PLACE OF BIRTH: Unrevealed

KNOWN RELATIVES: None
GROUP AFFILIATION: Formerly Scimitar, the Hand
EDUCATION: Unrevealed
FIRST APPEARANCE: Wolverine #59 (2008); (identified) Wolverine #60 (2008)

HISTORY: Phaedra's ability to bring the dead back to life drew the attention of Azrael, the angel of death. Azrael sought revenge on Wolverine (Logan/James Howlett) for taking more than his mortal share of lives, so Azrael allied with Phaedra despite finding her undoing of his work offensive. To that end, Phaedra infiltrated the ninja cult the Hand as a High Priestess and resurrected Wolverine for them after he had been slain by the Gorgon (Tomi Shishido); however, Phaedra secretly kept a piece of Wolverine's soul and fashioned it into the form of Shogun, whom she established as leader of a new terrorist group, Scimitar. She then lured Wolverine into a trap wherein Shogun killed Wolverine's new love Amir and defeated Wolverine by forcing him to ingest a bomb that Shogun then detonated, killing his physical form and sending his spirit to purgatory. There, his will sapped after losing another lover, Wolverine was finally defeated by Azrael and was stranded in purgatory. Aided by Earth's Sorcerer Supreme Dr. Strange, Wolverine's soul was freed and he set about confronting Phaedra. She gained an ally and a lover by resurrecting Wolverine's old foe Yakuza crime boss Lord Shingen Harada to oppose the hero, but Wolverine again slew Shingen, then struck a deal with Azrael to restore his soul in return for killing Phaedra, which Azrael was unable to do. Phaedra tried to bargain with Wolverine herself by offering to resurrect his love Mariko, but was slain after he rejected her offer.

| HEIGHT: 5'9" | WEIGHT: 136 lbs. | EYES: Blue | HAIR: Blonde |

ABILITIES/ACCESSORIES: Phaedra possessed the innate ability to bring the dead back to life, and could also manipulate the souls of those she resurrected.

INTELLIGENCE: 2 STRENGTH: 2 SPEED: 2
DURABILITY: 2 ENERGY PROJECTION: 3 FIGHTING SKILLS: 1

REAL NAME: Aldo Ferro
ALIASES: Vole, the Sicilian Mouse, il Topo Siciliano
IDENTITY: Secret
OCCUPATION: Independently wealthy; former crimelord, government operative
CITIZENSHIP: Italy

PLACE OF BIRTH: Unrevealed
KNOWN RELATIVES: None
GROUP AFFILIATION: Formerly Weapon X (multinational)
EDUCATION: Unrevealed
FIRST APPEARANCE: (Illusory) Wolverine #62 (1992); (full) Wolverine #64 (1992)

HISTORY: In the 1960s, Sicilian crime boss and mutant mastermind Aldo Ferro, then a robust and powerful man, learned of the Weapon X Project. Via connections between his crime family and ultra-covert US agencies, he met with project head Truett Hudson, aka "Prof. Thornton." Whereas Hudson used elaborate stage scenarios to implant false memories in Team X members, Ferro offered to directly implant more durable memories in exchange for Team X's age suppression treatment. Hudson agreed, and Ferro, now codenamed Vole, derived sadistic pleasure from linking Team X's implants to their pain receptors, but Hudson reneged on their bargain. When Team X disbanded, Ferro absconded with DNA from Wolverine (Logan/James Howlett) and spent years futilely trying to crack its genetic code. Ferro's wealth and resources bought him US government protection, and eventually he was believed dead. In recent years, Ferro, retired to an island retreat near Washington State, resolved to acquire fresh Wolverine DNA and arranged for Team X veteran Mastodon to lose his age suppression factor. Wolverine, Sabretooth, Silver Fox and others investigated and were lured to Ferro's island. Clad in armor that concealed his now withered form, Ferro fought the team as Psi-Borg, psionically guiding Sabretooth to apparently kill Silver Fox, but was himself attacked by a Shiva robot, another Weapon X legacy. Seriously wounded, he forced Sabretooth to escort him to safety. Canada, Psi-Borg departed and has not been seen since.

| HEIGHT: 5'10" | WEIGHT: 135 lbs. | EYES: Black | HAIR: Bald, formerly black |

ABILITIES/ACCESSORIES: Psi-Borg can create realistic illusions to seemingly alter his form and surroundings, implant false memories within human minds, generate psionic blasts, and seize mental control of others. His armor grants him superhuman strength, perhaps sufficient to lift 1 ton, corresponding speed, and sufficient durability to withstand armor-piercing bullets; it is unclear if it amplifies his psionic abilities.

INTELLIGENCE: 3 STRENGTH: 4 SPEED: 3 DURABILITY: 5
ENERGY PROJECTION: 6 FIGHTING SKILLS: 2

ILLUSORY SELF

Art by Mark Pacella with Mark Texeira (insets)

REAL NAME: Sapphire Styx (apparently)
ALIASES: None
IDENTITY: No dual identity
OCCUPATION: Mercenary, criminal
CITIZENSHIP: Madripoor

PLACE OF BIRTH: Presumably Madripoor
KNOWN RELATIVES: None
GROUP AFFILIATION: Former member of Roche's gang
EDUCATION: Unrevealed
FIRST APPEARANCE: Marvel Comics Presents #1 (1988)

HISTORY: A mutant life energy-vampire, Sapphire served Madripoor crimelord Roche. Spying on Princess Bar owner O'Donnell, she posed as bait for Wolverine (Logan/James Howlett) during an attack by Roche's gang and later attacked him in an alley using her "Kiss of Death," weakening him for her partner Razor-Fist (Douglas Scott), and assisting in Logan's capture. Sapphire reveled in the discovery that the imprisoned Logan's healing factor enabled her to repeatedly drain his life force. Logan escaped, but O'Donnell was captured, and Sapphire nearly drained him dry until Logan returned with Madripoor's new crimelord Tyger Tiger. Shooting Sapphire to save O'Donnell, Tyger was attacked by the succubus-like mutant, but after being bitten and then burned with a branding iron, Sapphire fled alongside Roche's Inquisitor. Later working alone, Sapphire stole a haul from the Yashida Clan, including possessions belonging to Logan's former lover, the late Mariko Yashida. Tyger set Logan on Sapphire's trail, but didn't tell him what Sapphire had stolen. After a short struggle, Logan retrieved the stolen goods. Tyger arranged further punishment for Sapphire, whose subsequent fate remains unrevealed.

KISS OF DEATH

| HEIGHT: 5'1" | WEIGHT: 165 lbs. | EYES: Grey | HAIR: Red |

ABILITIES/ACCESSORIES: Sapphire can drain other people's life force, weakening or even killing them; she generally does so by kissing her victim. The energy she drains enhances her strength and regenerates her body, making her stronger and more beautiful. An experienced markswoman, she sometimes carries a handgun.

INTELLIGENCE: 2 STRENGTH: 2/3* SPEED: 2 DURABILITY: 2/4*
ENERGY PROJECTION: 2 FIGHTING SKILLS: 1
*FILLED WITH DRAINED LIFE-FORCE

Art by John Buscema

SHIVA

REAL NAME: Shiva
ALIASES: None
IDENTITY: No dual identity
OCCUPATION: Assassin
CITIZENSHIP: None
PLACE OF CREATION: Unrevealed

KNOWN RELATIVES: None
GROUP AFFILIATION: US government; formerly Weapon X (multinational)
EDUCATION: Extent of programming unrevealed
FIRST APPEARANCE: Wolverine #50 (1992)

HISTORY: Decades ago, the Weapon X Project, tenth incarnation of the Weapon Plus Program, created the Shiva Scenario, a computer program using giant robots to kill Weapon X sleeper agents or renegade operatives if necessary. In recent years, former Weapon X operative Wolverine (Logan/James Howlett), a victim of Weapon X's memory alterations, investigated a Weapon X facility and inadvertently activated the Shiva Scenario; days later, under the direction of Weapon X head scientist Truett Hudson, aka "Prof. Thornton," a Shiva unit battled Wolverine. He destroyed it, then fought and destroyed a second Shiva unit. When Weapon X alumnus Silver Fox killed Hudson, several remaining Shivas activated and searched for additional Weapon X targets. Weeks later, two such targets, Sabretooth and John Wraith, each destroyed a Shiva, then joined forces with Wolverine and others to confront Psi-Borg (Aldo Ferro), telepathic creator of their memory implants and holder of many Weapon X secrets. During this conflict, a fifth Shiva attacked Psi-Borg and was also destroyed. Years later, when Wolverine regained his full memories, he invaded the White House to confront a high-level government official with unspecified ties to his manipulators, but a Shiva unit, acquired and activated by unidentified parties, arrived in a missile and slew the official. Using the Muramasa Sword, Wolverine destroyed the Shiva minutes later, but others presumably remain at large.

Art by Marc Silvestri

HEIGHT: 12' **WEIGHT:** 2000 lbs. **EYES:** Red **HAIR:** None

ABILITIES/ACCESSORIES: Shiva is an artificial intelligence inhabiting a robot body. When a Shiva unit is dismantled, Shiva's consciousness shunts to a new unit, of which an unrevealed but finite number exist. Each Shiva learns from its predecessor's errors, so it can never be defeated the same way twice. Each Shiva unit has superhuman strength (able to lift at least 40 tons), as well as superhuman speed, durability and reflexes. It can teleport, discharge plasma bursts or razor-sharp blades from its hands, project an electromagnetic force field, and emit electronic pulses to overwhelm former Weapon X members with genuine or implanted memories.

INTELLIGENCE: 2 **STRENGTH:** 5 **SPEED:** 4/7 (teleporter) **DURABILITY:** 7
ENERGY PROJECTION: 6 **FIGHTING SKILLS:** 4

SHREDDER

REAL NAME: Unrevealed
ALIASES: None
IDENTITY: Secret
OCCUPATION: Mercenary, assassin
CITIZENSHIP: Presumably Canada

PLACE OF BIRTH: Presumably Canada
KNOWN RELATIVES: None
GROUP AFFILIATION: None
EDUCATION: Unrevealed
FIRST APPEARANCE: Hulk/Wolverine: 6 Hours #1 (2003)

HISTORY: Operating out of a Canadian cemetery, the allegedly undefeated mercenary Shredder nearly slew a young Logan (James Howlett, later Wolverine) decades ago. More recently, past employer and drug trafficker Harry Galvano hired Shredder to recover drugs and money stolen by Sid and Whitie, who were flying to Mistassini, Canada. Pilot Margie White planned an early landing upon learning passenger Kyle Hatcher was suffering from a snake bite. The crooks objected, roughing up fellow passenger Bruce Banner when he intervened, triggering Banner's change into the monstrous Hulk. Surviving the resulting crash, Sid and Whitie forced Margie to lead them to Lake Vague, but she refused to help unless they took Kyle, too. While Banner joined Logan, who had been vacationing nearby, in trying to save Kyle and Margie, Shredder reached Lake Vague first, slaying the thieves' drop man after learning their location. Leaving a bloody trail as he tracked his prey, Shredder asked for more money upon learning of Wolverine's involvement, while Wolverine recognized Shredder's work on a pair of his victims. Shredder reached the thieves first and slew them both, but Margie stopped him from killing her and Kyle by promising payment from the drop man's nonexistent hidden safe. As Logan and Banner approached, Shredder tossed Kyle into a lake, occupying Banner while Logan crashed Shredder's departing boat. Shredder savagely slashed and impaled the dazed Logan, who ultimately severed Shredder's clawed hand, then left the killer to be attacked by a mountain lion. Wolverine and Banner jerry-rigged an anti-venom, saving Kyle's life.

Art by Scott Kolins

HEIGHT: 6'5" **EYES:** Red sclera and iris
WEIGHT: 190 lbs. **HAIR:** Sparse black hairs across a mostly bald head

ABILITIES/ACCESSORIES: Shredder's right hand was oversized, with each digit ending in sharp spikes, and could shred a person in seconds. He was an expert tracker and a lethal fighter, generally killing anyone he encountered in his missions, regardless of whether they helped him or not. He enjoyed torturing others. His face was horribly deformed, lacking lips and appearing as badly burned or otherwise scarred tissue stretched across a skull. He traveled via motorcycle.

INTELLIGENCE: 2 **STRENGTH:** 3 **SPEED:** 3 **DURABILITY:** 3
ENERGY PROJECTION: 1 **FIGHTING SKILLS:** 4

REAL NAME: Bolivar Trask
ALIASES: None
IDENTITY: No dual identity
OCCUPATION: Department of Defense advisor, anthropologist
CITIZENSHIP: USA
PLACE OF BIRTH: Turner County, South Dakota
KNOWN RELATIVES: Unidentified wife (deceased), Lawrence Trask (son, deceased), Tanya Trask (Sanctity, daughter), Donald Trask, Sr. (father, deceased), Simon Trask, Donald Trask, Jr. (brothers, deceased), Donald Trask III (nephew, deceased)
GROUP AFFILIATION: None
EDUCATION: Ph.D. in anthropology
FIRST APPEARANCE: X-Men #14 (1965)

HISTORY: Bolivar Trask was among the first learned men to realize the rise of mutants due to his own mutant offspring Tanya and Lawrence. After blocking Larry's power and memories, Bolivar, fearful other mutants would expose Larry, became obsessed with imprisoning them. With US government support, Bolivar developed the first Sentinels, robots made to serve humanity's needs and incarcerate mutants. Bolivar revealed the Sentinels' existence to the world during a televised debate with Professor Charles Xavier (secretly a mutant), but the Sentinels then refused to accept Bolivar's orders, having transferred their loyalties to Master Mold, the primary Sentinel. Master Mold tried to force Bolivar to help him manufacture new Sentinels independently, but seeing the mutant heroes of the X-Men oppose the Sentinels, Bolivar repented his beliefs and destroyed the Sentinel creation cubicles, killing himself and destroying Master Mold. Bolivar was found by Lawrence who blamed the X-Men for his father's death, ensuring a cycle of repeated attempts to perfect the Sentinels. More than a decade after Bolivar's death, Bastion exhumed his body and used the techno-organic Magus to infuse its transmode virus into the corpse, reanimating it. Bolivar joined the other infected anti-mutant zealots in Bastion's schemes.

TECHNO-ORGANIC FORM

HEIGHT: 5'10"	WEIGHT: 170 lbs.	EYES: Brown	HAIR: Brown

ABILITIES/ACCESSORIES: Bolivar Trask is skilled in anthropology, cybernetics and robotics; his inventions include the original (mark I) Sentinels and Master Mold. Bolivar's abilities since receiving the techno-organic virus are unrevealed, but include the power to conceal his inhuman appearance. The extent of Trask's autonomy (as opposed to Bastion's control), is unrevealed.

INTELLIGENCE: 5 **STRENGTH:** 2 **SPEED:** 2 **DURABILITY:** 6
ENERGY PROJECTION: 1 **FIGHTING SKILLS:** 1

Art by Bryan Hitch with Clayton Crain (inset)

REAL NAME: Tane
ALIASES: None
IDENTITY: Publicly known within Enclave; existence unknown to Earth's general populace
OCCUPATION: Tribune
CITIZENSHIP: Enclave
PLACE OF BIRTH: The Enclave, Himalayan Mountains, Tibet
KNOWN RELATIVES: None
GROUP AFFILIATION: Enclave
EDUCATION: Unrevealed
FIRST APPEARANCE: Wolverine: Killing (1993)

HISTORY: Tane was Tribune to a hidden Himalayan Enclave, who had splintered from the Inhumans due to opposition to Terrigen Mist usage. As cultural leader, Tane enforced the Enclave's Mandate that they stay isolated to remain pure and perfect, but he secretly sought to marry Serra, daughter of the Enclave's Matriarch, Nirissa, to found a dynasty and usurp Nirissa's power. As monstrous mutations arose in the Enclave's small gene pool, Nirissa pressured Tane to arrange the crossbreeding of Serra with the mutant Wolverine (Logan/James Howlett), intending for their offspring to inherit his healing factor. To this end, Tane influenced Logan to visit their Enclave; he further allowed Serra to overhear this plot, then manipulated her into fleeing into the frigid outland. As planned, Logan rescued Serra, but Tane secretly sent the monstrous Slith to slay him. Logan instead destroyed Slith and brought Serra back to the Enclave. As Serra began falling for Logan, Tane sought to kill Logan, purge Serra's memories of him, and make her his own; however, Logan challenged Tane to single combat. After preparing himself via a power-enhancing chemical infusion, Tane confronted Logan on the streets and caused Logan's body and mind to be wrought with pain. Tane then brutally battered his incapacitated foe, until Logan unleashed his berserker side; immune to the psychic pain Tane dealt, Logan stripped Tane of the lines that delivered the "juice" that empowered him. Slicing a scar into Tane's neck, Logan noted that if he were the animal Tane thought he was, Tane would be dead. Logan departed but gave Serra the means to contact him if she ever left the Enclave.

HEIGHT: 6'3"	WEIGHT: 210 lbs.	EYES: Unrevealed	HAIR: Black

ABILITIES/ACCESSORIES: Tane could mentally influence others, even halfway around the world. While he could directly manipulate most with little effort, strong-willed people such as Wolverine proved resistant to his control. He could also induce excruciating pain, and possibly other sensations at will. His abilities were enhanced by intravenous delivery of an unidentified chemical.

INTELLIGENCE: 3 **STRENGTH:** 3 **SPEED:** 2 **DURABILITY:** 2
ENERGY PROJECTION: 3 **FIGHTING SKILLS:** 3

Art by Kent Williams

UNCEGILA

REAL NAME: Unrevealed
ALIASES: Serpent-Thing, Witch-Serpent who dwells in the Heart of the World
IDENTITY: Secret; existence unknown to general public
OCCUPATION: Bane of Native American tribes
CITIZENSHIP: None

PLACE OF BIRTH: Unrevealed US location
KNOWN RELATIVES: Unidentified parasitic children
GROUP AFFILIATION: None
EDUCATION: Inapplicable; (as human) extensive training in magic
FIRST APPEARANCE: Marvel Comics Presents #95 (1991)

HISTORY: Untold millennia ago, an evil witch was transformed into the murderous monster Uncegila. In the early 20th century, Logan (James Howlett), working for the Hudson Bay Company, saved a Blackfoot youth from a bear corrupted by one of Uncegila's children after it blinded the boy. The Piegan Blackfoot cared for Logan, and after his wounds healed, an Uncegila-infected horse was found in the Blackfoot camp. Their shaman Old Wolf Heart told Logan that the Sioux had warned them of the coming of Uncegila. The next night the monster killed the Blackfoot camp's horses. Logan and the Blackfoot men tracked the witch-serpent, but she outsmarted them and returned to the camp to kill their women and children. Uncegila devoured She Watches the Sparrow Hawk, a woman Logan had fallen in love with, and then

MONSTER CHILD

disappeared into the ground within a second. The next morning Logan volunteered to kill the monster. Accompanied by the youth (now named Blind Owl), Logan found Uncegila sleeping in her mountain cave, but she awoke and attacked them along with her children. Blind Owl shot Uncegila in the eye with Logan's rifle, enraging the monster. Logan saved the boy and cut out the monster's heart with two blades. Reminded of the encounter by a dream years later, Logan rediscovered the cave containing Uncegila's bones.

Art by Todd Fox

HEIGHT: 38'	WEIGHT: 13 tons	EYE: Green	HAIR: Red & yellow (feathers)

ABILITIES/ACCESSORIES: Uncegila was granted longevity through her transformation. According to legend the mere sight of her drove people insane, but there was no real evidence for this. She crawled silently at top speeds of 100 mph through and above the ground. Slime secreted from her skin made her touch poisonous and corrosive. She could easily swallow a whole human or squash them with her weight. She made animals host for her parasitic children, which controlled and transformed the animals until the original form was barely recognizable.

INTELLIGENCE: 1/3* STRENGTH: 4 SPEED: 3 DURABILITY: 2
ENERGY PROJECTION: 1 FIGHTING SKILLS: 4
*AS HUMAN

ETHAN WARREN

REAL NAME: Ethan G. Warren
ALIASES: None
IDENTITY: No dual identity
OCCUPATION: Former soldier
CITIZENSHIP: USA

PLACE OF BIRTH: Unrevealed
KNOWN RELATIVES: Unidentified father (presumed deceased)
GROUP AFFILIATION: Formerly the US Army Air Forces
EDUCATION: Military training
FIRST APPEARANCE: Logan #1 (2008)

HISTORY: Ethan Warren discovered his mutant power shortly after puberty when he ran home after a mad dog chewed out his Achilles tendon. Concealing his abilities, he became a lieutenant in the US Army Air Forces. In May, 1945, his plane was shot down during a failed mission to sink the light cruiser Tone in Kure Harbor, and he and the other survivors were imprisoned in a Mukaishima work camp. Still hardy after three months while his fellow soldiers perished from starvation, disease and suicide, Warren was transferred to a military science base outside Hiroshima. Escaping alongside fellow prisoner Logan (James Howlett, later Wolverine), Warren tried to kill local villager Atsuko, believing her to be a secret assassin for Japan's Emperor. Logan stopped Warren and forced his departure, after which he and Atsuko became lovers. Warren subsequently shot Logan and slew Atsuko, but Logan healed and attacked Warren. Hiroshima's nuclear bombing ended their struggle, but Logan recovered and departed (his memories of these events soon lost), while Warren became a skeletal wraith, unable to leave the region. In recent years, Logan, his memories restored, returned to battle Warren, who tore out and consumed Logan's heart, which restored his human form. Surviving even this wound, Logan decapitated Warren, apparently killing him.

Art by Paco Diaz Luque

HEIGHT: 5'10"	WEIGHT: 165 lbs.	EYES: Blue	HAIR: Black

ABILITIES/ACCESSORIES: Warren's mutant powers granted him immunity to disease and to conventional injury. While he did not heal from wounds, he could not feel pain and would not bleed or be otherwise incapacitated unless the injury physically immobilized him. He could even function with severed tendons, though decapitation was apparently fatal. Hiroshima's nuclear explosion left him a fiery, clawed, wraith-like skeleton only able to access the Earthly plane with effort and unable to leave the village in which he mutated. In the latter state he was immune to aging and was selectively immaterial. Even after regaining human form he retained the ability to project fiery blasts.

INTELLIGENCE: 2 STRENGTH: 2 SPEED: 2 DURABILITY: 4
ENERGY PROJECTION: 3 FIGHTING SKILLS: 4

WHITE GHOST (EARTH-4011)

REAL NAME: John Howlett Jr.
ALIASES: Kitsunebi, Old Man, X
IDENTITY: Secret
OCCUPATION: Terrorist
CITIZENSHIP: Canada
PLACE OF BIRTH: Alberta, Canada
KNOWN RELATIVES: John Howlett Sr. (father, deceased), Elizabeth Howlett (mother, deceased), James Howlett (Logan/Wolverine, brother), Howlett (grandfather, surname unrevealed, deceased), others
GROUP AFFILIATION: Kanaguri cult
EDUCATION: No known formal education
FIRST APPEARANCE: (Behind the scenes) Wolverine: The End #1 (2004); (ghost image only) Wolverine: The End #2 (2004); (full) Wolverine: The End #3 (June, 2004)

HISTORY: Born in 1885 in the alternate Reality-4011, John Howlett's mutant powers surfaced at age 12 after seeing his mother kissing the gardener. Wounding his mother with his bone claws, John was institutionalized by his grandfather, while the public believed him to have died. John was eventually taken by researchers as their first subject, "X," and he developed additional powers before eventually escaping and slaying his captors. For many decades, John secretly watched his younger brother James, who had developed similar mutant powers, adopted the name Logan, was also mutated by Weapon X and became the hero Wolverine. By the late 21st century, as the White Ghost, John was worshipped by the Kanaguri cult, based atop Japan's Hiragana-san mountain. He also developed a terrorist sect, plotting to blow up Las Vegas, Nevada with a nuclear bomb to crumble the US economy, setting it up for a hostile takeover. John eventually had the long-retired Logan led to his mountain base, where he defeated his younger brother with his wraith-powers before revealing his true identity and embracing him. When John tried to recruit Logan into his plot, however, Logan pushed John from the mountaintop. Surviving, John traveled to Las Vegas to execute his terrorist plans, but Logan tracked him there. Logan's claws ultimately pierced John's heart, and John died telling Logan he was always proud of him.

HEIGHT: 5'3"
WEIGHT: 185 lbs.
EYES: Red (original color unrevealed)
HAIR: White (originally light brown)

ABILITIES/ACCESSORIES: Like Wolverine, the White Ghost had enhanced strength, speed, senses, healing, etc., as well as a slowed aging process. He could extend three bone claws from each forearm out through his wrists. He could also assume a ghost-like, intangible form, restoring his solid form at will.

INTELLIGENCE: 2 STRENGTH: 4 SPEED: 3 DURABILITY: 4
ENERGY PROJECTION: 1 FIGHTING SKILLS: 4

Art by Paco Diaz Luque

WHITE GHOST (MCLEISH)

REAL NAME: Roddy McLeish
ALIASES: Gweilo
IDENTITY: Publicly known
OCCUPATION: Assassin
CITIZENSHIP: UK
PLACE OF BIRTH: Broxburn, Scotland
KNOWN RELATIVES: Unidentified son
GROUP AFFILIATION: Unidentified assassins guild
EDUCATION: Unrevealed
FIRST APPEARANCE: Wolverine #119 (1997)

HISTORY: Killing his first man at age 13, McLeish developed a taste for murder, killing an average of 12 people a year for the next 37 years and earning a reputation as the world's best killer. In Hong Kong, McLeish adopted the alias "White Ghost," a literal translation of the anti-Caucasian slur Gweilo. There he became drinking buddies with Wolverine (Logan/James Howlett), whose superhuman abilities he observed in action. The Triads hired McLeish to kill the father of Logan's then girlfriend, Ai-Chia, but Logan crashed his motorcycle atop McLeish, breaking his spine, and Triad gunfire ignited the fuel. Believed dead, McLeish survived because his broken back caused him to limply go with the explosion's force. Regaining mobility over 10 years while his health continued to deteriorate with age, McLeish sent numerous assassins after Logan while leading him to an upstate New York cabin. McLeish goaded Logan into a berserker rage by revealing his murder of Ai-Chia. His healing factor largely depleted by the assassins' attacks, Logan was shot in the chest by McLeish with a poisoned Adamantium bullet. While McLeish claimed he had been grooming Logan to replace him as world's best killer, Logan derided McLeish before putting his fist under his chin and popping a claw on either side of his head. Before Logan could pop the lethal third claw, McLeish succumbed to age, injury and his alcohol-weakened heart. Logan burned McLeish's body.

HEIGHT: 6'1"
WEIGHT: 200 lbs.
EYES: Blue
HAIR: White

ABILITIES/ACCESSORIES: McLeish was a supremely skilled assassin, experienced with guns, various bladed weapons, explosives, etc., though his abilities deteriorated slightly with age. He was also a reasonably skilled ventriloquist and had an extremely high tolerance for alcohol, acquired via lifelong experience. Ten years after his injury, his health problems included a weak heart and presumably lung cancer. His back healed well enough that he could stand, though he was much more limited than he was at age fifty. When targeting Wolverine, he used an explosive packed with Adamantium shards.

INTELLIGENCE: 3 STRENGTH: 2/3* SPEED: 1/2*
DURABILITY: 1/2* ENERGY PROJECTION: 1 FIGHTING SKILLS: 4
*ABILITIES IN HIS PRIME

Art by Paco Diaz Luque

WOLVERINE: WEAPON X FILES

A brand-new, all-inclusive handbook for Hollywood's favorite mutant, spotlighting a complete biography of Wolverine! He may be in an acre of comics each month, but this is the only place to get the real score! Also featuring some of the Canucklehead's best allies — including Gambit, Maverick, Tyger Tiger and X-Force! And along for the ride are villains — the likes of Blob, Daken, Deadpool, Mastermind, Orphan Maker, Donald Pierce, the Purifiers, Sabretooth and S'ym! And more than four dozen other stars linked to our man Logan from Amiko to Silver Fox!

WOLVERINE ENCYCLOPEDIA VOL. 1 A-K

Introduction
Larry Hama

Text Writers
Paul Benjamin
Peter Sanderson
Dave Rios
Mark Robert Bourne

Design & Layout
Dan Danko

Cover
Adam Kubert
Jesse Delperdang

Cover Design
Joe Caponsacco

Assistant Editor
Mark Robert Bourne

Editors
Phil Crain
Dan Shaheen

Senior Editor
Mark Paniccia

Editor-in-Chief
Bob Harras

Special Thanks
Roger Bonas

WOLVERINE ON
BY LARRY HAMA

For a little guy, he comes with a lot of baggage. What is all this stuff about his secret and hidden past? What about those implanted memories and what happened during the time he was wandering around naked in Buffalo Wood? How come he only has one name? If the claws were always bone, why didn't he know they were there until after the adamantium was bound to his skeleton? What really happened between him and Cable? Do we really want to know the answers? Perhaps not. Maybe finding out all of that is like going up to your attic and discovering a photograph of your dad sitting on the verandas of the Havana Hilton with Lee Harvey Oswald, Jimmy Hoffa and Che Guevara. Or worse, finding a photo of your mom with her arm around George Hamilton.

I must admit that I am not a "continuity freak". I knew very little about the "Wolverine" character at the time I was asked to take on the scripting chores of his title. I sat myself down and read all the issues of "Wolverine" proper, including the precious incarnation by Frank Miller. I reread the early adventures in "Alpha Flight" and "Hulk" and much of the pertinent arcs in "X-Men".

There was quite a roster of comics luminaries represented in that first batch of reading; John Byrne, Chris Claremont, Bill Mantlo, Len Wein, Peter David, Jo Duffy, Archie Goodwin, Mark Gruenwald, just to mention the main scripters. (The list of pencilers and inkers would take up half this page.) Later on, I kept up by reading the additions made to the saga by the likes of Barry Windsor-Smith and Walt Simonson.

Like I said, I am not a continuity freak. I wasn't too troubled by the occasional contradictions in the back story or the inclusion in the canon of obfuscating dead-ends and odd frivolities. (I do, However take exception to the inference that Wolverine was ever afraid of Cyber! No WAY, bub!). All of that "plotting furniture" was as meaningless to me as the never- remembered McGuffin in "North by Northwest". I was, however struck by the consistency of characterization by a wide range of writers. This, in an industry where "personal takes" and wholesale makeovers by star writers are the norm. (At least Wolverine hasn't been killed yet!)

Through all the changes, travails and retcons, Logan has remained remarkably consistent in his stoic honesty, his simple loyalty and his inexorable will. We know full well that if he was our friend, he would not hesitate to come to our side in time of need. We never question the fact that in any given ethical choice situation, Logan would make the right and proper decision no matter how dire the consequences to himself.

These are powerful fantasies that transcend the mere "hero as a man of action" motif. These traits are all the more compelling because they are not slathered onto a strapping muscle-bound Adonis conforming to all the pre-set of western beauty. No. What we have is a five-foot-three inch hairy fireplug with a face like a potato and the temperament of a rabid pit bull, but oh, what a righteous fireplug he is.

I never felt that Wolverine's heroism lay in his ability to extrude adamantium claws and horizontally trisect his opponents. I think he is a hero simply because no matter what horrible things happen to him, he gets himself out of bed the next morning and keeps on going. Tragedy does not nail his palm to his forehead and cause him to bemoan his fate as others are want to do. He makes great big mistakes that ruin his life and he doesn't waste a second of his time in self-pity or recrimination. He lets it go and gets on with his life. How can we not admire this guy?

So how would you feel if you went up to your attic and found a photo of your parents sitting on a fence at the Calgary Stampede beside a little guy with sideburns in a plaid shirt and cowboy hat?

Larry Hama

ACANTI

A whale-like race of aliens that were enslaved by the Brood *(see Brood)* and used as living star-ships.

After the X-Men were infected by Brood eggs, Wolverine's heal-ing factor and adamantium skeleton enabled him to reject the egg's influence. Determined to kill his teammates if they should hatch into Brood, Wolverine was spared that decision when the prophet-singer of the Acanti race cured the X-Men.

ACOLYTES

The group of mutants known as the Acolytes came together to support Magneto in his quest for mutant supremacy over the human race. Wolverine has met the Acolytes in combat on many occasions *(see Magneto & Fabian Cortez).*

ADAMANTIUM

Adamantium is a nearly inde-structible metal alloy developed by the American scientist, Dr. Myron MacLain. Sometime after World War II, a Japanese scientist known as Lord DarkWind *(see Lord DarkWind)* developed a process by which adamantium could be bonded to human bone. However, Lord DarkWind's notes were stolen by some unknown party.

Years later, the top secret Weapon X program bonded adamantium to Wolverine's skeleton. The process gave Wolverine unbreakable bones. Were it not for Wolverine's mutant healing factor, the bond-ing process would certainly have killed him.

ADVERSARY

Known to the Cheyenne as "The Great Trickster," the Adversary is an ancient mystical being of immense power. His goal is to destroy Earth's dimension so he can remake it to his own liking. The Adversary used the "Great Gate" created by Forge *(see Forge)* years before to enter Earth's dimension. He then imprisoned Roma, *(see Roma)* guardian of the multiverse, within her own extra-dimensional fortress, the Starlight Citadel.

Wolverine and the X-Men, with Forge, invaded the Starlight Citadel to rescue Roma. During the rescue, Forge cast a spell that transformed the X-Men into pure energy, then used that energy to force the Adversary back through the Great Gate, sealing it shut behind him. The X-Men were thought to be dead, but were restored by Roma.

AGE OF APOCALYPSE

When Charles Xavier was acci-dentally killed by his future son, Legion, before he formed the X-Men, a new timeline was created.

In this world without Xavier, Magneto had formed the X-Men to fight the threat of the deadly mutant known as Apocalypse. In this new reality, Apocalypse has taken control of the North American continent, leading his mutant army on a bloody cru-sade to wipe out humanity.

Wolverine, known as Weapon X *(see Weapon X)*, along with Jean Grey and various alternate ver-sions of the X-Men, ultimately corrected the timeline with the help of the time-hopping Bishop, who was trapped in this violent alternate world.

ALBERT

Donald Pierce, the cyborg leader of the Reavers, designed Albert to be an exact android double of Wolverine. Teamed with a sec-ond android, Elsie Dee, the two were programmed to eliminate Wolverine.

Elsie, who would self-destruct when near Wolverine, was mis-takenly programmed with a maximum logic program that gave her a survival instinct. Not willing to sacrifice herself, Elsie used her programming to modify Albert's intelligence and capabili-ties. Nearly destroyed in battle with Wolverine, Albert rebuilt himself with kevlar, enhancing his durability. When Wolverine risked his life to save Elsie, she and Albert became his allies. Albert and Elsie are devoted to Wolverine and even traveled back in time after discovering that Wolverine might possibly have been killed in the distant past.

ALCHEMY AND THE TROLL ASSOCIATES

Tom Jones is called Alchemy because of his mutant ability to transmute elements. A group of trolls named Phiend, Phit, Phay, Phough and Phumm, known col-lectively as the Troll Associates, kidnapped Alchemy's mother which forced him to help them in their attempt to take over the world.

Excalibur and the X-Men came together to fight Alchemy and the Troll Associates. During the bat-tle, Alchemy temporarily trans-formed Wolverine's adamantium claws into rubber. With Alchemy's help, the heroes defeated the Troll Associates and saved Alchemy's mother.

ALHAZRED, ABDUL

Twice, Abdul Alhazred attempted to slay Tyger Tiger and take over her role as crimelord in Madripoor. Both times, Abdul and his men were defeated by Wolverine.

Alhazred can open a mystic gateway within his own body to free horrifying demons that he commands. Alhazred can also manipulate the human psyche to free a person's psychological demons. Wolverine fought against his inner demons and won, refusing to let the beast within him take over. The feed-back from Wolverine's resistance caused Alhazred to disappear into his own mystic gateway.

ALPHA FLIGHT

After reading about the formation of the Fantastic Four, the head of Department H, James Hudson *(see Guardian I and Department H)* formed Alpha Flight: a group of super-heroes composed mainly of mutants. Their first mission with Wolverine as their leader saw them defeat Egghead and the Eel, who were threatening the country with nuclear weapons. This resulted in the death of a member.

When Wolverine left to join the X-Men, Department H used the second generation team to bring him back. The team failed and it was later agreed to let him stay on as a member of the X-Men. Over the years both teams have helped each other on several occasions. After James Hudson apparently died, his wife, Heather, took his place as Guardian.

AMIKO

After the Secret Wars *(see Beyonder)*, Wolverine and the X-Men were teleported back to Earth. They appeared in Japan where they battled a giant dragon. Young Amiko's mother was killed in the devastation. Mariko Yashida and Wolverine took Amiko in and she became Mariko's ward.

After Mariko's death, Wolverine arranged for Amiko to live with foster parents. However, her foster parents were mentally abusing her and were frivolously spending the child support checks on themselves. Wolverine took Amiko from the couple and placed her in the care of the adventurer Yukio *(see Yukio)*. When Yukio is away on a mission, Amiko is left in the care of the the Silver Samurai.

Amiko sees Wolverine as "the Good Samurai" and longs to one day become a great and noble warrior as well.

ANDERSON, CHIEF MAGISTRATE

The "green and pleasant land" of Genosha owed its prosperity to the mutant slaves who were exploited to elevate the human population.

Chief Magistrate Anderson is the officer in charge of the Genoshan "Magistrate" police force. When the X-Men helped destroy the Genoshan system of mutant slavery, Chief Anderson and her Magistrates were their primary adversaries. Now that the Genoshan government is being restructured, Anderson is working to keep the peace in a land where one-time slaves are learning to live in harmony with their former masters.

ANGEL/ARCHANGEL

When he first met Wolverine, Warren Worthington III, the high-flying Angel, did not particularly care for Logan. Wolverine has always been somewhat lacking in social grace, but the true source of their animosity was a great deal more profound. Both harbored unrequited romantic feelings for Jean Grey. As a result, they sometimes clashed over what was in Jean's best interest, much to her chagrin.

Over the years, Angel and Wolverine became friends as well as teammates. Together, they joined forces with Gomurr the Ancient and Dr. Strange in a quest for the mystical liquid, the Crimson Dawn. They battled Tar, Keeper of the Crimson Dawn, and were able to use it to save the life of the X-Man, Psylocke (see Dr. Strange & Gomurr the Ancient).

Warren's life took a dramatic turn during a battle with the Marauders. Harpoon pinned Angel's wings against a wall. In the aftermath, Angel's wings were amputated. Apocalypse replaced Warren's wings and transformed him into Archangel.

Warren Worthington III, one of the original X-Men ultimately transformed to Archangel by Apocalypse

ANI-MEN, THE

Five scientists were recruited to form the group called the Ani-Men. None of the Ani-Men had superhuman powers until Count Nefaria transformed them into Ape-Man, Bird-Man, Cat-Man, Dragon Fly and Frog-Man, so they could take control of the North American Air Defense Command Center at Valhalla Mountain.

Only a short time after Xavier formed a new X-Men team, they thwarted Nefaria's *(see Count Nefaria)* plans. The resulting battle took the life of the X-Man, Thunderbird.

Dragonfly is the only current living member.

APOCALYPSE

The being known in ancient Egypt as En Sabah Nur has walked the Earth for countless centuries. Apocalypse is a mutant who has dedicated his immortal life to creating a world in which only the strongest will survive and humans are viewed as cattle. He is also responsible for transforming Angel into Archangel *(see Angel/Archangel).*

Apocalypse's goal to see the strongest mutants ruling over humankind has often brought him into conflict with Wolverine and the X-Men. Recently, a weakened Apocalypse was slain by his former servants, the Dark Riders, only to be resurrected by Genesis *(see Genesis).*

ARCADE

Arcade is a wealthy maniac who builds deadly amusement parks a.k.a. "Murderworlds." For a one million dollar charge, Arcade will lure any target into his Murderworld to face death.

Wolverine and the X-Men have faced a variety of Murderworlds and escaped. After killing his assistant for slashing his face, Arcade sought to frame Wolverine for this murder. Together, Wolverine and Gambit defeated Arcade and his ally, Mastermind II (the daughter of the original Mastermind), and proved Wolverine's innocence. Mastermind left Arcade in a permanent state of delusion.

The menacing mutant of mass mayhem known as Apocalypse

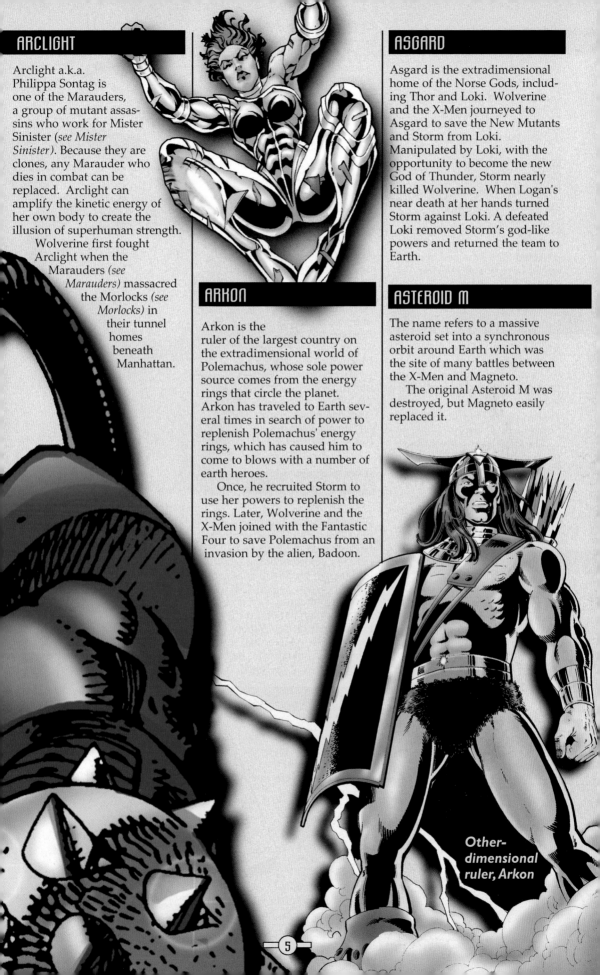

ARCLIGHT

Arclight a.k.a. Philippa Sontag is one of the Marauders, a group of mutant assassins who work for Mister Sinister (*see Mister Sinister*). Because they are clones, any Marauder who dies in combat can be replaced. Arclight can amplify the kinetic energy of her own body to create the illusion of superhuman strength.

Wolverine first fought Arclight when the Marauders (*see Marauders*) massacred the Morlocks (*see Morlocks*) in their tunnel homes beneath Manhattan.

ARKON

Arkon is the ruler of the largest country on the extradimensional world of Polemachus, whose sole power source comes from the energy rings that circle the planet. Arkon has traveled to Earth several times in search of power to replenish Polemachus' energy rings, which has caused him to come to blows with a number of earth heroes.

Once, he recruited Storm to use her powers to replenish the rings. Later, Wolverine and the X-Men joined with the Fantastic Four to save Polemachus from an invasion by the alien, Badoon.

ASGARD

Asgard is the extradimensional home of the Norse Gods, including Thor and Loki. Wolverine and the X-Men journeyed to Asgard to save the New Mutants and Storm from Loki. Manipulated by Loki, with the opportunity to become the new God of Thunder, Storm nearly killed Wolverine. When Logan's near death at her hands turned Storm against Loki. A defeated Loki removed Storm's god-like powers and returned the team to Earth.

ASTEROID M

The name refers to a massive asteroid set into a synchronous orbit around Earth which was the site of many battles between the X-Men and Magneto.

The original Asteroid M was destroyed, but Magneto easily replaced it.

Other-dimensional ruler, Arkon

AURORA

Jeanne-Marie Beaubier, like her twin brother Jean-Paul *(see Northstar)*, is a mutant with the ability to fly at incredible speeds and to generate incandescent bursts of light. Jeanne-Marie trained with James MacDonald Hudson at Department H. As Aurora, Jeanne-Marie became a founding member of Alpha Flight.

Ironically, one of Jeanne-Marie first missions was to capture Wolverine (the person that recruited her), who had abandoned Department H to join the X-Men.

AUSTRALIA

After their nationally televised "death" in Dallas *(see Adversary)*, Wolverine and the X-Men let the world believe they were dead. Their strategy was to gain a greater amount of freedom and the element of surprise.

The X-Men used the former headquarters of the Reavers *(see Reavers)*, a deserted town in the Australian outback, as their base. From there, the silent mutant Gateway could teleport them to any destination in the world.

AVALANCHE

Dominic Petros is a mutant who can generate powerful waves of vibration from his hands that create earthquake-like effects within a limited area.

Avalon--Magneto's former haven built partially from Cable's satellite Greymalkin

A member of the second Brotherhood of Evil Mutants, Avalanche first fought Wolverine and the X-Men during an assassination attempt on Senator Robert Kelly *(see Kelly, Senator Robert)*.

AVALON

Cable's massive, futuristic satellite, Greymalkin, was thought to be destroyed until Magneto restored a portion of the satellite for his own purposes. Magneto planned to use Avalon as a haven for mutants, a separate and sovereign nation for the homo-superior race. When Exodus fought Holocaust in Avalon, the fallout from their battle destroyed the satellite.

AVENGERS

As one of the Earth's foremost teams of super heroes, the Avengers were dedicated to protecting humanity against threats beyond the capability of conventional peacekeeping forces. Over the years the Avengers roster has featured some of the greatest heroes to walk the earth: from Captain America and Thor to the Vision and Iron Man Wolverine, both alone and with the X-Men, fought beside the heroic Avengers on many occasions.

AVENGERS ASSEMBLE!

BAMF

In a bedtime story Kitty Pryde (see Pryde, Kitty) told young Illyana Rasputin (while Wolverine and the X-Men listened at the door), Bamf was a tiny, cute, and very flirtatious version of Nightcrawler. Later, Nightcrawler traveled to an alternate dimension where Bamf and his race actually existed.

BANSHEE

Sean Cassidy is a mutant with a sonic scream that can easily shatter steel and which allows him to fly. Banshee, a former Interpol agent, was recruited to help Cyclops rescue the original X-Men from the menace of Krakoa (see Krakoa the Living Island).

Banshee is now the Headmaster of Xavier's School for Gifted Youngsters, home of Generation X (see Generation X).

BARAN, PRINCE

Prince Baran was the ruler of Madripoor (see Madripoor).

Baran was often involved in attempts on Wolverine's life. He staged the slaughter of Wolverine's friends at the Princess Bar. Soon, Baran found himself at Wolverine's mercy. While attempting to flee, Baran was shot.

BEAST

Dr. Henry "Hank" McCoy is one of the original X-Men. In contrast to his animal-like appearance and bestial agility, he is an erudite, well-read biochemist with a great love for Shakespeare.

After Magneto leeched the adamantium from Wolverine's skeleton, the Beast extensively catalogued the changes in Logan's physiology. Beast deduced that Wolverine was regressing into a more feral state because of the trauma caused by losing his adamantium (see Wolverine).

BELASCO

Belasco is a 13th century sorcerer who gained mystical power by making a pact with the extradimensional beings, the Elder Gods.

Exiled to the realm of Limbo, he battled and defeated the X-Men of an alternate Earth. Later, he fought the true X-Men and Wolverine in Limbo.

BEYONDER

Originally, the being known as the Beyonder was the collective whole of another universe dubbed the "Beyond-Realm." When the Beyonder discovered there were other universes he became curious and gathered many superhuman heroes and villains, including Wolverine, to fight a "Secret War." For the Secret War, the Beyonder created a "Battle World" in a distant galaxy. After the war, the X-Men teleported to Japan where Wolverine became guardian to Amiko (See Amiko).

Later, the Beyonder took on a physical form and came to Earth to study the nature of desire. Seeing the threat posed by the whimsical and omnipotent Beyonder, Wolverine and the other heroes of earth confronted the Beyonder. In the end, the Beyonder was destroyed by the Molecule Man while he was attempting to become mortal.

BINARY

While Logan worked in Canada's Department H, his contact in the American intelligence community was agent Carol Danvers, whom he nicknamed "Ace."

Years later, Danvers was genetically altered by a Kree called Captan Marvell and gained superpowers. She joined the Avengers as Ms. Marvel, until her powers and memories were absorbed by Rogue while she

was still a member of the Brotherhood of Evil Mutants. After this traumatic event, Danvers lived with the X-Men for a short time, but she had no memory of her prior relationship with Wolverine. Professor Xavier restored Danvers' memories, but he was unable to restore the emotional connections associated with them. When the X-Men were abducted by the alien Brood (*see Brood*), Danvers was exposed to energies that triggered her transformation into Binary. As Binary, Danvers helped Wolverine and the X-Men defeat the Brood. Presently, Binary is a member of the Starjammers (*see Starjammers*).

He asked to join the X-Men, who are considered legends in his era, to prevent an unknown "X-traitor" from destroying the team. Bishop, like Wolverine, is a warrior who is willing to take a life in combat. Since joining the X-Men, he has learned to control his killer instincts.

Wolverine returned at the request of Lucy Crim (*see Crim, Lucy*). Blackheart was once again thwarted and the town was returned to normal. Blackheart returned to his father's realm where he killed Mephisto.

Blackheart, ruling prince of Hell.

BLACKHEART

Blackheart was the son of Mephisto, ruler of Hell. Blackheart summoned Ghost Rider, The Punisher and Wolverine to the town of Christ's Crown to help him overthrow his father. The trio of heroes refused and defeated him.

Later, Blackheart returned to Christ's Crown and possessed the townspeople (*see Corrupt, The*). Punisher, Ghost Rider and

BISHOP

Born seventy years in the future, Bishop was a member of a mutant police force, the X.S.E. (Xavier's Security Enforcers).

Bishop has the mutant ability to absorb and rechannel projected energy, and is well trained in many forms of combat. Bishop came to the twentieth century in pursuit of the mutant villain, Fitzroy (*see Fitzroy*).

BLACK KING

Sebastian Shaw is a mutant who can absorb energy and metabolize it to enhance his own strength to superhuman levels. Shaw became known as the Black King, leader of the Inner Circle of the Hellfire Club (*see Hellfire Club*).

In its quest to achieve world domination through economic and political means, the Inner Circle often clashed with Wolverine and the X-Men. Shaw was believed to be dead, slain by his son Shinobi Shaw (*see Shaw, Shinobi*). He has since resurfaced, but has yet to reclaim his throne as leader of the Hellfire Club's Inner Circle.

BLACK QUEEN

The Black Queen of the Hellfire Club is a several millennia-old mutant External called Selene. As a member of the Inner Circle of the Hellfire Club and on her own, Selene has battled Wolverine and his allies often. Once, Wolverine nearly killed Rachel Summers *(see Phoenix II)* to stop her from making the mistake of murdering Selene in cold blood.

BLACK SHADOW

The Black Shadow was a destructive being of pure energy manifested by a mysterious schizophrenic mutant in China.

The Black Shadow destroyed everything in its path, only to be driven away each time by the White Shadow, another manifestation of the mutant's psychosis. The nameless mutant ended his madness by throwing his physical body onto Wolverine's claws, killing himself.

BLACK TOM

Thomas Samuel Eamon Cassidy is the older cousin of Sean Cassidy, the Banshee *(see Banshee)*.

Black Tom once used a wooden shillelagh (an Irish cane or club) to focus his mutant energy blasts.

However, to enhance his abilities, he implanted wood into his body to conduct his power directly. The results were disastrous. The wood within him has spread throughout his body like a cancer, and unless stopped, it will kill him.

Teamed with his partner in crime, Juggernaut *(see Juggernaut)*, Black Tom has clashed with Wolverine and the X-Men numerous times.

BLACK WIDOW

Natalia "Natasha" Alianovna Romanoff is a descendant of Russia's royal family. Logan first met Natasha in Madripoor in 1941, when he and a young Captain America *(see Captain America)* rescued her from Baron Wolfgang von Strucker and the secret organization, The Hand *(see Baron Wolfgang von Strucker & Hand, The)*. Natasha was later trained to be a field agent for the KGB.

As the Black Widow, Natasha is an accomplished martial artist and master of espionage. Eventually, she left the KGB to become one of the Avengers.

She and Wolverine have fought as allies often and have even faced The Hand's assassins together. To this day, the Black Widow still calls Wolverine "Little Uncle."

BLAZE, JOHNNY

Johnny Blaze was once a daredevil motorcycle performer who called upon the dark lord Mephisto to save a dying friend in exchange for his soul. Blaze was bonded with the demon Zarathos, creating the Ghost Rider. Many years later, Zarathos' soul was transferred to the Crystal of Souls, freeing Blaze of the curse.

Years later, for a short period, he joined Dr. Strange's Secret Defenders along with Wolverine, Spider-Woman II and Darkhawk to vanquish Dreadlox *(see Dreadlox)*.

BLOB

Once a circus performer, Fred J. Dukes decided his mutant powers would be more useful in a life of crime. The Blob is so massive and obese that he is virtually immovable and highly resilient. His epidermis has proven to be resistant to even Wolverine's adamantium claws.

Both on his own and as a member of the Second Brotherhood of Evil Mutants and Freedom Force *(see Freedom Force)*, Blob has often clashed with Wolverine.

BLOCKBUSTER

Blockbuster is the superhumanly strong powerhouse of the Marauders.

Blockbuster was killed during the massacre of the Morlocks. He and the other "dead" Marauders have since returned to life through the clones created with Mr. Sinister's *(see Mr. Sinister)* bioengineering technology.

Former Ghost Rider, Johnny Blaze

Vampyric villain Bloodscream

BRASS

Sean Watanabe is the son of martial arts instructor, Yuji Watanabe. After the death of his girl-friend at the hands of the Mandarin, Sean became Brass. Sean's vendetta brought him togeth-er with Wolverine and Ghost Rider in a battle against Mandarin's ser-vant, Deathwatch *(see Deathwatch)*.

BLOODSCREAM

In 1944, at the Battle of Normandy, the vampire known as Bloodscream first met Logan. Fifty years later, Bloodscream crossed paths with Logan in Madripoor.

With his partner, Roughouse, he had been hired by Prince Baron and General Coy to kill Tyger Tiger and Wolverine.

Seeking Wolverine's blood to cure himself of vampirism, Bloodscream joined with Cylla *(see Cylla)* to track Wolverine. Wolverine struck Bloodscream down with the Honor Sword of the Clan Yashida *(see Honor Sword of the Clan Yashida)*, a sword forged from a meteorite. Wolverine left Bloodscream for dead. However, Bloodscream lived and joined the androids Albert and Elsie Dee *(see Albert and Elsie Dee)* in a quest for Wolverine.

BLOOD SHADOW

Blood Shadow was the leader of The Coven. The Coven planned to take over the Temple of the Sun so they could usher in an "age of darkness." When Blood Shadow telepathically probed Wolverine, he trig-gered a berserker rage. This caused Wolverine to lose control and kill Blood Shadow.

BOKENGA, LIEUTENANT

Lt. Bokenga was the Head of Conglese Military Security for the African expedition on which the Punisher *(see Punisher)* and Wolverine stopped a group of gorilla poachers.

BOX

The original Box was the para-plegic Roger Bochs, who invent-ed the humanoid robot he jok-ingly nicknamed "Box" as a pun on his name. Bochs was able to phase into Box so that the robot's body became his own.

The Box robot is incredibly strong and is equipped with jets that enabled it to fly. Many dif-ferent people have taken the mantel of Box and because of their affiliation with Alpha Flight, they have fought beside Wolverine.

BRADDOCK, BRIAN

Also known as Captain Britain or Brittanic, Brian Braddock is one of England's greatest heroes.

A mutant possessed of incredible strength, resistance to injury, and the power of flight, Braddock is the twin brother of the X-Man called Psylocke *(see Psylocke)*. He is a founding member of Excalibur *(see Excalibur)*, and longtime ally of Wolverine.

BROOD

The Brood are an alien race with a hive mentality. Some Brood function as warriors, other as workers, and others as breeders. Though there are many Brood queens who command their own hives, the Empress of the Brood rules over the entire race.

The Brood procreate by implanting eggs into host bodies. Only the strongest of host bodies are worthy of the egg of a Brood Queen. The Brood have fought the X-Men and Wolverine many times *(see Acanti, Shi'ar Empire, Deathbird, Connover, Reverend William and Hannah)*.

BUSHWACKER

A former priest and CIA opera-tive, Bushwacker's right arm was bionically altered to function as a gun. Wolverine learned that Bushwacker was killing mutants whose low-level powers helped them to excel in the arts.

Daredevil *(see Daredevil)* and Wolverine fought Bushwacker and captured him. Wolverine was so enraged at Bushwacker's actions that Daredevil had to stop him from killing Bushwacker so that he could be turned over to the police.

CABLE

The man called Cable is Nathan Christopher Summers, also known as Nathan Dayspring, the Askani Son. The son of Cyclops and Madlyne Pryor, he was born in the present, but raised in the future.

Cable is a powerful warrior who is as comfortable using his futuristic weapons as he is with his psionic and telepathic powers.

A time-traveler, Cable spent several years as a mercenary in the time before Logan became Wolverine, where they met several times. What actually happened during those encounters has yet to be revealed, but the next time the two met in Madripoor it was obvious Wolverine had an intense dislike for Cable.

Time-travelling Cable

Wolverine and Cable fought side-by-side, but Wolverine still held his grudge for some time. During the battle in which the X-Men vanquished the threat of the Phalanx, Wolverine saw that Jean Grey *(see Grey, Jean)* cared deeply for Cable (she and Cyclops were displaced in time to raise Cable in the distant future). Out of his love for Jean, Logan chose to reconcile with Cable and they have been allies ever since.

CADRE

The aliens called the Cadre were almost successful in their attempt to take control of the Shi'ar Empire. The Cadre's leader called his people "Warskrulls." The Warskrulls' technology allowed them to mimic not only other people's forms, but their superhuman powers as well.

The Cadre replaced Professor Charles Xavier and used him to control Lilandra, Majestrix of the Shi'ar. When the X-Men came to rescue Professor Xavier, Wolverine sensed that the Xavier Warskrull was not the true Xavier and killed him. Wolverine, like several other X-Men, was captured and replaced with a Warskrull.

In the end, the X-Men defeated the Cadre and returned to Earth with Professor Xavier.

CALIBAN

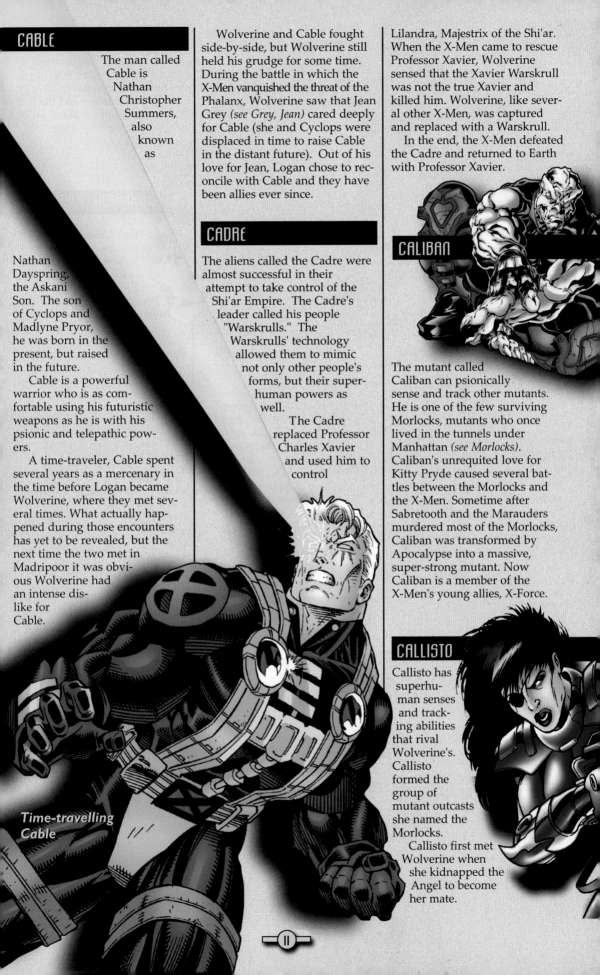

The mutant called Caliban can psionically sense and track other mutants. He is one of the few surviving Morlocks, mutants who once lived in the tunnels under Manhattan *(see Morlocks)*. Caliban's unrequited love for Kitty Pryde caused several battles between the Morlocks and the X-Men. Sometime after Sabretooth and the Marauders murdered most of the Morlocks, Caliban was transformed by Apocalypse into a massive, super-strong mutant. Now Caliban is a member of the X-Men's young allies, X-Force.

CALLISTO

Callisto has superhuman senses and tracking abilities that rival Wolverine's. Callisto formed the group of mutant outcasts she named the Morlocks.

Callisto first met Wolverine when she kidnapped the Angel to become her mate.

**Human "cannonball"
Sam Guthrie**

and can breathe on land or underwater. Ch'od is one of the Starjammers (*see Starjammers*), a team of space pirates who operate in the Shi'ar Galaxy.

The Starjammers and the X-Men are longtime allies, so Ch'od and Wolverine have fought together many times.

CHAMPION, IMUS

Imus Champion is a wealthy criminal whose body is deteriorating at a rapid rate. Champion hired the mercenary Le Peregrine to kidnap Lynx, whose blood contained the cure-all Panacea drug.

Wolverine, Champion, Le Peregrine, and the Black Widow freed Lynx, but Champion escaped.

CHAMPION OF THE UNIVERSE

The Champion of the Universe is one of the Elders of the Universe, who chose to perfect himself in the area of physical combat. The Champion is immortal, virtually invulnerable, and is stronger than even the Hulk.

Master of an untold number of fighting styles, the Champion came to Earth and kidnapped the strongest of the super heroes, so he could challenge them to a boxing match. When Colossus was taken, Wolverine and Cyclops attempted to rescue him. However, they could not penetrate the Champion's force field and had to watch helplessly as the Champion beat Colossus and Earth's other heroes.

CANNONBALL

Sam Guthrie has the power to fly at high speeds by generating a powerful blast of energy behind him and to generate a "blast field" that makes him invulnerable while flying. These powers earned Sam the name Cannonball.

As a founding member of the New Mutants, Cannonball received a great deal of training from Wolverine. This training served Sam well as deputy leader of X-Force. Sam is the first, and presently the only, member of the New Mutants to graduate to the X-Men. On one of his earliest missions as an X-Man, Cannonball helped save Wolverine from Genesis in a battle that left Wolverine in a regressed, feral state.

CAPTAIN AMERICA

The Avenger called Captain America was known as one of the world's greatest heroes. During World War II, Steve

Rogers was injected with the Super Soldier serum to become a symbol of the American dream, Captain America. Captain America and Logan first met in Madripoor in 1941. Together, they saved a young girl named Natasha Alianovna Romanoff (*see Black Widow*) from The Hand and Baron Wolfgang von Strucker.

Wolverine and Captain America have fought side-by-side against the likes of Dredmund Cromwell, Tess-One and the Overrider. In their last battle together, Wolverine and Captain America fought together against Onslaught (*see Onslaught*).

CH'OD

Ch'od is an amphibious Saurid from the planet Timor who possesses superhuman strength

CHANG

Chang was the Madripoor branch office expediter for Landau, Luckman and Lake *(see Landau, Luckman and Lake)*. Wolverine knew Chang from his secret agent days with Landau, Luckman and Lake and was one of the few people he called friend. Chang was killed by Bloodscream and Roughhouse *(see Bloodscream and Roughhouse)*.

CHARLIE

Wolverine's pet name Charlie is short for "Charlemagne." Charlie was a freelance intelligence operative during the Cold War. She was a close friend and lover to Logan before he became Wolverine.

Later, as Wolverine, he rescued Charlie from a KGB double-cross. Charlie disappeared, only to resurface many years later, murdering KGB operatives. She hoped her actions would bring Logan to kill her before the KGB could get to her. Instead, she attracted both Wolverine and Spider-Man to East Berlin.

Mortally wounded by Wolverine's claws, Charlie was accidentally killed by Spider Man *(see Spider-Man)*.

CHENEY, LILA

Lila Cheney is a popular rock musician who has the mutant power to teleport over interstellar distances. she has a rep-utation in several galaxies as a phenomenal musician and an even better thief.

When a group of Skrulls called the Cadre *(see Cadre, the)* infiltrated and took control of the Shi'ar Empire, Lila used her powers to transport Wolverine and the X-Men to the Shi'ar homeworld. There, they defeated the Skrulls, saving Lilandra, Professor Charles Xavier, and the entire Shi'ar Empire.

CHIEF EXAMINER

The Chief Examiner was a computerized construct that came to Earth to gather data on the powers of Earth's super heroes. Its purpose was to use those powers to create a champion who could defend his distant planet from destruction by an invading power.

Disrupted by Magneto's powers, the Chief Examiner attacked the X-Men and transformed Wolverine into stone. Magneto and Rogue defeated the Chief Examiner and restored it to normal operational status, saving Wolverine and returning him to human form.

CHIMERA

To gain information on Wolverine and his regressive state *(see Wolverine)*, Chimera killed almost an entire branch office of the multidimensional holding firm Landau, Luckman, and Lake *(see Landau, Luckman, and Lake)*. When confronted by Wolverine, she was forced to flee after being wounded in the battle.

CHROME

The Acolyte known as Chrome was with Fabian Cortez when Magneto's Acolytes were formed. Chrome fought against Wolverine and the X-Men in Genosha in the Acolytes' first battle. He died while saving Magneto during the destruction of Asteroid M.

CLAN DESTINE

The Clan Destine is a family of immortals all of whom have superhuman powers and are all the children of the invulnerable immortal, Adam Destine.

The X-Men and the Clan Destine once joined forces to fight the extradimensional demon called Synraith.

Wolverine and Adam met in battle and recognized each other. Adam and Wolverine each thought the other had been killed in the explosion of a mountain fortress many years ago.

Chimera, arch-nemesis of Landau, Luckman and Lake

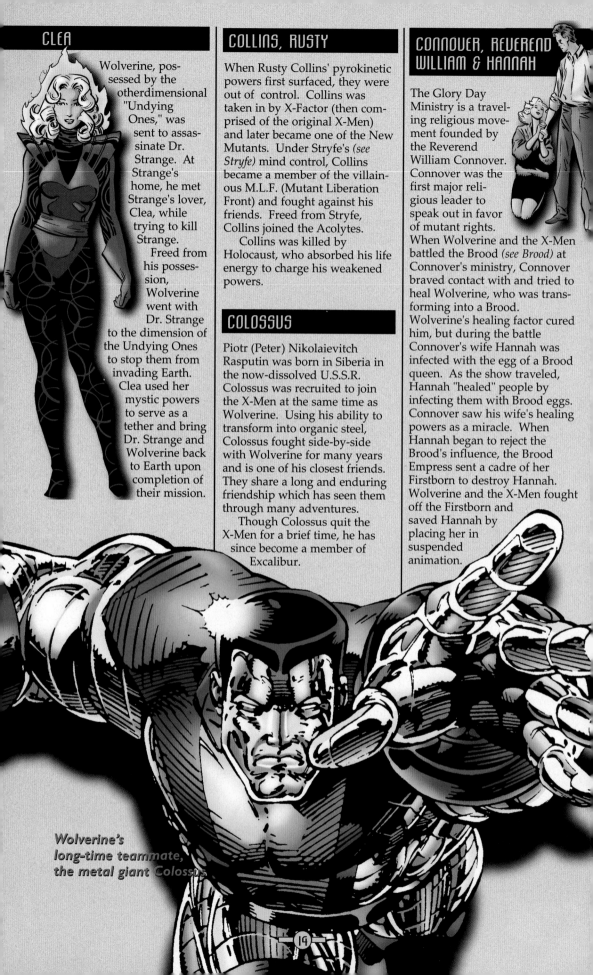

CLEA

Wolverine, possessed by the otherdimensional "Undying Ones," was sent to assassinate Dr. Strange. At Strange's home, he met Strange's lover, Clea, while trying to kill Strange.

Freed from his possession, Wolverine went with Dr. Strange to the dimension of the Undying Ones to stop them from invading Earth. Clea used her mystic powers to serve as a tether and bring Dr. Strange and Wolverine back to Earth upon completion of their mission.

COLLINS, RUSTY

When Rusty Collins' pyrokinetic powers first surfaced, they were out of control. Collins was taken in by X-Factor (then comprised of the original X-Men) and later became one of the New Mutants. Under Stryfe's *(see Stryfe)* mind control, Collins became a member of the villainous M.L.F. (Mutant Liberation Front) and fought against his friends. Freed from Stryfe, Collins joined the Acolytes.

Collins was killed by Holocaust, who absorbed his life energy to charge his weakened powers.

COLOSSUS

Piotr (Peter) Nikolaievitch Rasputin was born in Siberia in the now-dissolved U.S.S.R. Colossus was recruited to join the X-Men at the same time as Wolverine. Using his ability to transform into organic steel, Colossus fought side-by-side with Wolverine for many years and is one of his closest friends. They share a long and enduring friendship which has seen them through many adventures.

Though Colossus quit the X-Men for a brief time, he has since become a member of Excalibur.

CONNOVER, REVEREND WILLIAM & HANNAH

The Glory Day Ministry is a traveling religious movement founded by the Reverend William Connover. Connover was the first major religious leader to speak out in favor of mutant rights. When Wolverine and the X-Men battled the Brood *(see Brood)* at Connover's ministry, Connover braved contact with and tried to heal Wolverine, who was transforming into a Brood. Wolverine's healing factor cured him, but during the battle Connover's wife Hannah was infected with the egg of a Brood queen. As the show traveled, Hannah "healed" people by infecting them with Brood eggs. Connover saw his wife's healing powers as a miracle. When Hannah began to reject the Brood's influence, the Brood Empress sent a cadre of her Firstborn to destroy Hannah. Wolverine and the X-Men fought off the Firstborn and saved Hannah by placing her in suspended animation.

Wolverine's long-time teammate, the metal giant Colossus

COOPER, DR. VALERIE

As mutants and superhumans became more prevalent in society, Dr. Valerie Cooper chose to dedicate her political career to providing the United States government with some measure of control over these superhumans. Cooper became the chairperson of the Presidential Commission on Superhuman Activities and transformed the former Brotherhood of Evil Mutants into a government-sanctioned team, Freedom Force (see Freedom Force). Many of Freedom Force's missions brought them into conflict with Wolverine and the X-Men. The criminal members of Freedom Force proved too unreliable and the team lost its sanction. Cooper then worked with allies and former members of the X-Men to form the government-sanctioned mutant team, X-Factor (see X-Factor).

CORBEAU, DR. PETER

A longtime ally of the X-Men, Corbeau was working for NASA when Stephen Lang's Sentinels captured Wolverine, Banshee, and Jean Grey. Corbeau scheduled a space shuttle launch and smuggled the rest of the X-Men on board as his crew. Corbeau flew the X-Men to S.H.I.E.L.D.'s orbital platform, where they fought Lang and his Sentinels.

CORNELIUS, DR.

Dr. Cornelius was the medical specialist responsible for the Weapon X project that laced Wolverine's bones with adamantium. He was also responsible for the mental programming that wiped out most of Logan's memories (see Weapon X).

CORPORAL EBAMBE

Corporal Ebambe was a gorilla poacher who was in league with Norma Wyeth (see Wyeth, Norma). When Wolverine met the Punisher in Africa, they stopped Wyeth and Ebambe.

Wolverine left Ebambe wounded in the jungle, prey for the animals he once hunted.

CORRIGAN, ARCHIE

The proprietor of South Seas Skyways in Madripoor, Archie flew cargo for the crimelord Tyger Tiger.

Despite threats from rival crimelord General Coy, Archie remained loyal to Tyger and her friend, Wolverine. Archie and Wolverine destroyed one of General Coy's opium shipments, preventing Coy from taking over as the primary crimelord in Madripoor. Archie was clawed to death in the Princess Bar by assassins who had been hired by General Coy and Prince Baran (see General Coy and Prince Baran).

CORRUPT, THE

Citizens of the town known as Christ's Crown were called the Corrupt after Blackheart (see Blackheart) took possession of their minds.

CORSAIR

When the X-Men called Cyclops and Havok were only children, their father was taken by the mad Shi'ar Emperor D'Ken (see D'Ken). D'Ken killed their mother and made Major Christopher Summers a slave.

In the Shi'ar slave pits, Summers met a group of slaves who escaped with him to become the Starjammers. Calling himself Corsair after the legendary swashbucklers of Earth, Summers leads the Starjammers in acts of piracy against the Shi'ar Empire.

Corsair and Wolverine met when the X-Men and the Starjammers fought together against the Shi'ar Imperial Guard.

CORTEZ, FABIAN

When Magneto decided to separate himself from the problems of Earth, Fabian Cortez convinced him to fight for the rights of mutants. As a result, the Acolytes (see Acolytes) were formed.

Cortez has used his ability to amplify the powers of others beyond their control to fight Wolverine, the X-Men, and the Avengers. He was exiled from the Acolytes after he betrayed Magneto.

COUNT NEFARIA

The descendant of a long line of Italian noblemen, Count Lichino Nefaria built a powerful organization within the international crime syndicate known as the Maggia. With the help of his

Swashbuckling father of Cyclops and leader of the Starjammers, Corsair

Ani-Men *(see Ani-Men)*, Nefaria seized control of the North American Air Defense Command Center at Valhalla Mountain in Colorado. His plan to threaten every nation on Earth with America's nuclear arsenal was foiled by Wolverine and the X-Men.

COURIER

Courier was a German intelligence operative who used his power to generate bio-electric currents to serve his country until his country betrayed him.

Courier met Wolverine after German technology developed a Panacea drug that would cure all diseases, leaving the world hopelessly overpopulated. When the drug was injected into Lynx, Courier's mission was to bring her back to Germany. On his mission, Courier worked with Wolverine, Le Peregrine, and the Black Widow *(see Champion, Imus)*.

COY, GENERAL

Nguyen Ngoc Coy was a former general in the South Vietnamese army, who traveled to Madripoor in an attempt to seize control by killing its newest crimelord, Tyger Tiger. Wolverine, as Patch, protected Tyger from Coy and helped her cement her position as crimelord in Madripoor.

After a failed attempt to slay Wolverine, Coy and Prince Baran of Madripoor found themselves at Wolverine's mercy. Coy blamed the massacre of Wolverine's friends on Baran, then shot him in the head to

appease Wolverine. Coy was then shot by Tyger Tiger.

CRIM, LUCY

When her town was overtaken by Blackheart, Lucy Crim contacted Wolverine, Ghost Rider and Punisher telepathically for help. The heroes defeated Blackheart and the town of Christ's Crown was returned to normal *(see Christ's Crown and Corrupt, The, Blackheart)*.

CROMWELL, DREDMUND

The master of Druid magic known as Dredmund worked with Dr. Nightshade to artificially engineer a race of werewolves. The werewolf community was discovered by Captain America, Dr. Druid, and Wolverine. Attempts to transform Wolverine into a werewolf failed, but Dr. Nightshade did release his feral side and pit him against Captain America.

Dredmund and his allies were defeated by Wolverine, Captain America, and Dr. Druid.

CULLODEN, ZOE

Known as "The Expediter," Zoe Culloden handles Wolverine's account for the multidimensional firm, Landau, Luckman and Lake. Zoe was rescued from an orphanage in Bucharest by Chang and trained to be his successor.

Zoe and her partner, Noah, maintained constant surveillance on Wolverine to monitor his feral regression. Zoe manipulated the events leading up to Wolverine's encounter with Genesis to meet the hidden agenda of Landau, Luckman and Lake *(see Genesis, Chang, Landau, Luckman and Lake)*.

Zoe Culloden, account manager fo Landau, Luckman and Lake, a.k.a The Expediter

CYBER

Many years ago, Cyber and Wolverine had a falling out over a woman. This led to a confrontation in which Cyber did something so terrible to Logan that Wolverine has suppressed the memories. As a result, Wolverine has never revealed the true circumstances of his first meeting with Cyber.

Cyber had adamantium skin and razor-sharp claws at the tips of his fingers, which were coated with a powerful hallucinogen.

Cyber faced Wolverine in his attempt to take over Madripoor's criminal underground. This plan failed when Wolverine gouged out Cyber's left eye and dropped him into a truck filled with his hallucinogenic drug, which merged with his bio-system, causing him to drift between reality and hallucinations.

Much later, Cyber tracked down Wolverine to steal Wolverine's adamantium skeleton. Realizing that Wolverine no longer had an adamantium skeleton, Cyber snapped off the bone claws on Wolverine's right hand. Much later, the Dark Riders took Cyber to Genesis, who killed Cyber so that he could use Cyber's adamantium skin to restore Wolverine's skeleton.

X-Men's leading man, Cyclops

CYCLOPS

Scott Summers was the first member of the original team of X-Men. As Cyclops, he can convert solar energy into "optic blasts," powerful beams of concussive energy that he releases from his eyes.

When the original X-Men were captured by Krakoa the Living Island *(see Krakoa the Living Island)*, Cyclops led Wolverine and the new X-Men on a rescue mission. At this time, Wolverine had little control over his violent nature and often clashed with Cyclops.

Their relationship was further strained by Wolverine's romantic feelings for Cyclops' longtime girlfriend (and now wife), Jean Grey *(see Grey, Jean)*. However, over their many years as teammates, Cyclops and Wolverine have set aside their differences to become close friends.

CYLLA

A cyborg created by Donald Pierce *(see White King)*, Cylla was built to destroy Wolverine. Formerly a pilot, Cylla Markham became a cyborg after her body was badly injured and left crippled. Of course, Cylla never managed to fulfill her quest to murder Wolverine.

Betrayed by her "ally" Bloodscream *(see Bloodscream)*, Cylla died to feed Bloodscream's vampiric need for life energy.

CYPHER

Douglas Ramsey was a member of the New Mutants with the power to translate and speak any language. Though he received some physical training from Wolverine, Cypher rarely participated in intensive combat training.

Doug Ramsey sacrificed his life in battle saving the life of his teammate, Wolfsbane. Cypher's body was later used as part of the template for the Phalanx (see Phalanx) created being called Douglock.

D'ALEXIS, AMBER

Amber D'Alexis was the lover of both Jake Fury, the original Scorpio, and his brother Nick Fury. After Jake's suicide, Amber trained her son, Mikel, to kill Nick Fury because she blamed him for Jake's death.

Wolverine had to kill Amber when she attempted to shoot Mikel and Nick (*see Fury, Nick*).

D'KEN

When D'Ken's older sister, Deathbird, was denied her birthright to the throne of the Shi'ar Empire, D'Ken became Emperor.

D'Ken was insane and tried to use the power of the M'Kraan Crystal to his own ends. Knowing that the power of the crystal, once unleashed, would destroy the entire universe, D'Ken's younger sister, Lilandra, decided to stop him. The X-Men aided her and managed to save the universe from destruction. Lilandra became Majestrix, ruling the Shi'ar Empire in D'Ken's place.

DAI-KOMO

Dai-Komo was a Yakuza drug lord who created a highly addictive drug called Thunderbolt. Thunderbolt gave superhuman strength and euphoria to its user, followed by death.

Thunderbolt-charged assassins nearly killed Wolverine, but he survived to hunt down Dai-Komo. When Wolverine found him, Dai-Komo had already been slain by the rogue assassin, Reiko (*see Reiko*).

DAREDEVIL

Daredevil is actually a blind lawyer named Matt Murdock. Daredevil was trained in combat by the mysterious man called Stick. Daredevil's enhanced senses rival those of Wolverine.

Wolverine and Daredevil first met on the trail of Lord Dark-Wind (*see Lord DarkWind*), whose adamantium bonding process gave Daredevil's foe, Bullseye, an adamantium spine.

From the beginning, Daredevil was uneasy with Wolverine's ferocity and willingness to kill in battle. When they faced the mutant-killing mercenary called Bushwacker (*see Bushwacker*), Daredevil twice stopped Wolverine from killing their enemy.

DARKHAWK

Chris Powell is a high school student whose mysterious amulet transforms him into Darkhawk.

Darkhawk's armor is bulletproof, enhances his strength, allows him to fly and to fire energy blasts. Darkhawk and Wolverine fought together as Secret Defenders (*see Secret Defenders*) against the forces of Macabre.

Blind lawyer turned super-hero, Daredevil

DARKSTAR

Laynia Petrovna and her twin brother Nicolai Krylenko (see Vanguard) both served the U.S.S.R. as members of the Soviet Super Soldiers. A former member of the Champions of Los Angeles, Darkstar can manipulate the extradimensional energy called the Darkforce to fly, teleport and create objects of solid Darkforce energy.

Though she and the Soviet Super Soldiers have occasionally been manipulated to fight against Wolverine and the X-Men, their common bond as mutants has more often made them allies.

DARK RIDERS

The original Dark Riders were Inhumans gathered by Apocalypse to aid him in his quest for a world in which only the strong survive. Wolverine has fought several different variations of the Dark Riders under the leadership of Apocalypse, Stryfe, and finally Genesis.

After Genesis' machinations left Wolverine in a feral state, Wolverine killed many of the Dark Riders.

DAZZLER

Alison Blaire, taking the stage name Dazzler, used her mutant powers to create a fantastic light show to accompany her music. Dazzler first met Wolverine when the X-Men rescued her from agents of the Hellfire Club (see Hellfire Club).

Eventually, Dazzler became one of the X-Men and fought alongside Wolverine and the rest of the team. Dazzler left the team with Longshot (see Longshot) to help him battle tyranny in his native dimension, the Mojoverse (see Mojo).

DEATHBIRD

Deathbird was the firstborn of the ruling family of the Shi'ar Empire. Unlike most Shi'ar, Deathbird is an evolutionary throwback who retained many of her avian qualities, including functional wings. Because she was exiled as a criminal, Deathbird's place on the throne of the Empire went to her brother D'Ken (see D'Ken).

On Earth, Deathbird and her allies, the Brood (see Brood), fought Wolverine and the X-Men. After Lilandra took D'Ken's place as the ruler of the Shi'ar, Deathbird forged an alliance with the alien Badoon and Brood, usurping control of the Shi'ar Empire.

The Cadre (see Cadre), a group of Skrulls who used technology to mimic superhuman powers as well as forms, took control of Professor Xavier and Lilandra. With the Cadre's help, Lilandra took the throne from Deathbird so that the Cadre could control the Shi'ar Empire. With the help of Wolverine and the X-Men, Deathbird defeated the Cadre. Deathbird left the Shi'ar Empire to Lilandra, apparently happy to abdicate the throne she had fought so hard to obtain.

DEATHLOK

The cyborg known as Deathlok encountered Wolverine when they battled a duplicate robot of Dr. Doom called the MechaDoom.

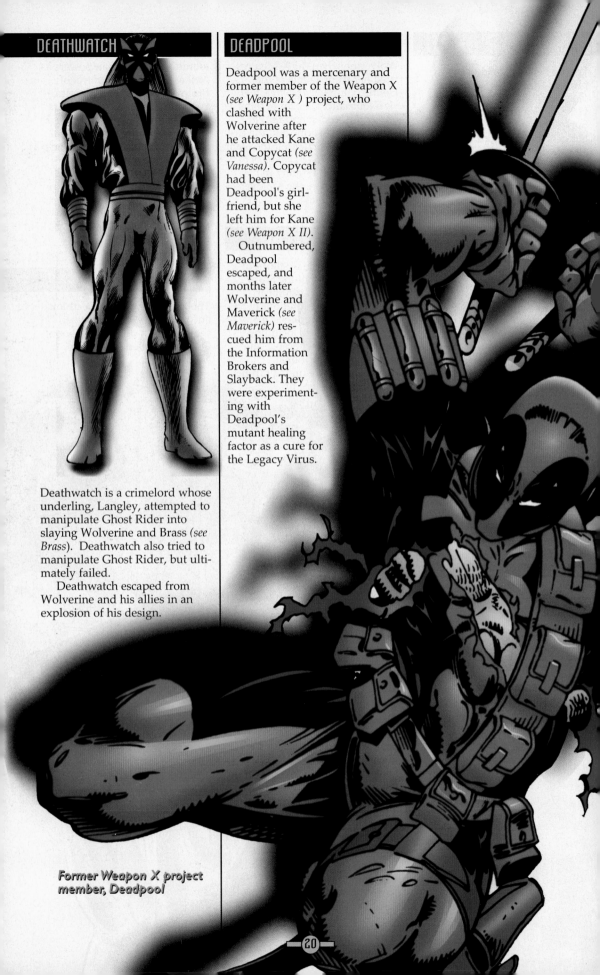

DEATHWATCH

Deathwatch is a crimelord whose underling, Langley, attempted to manipulate Ghost Rider into slaying Wolverine and Brass (*see Brass*). Deathwatch also tried to manipulate Ghost Rider, but ultimately failed.

Deathwatch escaped from Wolverine and his allies in an explosion of his design.

DEADPOOL

Deadpool was a mercenary and former member of the Weapon X (*see Weapon X*) project, who clashed with Wolverine after he attacked Kane and Copycat (*see Vanessa*). Copycat had been Deadpool's girl-friend, but she left him for Kane (*see Weapon X II*).

Outnumbered, Deadpool escaped, and months later Wolverine and Maverick (*see Maverick*) rescued him from the Information Brokers and Slayback. They were experimenting with Deadpool's mutant healing factor as a cure for the Legacy Virus.

Former Weapon X project member, Deadpool

DECIMATOR

When Wolverine worked with the Secret Defenders (*see Secret Defenders*), he fought Decimator. Decimator was one of the henchmen for Macabre (*see Macabre*).

DEPARTMENT H

The Canadian Prime Minister worked with James MacDonald Hudson (*see Guardian I*) to create Department H, a secret research and development division of the Ministry of Defense. Department H resources were used to rehabilitate Logan after his skeleton was laced with adamantium. Department H also funded the creation of Alpha Flight (*see Alpha Flight*).

When Wolverine left Canada to become an X-Man, Department H once sent Weapon Alpha (who later became Guardian), and then all of Alpha Flight, to retrieve Wolverine. Recently, Department H was closed down when funding was cut off, leaving Alpha Flight to work independently from the government.

DER JARRMACHT

Before Nightcrawler joined the X-Men, he was a member of the German traveling circus, Der Jarrmacht.

Years later when Nightcrawler returned to Germany, his friends claimed to be having trouble with monsters who roamed the area. Together, Wolverine and Nightcrawler learned that there was a clan of monsters, the Neuri, living in disguise among the villagers. Der Jarrmacht had themselves genetically altered so that they could destroy the monsters. Because the Neuri were pacifists, Nightcrawler and Wolverine fought to defend them from Der Jarrmacht.

In the end, the Neuri allowed themselves to be slain so that they would no longer have to live among people who feared and hated them.

DESTINY

Though blind, Irene Adler could psionically see the future. Destiny was Mystique's closest friend and helped her create the second Brotherhood of Evil Mutants. When the Brotherhood gained the sanction of the United States government and became Freedom Force (*see Freedom Force*), Destiny remained a member.

Though Destiny was later murdered by Professor Charles Xavier's son, Legion, she used her powers to save the life of Forge (*see Forge*) from Legion.

DIAMOND LIL

Lillian Crawley is virtually impervious to harm with diamond-hard skin. As a Gamma Flight trainee, Diamond Lil was trained by Canada's Department H. Lil became a member of Omega Flight and fought against Alpha Flight in the battle that left James MacDonald Hudson apparently dead (*see Guardian I*).

Diamond Lil later reformed and became a member of Alpha Flight.

DIRT NAP

Dirt Nap has the power to absorb other living beings and take their forms. Dirt Nap tried to absorb Wolverine, but could not metabolize him because of his mutant healing factor. Dirt Nap fled from Wolverine by taking the form of a rat.

Dirt Nap is the only Dark Rider (*see Dark Riders*) to survive Wolverine's feral regression at the hand of Genesis (*see Genesis*).

DOC SAMSON

Dr. Leonard Samson was transformed by gamma radiation into a superstrong, invulnerable, green-haired psychiatrist.

Doc Samson has little desire to be a super hero and has used his strength primarily in his efforts to cure the Hulk (*see Hulk*). However, Doc Samson and Wolverine once worked together to stop an alien invasion from entering Earth through a teleportation gateway.

Samson serves as psychiatric counsel to the government-sanctioned mutant team, X-Factor (*see X-Factor*).

DOMINO

Domino is a mutant whose power causes things to "fall into place" for her, presumably through some psionic manipulation of probability fields. Domino worked as a mercenary for many years and is an expert in sharpshooting and hand-to-hand combat.

As a member of X-Force (*see X-Force*), Domino has fought beside Wolverine many times.

DRACULA

Wolverine and the X-Men fought the legendary vampire Count Dracula when he took Storm as his consort against her will. However, Storm's transformation into a vampire could not be completed, as she refused to take a human life. Rejected, Dracula relinquished his hold on Storm.

Later, Dracula made Rachel Van Helsing, the last descendant of his ancient enemy, Abraham Van Helsing, his consort. Dracula then abducted Storm, hoping her skills as a thief would allow her to steal and destroy the Darkhold, a mystical book containing a spell that kills vampires.

The X-Men defeated Dracula, but Rachel Van Helsing was still a vampire. At her request, Wolverine killed Rachel with a wooden stake. Dracula was destroyed by Dr. Strange using the Darkhold.

Crazed with delusions of world domination, the devious Dr. Doom

DR. DOOM

Ruler of the small Balkan nation of Latveria, Dr. Victor Von Doom has proved relentless in his quest to rule the world. Doom's lust for power has brought him into conflict with many of Earth's heroes, including Wolverine and the X-Men.

Several times, Dr. Doom has allied himself with Earth's heroes against common enemies, but he has ultimately served only his own agenda. Doom was apparently killed in the battle with Onslaught *(see Onslaught)*, forced against his will to sacrifice his life. The sacrifice helped save the world he had always longed to rule.

DREADLOX

In service to Macabre (see Macabre), Dreadlox used her power to make people see visions of their worst nightmares. Dreadlox and her teammates were defeated by Wolverine on the first mission of the Secret Defenders (see Secret Defenders).

DR. NEUTRON

When Wolverine and Havok (see Havok) vacationed together in Mexico, Dr. Neutron's minions attacked them. Neutron's plan was to manipulate Havok into using his powers to supercharge General Meltdown's (see General Meltdown) to his fullest potential.

Dr. Neutron failed, but he, unlike his allies General Meltdown and Skarlett MacKenzie, survived.

DR. STRANGE

Dr. Stephen Strange is the Sorcerer Supreme of Earth's dimension and its protector against all mystical threats. Dr. Strange has aided Wolverine and the X-Men against a variety of supernatural dangers.

Once, Wolverine nearly killed Dr. Strange while possessed by the otherdimensional Undying Ones (see Undying Ones). Wolverine and Archangel followed Gomurr the Ancient and Dr. Strange on their quest to save Psylocke. Dr. Strange also recruited Wolverine as a "Secret Defender" to help defeat Dreadlox and Macabre.

Earth's Supreme Sorcerer, the mysterious Dr. Strange

EEL

The Eel was a mercenary whose battle suit generated powerful blasts of electricity.

Before Alpha Flight (see Alpha Flight) was fully formed, Wolverine led a team of potential members and trainees into battle against Eel and his companions. Eel and other criminals were hired by Egghead in an extortion plan that threatened New York City with nuclear annihilation. Eel and the others were defeated.

The electrifying Eel—one of the first opponents of the early roster of Alpha Flight

EGGHEAD

Early in his career, the criminal mastermind Egghead threatened to use a nuclear missile to destroy New York City. Egghead had hired several costumed criminals to protect the missile, which was to be launched from Canadian soil.

Though the Alpha Flight team was not yet fully formed, Wolverine led the trainees into battle against Egghead and his men. Wolverine and the early version of Alpha Flight managed to foil Egghead's plan.

ELECTRON

A member of the Royal Elite of the Shi'ar Imperial Guard, Electron served the ruling power of the Shi'ar Empire (see Lilandra, D'Ken & Shi'ar Empire).

ELEKTRA

Elektra was the former lover of Daredevil (see Daredevil) and an assassin who was killed by Bullseye. She was resurrected by The Hand, a secret organization to which she formerly belonged (see Hand, The).

Taught by the same clan that taught Daredevil his fighting skills, Elektra tries to pass her skills to Wolverine. She is trying to teach these mystic arts to him in the hope that it will bring him back his humanity and subdue his bestial urges.

ELSIE DEE

(See Albert).

EPSILON RED

Epsilon Red was a genetically altered astronaut whom Wolverine was sent to assassinate in his days as a CIA operative. Those orders were canceled, and the team withdrew before completing the mission.

In the present, Epsilon Red helped Wolverine clear up some of his past.

ERIC THE RED

Erik the Red was a member of the Shi'ar who attempted to kill Charles Xavier with the help of a brainwashed Havok and Polaris.

After Erik was defeated and Havok and Polaris freed, the X-Men next encountered Eric The Red when he assisted D'Ken in overthrowing Lilandra. When Lilandra sought refuge with the X-Men, Erik convinced Firelord (see Firelord) to attack the team while he retrieved Lilandra. After returning her to D'Ken, Erik escaped when the X-Men defeated D'Ken (see D'Ken).

EXCALIBUR

Excalibur is a group of mutants operating from Xavier's Muir Island facility. Three of Excalibur's members, Nightcrawler, Shadowcat and Colossus, were former teammates of Wolverine's.

Anytime the need arises, they are willing to give each other a hand. Recently they helped the X-Men in defeating the technobeings known as the Phalanx (see

Phalanx).

Members include Captain Britain, Megan, Phoenix II, Nightcrawler, Shadowcat, Colossus, Wisdom and Widget. (see Nightcrawler, Pryde, Kitty, Colossus, Phoenix II, Brian Braddock).

EXODUS

Exodus was Magneto's right-hand man in the Acolytes (see Acolytes). After a fierce battle with the X-teams, Charles Xavier (see Xavier, Charles) mind-wiped Magneto. Exodus then became the self-proclaimed voice of the comatose Magneto (see Magneto).

Exodus, faithful follower of Magneto's dream of mutant superiority.

EXPEDITER, THE

The title of Expediter has been used by Johnny Wraith, Carlysle Kestrel and Zoe Culloden. All were agents or expediters of the inter-reality firm of Landau, Luckman and Lake (see Landau, Luckman & Lake) this firm's agents were used for surveillance and rescue missions. (See Culloden, Zoe, Chang, Wraith, Johnny)

FAMINE

Apocalypse transformed a young, anorexic girl, Autumn Rolfson into one of his Four Horsemen. She used her power to turn organic matter into dust to serve Apocalypse's will. She and the Horsemen have fought Wolverine and the X-Men many times. Wolverine has battled her and the other Horsemen with the X-Men.

FANG

Fang joined the Imperial Guardsmen of the Shi'ar Empire under the rule of Emperor D'Ken (see D'Ken). D'Ken used the Guard to defeat the X-Men, who had come to the aid of the exiled leader, Lilandra. Fang was later killed when he was implanted by the Brood (see Brood). Fang proved a worthy opponent in his clash with Wolverine.

FANTASTIC FOUR

The superhero team known as Fantastic Four, comprised of Mr. Fantastic, Invisible Woman, Human Torch and the Thing,

fought alongside Wolverine during the various Infinity crusades.

Later a fugitive Skrull named De'Lila (see Skrull) overtook the team and supposedly killed them in her quest for a techno egg. Disguised as the Invisible Woman, she enlisted Wolverine, Ghost Rider, Hulk and Spider-Man to become the new Fantastic Four soon after, the heroes caught onto her scheme and defeated her, saving the original FF.

FENRIS

Andrea and Andreas Strucker are the twin children of the Nazi war criminal Baron Wolfgang von Strucker (see Strucker, Baron Von). When the siblings hold hands, they are able to generate powerful blasts of energy.

Endowed by their father with super powers, Fenris fought Wolverine and the X-Men when they attempted to kill Magneto while he was on trial before the World Court. Since then, Fenris has returned several times to battle the X-Men.

FERAL

The mutant known as Feral and her team X-Force were captured by Wolverine after it appeared that X-Force team leader, Cable, was responsible for the attempted assassination of Charles Xavier. When Cable was cleared of the charges X-Force was released.

Recently Feral left X-Force and is currently wanted for questioning by the government for murder.

Feline mutant and former X-Force member, Feral

FIRELORD

Firelord, a former herald of Galactus was convinced by Erik the Red (*see Erik the Red*) that the X-Men were harboring a fugitive of the Shi'Ar Empire.

After being defeated by the Phoenix, Firelord realized he was being used as pawn by Erik the Red, who kidnapped Lilandra while he battled. When the other X-men returned from vanquishing D'Ken, Firelord apologized for attacking them.

FIRESTAR

Firestar was recruited by the White Queen's Massachusetts Academy and became a member of the Hellions (*see Hellions*). Unknowingly, she had also become a pawn of Thunderbird II and fought with the X-Men. After the Hellions were killed (*see Fitzroy*), she left to join The New Warriors.

FETISH

Fetish was a member of The Coven who fought Wolverine on the island of Koma Koi (*see Koma Koi*).

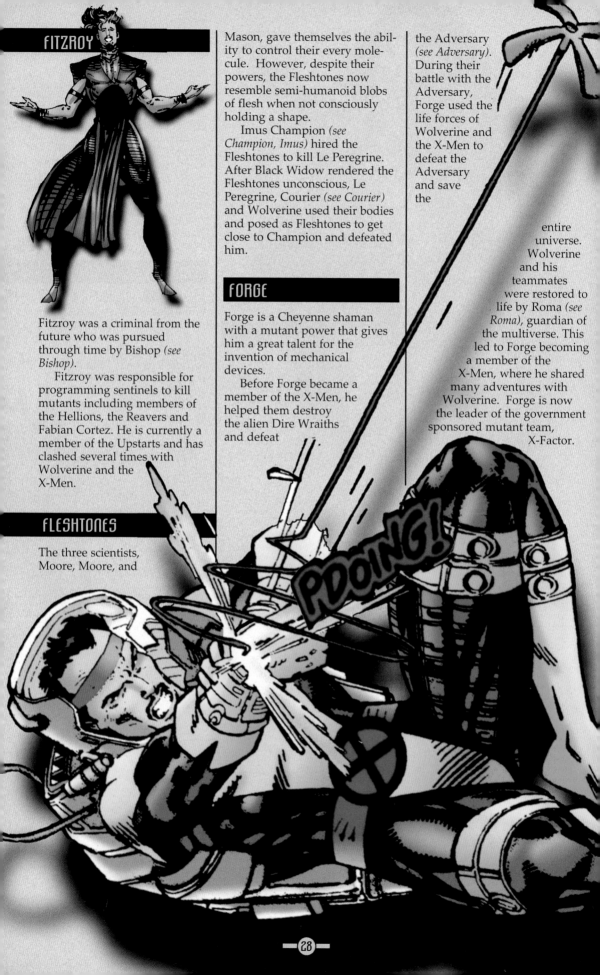

FITZROY

Fitzroy was a criminal from the future who was pursued through time by Bishop *(see Bishop)*.

Fitzroy was responsible for programming sentinels to kill mutants including members of the Hellions, the Reavers and Fabian Cortez. He is currently a member of the Upstarts and has clashed several times with Wolverine and the X-Men.

FLESHTONES

The three scientists, Moore, Moore, and Mason, gave themselves the ability to control their every molecule. However, despite their powers, the Fleshtones now resemble semi-humanoid blobs of flesh when not consciously holding a shape.

Imus Champion *(see Champion, Imus)* hired the Fleshtones to kill Le Peregrine. After Black Widow rendered the Fleshtones unconscious, Le Peregrine, Courier *(see Courier)* and Wolverine used their bodies and posed as Fleshtones to get close to Champion and defeated him.

FORGE

Forge is a Cheyenne shaman with a mutant power that gives him a great talent for the invention of mechanical devices.

Before Forge became a member of the X-Men, he helped them destroy the alien Dire Wraiths and defeat the Adversary *(see Adversary).* During their battle with the Adversary, Forge used the life forces of Wolverine and the X-Men to defeat the Adversary and save the entire universe. Wolverine and his teammates were restored to life by Roma *(see Roma),* guardian of the multiverse. This led to Forge becoming a member of the X-Men, where he shared many adventures with Wolverine. Forge is now the leader of the government sponsored mutant team, X-Factor.

PDOING!

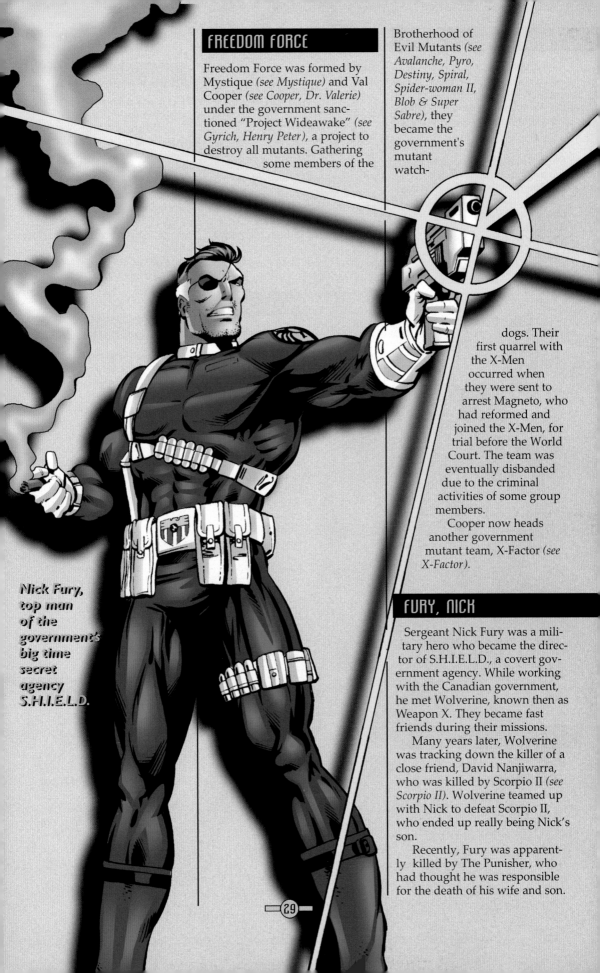

FREEDOM FORCE

Freedom Force was formed by Mystique *(see Mystique)* and Val Cooper *(see Cooper, Dr. Valerie)* under the government sanctioned "Project Wideawake" *(see Gyrich, Henry Peter)*, a project to destroy all mutants. Gathering some members of the Brotherhood of Evil Mutants *(see Avalanche, Pyro, Destiny, Spiral, Spider-woman II, Blob & Super Sabre),* they became the government's mutant watch-dogs. Their first quarrel with the X-Men occurred when they were sent to arrest Magneto, who had reformed and joined the X-Men, for trial before the World Court. The team was eventually disbanded due to the criminal activities of some group members.

Cooper now heads another government mutant team, X-Factor *(see X-Factor).*

Nick Fury, top man of the government's big time secret agency S.H.I.E.L.D.

FURY, NICK

Sergeant Nick Fury was a military hero who became the director of S.H.I.E.L.D., a covert government agency. While working with the Canadian government, he met Wolverine, known then as Weapon X. They became fast friends during their missions.

Many years later, Wolverine was tracking down the killer of a close friend, David Nanjiwarra, who was killed by Scorpio II *(see Scorpio II).* Wolverine teamed up with Nick to defeat Scorpio II, who ended up really being Nick's son.

Recently, Fury was apparently killed by The Punisher, who had thought he was responsible for the death of his wife and son.

GAMBIT

Remy LeBeau is a Cajun-born mutant who grew up in the New Orleans' Thieves Clan. Gambit, like Wolverine, has a long history with Sabretooth, none of it good.

Together, Gambit and Wolverine faced Arcade and Mastermind II (the daughter of the original Mastermind) in London (see Arcade). Gambit has used his mutant power to charge objects with kinetic energy to fight often alongside Wolverine. Gambit is also well known at Logan's favorite hangout, the Princess Bar (see Princess Bar) in Madripoor (see Madripoor).

GARNOFF, FATHER ALEX

Father Alex Garnoff is a member of the Soviet Super Soldiers (see Soviet Super Soldiers) who traveled with Darkstar (see Darkstar) to Siberia to investigate a series of strange occurrences. Upon their arrival, they were attacked by the Skinner of Souls (see Skinner of Souls), who then wiped their minds clean and imprisoned them.

Colossus, Wolverine, Psylocke and Iceman happened to be nearby and defeated the Skinner of Souls, freeing Garnoff and Darkstar.

GATEWAY

The aborigine called Gateway can create teleportation portals capable of transporting people through space, time, and between dimensions.

The X-Men befriended Gateway while in the Australian (see Australia) outback. While they lived in Australia, Gateway teleported the X-Men to whatever destination they wished. He also teleported Wolverine to Madripoor, where Logan became known as Patch. Though he almost never speaks and has revealed little about himself, Gateway has been an important ally to Wolverine. Gateway presently lives at Professor Xavier's School for Gifted Youngsters, home to

GAMESMASTER

The Gamesmaster is an omnipath who formed the group of villains known as the Upstarts. The Upstarts participated in the Gamesmaster's twisted contest in which they accumulated points for killing mutants. The winner would become the leader of the team.

The Gamesmaster's game had far-reaching effects on the X-Men.

Generation X.

GEIST

Geist was a scientist who worked for the Nazis during World War II. Sustained by a cybernetic body, Geist was hired by the small country of Terra Verde to create a super hero for them. Geist experimented on an unwilling Roughouse (see Roughouse) with a special form of cocaine that made its user stronger than any human.

Wolverine, who was seeking to free Roughouse, defeated Geist.

GENOSHA

Genosha is an island nation located in the Indian Ocean, east of Africa.

For many years, Genosha enjoyed economic wealth by using mutants as slave labor. That all changed when the X-Men with the help of Jennifer Ransome and Philip Moreau overthrew the Genoshan government. In the aftermath, Wolverine pledged that if Philip Moreau could not end Genoshan slavery peacefully, he and the X-Men would return to dismantle the Genoshan government by force. Since then, Wolverine and the X-Men have returned to Genosha several times, fighting the likes of Cameron Hodge (see Hodge, Cameron) and also the Acolytes (see Acolytes).

GENERAL MELTDOWN

The Russian General Meltdown and his ally, Dr. Neutron, planned to use Havok to charge Meltdown to his fullest potential. Neutron's men attacked Wolverine and Havok on their Mexican vacation and manipulated the heroes into fighting against each other. However, Havok and Wolverine worked together to destroy General Meltdown and avert nuclear disaster.

GENE NATION

Wolverine and the X-Men believed the Morlocks were dead when Mikhail Rasputin (*see Rasputin, Mikhail*) apparently committed suicide and took them all with him. However, Mikhail transported the Morlocks to another dimension where time flowed more quickly than on Earth.

The children of the Morlocks were angry at having been exiled from Earth and returned seeking vengeance on the human race as the Gene Nation.

Wolverine and the X-Men stopped Gene Nation, but only at the cost of their leader Marrow's life. Members include: Hemingway, Marrow, Sack, Reverb and Vessel.

GENERATION X

Generation X are the newest and youngest students of Professor Charles Xavier's dream of peaceful mutant/human coexistence. At Xavier's School for Gifted Youngsters (formerly Xavier's Massachusetts Academy), the students study a conventional curriculum as they learn to control their mutant powers. The students (Chamber, Husk, Jubilee, Monet St. Croix, Mondo, Penance, Skin & Synch) are overseen by Banshee (*see Banshee*) and White Queen (*see White Queen*).

Wolverine has visited the school as a guest lecturer on fighting skills and is a close friend of Jubilee (*see Jubilee*).

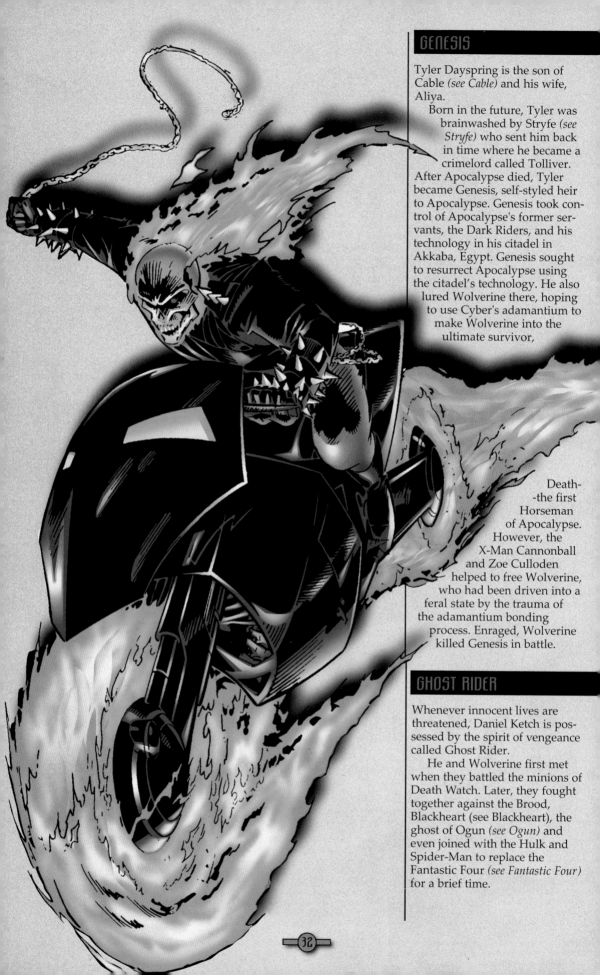

GENESIS

Tyler Dayspring is the son of Cable (*see Cable*) and his wife, Aliya.

Born in the future, Tyler was brainwashed by Stryfe (*see Stryfe*) who sent him back in time where he became a crimelord called Tolliver. After Apocalypse died, Tyler became Genesis, self-styled heir to Apocalypse. Genesis took control of Apocalypse's former servants, the Dark Riders, and his technology in his citadel in Akkaba, Egypt. Genesis sought to resurrect Apocalypse using the citadel's technology. He also lured Wolverine there, hoping to use Cyber's adamantium to make Wolverine into the ultimate survivor,

Death--the first Horseman of Apocalypse. However, the X-Man Cannonball and Zoe Culloden helped to free Wolverine, who had been driven into a feral state by the trauma of the adamantium bonding process. Enraged, Wolverine killed Genesis in battle.

GHOST RIDER

Whenever innocent lives are threatened, Daniel Ketch is possessed by the spirit of vengeance called Ghost Rider.

He and Wolverine first met when they battled the minions of Death Watch. Later, they fought together against the Brood, Blackheart (see Blackheart), the ghost of Ogun (*see Ogun*) and even joined with the Hulk and Spider-Man to replace the Fantastic Four (*see Fantastic Four*) for a brief time.

Jean Grey, a woman who always has a place in Logan's heart

GLADIATOR

Gladiator is the Praetor (leader) of the Shi'ar Imperial Guard. The Imperial Guard's members come from various planets in the Shi'ar Empire *(see Shi'ar Empire)* and are an elite force who serve and protect the ruler of the Empire.

By far the most powerful member of the Guard, Gladiator can fly, is superhumanly strong, resistant to injury and can generate intense heat beams from his eyes. Gladiator and the Imperial Guard first fought the X-Men on the orders of the mad Emperor D'Ken. D'Ken was replaced by Majestrix Lilandra Neramani, an ally of the X-Men and Professor Charles

Xavier's lover. When Lilandra decided to take action against the threat of the Phoenix, the X-Men opposed her. The matter was to be decided in a trial by combat, and the Imperial Guard again fought Wolverine and the X-Men. Gladiator has clashed with the X-Men several other times, always out of loyalty to the ruler of the Shi'ar Empire.

GREY, JEAN

Jean Grey was one of the original X-Men. Her psionic power earned her the name Marvel Girl.

Wolverine's first mission as one of the X-Men was to help rescue the original X-Men from Krakoa the Living Island *(see Krakoa the Living Island).* Logan

was instantly attracted to Jean Grey and fell in love with her almost immediately. Wolverine's feelings for Jean only added to the friction between him and Cyclops, who was both Jean's boyfriend and the X-Men's team leader.

Eventually, Logan resigned himself to the fact that he and Jean would never be together, but never stopped loving her. That bond of love was never more apparent than after Magneto leeched the adamantium from Wolverine's bones.

The X-Men escaped on the Blackbird, which had been damaged and was flying out of control. Wolverine had been declared medically dead by the Blackbird's medical scanners when Jean was pulled from the plane by the wind. Wolverine miraculously returned from the edge of death to rescue Jean.

Though he did not officially attend Jean's marriage to Cyclops, he was there, watching from the treeline.

Nate Grey was created in an alternate reality where Charles Xavier's premature death led to an "Age of Apocalypse" *(see Age of Apocalypse)*. Mister Sinister *(see Mr. Sinister)*, one of Apocalypse's most trusted servants, used the DNA of Scott Summers and Jean Grey to create a weapon against Apocalypse which became Nate Grey, the X-Man. Nate Grey has vast telepathic and telekinetic powers. Grey was one of a handful of beings to survive the destruction of that parallel Earth by making his way into the X-Men's Earth.

Like Wolverine in his early days as an X-Man, Nate Grey has little self-control and is reluctant to trust others. He eventually came to trust the X-Men and fought with them against Onslaught *(see Onslaught)*.

GROUNDHOG

Detective Sean Benard was attacked by a group of corrupt police officers when they learned that he had reported them to Internal Affairs. Benard was saved by Logan, who recruited him to join Alpha Flight.

Wolverine led Alpha Flight with Benard into battle against Egghead *(see Egghead)*, who threatened to blow up New York with a nuclear bomb. Benard quit the team after a team member sacrificed himself to stop the missile.

GUARDIAN I

James MacDonald Hudson created Department H, a top secret research and development agency within the Canadian Ministry of Defense. There, Hudson created a battle suit that allowed him to fly, project a force field, and fire powerful beams of energy by manipulating Earth's electro-magnetic field.

While on their honeymoon, Hudson and his bride, Heather, were attacked by Logan in Canada's Buffalo Wood National Park. He had been driven into a feral state by the trauma of the Weapon X program. James and Heather managed to subdue Logan and helped him regain his human personality over time. With Logan, Hudson formed Canada's first super team, Alpha Flight.

When Wolverine left Department H to become an X-Man, Hudson attempted to bring Wolverine back by force. The attack failed and he nearly killed Dr. Moira MacTaggert in the battle. Guilt-ridden, Hudson took the name Vindicator and led Alpha Flight against the X-Men in another attempt to reclaim Wolverine. This mission failed, but afterwards the X-Men and Alpha Flight became allies. After Department H was disbanded by the Canadian government, Alpha Flight continued working as a team. Hudson changed his name to Guardian. After nearly dying in combat, he returned to scientific research.

Despite their conflicts in the past, Hudson remains one of Logan's closest friends.

GUARDIAN II

Heather McNeil Hudson quit her job to be with the man she loved, James MacDonald Hudson. On their honeymoon, Heather and James were attacked by a feral Logan, crazed by the trauma of the Weapon X program. Together, they nursed Logan back to health, which ultimately led to the formation of Alpha Flight (*See Guardian I and Alpha Flight*).

Logan fell in love with Heather, but he knew that her feelings for him were purely maternal. When Professor Xavier offered Wolverine the chance to join the X-Men, Wolverine accepted. Logan saw membership in the X-Men as an opportunity to overcome his longing for Heather.

After being disbanded by the Canadian government, Alpha Fight continued working as a team. After her husband's apparent death, Heather served as Alpha Flight's team leader. Eventually, Heather donned a reconstructed version of Guardian's battlesuit and took the name Vindicator. Heather sought training from Wolverine when they first encountered Lady Deathstrike.

When James MacDonald Hudson "returned from the dead," Heather became known as Guardian and James took the name Vindicator.

Heather now works with her husband on various research projects, and has used her battle suit to aid Logan many times.

GOMURR THE ANCIENT

Known long ago as Gomurr the Impetuous, he possesses powerful mystical abilities, well-honed fighting skills and a personality replete with both wisdom and humor. Gomurr and Wolverine have known each other for a very long time, but went many years without contact.

After Psylocke (*see Psylocke*) was mortally wounded by Sabretooth (*see Sabretooth*), Gomurr led Wolverine, Archangel, and Dr. Strange to meet Tar (*see Tar*), protector of the Crimson Dawn. The power of the Crimson Dawn healed Psylocke but left her altered on a fundamental level.

GYRICH, HENRY PETER

Henry Peter Gyrich is a member of the United States National Security Council who works for the government's Project Wideawake. Project Wideawake works to regulate the activities of superhumans and mutants within the United States. Project Wideawake was responsible for drafting the former Brotherhood of Evil Mutants to become Freedom Force (*see Freedom Force*).

HAND, THE

The Hand is a group of religious ninja assassins who have attempted to kill Wolverine many times. The Hand ninjas are deadly warriors and assassins. When a Hand ninja is slain, the body disintegrates. The Hand was once led by Lord Shingen Harada and later, by the Mandarin. The Hand now follows Matsuo Tsurayaba.

HARPOON

Harpoon is an Inuit Eskimo with the ability to generate deadly harpoons of pure energy.

Harpoon and the Marauders (see Marauders) battled against Wolverine during the massacre of the Morlocks beneath the streets of Manhattan. The Marauders work for Mr. Sinister (see Mr. Sinister) and can be replaced upon death with exact genetic duplicates.

HARRIERS

The Harriers are a team of highly trained mercenaries who once worked for S.H.I.E.L.D. and claim to be capable of defeating a team as powerful as the Avengers. Sergeant-Major Harry Malone is a retired Royal Marine commando and the leader of the Harriers.

The Harriers, known as Shotgun and Axe first fought Wolverine in the "Golden Triangle" near the headwaters of the Mekong Delta. Though they claimed to have been hired to protect General Coy's opium shipment, the Harriers were actually working undercover for the D.E.A. Later, the Harriers were hired to capture Wolverine, Psylocke, and Jubilee. After a pitched battle, Psylocke, Jubilee, and the Harriers learned that the whole mission was actually a training session set up by Hardcase and Wolverine.

The Harriers' code-names describe their specialties: Axe, Blindside, Hardcase, Lifeline, Longbow, Piston, Ranger, Shotgun, Timebomb, and Warhawk.

HAVOK

Alex Summers is the younger brother of Scott Summers (see Cyclops). Havok was one of the X-Men who was rescued by Wolverine and the new X-Men team from Krakoa the Living Island (see Krakoa the Living Island).

Havok absorbs and metabolizes solar and cosmic energy and then releases it in incredibly destructive plasma blasts. Wolverine and Havok have worked together for years as members of the X-Men.

Logan and Alex became much closer during a vacation they took together in Mexico. Their vacation time was cut short when General Meltdown, Dr. Neutron, and Quark (A.K.A. Skarlett MacKenzie and lover of Alex's) manipulated the heroes to fight against each other. The villains planned to enrage Havok to the point where he would use his full power on General Meltdown, charging Meltdown's nuclear powers to their maximum potential. Instead, Havok and Wolverine worked together to destroy Meltdown and avert nuclear disaster. Though Logan knew that Skarlett had been manipulating Havok on behalf of General Meltdown (who vaporized her), Logan chose to let Havok believe that the woman he had fallen in love with was truly brave and compassionate.

HELLFIRE CLUB

The Hellfire Club was created in England in the 1760's as a social organization for the British elite. The American branch of the club is publicly known as a place for America's elite to meet and discuss political and business allegiances. Unknown to the general public, the leaders of the Hellfire Club are mutants. Known as the Inner Circle, these mutants are engaged in a conspiracy to rule the world through economic and political power.

Wolverine and the X-Men first battled the Inner Circle when Jason Wyngarde, the original Mastermind, sought to gain membership in the Inner Circle by taking control of the original Phoenix *(see Phoenix)*. Wyngarde's psionic tampering triggered Phoenix's transformation into the Dark Phoenix.

Through the years, Wolverine has often clashed with the Hellfire Club. The membership of the Hellfire Club's Inner Circle has gone through many changes *(see Black Queen, Black Bishop, Shinobi Shaw, Tessa, White Bishop & White Queen)*.

HELLIONS

The Hellions were a team of adolescent mutants who were recruited by Emma Frost, the White Queen, so that they might serve the Inner Circle of the Hellfire Club *(see Hellfire Club & White Witch)*. Emma secretly instructed them in the use of their superhuman powers at her private school, the Massachusetts Academy.

Members included Beef, Bevatron, Catseye, Empath, Jetstream, Roulette, Tarot, Thunderbird II (now known as Warpath) and, briefly, Firestar. The team came to an end when most of its members were slaughtered by Trevor Fitzroy's sentinels.

HEPZIBAH

A member of the Mephitisoid race, Hepzibah's name cannot be pronounced by humans. Corsair *(see Corsair)* gave her the name Hepzibah when they met in the Shi'ar slave pits. Like Wolverine, Hepzibah has enhanced night vision, a superhuman sense of smell, and retractable claws.

As one of the Starjammers *(see Starjammers)*, Hepzibah is a long-time ally of Wolverine and the X-Men.

HERCULES

The Hercules of Greek legend and the Avengers met Wolverine in a bar, where the two fought. In the end, the two became friends and took advantage of the empty bar by having a few free beers.

HINES, MISS

Miss Hines was responsible for monitoring and recording the Weapon X project *(see Weapon X project)* that laced Wolverine's bones with adamantium. The trauma of the adamantium bonding process drove Logan into an animalistic rage that led to him to slaughter everybody involved, except Hines.

Later, Hines worked for the U.S. Department of Agriculture in the Pest Control Division. The division is a cover for the covert department that ran the Weapon X project.

Hines was killed by the Psi-Borg, Aldo Ferro.

HOBGOBLIN

The name "Hobgoblin" has been used by several individuals over the years. It is the English equivalent of the name of the shape-changing member of the Shi'ar Imperial Guard *(see Shi'ar Imperial Guard)*, who is now known as Shape-Shifter.

The name "Hobgoblin" was also adopted by an unknown criminal who appropriated and adapted the costume and weaponry of the original Green Goblin. This Hobgoblin convinced the world that he was actually reporter Ned Leeds, who was killed in Germany while Wolverine and Spider-Man were there investigating the murders of several C.I.A. operatives.

HODGE, CAMERON

A childhood friend of Warren Worthington, the Angel *(see Angel/Archangel)*, Cameron Hodge was hired by the original X-Men to manage the original X-Factor *(see X-Factor)*. However, Hodge actually despised Worthington and founded the Right, a small army of armored warriors, to destroy all mutants.

Later, converted into a cyborg, Hodge allied himself with the rulers of Genosha, a nation in which mutants were enslaved. It was there that he first clashed with

Wolverine. Still later, Hodge was absorbed into the techno-organic alien race known as the Phalanx *(see Phalanx)*.

HONOR SWORD OF THE CLAN YASHIDA

Mariko Yashida, now his deceased lover, gave Wolverine the Honor Sword of the

Clan Yashida, marking him as the guardian of the honor of her clan. The blade is said to have been forged from meteorite iron by demon smiths in the caves of Kyushu.

Using the sword's ability to act as a lode-stone,

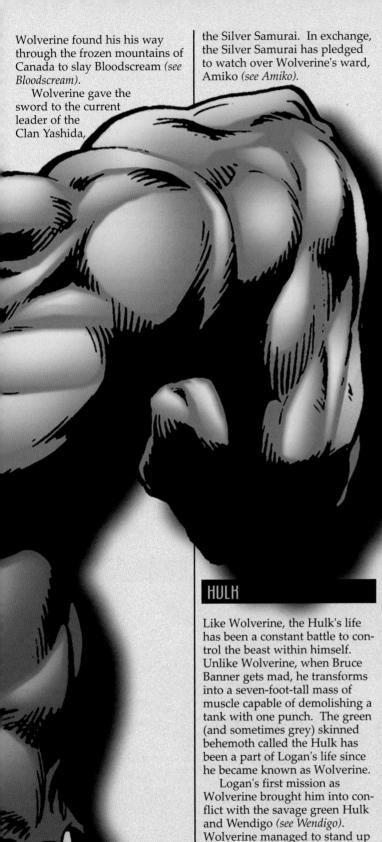

Wolverine found his his way through the frozen mountains of Canada to slay Bloodscream (see Bloodscream).

Wolverine gave the sword to the current leader of the Clan Yashida, the Silver Samurai. In exchange, the Silver Samurai has pledged to watch over Wolverine's ward, Amiko (see Amiko).

HULK

Like Wolverine, the Hulk's life has been a constant battle to control the beast within himself. Unlike Wolverine, when Bruce Banner gets mad, he transforms into a seven-foot-tall mass of muscle capable of demolishing a tank with one punch. The green (and sometimes grey) skinned behemoth called the Hulk has been a part of Logan's life since he became known as Wolverine.

Logan's first mission as Wolverine brought him into conflict with the savage green Hulk and Wendigo (see Wendigo). Wolverine managed to stand up to both monsters, despite their enormous power. Over the years, Wolverine has encountered the Hulk under a variety of circumstances.

As Patch, Logan first encountered the less savage, more cunning, grey-skinned Hulk. Wolverine fought against the Hulk when he accidentally smashed through the wing of a commercial jet. However, Wolverine fought alongside the Hulk, Spider-Man and Ghost Rider as the Fantastic Four for a brief time (see Fantastic Four). Both Wolverine and the Hulk fought against Onslaught, at which time Bruce Banner was separated from the Hulk.

HUNTER FROM DARKNESS

The Hunter from Darkness is one of a species of large, wolf-like creatures that inhabit Buffalo Woods National Park in the Canadian North Woods. The Blackfoot Indians believe the Hunters to be forest spirits.

Years ago, Wolverine found one particular Hunter from Darkness and freed his foot from a steel trap. This Hunter still remembers Wolverine with gratitude.

HUSSAR

An alien belonging to the Shi'ar Imperial Guard (see Shi'ar Imperial Guard), Hussar wields a "neuro-whip" that adversely affects the nervous system of her target.

She came into conflict with Wolverine when she joined a conspiracy against Shi'ar Princess-Majestrix Lilandra (see Lilandra). She has since rejoined the Guard.

HYDRA

Originally a secret criminal society in World War II Japan, Hydra was transformed by the Nazi war criminal Baron Wolfgang von Strucker (see von Strucker, Baron Wolfgang) into the world's most powerful and dangerous subversive organization. Its goal for over half a century has been world domination. Wolverine's former lover, Silver Fox, is a member of Hydra.

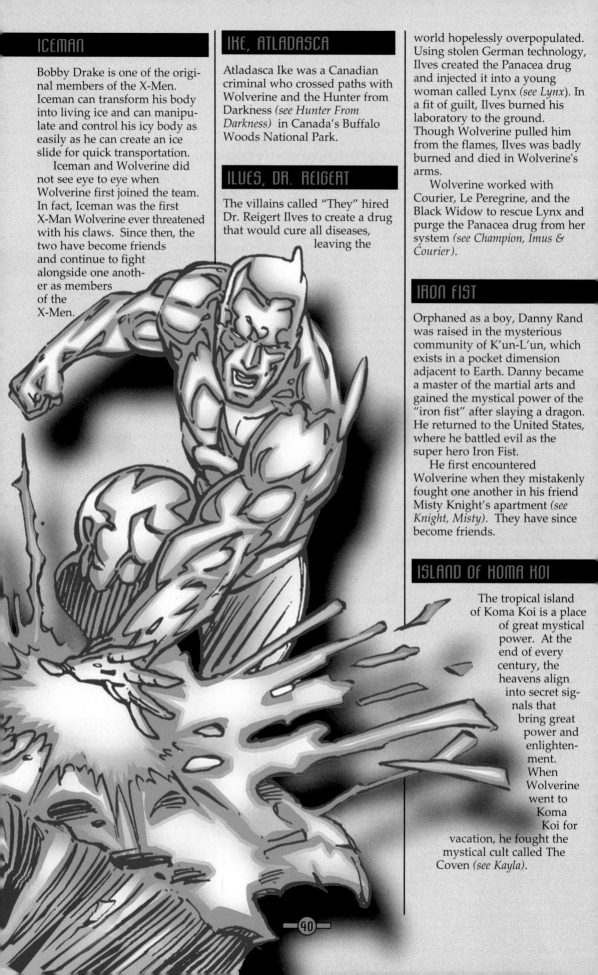

ICEMAN

Bobby Drake is one of the original members of the X-Men. Iceman can transform his body into living ice and can manipulate and control his icy body as easily as he can create an ice slide for quick transportation.

Iceman and Wolverine did not see eye to eye when Wolverine first joined the team. In fact, Iceman was the first X-Man Wolverine ever threatened with his claws. Since then, the two have become friends and continue to fight alongside one another as members of the X-Men.

IKE, ATLADASCA

Atladasca Ike was a Canadian criminal who crossed paths with Wolverine and the Hunter from Darkness *(see Hunter From Darkness)* in Canada's Buffalo Woods National Park.

ILVES, DR. REIGERT

The villains called "They" hired Dr. Reigert Ilves to create a drug that would cure all diseases, leaving the world hopelessly overpopulated. Using stolen German technology, Ilves created the Panacea drug and injected it into a young woman called Lynx *(see Lynx)*. In a fit of guilt, Ilves burned his laboratory to the ground. Though Wolverine pulled him from the flames, Ilves was badly burned and died in Wolverine's arms.

Wolverine worked with Courier, Le Peregrine, and the Black Widow to rescue Lynx and purge the Panacea drug from her system *(see Champion, Imus & Courier)*.

IRON FIST

Orphaned as a boy, Danny Rand was raised in the mysterious community of K'un-L'un, which exists in a pocket dimension adjacent to Earth. Danny became a master of the martial arts and gained the mystical power of the "iron fist" after slaying a dragon. He returned to the United States, where he battled evil as the super hero Iron Fist.

He first encountered Wolverine when they mistakenly fought one another in his friend Misty Knight's apartment *(see Knight, Misty)*. They have since become friends.

ISLAND OF KOMA KOI

The tropical island of Koma Koi is a place of great mystical power. At the end of every century, the heavens align into secret signals that bring great power and enlightenment. When Wolverine went to Koma Koi for vacation, he fought the mystical cult called The Coven *(see Kayla)*.

JACK

Jack is a member of Canada's secret intelligence division, Department H (*see Department H*) and a friend of Wolverine.

Recently, Jack, Wolverine, and the Punisher joined forces against a band of criminals on an oil platform in the Pacific Ocean.

JAMIL

Trained as a thief by Storm's former mentor, Achmed El-Gibar, Jamil left to serve the "External" called Candra. Jamil later became the guide to the spatial-shifting citadel of Apocalypse.

Jamil led Wolverine to Apocalype's haven, where Genesis attempted to bond Cyber's adamantium to Wolverine's skeleton (*see Genesis & Cyber*). The attempt failed, leading to the death of Genesis and the destruction of the citadel.

JONES, RICK

A longtime sidekick of the Hulk, Rick Jones encountered Wolverine after he battled the Hulk (*see Hulk*), who accidentally downed an airliner while airborne. The incident just ended up being a huge misunderstanding.

Recently when the Hulk traveled to the future, an older Rick Jones accidently impaled himself on the claws of Wolverine's skeleton. Whether or not this is truly how the death of Rick Jones occurs remains to be seen.

JUBILEE

After the murder of her parents, Asian-American teenager Jubilation Lee earned money performing stunts with her mutant power to create "fireworks" of energy at a Southern California mall. After being rescued by Rogue, Storm and Jean Grey from a mutant attack, Jubilee returned with them to their Australian base (*see Australia*). Upon her arrival, Jubilee helped rescue Wolverine after he was ambushed by the Reavers (*see Reavers, The*).

Soon after, Wolverine became a like big brother to the young girl--acting as both a close friend and mentor. She became a member of the X-Men and continued to team up with Wolverine on many adventures. Recently, however, Professor Charles Xavier had her join the new team of teenage mutants, Generation X (*see Generation X*).

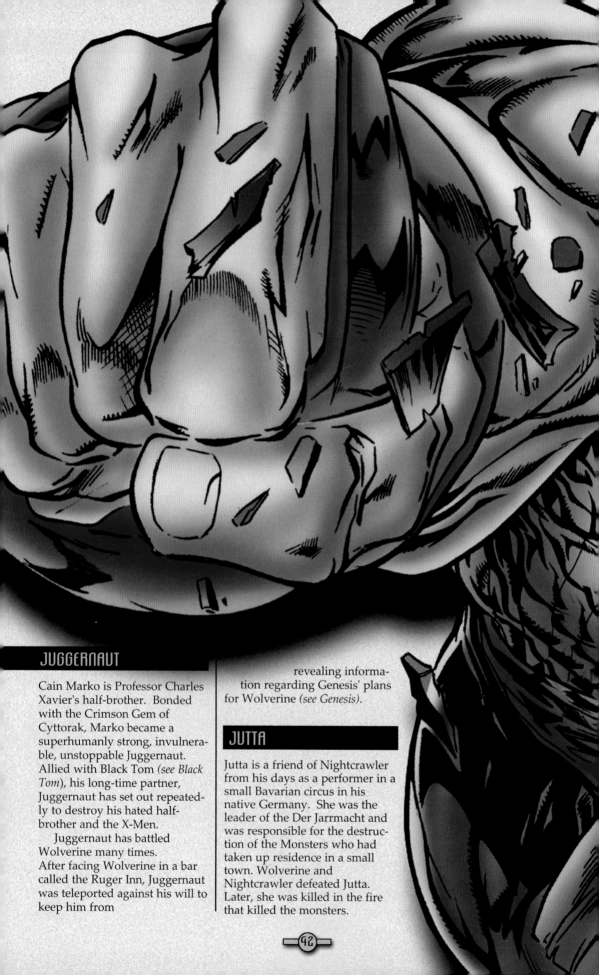

JUGGERNAUT

Cain Marko is Professor Charles Xavier's half-brother. Bonded with the Crimson Gem of Cyttorak, Marko became a superhumanly strong, invulnerable, unstoppable Juggernaut. Allied with Black Tom (*see Black Tom*), his long-time partner, Juggernaut has set out repeatedly to destroy his hated half-brother and the X-Men.

Juggernaut has battled Wolverine many times. After facing Wolverine in a bar called the Ruger Inn, Juggernaut was teleported against his will to keep him from revealing information regarding Genesis' plans for Wolverine (*see Genesis*).

JUTTA

Jutta is a friend of Nightcrawler from his days as a performer in a small Bavarian circus in his native Germany. She was the leader of the Der Jarrmacht and was responsible for the destruction of the Monsters who had taken up residence in a small town. Wolverine and Nightcrawler defeated Jutta. Later, she was killed in the fire that killed the monsters.

The invulnerable
Juggernaut

KARMA

A founding member of the New Mutants, Xi'an Coy Manh can psionically possess the minds of others. Karma's uncle is Wolverine's enemy, the Madripoor crimelord General Nguyen Ngok Coy (see General Coy).

Karma left the New Mutants before they became X-Force (see X-Force) to search for her missing siblings, Leong and Nga. While searching, she worked for her uncle for a brief time, surreptitiously aiding Wolverine.

KAYLA

Kayla was a priestess whom Wolverine met on the Island of Koma Koi. Kayla enlisted Wolverine to help defend the Temple of the Sun from the demonic cult called The Coven. Wolverine defeated the Coven and returned the mystical gem called the Tear of Heaven to the Temple of the Sun. His actions ensured the dawn of an age of enlightenment.

KELLY, SENATOR ROBERT EDWARD

A member of the United States Senate, Robert Edward Kelly has long regarded the growing number of superhuman mutants as a threat to national security and has promoted legislation such as the "Mutant Registration Act" in attempts to cope with that supposed threat.

Nevertheless, Kelly is a man of honor and principles who does not want innocent mutants to come to harm, in sharp contrast to anti-mutant bigots like Graydon Creed.

KIERROK

Kierrok the Damned is one of the N'Garai and a child of the extradimensional race of demons called the Elder Gods.

Long after his first encounter with Wolverine which ended in defeat, Kierrok began sending scouts through a mystical cairn. Together, Wolverine and Nightcrawler battled Kierrok in his own dimension. Wounded by the savage Wolverine, Kierrok had his demons lured the two X-Men back to Earth and then obliterated the cairn so that Wolverine could not return to destroy him.

KNIGHT, MISTY

New York City policewoman Misty Knight lost her right arm due to an explosion. Equipped with a new bionic arm, Knight and her friend Colleen Wing (see Wing, Colleen) founded the detective agency Nightwing Restorations. They are also known as the Daughters of the Dragon.

Knight first encountered Wolverine and the X-Men when the latter mistakenly fought her ally and lover Iron Fist in the apartment she shared with Jean Grey (see Grey, Jean).

KNIGHTS OF HELLFIRE

The Knights of Hellfire are masked, uniformed mercenaries who work as guards and enforcers for the Inner Circle of the Hellfire Club (see Hellfire Club).

When Mastermind mentally compelled the first Phoenix to become the Inner Circle's Black Queen, a lone Wolverine invaded their mansion and battled many of the Knights. He inflicted wounds on three Knights, Cole, Macon and Reese, that would have proved fatal had the three not been converted into cyborgs.

These three later joined The Reavers (see Reavers, The), but were killed by Trevor Fitzroy's (see Fitzroy) sentinels in a final climactic battle.

KRAKOA THE LIVING ISLAND

Krakoa the Living Island was actually an enormous, mutated, sentient living entity that appeared to be an island. It captured most of the original X-Men and held them prisoner there, feeding on their life energies. Professor Charles Xavier recruited a new team of X-Men, including Wolverine, who successfully rescued the original team and forced Krakoa to flee into outer space.

KULAN GATH

A sorcerer of the prehistoric Hyborian Age, Kulan Gath was an enemy of the adventurers Conan the Barbarian and Red Sonja. In recent times Kulan Gath's spirit has taken possession of human hosts and done battle with super heroes including Spider-Man and the X-Men.

I • N • D • E • X

Everything you ever wanted to know about one of the most popular members of the outlaw band of mutants known as the X~men: The feral and ferocious WOLVERINE!

In this first volume, find out about the people, places and things that have affected this mysterious, yet popular mutant's life. A must for every WOLVIE fan!!!

VOL. 2

Wolverine Encyclopedia
Vol 2 L-R

Writers
Peter Sanderson
Mark Robert Bourne
Paul Benjamin
Jerald DeVictoria

Cover
Anthony Winn
Danny Miki

Cover Design
Joe Caponsacco

Design and Layout
Dan Danko

Technical maps
Eliot Brown

Coloring
Andy Walton
Malibu Coloring

Editorial Assistant
Mark Robert Bourne

Associate Editors
Phil Crain
Dan Shaheen

Editor
Mark Paniccia

Editor in Chief
Bob Harras

Special Thanks
Roger Bonas
Drew Harris
Jennel Cruz

EDITORIAL by Mark Panicca

As you say when you don't know how to start an editorial about a character as complex as Wolverine, "Where do you start?" This guy's all over the map...and the maps of several different time lines and dimensions. He's also been around for a while...a long while (we think).

Where it started for me was when Marvel Editor-in-Chief extraordinaire and fellow coffee guru, Bob Harras, called me up and said, "The Wolverine Encyclopedia. It's yours." When I got off the phone, I didn't know whether to be happy or sad. This was a great opportunity to work on an X-Men-related project, a character who was a fave of mine for many a year. But there sure was a lot of homework included. I suddenly found myself fending off a minor panic attack at the mere thought of all the research involved. Was I back in college? Did somebody say something about a term paper due this morning? I mean, Wolverine has been just about everywhere except...well, he *has* been everywhere, and I've got the feeling he has more passports to more places than we currently know about.

The beauty of this character is that for as much as we know about him and read of his adventures, there's still an air of mystery that keeps us coming back for more. He's been a favorite of mine since the early Claremont/Byrne days of Uncanny X-Men, and it's really been an interesting project for all of us who have worked on it. I found myself reminiscing quite heavily while reading and re-reading these entries. Despite whatever obstacles have plagued us, we all had a great time working on it mainly due to the sentimental value of Logan, Patch, Wolvie or whatever you prefer to call him. So here's Volume 2 of the Wolverine Encyclopedia. Enjoy, learn and keep having fun, true believer!

LADY DEATHSTRIKE

Yuriko Oyama was the daughter of the late Lord DarkWind *(see Lord DarkWind)*, a Japanese scientist who developed a process for bonding the unbreakable metal, Adamantium to human bone. Believing that her father's secret process had been stolen and used on Wolverine's skeleton, Lady Deathstrike conceived an irrational hatred for Wolverine. She was converted into a cyborg by Spiral *(see Spiral)*, with later modifications by Donald Pierce *(see Pierce, Donald)*. Her skeleton was laced with Adamantium, and she was endowed with razor-sharp, Adamantium fingers on each hand. She is a former member of the Reavers *(see Reavers)*. Her feud with Wolverine apparently came to an end when she learned that the Adamantium had been leached from his body.

LANG, STEPHEN

Believing mutants to be the ultimate threat to humanity, Stephen Lang obtained the financial support of the "Council of the Chosen," later known as the Inner Circle of the Hellfire Club *(see Hellfire Club)*, to construct giant Sentinel robots that he used to combat X-Men and other mutants. These Sentinels have mutant-hunting/tracking abilities and are considered the ultimate adversary for mutantkind.

Lang apparently perished when his space station base was demolished. However, Lang was actually absorbed into the alien group entity known as the Phalanx *(see Phalanx)*. Unlike other human beings assimilated into the Phalanx, Lang was allowed to retain his independent consciousness. He directed the Phalanx in its many battles with the X-Men.

LEGION

David Charles Haller was the illegitimate son of Professor Charles Xavier and Gabrielle Haller. A mutant with enormous psionic powers, David spent most of his young life in a catatonic state. His name, "Legion," refers to the multiple personality disorder that has afflicted him for years.

After his multiple personalities were merged, Legion journeyed twenty years back in time, planning to kill Magneto at a critical moment in his life in an effort to change history for the better. Instead, Legion inadvertently slew Xavier, thereby creating the alternate timeline known as "The Age of Apocalypse" where Earth lay in devastation and Apocalypse ruled North America *(see Age of Apocalypse)*. Wolverine was known as the freedom fighter Weapon X. In this timeline, Wolverine fought alongside Jean Grey against the tyranny of Apocalypse.

Legion himself perished when the original timeline was restored.

LILANDRA

Princess of the ruling family of the alien Shi'ar race and consort to Charles Xavier, Lilandra Neramani first encountered Wolverine and the X-Men when she came to Earth to seek Charles Xavier's help in opposing her tyrannical brother, the Emperor D'Ken *(see D'Ken)*. Lilandra has remained an ally of the X-Men ever since, although she did stand against the X-Men at the trial of Phoenix. The trial resulted in the X-Men battling the Shi'ar guard and the eventual death of the Phoenix.

LOCKHEED

Lockheed is a small, winged, alien reptile who, like the dragons of legend, can exhale flame. The X-Man Kitty Pryde first encountered Lockheed on a Brood-dominated planet *(see Brood)*. Fond of his new friend Kitty, Lockheed has remained Kitty's companion ever since, first in the X-Men and now in Excalibur.

LONGSHOT

Longshot is a humanoid created by the genetic engineer Arize on "Mojoworld" *(see Mojoworld)*, a planet in another dimension where society is ruled by the whims of television. He fled to Earth in order to escape that planet's mad dictator, Mojo, and for a time served in the X-Men. With former X-Man, Dazzler *(see Dazzler)*, he continues to battle Mojo and Mojo II: The Sequel.

LOKI

The Norse god of mischief and evil, Loki, is a prince of Asgard, an extradimensional realm inhabited by near-immortal superhuman beings who were once worshiped as gods by the Vikings. Loki was the son of Laufey, king of the Storm Giants. He was adopted by Odin, King of Asgard, after he slew Laufey in battle. Despite Loki's repeated betrayals of Odin, the high father still calls Loki son.

Possessing great magical powers, Loki has long sought to destroy his foster brother, the Thunder God Thor, and seize the throne of Asgard. Loki clashed with the X-Men and New Mutants when the mutant teams joined forces with Alpha Flight and later when the X-Men traveled to Asgard.

Through the years, Loki has turned his attentions to Earth in hopes of destroying the adopted home of his hated foster brother Thor. One of the most notable of Loki's machinations resulted in the formation of the Avengers as Loki used the Hulk to create havoc on earth.

LORD DARKWIND

The notable Japanese scientist Lord DarkWind was the architect of the bonding process, used on Wolverine, that affixes Adamantium to the subject's skeleton *(see Adamantium)*. The process successfully bonds the molecules of the Adamantium with the molecules of the bone tissue. Darkwind's daughter, Lady Deathstrike *(see Lady Deathstrike)*, sought Wolverine years after her father's death. She believed that Wolverine had played a role in the pilfering of her father's bonding process. Lady Deathstrike and Wolverine are the only know survivors of the bonding process.

LORD SHINGEN

The head of the Yashida crime family of the Japanese Yakuza, Lord Shingen was also the father of Mariko Yashida *(see Yashida, Mariko)*, a woman with whom

Wolverine fell deeply in love. Although Shingen defeated him in their first battle, Wolverine was forced to slay the crimelord. After Shingen's death Wolverine and Mariko became engaged.

LUPO

Lupo is one of the Savage Land Mutates, natives who were subjected to genetic engineering by Magneto. In Lupo's case, he was endowed with the psionic ability to control certain animals. Lupo's abilities center around wolves and other wild dogs. Another Savage Land Mutate, Brainchild, mutated Lupo even further, giving him a wolf-like appearance. Wolverine has come into contact with Lupo and other members of the Savage Land Mutates during his many travels to the Savage Land.

LYNX

Born without an immune system and with a bestial appearance, the girl known only as Lynx was raised by scientists in a germ-free environment without any human contact. As a result of her mistreatment, she has a feral personality and is incapable of speaking a human language.

Dr. Reigert Ilves used Lynx as a subject for an experimental serum that he hoped would cure all known diseases. She aided Wolverine and the Black Widow in battling Ilves' employers, a subversive organization called the Third Person. Wolverine set her free in the Canadian North Woods. She mistakenly believes him to be her mate.

MACABRE

Macabre and her companions began as an extra-dimensional, sentient virus that developed into separate personalities when it gestated within human bodies. Macabre, who could grant temporary youth to the aged, used her power to build a crime syndicate in Phoenix, Arizona. Wolverine, Darkhawk, Spider-Woman, Nomad and Dr. Strange defeated Macabre and her servants on their first mission as the Secret Defenders.

MacTAGGERT, MOIRA

Dr. Moira MacTaggert is one of the world's leading geneticists and heads the Mutant Research Center at Muir Island, located off the coast of Scotland. She met Charles Xavier when they were both students and, for a time, they were engaged to be married. She instead wed Joseph MacTaggert and sometime later bore his son, the mutant Proteus. Proteus later became an enemy of the X-Men. She and Xavier have remained close friends and partners over the years, and she is a staunch ally of Wolverine. Currently she devotes herself to seeking a cure for the Legacy Virus, with which she herself is infected.

MALICE

Malice was a being who existed in the form of "pure consciousness" and could take mental possession of other beings. She first fought Wolverine when she took possession of the Dazzler (see Dazzler) and battled the X-Men. She was also a member of Mister Sinister's Marauders while inhabiting the body of Polaris. After the mutant massacre and the defeat of the Marauders, Malice remained in hiding until she perished after clashing with Havoc and Polaris of the government-sanctioned mutant team, X-Factor.

MADRIPOOR

Madripoor is an island in the South Pacific which has become notorious as an international center of crime. The island is divided into two areas, the prosperous Hightown, where the ruling monarch, Prince Baran (see Baran, Prince), lives, and crime-ridden Lowtown. The two dominant crimelords in Madripoor are Wolverine's ally Tyger Tiger (see Tyger Tiger) and his enemy General Coy (Coy, General). For years Wolverine frequently operated in Madripoor under the alias "Patch," and was co-owner of Lowtown's Princess Bar. Wolverine does not frequent Madripoor any more since the recent murders of his friends, Archie Corrigan (see Corrigan, Archie) and O'Donnell, his co-partner in the Princess Bar (see Madripoor map on page 80).

MADROX

Jamie Madrox is also known as the Multiple Man, a mutant who has the power to create duplicates of himself at will. For a long time Madrox worked as Moira MacTaggert's assistant at the Mutant Research Center on Muir Isle. Later he was a founding member of the second version of X-Factor (see X-Factor).

One of Madrox's bodies died due to the Legacy Virus, but others have recently turned up alive and healthy. Madrox has been an ally of Wolverine since they first met during the first conflict with Proteus on Muir Isle.

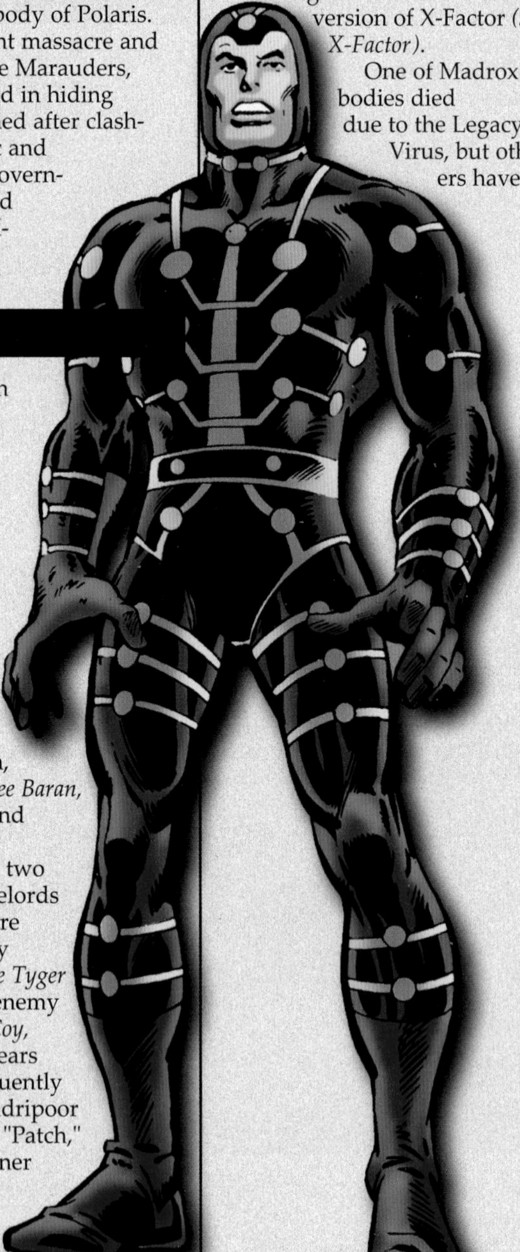

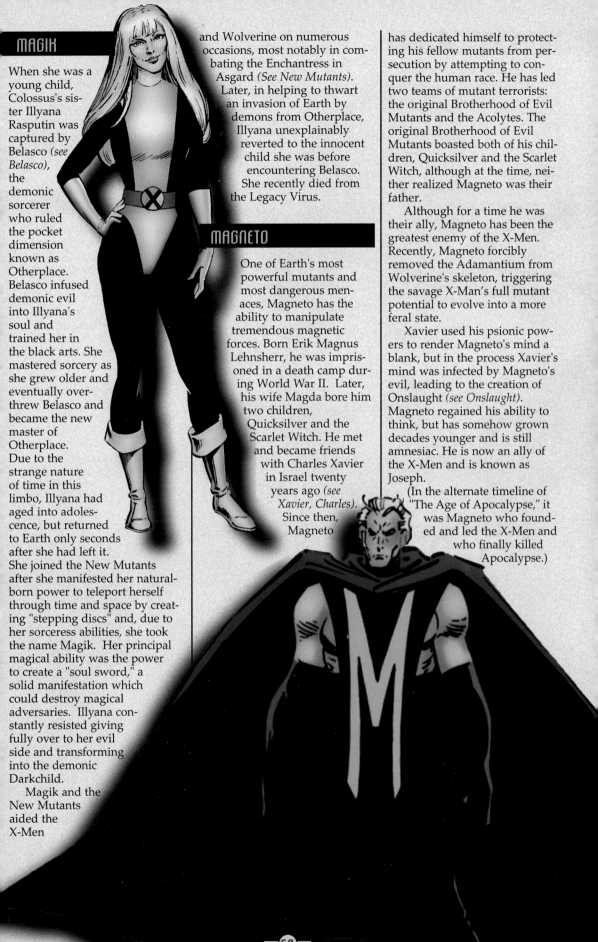

MAGIK

When she was a young child, Colossus's sister Illyana Rasputin was captured by Belasco (see Belasco), the demonic sorcerer who ruled the pocket dimension known as Otherplace. Belasco infused demonic evil into Illyana's soul and trained her in the black arts. She mastered sorcery as she grew older and eventually overthrew Belasco and became the new master of Otherplace. Due to the strange nature of time in this limbo, Illyana had aged into adolescence, but returned to Earth only seconds after she had left it. She joined the New Mutants after she manifested her natural-born power to teleport herself through time and space by creating "stepping discs" and, due to her sorceress abilities, she took the name Magik. Her principal magical ability was the power to create a "soul sword," a solid manifestation which could destroy magical adversaries. Illyana constantly resisted giving fully over to her evil side and transforming into the demonic Darkchild.

Magik and the New Mutants aided the X-Men and Wolverine on numerous occasions, most notably in combating the Enchantress in Asgard (See New Mutants). Later, in helping to thwart an invasion of Earth by demons from Otherplace, Illyana unexplainably reverted to the innocent child she was before encountering Belasco. She recently died from the Legacy Virus.

MAGNETO

One of Earth's most powerful mutants and most dangerous menaces, Magneto has the ability to manipulate tremendous magnetic forces. Born Erik Magnus Lehnsherr, he was imprisoned in a death camp during World War II. Later, his wife Magda bore him two children, Quicksilver and the Scarlet Witch. He met and became friends with Charles Xavier in Israel twenty years ago (see Xavier, Charles). Since then, Magneto has dedicated himself to protecting his fellow mutants from persecution by attempting to conquer the human race. He has led two teams of mutant terrorists: the original Brotherhood of Evil Mutants and the Acolytes. The original Brotherhood of Evil Mutants boasted both of his children, Quicksilver and the Scarlet Witch, although at the time, neither realized Magneto was their father.

Although for a time he was their ally, Magneto has been the greatest enemy of the X-Men. Recently, Magneto forcibly removed the Adamantium from Wolverine's skeleton, triggering the savage X-Man's full mutant potential to evolve into a more feral state.

Xavier used his psionic powers to render Magneto's mind a blank, but in the process Xavier's mind was infected by Magneto's evil, leading to the creation of Onslaught (see Onslaught). Magneto regained his ability to think, but has somehow grown decades younger and is still amnesiac. He is now an ally of the X-Men and is known as Joseph.

(In the alternate timeline of "The Age of Apocalypse," it was Magneto who founded and led the X-Men and who finally killed Apocalypse.)

MAGNUM, MOSES

Moses Magnum was once the corrupt head of the Deterrence Research Corporation. Apocalypse granted Magnum superhuman strength and the power to trigger earth-quakes. Magnum battled Wolverine and the X-Men when the team traveled to Japan from the Savage Land. At first, the Japanese hero Sunfire attacked the X-Men, thinking they were responsible for the earthquakes. Later he fought alongside Wolverine and the X-Men against Magnum.

MAI

Mai, whose last name is unknown, is a young Chinese woman whose husband and child were killed by the menace called the Black Shadow (*see Black Shadow*). Wolverine joined her in hunting the creature down.

MANDARIN

Years ago the Chinese nobleman now known as the Mandarin discovered a crashed alien starship and mastered its advanced technology as well as the ten power rings he found within. Since that time the Mandarin has repeatedly attempted to conquer the world, only to be thwarted time and time again by his archenemy, Iron Man.

The Mandarin first became Wolverine's enemy when he and the scientist Matsuo Tsurayaba transformed Psylocke into the Mandarin's slave, Lady Mandarin, and sent her to kill Wolverine (*see Psylocke*).

MANDROID

Mandroid is a large armored battlesuit worn by S.H.I.E.L.D. agents in order to combat super-human adversaries. Moses Magnum sent men in purloined Mandroid battlesuits to fight Wolverine and the X-Men during one of the team's trips to Japan.

MARAUDERS

The Marauders were a team of mutants who operated as assassins on behalf of Mr. Sinister *(see Mr. Sinister)*. Members included Arclight, Blockbuster III, Harpoon, Malice III, Prism, Riptide, Sabretooth, Scalphunter, Scrambler and Vertigo II. Wolverine and the X-Men first battled the Marauders when Mister Sinister had the mutant assassins execute the "Mutant Massacre," the systematic slaughter of the population of the Morlocks *(see Morlocks)*. As genetically constructed clones, the Marauders can be replaced by Mr. Sinister if killed or otherwise damaged in battle. The result is an endless supply of deadly killers.

MARROW

Wolverine and the X-Men believed the surviving Morlocks to be dead when Mikhail Rasputin apparently committed suicide and killed the Morlocks in the process. In reality, Mikhail transported the Morlocks to another dimension where time flowed more quickly than on Earth. A young girl named Sarah and the children of the Morlocks were angry at having been exiled from Earth and returned seeking vengeance on the entire human race.

Sarah chose the name Marrow because of her exposed skeletal structure. Different parts of her anatomy can be torn off and used as daggers. Marrow surgically attached a bomb to her heart that could only be stopped by her death. Wolverine and the X-Men watched as Storm defeated Marrow in single combat. In the end, Storm was forced to kill Marrow to save the lives of innocent subway travelers.

MASQUE

Masque is a Morlock who has the mutant power to alter a person's facial features by touching them. Wolverine has clashed with Masque more than once, most notably when the X-Men rescued Power Pack, a team of super-heroic children, from him.

MASTERMIND

The original Mastermind was a mutant named Jason Wyngarde, who had the power to create illusions. He was a member of Magneto's original Brotherhood of Evil Mutants. Later, he joined the Hellfire Club's Inner Circle and used his powers to brainwash, torture and corrupt the original Phoenix, manipulating her into becoming the Club's Black Queen. This mental subversion inadvertently triggered Phoenix's transformation into the Dark Phoenix *(see Phoenix I)*. Still later, he mentally manipulated Mariko Yashida into rejecting Wolverine as her fiancé.

Mastermind finally died from the Legacy Virus, but his daughter Martinique Jason inherited his powers and adopted his alias.

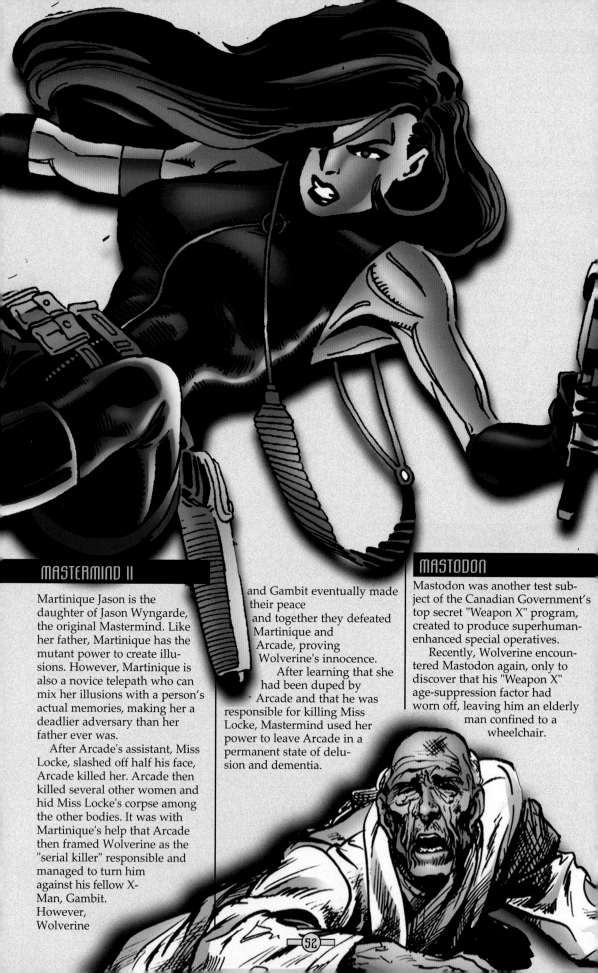

MASTERMIND II

Martinique Jason is the daughter of Jason Wyngarde, the original Mastermind. Like her father, Martinique has the mutant power to create illusions. However, Martinique is also a novice telepath who can mix her illusions with a person's actual memories, making her a deadlier adversary than her father ever was.

After Arcade's assistant, Miss Locke, slashed off half his face, Arcade killed her. Arcade then killed several other women and hid Miss Locke's corpse among the other bodies. It was with Martinique's help that Arcade then framed Wolverine as the "serial killer" responsible and managed to turn him against his fellow X-Man, Gambit. However, Wolverine and Gambit eventually made their peace and together they defeated Martinique and Arcade, proving Wolverine's innocence.

After learning that she had been duped by Arcade and that he was responsible for killing Miss Locke, Mastermind used her power to leave Arcade in a permanent state of delusion and dementia.

MASTODON

Mastodon was another test subject of the Canadian Government's top secret "Weapon X" program, created to produce superhuman-enhanced special operatives.

Recently, Wolverine encountered Mastodon again, only to discover that his "Weapon X" age-suppression factor had worn off, leaving him an elderly man confined to a wheelchair.

McCABE, LINDSAY

Actress Lindsay McCabe is the friend and confidante of Jessica Drew, the original Spider-Woman. Lindsay became Jessica's partner in her private detective agency, based in San Francisco. For a time Drew and McCabe operated in Madripoor (*see Madripoor*), where they were frequent allies of Wolverine.

McCOY

McCoy, also known as the "Dark Beast," was created in an alternate reality where Charles Xavier's premature death led to an "Age of Apocalypse." In this twisted alternate reality, Apocalypse ruled the North American continent. There, Henry McCoy, a beast in temperament as well as appearance, conducted hideous experiments on mutants and humans for Sinister. When that alternate reality was destroyed, McCoy was thrown back in time and into the restored timeline. He appeared sometime before the formation of the Morlocks and was instrumental in their creation.

For a time, McCoy infiltrated the X-Men by impersonating the real Beast (*Dr. Henry McCoy*), deceiving even Wolverine's enhanced senses. McCoy's subterfuge ended when Onslaught attacked the X-Men and McCoy escaped to hatch a new plan.

MAVERICK

David North, alias Maverick, was another test subject in the Canadian government's top secret "Weapon X" program. He once possessed the mutant power to absorb kinetic impacts, within certain limits, without injury to himself. Maverick was the partner of both Wolverine and Sabretooth when the trio were C.I.A. agents in the 1960s.

Maverick has discovered he is infected with the Legacy Virus and has asked Wolverine as a favor to end his life. Wolverine refused and Maverick has come to terms with his fatal ailment.

Excalibur).
She first met
Wolverine when her
lover Captain Britain *(see
Braddock, Brian)* joined
forces with the X-Men to
battle the Phalanx *(see
Phalanx)*.

MEAN

Kitty Pryde of the X-Men once
told the child Illyana Rasputin a
fairy tale in which Wolverine
was a character who was remi-
niscent of the Tasmanian
Devil and who seemed to have
an insatiable craving for beer and
cigars. Telling people to "Just call
me Mean," he apparently had no
real name. Astonishingly,
Nightcrawler once journeyed to
an extradimensional world in
which Mean and the other

characters from Kitty's fairy tale
actually existed *(see Bamf)*.

MEGGAN

Meggan is a shapechanging
mutant. As her features suggest, she is able to trace her
heritage from the faerie
of British
legend.
She is a founding
member of the
British super
hero team
Excalibur
*(see

MESMERO

The real name of Mesmero is
unknown. Mesmero is a green-
skinned mutant with superhuman hypnotic powers. He once
mesmerized the members of the
X-Men into losing their memories and true personalities and
becoming performers in his traveling circus. He cast Wolverine
as the animalistic beast-man in
his sideshow.
    The Beast arrived on the
scene and was shocked to see the
X-Men performing in the center
ring and as sideshow

freaks. When the Beast attempted to free the X-Men, he was knocked unconscious by a mesmerized Colossus. Seeing the Beast being captured jarred Wolverine's memory.

It was Wolverine who fought free of Mesmero's influence and helped the other X-Men break Mesmero's spell and regain their freedom.

Returned to their senses, the X-Men confronted Mesmero. It was then revealed that Mesmero had been fooled into this deed and Magneto was the real villain behind this attempt to destroy the X-Men.

Mesmero began his career by taking control of a large number of latent mutants, including Lorna Dane. At the time, Mesmero believed that he was in the employ of Magneto, but it was later revealed that it was in fact a robot verson of Magneto.

In what was perhaps his most humiliating defeat, Mesmero gained control of Excalibur, but in turn was defeated by the dragon Lockheed and the students from St. Searle's School For Young Ladies.

In addition, Mesmero has served as the Deputy Leader of the Demi-Men.

MICROVERSE

On a mission with the X-Men, Wolverine travelled to a subatomic dimension called the Microverse when the evil being called "The Entity" appeared and began randomly destroying worlds. An inhabitant of the Microverse had tracked the entity to its source in the Macroverse (Earth's dimension). The Entity was, in reality, the first manifestation of the dark side of Professor Charles

Xavier's personality. Together, the X-Men fought alongside the freedom fighters of the Microverse and defeated the Entity, restoring control to Professor Xavier's true personality. The Microverse's heroes are:
Bug: A humanoid Insectivorid with great agility and a battle lance that fires powerful energy blasts.

Commander Arcturus Rann: The leader of the Microverse's freedom fighters. He is a master strategist and warrior skilled in all forms of hand-to-hand combat.

Fireflyte: Fireflyte is a tiny, fairylike psionic songstress whose melodies attune her to the binding energy of the Microverse known as the Enigma Force.

Huntarr: Bred for battle, Huntarr can transform his body into a variety of weapons.

Marionette: Marionette was a pampered princess who became an expert warrior to help the freedom fighters overthrow a vicious dictatorship.

MIMIC

An accident in his father's lab gave Calvin Rankin the power to mimic the physical, intellectual and psionic abilities of anyone he encountered. As the Mimic, Rankin was briefly a member of the original X-Men. He was believed to be dead after he absorbed massive amounts of gamma radiation from the Hulk. Left for dead, Rankin survived because his mutant power allowed him to mimic the mutant healing factor of Wolverine, who had been in the area hunting the Hulk. Rankin's powers were altered by his near death and caused him to

take on Wolverine's powers, appearance and feral nature.

Years later, Wolverine and the Hulk fought Rankin, who had lost control and reverted to a beast-like state. Wolverine taught Rankin a form of meditation in the hopes that it would teach him to control his powers as it had helped Wolverine control his own feral nature. The Mimic told Hulk that his father's experiments involved the integration of adamantium into the human body, but a connection to the Weapon X project or Wolverine's adamantium skeleton has not yet been revealed.

MIRAGE

Dani Moonstar, formerly known as Psyche and Moonstar, is an adolescent Native American mutant with the mental power to project solid three-dimensional images drawn from the minds of others and based upon her target's darkest fears. Later, she also learned how to project an image of a person's deepest fantasy.

During a trip to Asgard (see Asgard) she became one of the Valkyries. Recently she began using "neural arrows" with which she can cause victims to experience their greatest fears.

As a founding member of the New Mutants (see New Mutants), she was an occasional ally of Wolverine and the X-Men, most notably against the Enchantress in Asgard.

MISS LOCKE

Miss Locke was a mercenary who worked for the killer-for-hire Arcade (see Arcade). After the sadistic Miss Locke slashed off half Arcade's face, he killed her. Arcade and his ally at the time, Mastermind II, framed Wolverine for Miss Locke's murder (see Mastermind II). Along with his fellow X-Man, Gambit (see Gambit), Wolverine defeated Arcade and Mastermind II, discovering Miss Locke's true fate and realized that Arcade had duped her into believing that Wolverine had killed Miss Locke. Mastermind II avenged Miss Locke's death by leaving Arcade in a permanent state of delusion and dementia.

M'KRAAN CRYSTAL

The M'kraan Crystal is a gigantic, powerful object once located on a planet in the Shi'ar Galaxy that, because of the massive neutron galaxy contained within it, possesses the potential to obliterate the entire universe. The M'Kraan Crystal was the holding place for the Phoenix force and it is also a nexus of realities. Wolverine and the X-Men fought to prevent the mad Shi'ar Emperor D'ken (see D'Ken) from seizing control of the Crystal.

In "The Age of Apocalypse" (see Age of Apocalypse) time-line, Bishop (see Bishop) dove through that reality's M'kraan Crystal to travel back in time to prevent Legion (see Legion) from killing Charles Xavier.

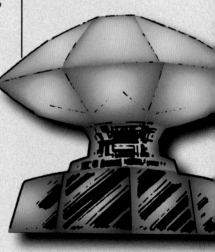

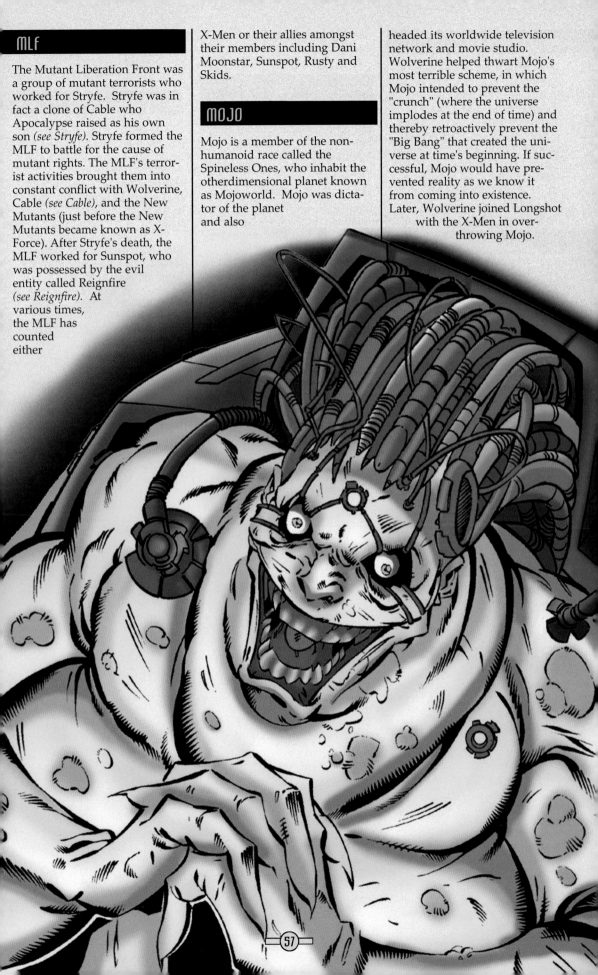

MLF

The Mutant Liberation Front was a group of mutant terrorists who worked for Stryfe. Stryfe was in fact a clone of Cable who Apocalypse raised as his own son *(see Stryfe)*. Stryfe formed the MLF to battle for the cause of mutant rights. The MLF's terrorist activities brought them into constant conflict with Wolverine, Cable *(see Cable)*, and the New Mutants (just before the New Mutants became known as X-Force). After Stryfe's death, the MLF worked for Sunspot, who was possessed by the evil entity called Reignfire *(see Reignfire)*. At various times, the MLF has counted either

X-Men or their allies amongst their members including Dani Moonstar, Sunspot, Rusty and Skids.

MOJO

Mojo is a member of the non-humanoid race called the Spineless Ones, who inhabit the otherdimensional planet known as Mojoworld. Mojo was dictator of the planet and also

headed its worldwide television network and movie studio. Wolverine helped thwart Mojo's most terrible scheme, in which Mojo intended to prevent the "crunch" (where the universe implodes at the end of time) and thereby retroactively prevent the "Big Bang" that created the universe at time's beginning. If successful, Mojo would have prevented reality as we know it from coming into existence. Later, Wolverine joined Longshot with the X-Men in overthrowing Mojo.

MOJO II

Mojo II, also known as Mojo II: The Sequel, is a clone of the original Mojo. When Wolverine joined with Mojo II, Longshot and the X-Men in overthrowing the original Mojo, Mojo II was able to take over the rulership of Mojoworld. Currently, Mojo II: the Sequel has been deposed and battles Mojo for control of the Planet.

MOJOWORLD

Mojoworld is a planet whose existence is dependent on television. Mojoworld's tyrant rulers all live or die depending on their ratings. Wolverine and other X-Men have been forcibly taken to this planet on several occasions for the amusement of Mojo and the general populace of Mojoworld.

Both Longshot and Mojo II: the Sequel *(see Mojo II)* have at one time ruled the planet, but cur-rently the original Mojo controls the throne.

MOLECULE MAN

Owen Reece was a lowly lab technician until an accident gave him the power to psionically manipulate all known forms of matter and energy on an atomic level. That accident opened a portal into the otherdimensional home of the Beyonder.

When the Beyonder gathered some of Earth's greatest heroes and villains, including Wolverine, to fight his "Secret Wars" *(see Beyonder)*, Molecule Man sided with the villains against Wolverine and his allies. Later, when the Beyonder took on a physical form and came to Earth to study the nature of desire, Molecule Man helped Earth's heroes combat the Beyonder. Reece pro-jected the Beyonder's energy into another dimension where it formed a new pocket-universe.

MOLE MAN

A pathetic misfit in human society, the man now known as the Mole Man discovered and mastered a vast network of caverns and the strange humanoid race, the Molian Subterranean, as well as the huge monsters that inhabited it.

Wolverine first entered the Mole Man's realm when he served as a member of the "new" Fantastic Four alongside Spider-Man, the Hulk and Ghost Rider *(see Fantastic Four)*.

MONKEYWRENCH

Johnny Bloodcede, alias Monkeywrench, was a fanatical member of the Nature Defense League, a band of terrorists fighting for ecological causes. Wolverine went after him when he kidnapped Alice Hoff, the daughter of a friend of Charles Xavier.

MONSTERS

The "Monsters" were a community of grotesque but peaceful people, probably mutants, whom Wolverine and Nightcrawler tried to protect. Persecuted by Nightcrawler's old circus friend Jutta (see Jutta and Der Jarrmacht) and the frightened citizens of a small town in Germany, the Monsters died in a fire started by the frightened townspeople in an old abandoned castle.

MOONHUNTER AND THE NIGHT PATROL

Moonhunter worked for Dredmund Cromwell (see Cromwell, Dredmund), who was attempting to create a race of werewolves. Moonhunter and a team of artificially engineered werewolves called the "Night Patrol" had the job of tracking

down and controlling escaped experimental werewolves. Moonhunter abducted Wolfsbane, believing her to be a rogue werewolf from Cromwell's colony. When Moonhunter and his allies were defeated by Wolverine and Captain America, the artificial werewolves were returned to normal.

MOREAU, DAVID

David Moreau, better known as "the Genegineer," was the head scientist responsible for locating and enslaving mutants for the Genoshan government. It was he who supervised the imprisonment of Wolverine and Rogue when they were forcibly transported to Genosha (see Genosha). After journeying to a Genoshan prison camp for mutants, his son Philip became a prominent freedom fighter for the Genoshan mutants.

MORLOCKS

The Morlocks were a community of mutant outcasts who lived in a network of tunnels underneath New York City. They were led by Callisto (see Callisto) until she was bested in combat by Storm. Storm then became their leader by right of battle. Other prominent Morlocks included Caliban (see Caliban), Masque, Sunder, Annalee, Erg, Piper and the Healer.

Most of the Morlock population was slaughtered by the Marauders during the "Mutant Massacre". After the "Age of Apocalypse," it was revealed that McCoy, the Dark Beast (see McCoy) from that reality, used his twisted genetic talents to create the majority of the mutant outcasts.

MR. FANTASTIC

Reed Richards, also known as Mr. Fantastic, is the leader of the Fantastic Four, a group of individuals who gained their powers from a cosmic ray mishap during a rocket launch (see Fantastic Four). Richards is arguably the greatest scientific mind alive

today. He has the superhuman ability to stretch his body to great lengths and into various shapes.

Wolverine and Mr. Fantastic once battled Doctor Doom alongside their respective teams, the X-Men and the Fantastic Four. As a member of a substitute Fantastic Four team, Wolverine also aided Mr. Fantastic and the original members in an encounter with the Mole Man in Subterranea.

MR. JIP

Mr. Jip was the first pupil of Earth's Sorcerer Supreme, Doctor

Strange's mentor, the Ancient One. Mr. Jip, however, turned his mastery of sorcery to evil ends; in the process his body became huge and misshaped. The X-Men were used by Mr. Jip to collect three mysterious stones which, at the same time, were sought by the Serpent Society. The X-Men defeated the Society and claimed the stones. When they were put into Mr. Jip's possession, they were stolen by Sidewinder, who had a deal with the Atlantians, Ghaur and Llyra. The two had planed to use the mysterious stones in their quest for the Serpent's Crown.

MR. SINISTER

Originally a biologist in Victorian England who developed advanced theories on human evolution, Nathaniel Essex allied himself with Apocalypse *(see Apocalypse)*, who later trans-

formed Essex into the creature that would come to be known as Mr. Sinister. As Sinister he was responsible for the creation of Madelyne Pryor *(see Pryor, Madelyne)*, the clone of Jean Grey *(see Jean Grey)* who later became the evil Goblin Queen. Sinister ordered the Marauders (whom he was responsible for creating) to perpetrate the "Mutant Massacre" of the Morlocks *(see Morlocks and McCoy)*. He first directly combatted Wolverine and the X-Men during the "Inferno" crisis, an invasion of demon mutants created by Sinister and the demon Sym *(see Sym)*.

MUIR ISLE

Muir Isle is an island off the coast of

Scotland where Dr. Moira MacTaggert has established her Mutant Research Center. Wolverine has often visited the center on X-Men business. It has also been used as Excalibur's base and as a vacation spot for the X-teams.

MURDERWORLD

Murderworld is the name given by the wealthy and crazed assassin, Arcade *(see Arcade)* to his various secret installations. They resemble amusement

parks, but are filled with death traps, in which Arcade imprisons his victims and adversaries, including Wolverine and the X-Men.

MYSTIC WORM

The Mystic Worm was an immense, serpent-like creature that threatened the Canadian Indians' homes back in the 1800s.

During a "dream" that Wolverine had while hiking through the Canadian outback, he recalled saving a young Indian boy from trappers.

Being wounded himself, the boy's tribe took him in and nursed him back to health. The Shaman told Logan stories of a Mystic Worm that had been terrorizing the tribe and when it finally appeared it killed a squaw that Logan had feelings for. Logan and the Indian boy tracked the Mystic Worm to its cave where they killed it. After waking from his dream, Logan found the cave and the skeletal remains of the worm. Based on the fact that Logan has memory implants, it is impossible to tell if these event ever truly occurred. If so, Logan would be over 100 years old.

MYSTIQUE

Also known as Raven Darkholme, Mystique is a mutant shapechanger. She is the former lover of Wolverine's

arch-foe Sabretooth, the mother of Nightcrawler *(see Nightcrawler)* and Greydon Creed, as well as the foster mother of Rogue. Wolverine first encountered her when she led her terrorist organization, the third Brotherhood of Evil Mutants, in an attempt to assassinate Senator Robert Kelly *(see Kelly, Senator Robert)*. Later, Mystique and her Brotherhood became Federal Government operatives for Freedom Force *(see Freedom Force)*. Under this name they again repeatedly fought Wolverine and the X-Men, most notably in Dallas during the conflict with the evil mystic Adversary. Subsequently, Mystique became an ally of Wolverine and the X-Men, when she aided him in preventing Mojo's scheme to block the "Big Bang" that created the universe. Most recently, Mystique returned to criminality, but was forced to serve as a member of X-Factor. *(see X-Factor)*.

N'ASTIRH

N'astirh is a demon from the extradimensional limbo known as Otherplace. The crimson demon led his fellow Otherplace demons in the invasion of Manhattan known as the "Inferno." He was defeated by Wolverine, the X-Men and the original X-Factor and he was apparently destroyed.

NEW MUTANTS

The New Mutants were the second generation of adolescent mutants organized by Professor Charles Xavier. Members included Cannonball, Cypher, Karma, Magik, Magma, Mirage, Sunspot, Warlock and Wolfsbane. With the formation of the New Mutants, Xavier used the young team to aid the X-Men in combat whenever the senior group was overpowered. Most notably the two teams joined forces against the Enchantress and Loki in Asgard *(see Asgard and Loki)* where the New Mutants were kidnapped but then rescued by the X-Men. Eventually Cable *(see Cable)* reorganized the remaining members of the New Mutants into X-Force *(see X-Force).*

Before Cable recruited them into X-Force, Magneto was for a time the headmaster of the New Mutants. In an effort to embrace Charles Xavier's vision of human/mutant unity, Magneto agreed to lead the New Mutants. Despite his efforts, the team never fully embraced him and Magneto could never earn the loyalty he would need to lead the New Mutants. In the end, Magneto left the group to pursue h own path.

NEW WARRIORS

The New Warriors was a team of young costumed crimefighters whose members included Firestar, Namorita, Night Thrasher, Nova, Rage, Silhouette and Speedball, among others. They battled alongside Wolverine and many other super heroes in the "Infinity War." Members Firestar, Justice, Timeslip, Kymaera and Night Thrasher have been revealed as mutants.

N'GARAI

The N'garai are a race of other-dimensional demons who ruled Earth in prehistoric times. Trapped in another dimension, they have repeatedly sought to cross the dimensional barriers back to Earth and reconquer it. Wolverine has twice been instrumental in defeating one of their leaders, Kierrok.

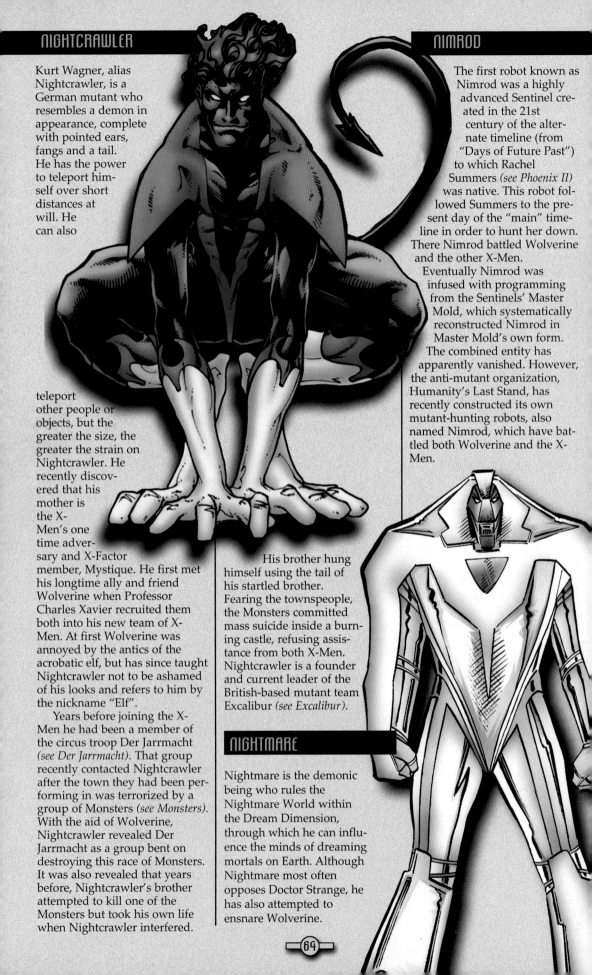

Kurt Wagner, alias Nightcrawler, is a German mutant who resembles a demon in appearance, complete with pointed ears, fangs and a tail. He has the power to teleport himself over short distances at will. He can also teleport other people or objects, but the greater the size, the greater the strain on Nightcrawler. He recently discovered that his mother is the X-Men's one time adversary and X-Factor member, Mystique. He first met his longtime ally and friend Wolverine when Professor Charles Xavier recruited them both into his new team of X-Men. At first Wolverine was annoyed by the antics of the acrobatic elf, but has since taught Nightcrawler not to be ashamed of his looks and refers to him by the nickname "Elf".

Years before joining the X-Men he had been a member of the circus troop Der Jarrmacht (see Der Jarrmacht). That group recently contacted Nightcrawler after the town they had been performing in was terrorized by a group of Monsters (see Monsters). With the aid of Wolverine, Nightcrawler revealed Der Jarrmacht as a group bent on destroying this race of Monsters. It was also revealed that years before, Nightcrawler's brother attempted to kill one of the Monsters but took his own life when Nightcrawler interfered.

His brother hung himself using the tail of his startled brother. Fearing the townspeople, the Monsters committed mass suicide inside a burning castle, refusing assistance from both X-Men. Nightcrawler is a founder and current leader of the British-based mutant team Excalibur (see Excalibur).

Nightmare is the demonic being who rules the Nightmare World within the Dream Dimension, through which he can influence the minds of dreaming mortals on Earth. Although Nightmare most often opposes Doctor Strange, he has also attempted to ensnare Wolverine.

The first robot known as Nimrod was a highly advanced Sentinel created in the 21st century of the alternate timeline (from "Days of Future Past") to which Rachel Summers (see Phoenix II) was native. This robot followed Summers to the present day of the "main" timeline in order to hunt her down. There Nimrod battled Wolverine and the other X-Men.

Eventually Nimrod was infused with programming from the Sentinels' Master Mold, which systematically reconstructed Nimrod in Master Mold's own form. The combined entity has apparently vanished. However, the anti-mutant organization, Humanity's Last Stand, has recently constructed its own mutant-hunting robots, also named Nimrod, which have battled both Wolverine and the X-Men.

N'KOTHA

N'kotha was an entity who was part of the Phalanx *(see Phalanx)*, an alien techno-organic race with a group mind that assimilated members of the races of other worlds it intended to conquer. N'kotha clashed with Wolverine in the course of the Phalanx's battle with the X-Men, X-Factor, X-Force, Excalibur and the members of the team that would eventually become Generation X *(see Generation X)*.

NOMAD

As a boy, Jack Monroe acquired enhanced strength and agility from a recreation of Captain America's "super-sol-dier formula." He adopted the name and costume of the original Captain America's deceased partner, Bucky. His older partner became the new Captain America, since the original (Steve Rogers) was then missing and believed to be dead. Both Monroe and the new Captain went insane because of the formula and the government placed them in suspended animation.

Years later, Monroe was revived and, as an adult, eventually became the vigilante known as Nomad. He is now once more in suspended animation. Nomad was a member of the Secret Defenders *(see Secret Defenders)* alongside Wolverine.

NORAD

NORAD (North American Air Defense) is the United States military organization that has its war base in Valhalla Mountain in the Colorado Rockies. On his second mission with the "new" X-Men, Wolverine traveled there to help them stop Count Luchino Nefaria *(see Count Nefaria)*, who had seized the base and was threatening to launch America's entire nuclear missile arsenal.

Years later, Wolverine and the X-Men returned to Valhalla Mountain to confront Thunderbird II (now known as Warpath).

NORTHSTAR

Jean-Paul Beaubier is a French-Canadian mutant with the power to move at superhuman

speed. He and his twin sister, Aurora *(see Aurora)*, are both members of Alpha Flight *(see Alpha Flight)*, the Canadian team of superhuman operatives to which Wolverine once belonged. After Wolverine left Canada's Department H *(see Department H)*, Northstar was among the members of Alpha Flight who attempted to return Wolverine to the Canadian government after he left to join the X-Men. A vain and arrogant hero, Northstar's overconfidence can be considered both his greatest strength and weakness.

NYOIRIN

Lord Nyoirin was the Japanese crimelord who employed Kwannon, the ninja assassin whose consciousness was transferred into Psylocke's original body *(see Psylocke)*. He is now deceased.

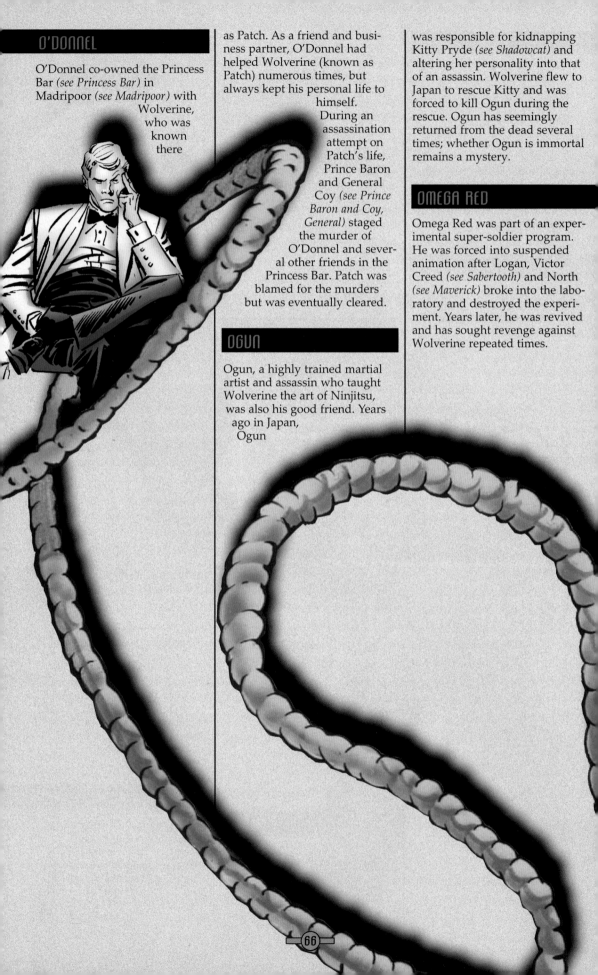

O'DONNEL

O'Donnel co-owned the Princess Bar *(see Princess Bar)* in Madripoor *(see Madripoor)* with Wolverine, who was known there as Patch. As a friend and business partner, O'Donnel had helped Wolverine (known as Patch) numerous times, but always kept his personal life to himself.

During an assassination attempt on Patch's life, Prince Baron and General Coy *(see Prince Baron and Coy, General)* staged the murder of O'Donnel and several other friends in the Princess Bar. Patch was blamed for the murders but was eventually cleared.

OGUN

Ogun, a highly trained martial artist and assassin who taught Wolverine the art of Ninjitsu, was also his good friend. Years ago in Japan, Ogun was responsible for kidnapping Kitty Pryde *(see Shadowcat)* and altering her personality into that of an assassin. Wolverine flew to Japan to rescue Kitty and was forced to kill Ogun during the rescue. Ogun has seemingly returned from the dead several times; whether Ogun is immortal remains a mystery.

OMEGA RED

Omega Red was part of an experimental super-soldier program. He was forced into suspended animation after Logan, Victor Creed *(see Sabertooth)* and North *(see Maverick)* broke into the laboratory and destroyed the experiment. Years later, he was revived and has sought revenge against Wolverine repeated times.

ONSLAUGHT

Magneto and Charles Xavier were once friends who shared opposite opinions of the Homo superior role. After many years of disagreements and battles, Xavier wiped Magneto's mind clean, sending him into a coma-like state. During this encounter, part of the evil ego of Magneto was transferred unknowingly into Xavier's mind. The combining of the two personalities began the formation of the entity known as Onslaught.

This entity sought the domination and destruction of humankind. During a fierce battle with the heroes of Earth,

Onslaught was defeated, but at the cost of many of the Earth's greatest heroes' lives. Charles Xavier was freed of the mental bond, but lost his telepathic abilities *(see Xavier, Charles)*.

ORACLE

Oracle was a member of the Shi'ar Imperial Guard who fought the X-Men when they attempted to

free Shi'ar princess, Lilandra *(see Lilandra)*, from the clutches of her brother, Emperor D'Ken *(see D'Ken)*. She physically fought Wolverine in this battle, but was defeated. After the Emperor D'Ken was overthrown, Oracle continued to serve Lilandra in the Shi'ar Imperial Guard.

OVERRIDER

Richard Rennselaer is a retired SHIELD agent whose son, Johnny Rennselaer, suffers from a condition called nuclear psychosis. Nuclear psychosis is a fear of nuclear annihilation so severe that it causes the victim to completely withdraw from reality. Rennselaer planned to use his mutant power to override electrical systems in order to take control of America's nuclear arsenal and render it useless by launching the missiles into the ocean. Rennselaer's plan was thwarted by Wolverine and Captain America *(see Captain America)*, who teamed up to stop him.

OZYMANDIAS

Former ruler of the domain now under Apocalypse's control, Ozymandias remains forever trapped in a stone-like form, a punishment inflicted upon him by a young Apocalypse. He is now the official documenter of mutant history, namely the history of Xavier. Recently, Ozymandias was forced to destroy several documents when Cyclops, Jean Grey and Wolverine found their way into the hidden cavern where most of his records were kept.

PATCH

Because the world believed Wolverine and the X-Men to be dead (*see Adversary and Australia*), Wolverine called himself Patch during his non-costumed adventures in Madripoor (*see Madripoor*). As Patch, Wolverine wore a patch over his left eye and refrained from using his claws in front of witnesses. Though there were some people who knew Patch's true identity, Logan's friends chose to respect his desire for secrecy.

PHALANX

The Phalanx is a group of techno-organic aliens bent on destroying the human race and taking over Earth as their new home. Several anti-mutant humans have joined the collective mind of the Phalanx including Cameron Hodge and Stephen Lang (*see Hodge, Cameron and Lang, Stephen*). Although the Phalanx is a combined intelligence, Lang has been allowed to exist as a single mind, outside of the group intellect. Wolverine and the X-Men thwarted the Phalanx's last invasion attempt.

PHOENIX I

The entities known as Phoenix first appeared on Earth after they encountered a doomed shuttle piloted by Jean Grey (*see Grey, Jean*) who was known at that time as Marvel Girl. This entity took over Grey's form and saved the X-Men, who had just escaped from Stephen Lang's crazed schemes (*see Lang, Stephen*). In the form of Marvel Girl, the Phoenix shielded the other X-Men while the shuttle reentered Earth's atmosphere.

While impersonating Jean Grey, the entity chose the name Phoenix. Eventually, Phoenix came under the influence of Mastermind, who corrupted the being and released its darker, evil personality.

Sudden changes in personality became the norm for Phoenix. During a joy ride through the galaxy, she destroyed a small planet and used the energy in order to return to Earth. After the Shi'ar Empire (*see Shi'ar Empire*) demanded that "Jean Grey" pay for her crime, the X-Men challenged the Shi'ar to a fight for her life. The X-Men and the Shi'ar guard fought in an oxygen-enclosed area of the moon. The battle was fierce, but the X-Men found themselves outmatched. Finally, only Cyclops and Phoenix remained undefeated. The two sought shelter to regroup. Fearing she might do something unpredictable again, Phoenix killed herself at this point. Years later, the real Jean Grey was revived from the Hudson Bay in the cocoon created by the Phoenix force.

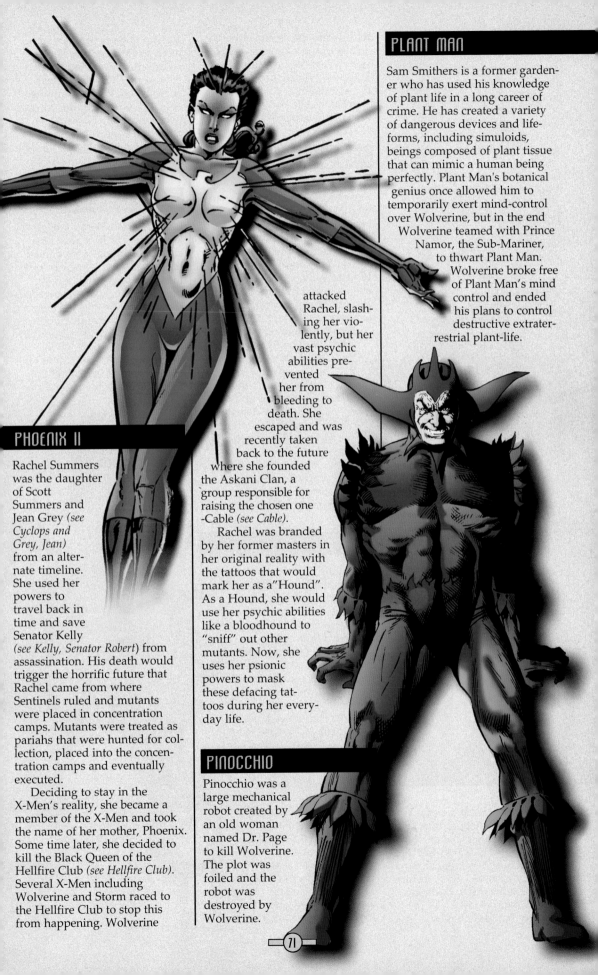

PLANT MAN

Sam Smithers is a former gardener who has used his knowledge of plant life in a long career of crime. He has created a variety of dangerous devices and life-forms, including simuloids, beings composed of plant tissue that can mimic a human being perfectly. Plant Man's botanical genius once allowed him to temporarily exert mind-control over Wolverine, but in the end Wolverine teamed with Prince Namor, the Sub-Mariner, to thwart Plant Man. Wolverine broke free of Plant Man's mind control and ended his plans to control destructive extraterrestrial plant-life.

PHOENIX II

Rachel Summers was the daughter of Scott Summers and Jean Grey (see Cyclops and Grey, Jean) from an alternate timeline. She used her powers to travel back in time and save Senator Kelly (see Kelly, Senator Robert) from assassination. His death would trigger the horrific future that Rachel came from where Sentinels ruled and mutants were placed in concentration camps. Mutants were treated as pariahs that were hunted for collection, placed into the concentration camps and eventually executed.

Deciding to stay in the X-Men's reality, she became a member of the X-Men and took the name of her mother, Phoenix. Some time later, she decided to kill the Black Queen of the Hellfire Club (see Hellfire Club). Several X-Men including Wolverine and Storm raced to the Hellfire Club to stop this from happening. Wolverine attacked Rachel, slashing her violently, but her vast psychic abilities prevented her from bleeding to death. She escaped and was recently taken back to the future where she founded the Askani Clan, a group responsible for raising the chosen one -Cable (see Cable).

Rachel was branded by her former masters in her original reality with the tattoos that would mark her as a"Hound". As a Hound, she would use her psychic abilities like a bloodhound to "sniff" out other mutants. Now, she uses her psionic powers to mask these defacing tattoos during her everyday life.

PINOCCHIO

Pinocchio was a large mechanical robot created by an old woman named Dr. Page to kill Wolverine. The plot was foiled and the robot was destroyed by Wolverine.

PLASMA

The leader of a religious cult, Plasma, along with her Trackers, fought Havok (see Havok) in the Australian outback. Wounded in battle, she was left for dead by the Trackers. Havok took her in and the two fell in love. The Trackers returned a short time later and kidnapped Plasma. With Wolverine, Havok tried to rescue her, but she had turned on her former lover. The Trackers were defeated, but Plasma escaped.

POLARIS

Polaris was a member of the X-Men who were held captive by Keirrok the Living Island (see Keirrok the Living Island). She and the other members were rescued by a new team of X-Men, including Wolverine. Afterwards she and her fiancé, Havok, left the team but both eventually returned to the group, either as an ally or foe. On one such occasion, Polaris was possessed by Malice (see Malice), a member of the Marauders (see Marauders). Eventually, she was freed and now is a member of X-Factor (see X-Factor).

PORCUPINE

The Porcupine was a mercenary whose quill-covered battle suit housed a variety of weapons, including gas and poisonous darts. Before Alpha Flight (see Alpha Flight) was fully formed, Wolverine led a team of potential members and trainees into battle against Porcupine and his companions.

Porcupine and other criminals were hired by Egghead (see Egghead) in an extortion plan that threatened New York City with nuclear annihilation. Porcupine and the others were defeated. Years later, Porcupine was slain when he accidentally fell on his own quill during a battle between the Serpent Society and Captain America.

POST

Although little is known about the humanoid known as Post, it is clear that he is an extremely dangerous foe. He was sent by Onslaught to test the X-Men's fighting abilities, powers and loyalties to each other. After almost destroying the team, Post disappeared, having all the data he needed on the X-Men.

POWER MAN

Power Man was a mercenary with the powers of superhuman strength and nigh-invulnerability.

Before Alpha Flight was fully formed, Wolverine led a team of potential members and trainees into battle against Power Man and his companions. Power Man and other criminals were hired by Egghead (see Egghead) in an extortion plan that threatened New York City with nuclear annihilation. Power Man was defeated along with the others. Because his powers had been altered to allow him to grow to gigantic proportions, Power Man now calls himself Goliath.

POWER MAN

Luke Cage is a Hero for Hire well known for his steel-hard skin and super strength. He gained his powers after being exposed to molten steel while serving time in prison. Once he escaped from prison, he decided to use his powers as a troubleshooter in New York. With his partner Iron Fist, he aided the X-Men in destroying the Living Monolith's plan to steal an exhibit of Egyptian artifacts.

POWER PACK

Power Pack was a group composed of two brothers and two sisters who gained their powers when an alien Smart Ship, "Friday" crashed near their home. Inadvertently, they began to use their powers as super heroes and called themselves Power Pack. Over the years, they have helped and befriended several heroes including Kitty Pryde (see Shadowcat) and Wolverine, whom they met in the Morlock (see Morlocks) tunnels during the Mutant Massacre. Alex is now a member of the New Warriors and fought beside Wolverine during the Infinity War.

PRESS GANG

Before the X-Men helped overthrow the Genoshan (see Genosha) government, Genoshan law did not allow citizens to migrate to other countries. Many fled this oppression. The Press Gang was a team of Genoshan mutants who were hired to retrieve Genoshan refugees. While retrieving Jenny Ransome, the Press Gang also took her friend, Madelyne Pryor Summers. Wolverine and the X-Men fought the Press Gang during the rescue.

PRINCESS BAR

Located in a rather seedy part of Madripoor (see Madripoor), the Princess Bar is co-owned by Patch (see Patch). The Bar was closed after the murder of several regulars by the hired assassins of General Coy and Prince Baron (see Coy, General and Baron, Prince and Princess Bar map on page 81).

PRISM

Prism is a member of the infamous Marauders (see Marauders), who during an attack on the Morlocks (see Morlocks) was shattered by Jean Grey's telepathic powers. Since then Prism has been cloned and has fought members of the X-teams on several occasions.

PROFESSOR

The man known only as the Professor was in charge of the Weapon X project that laced Wolverine's bones with adamantium (see Weapon X Project and adamantium). The trauma of the adamantium bonding process drove Logan into an animalistic rage, in which state he cut off the Professor's hand. Years later, Wolverine tracked down the Professor at the U.S. Department of Agriculture in the Pest Control Division. This division is a cover for the covert department that formerly ran the Weapon X project. The Professor was killed by Silver Fox in the Windsor, Ontario warehouse that stored the Shiva robots (see Shiva).

PROJECT, THE

The Project was a U.S. government operation developed to take volunteers and transform them into killers by programming their minds through visual and drug-induced suggestion. Typhoid Mary (see Typhoid Mary) and a man named Roberts are two of the known volunteers. The project was created by a man named Trevor who has since been killed by Wolverine.

PROTEUS

Proteus is a psionic-energy being who possesses a human body. When the energy is spent the body is destroyed and Proteus has to find another host body. Moira MacTaggert's (see MacTaggert, Moira) son was one host. He held her hostage until the X-Men and Wolverine came to rescue her. After he was destroyed, Proteus was passed to her husband who was slain by Colossus. Recently, Proteus returned and

fought the X-Men, X-Factor and the New Warriors (see New Warriors). However, in the end he committed suicide.

PSI-BORG

Aldo Ferro was a crime lord called "Il Topo Siciliano" (the Sicilian Mouse) who once owned nearly half of the land and businesses in Cuba. During the Weapon X experiment, Ferro used his telepathic powers to implant false memories in Wolverine and other victims. Ferro linked the false memories to the pain receptors of his victims not only because it was more effective, but because he enjoyed inflicting pain on others.

When one of the Weapon X victims, the man called Mastodon, began to age rapidly, Wolverine joined Maverick, Sabretooth, Silver Fox, and John Wraith (plus Jubilee and Miss Hines) to make sure their own age-suppression factors would not break down. They faced Ferro in his stronghold and found a ring of computers that functioned to help Ferro develop an age suppression factor of his own. Before Ferro was defeated, he revealed to Wolverine that his memories of the time he spent with Silver Fox as a boy were real and not implants.

PUNISHER

The Punisher is a vigilante who was involved in stopping a poaching epidemic in Africa. Wolverine was also on the trail and he and the Punisher clashed after Logan mistook the Punisher for a poacher. The real poachers were later revealed and the two heroes met years later when Blackheart (see Blackheart) took over the town of Christ's Crown.

PSYLOCHE

The British-born Elisabeth "Betsy" Braddock was enlisted by the X-Men to help fight the Marauders during the "Mutant Massacre" of the Morlocks. After going through the Siege Perilous, she was discovered by the Mandarin and Matsuo Tsurayaba who attempted to use her to heal the soul and mind of Matsuo's assassin lover, Kwannon. Kwannon was left with some of both her own and Betsy's minds, and Betsy's original body was left a blank slate.

Wolverine was instrumental in rescuing Betsy's new body from the Mandarin's brainwashing. Betsy stayed with the X-Men for several years, until her original body returned infected with the Legacy Virus. One of her last actions was helping to cleanse the memories of Kwannon from Betsy's new body. Recently, Betsy was nearly disemboweled by Sabretooth, but Wolverine and Archangel saved her life by exposing her soul to the Crimson Dawn. The full effect of this remains to be seen.

PUCK

Nearly a century old, Puck, whose real name is Eugene Judd, is a longstanding member of Alpha Flight (see Alpha Flight), although he never served directly with Wolverine. Before becoming a member, Puck often found himself in the same trouble spots as Logan. Sometimes, they were on different sides, but they only met face-to-face recently. A "time twister" took them back to 1937 Spain where they fought beside Ernest Hemingway and Spanish partisans against both Nazis and Lady Deathstrike (see Lady Deathstrike). Soon after Wolverine lost his adamantium, Puck and Heather Hudson (see Guardian II) helped Logan defend himself against Lady Deathstrike.

PYRO

St. John Allerdyce was one of Mystique's recruits for her Brotherhood of Evil Mutants. His control over all flame allows him to shape any object or creature out of flame. He has clashed repeatedly with the X-Men, both in the Brotherhood and Freedom Force, a government team of mutants. He contracted the Legacy Virus and planned to live out his final days at Jonathan Chambers' Florida compound. Then, during the last phase of his Legacy Virus sickness, he went on a rampage. Near death, he was whisked away in a mound of earth by Avalanche. Mystique has recruited him for an unknown plan involving X-Factor (see X-Factor).

QUARTERMAIN, CLAY

Clay Quartermain was an agent for SHIELD for several years and in several capacities. Though for a long time he was thought to be dead, it was recently revealed that he had been kept in cold storage in the depths of SHIELD headquarters. As a high-ranking officer under Nick Fury (see Fury, Nick), he had dealings with Logan several times under the auspices of SHIELD. While aiding the Hulk (see Hulk) to destroy a stockpile of Gamma Bombs, Quartermain found himself faced with the unenviable task of breaking up a fight between the Hulk and Wolverine.

QUICKSILVER

Pietro Maximoff was one of the earliest foes of the X-Men but reformed to join the Avengers (see Avengers) as well as the Inhumans and X-Factor. His background with Magneto and history of being mentally manipulated has always left him a mutant walking on the edge between hero and villain. Recently, he had found a place with X-Factor and was working through his marital problems with his wife, Crystal, but the Onslaught affair robbed him of both his wife and sister, the Scarlet Witch. He is currently staying with the X-Men. He has a daughter, Luna, who has so far shown no evidence of mutant powers.

RANCOR

Rancor is the descendant of Wolverine in the alternate future universe of the Guardians of the Galaxy. She is a strong opponent of the Guardians both as ruler of the planet Haven and slavemaster of the Inhumans on the Blue Area of the moon. Besides her feral abilities and healing factor, she often uses one of Wolverine's adamantium blades as a weapon. Apparently, the claw was ripped off by Gladiator (see Gladiator) of the Shi'ar Imperial Guard. She had a child with the Guardian Talon as the unwilling genetic father in order to preserve the heritage of Wolverine's bloodline.

RAZA

Raza Longknife is a Shi'ar member of the Starjammers (see Starjammers) and has fought alongside the X-Men against various interstellar foes, notably the Shi'ar empires ruled by D'Ken and Deathbird, the Brood, and the Cadre. Raza first met the X-Men while helping them assault the M'Kraan Crystal (see M'Kraan Crystal) and defeat the evil Shi'ar emperor D'Ken. Although Raza's personal motives have sometimes put him at odds with the Starjammers, he still serves with them. He was once a guest of the X-Men at their headquarters, which at that time was Magneto's abandoned island base in the Atlantic.

RAZOR-FIST

The Razor-Fist Wolverine faced was the second mercenary to take that guise. Both of his hands were amputated and replaced with steel blades. While working for the crimelord Roche in Madripoor (see Madripoor), he was ordered to capture "Patch," which he did with the aid of Sapphire Styx (see Sapphire Styx). After Logan escaped there was a rematch, but Logan was still groggy from his interrogation and could not adequately defend himself. He was swept over a waterfall, seemingly to his death. Logan survived, and returned to fight Razor-Fist. Although left for dead, Razor-Fist survived and is currently a freelance mercenary.

REAPER

Pantu Hurages was a member of Stryfe's and Reignfire's Mutant Liberation Fronts (see MLF). Besides his superhuman agility and endurance, he can induce a paralytic state just by touching his opponent or by using a conductive material such as his scythe. As a member of the MLF, he has fought many of the X-Teams, including the New Mutants, X-Men, X-Factor, and X-Force. He has an intense rivalry with Shatterstar, who has severed both of his hands.

REAVERS

The Reavers were a group of cyborg thieves who had a base in Australia. After the X-Men defeated them, they took the Reavers' base for themselves. Some of the few remaining members joined forces with Donald Pierce (see Pierce, Donald), Lady Deathstrike (see Lady Deathstrike), and Cole, Macon, and Reese, three former Knights of the Hellfire Club who had been badly mauled by Wolverine and forced to turn to cybernetics to survive. They launched several attacks on the X-Men in general and on Wolverine in particular, including the creation of the androids Elsie Dee and Albert and the Cyborg Cylla. The Reavers, save Lady Deathstrike, were all presumed slain by Trevor Fitzroy's Sentinels.

REIKO

The assassin named Reiko worked for the Yakuza drug lord Dai-Komo, who (see Dai-Komo) created a highly addictive drug called Thunderbolt. It conferred superhuman strength and euphoria on its user, shortly followed by death. Despite Reiko's affiliation with Wolverine's adversaries, Wolverine spared her life. Reiko then killed Dai-Komo. Because Dai-Komo had connections to the Hand, Reiko was punished by Matsuo Tsurayaba. Matsuo blinded Reiko, promising to restore her sight if she killed Jubilee. When Reiko learned that Jubilee was an ally of Wolverine, she reneged on her contract and tried to flee the Hand. In her attempt to leave Japan, Reiko was taken against her will by Silver Fox and HYDRA. Finally, Reiko was tricked by Matsuo into poisoning Wolverine's true love, Mariko Yashida. When Reiko learned that she had betrayed Wolverine, to whom she owed a debt of honor, she ended her own life.

RHINO

The Rhino is a mercenary thug who possesses superhuman strength, speed, stamina and resistance to injury. Before Alpha Flight (see Alpha Flight) was fully formed, Wolverine led a team of potential members and trainees into battle against Rhino and his companions. Rhino and other criminals (see Porcupine and Power Man) were hired by Egghead in an extortion plan that threatened New York City with nuclear annihilation. Rhino and the others were defeated.

RICHARDS, FRANKLIN

As the son of Reed and Susan Richards, Franklin had the potential for power beyond that of most mutants. Despite the efforts of his father (see Mr. Fanastic) to restrain his powers, they began to emerge at an early age. As a member of Power Pack, Franklin fought alongside Wolverine several times. Professor Xavier kept a close eye on his progress, and when Onslaught emerged, Franklin Richards was manipulated into aiding Onslaught's plans. Now that his parents are missing, Franklin has gone to live with Generation X. In a future alternate reality, Franklin is a member of the X-Men during their final stand against the Sentinels.

RIPTIDE

Riptide was one of the Marauders (see Marauders) who took part in the "Mutant Massacre" of the Morlocks. His power to spin at superhuman speed allowed him to hurl volleys of ordinary projectiles with hurricane force. His barbarism led to his own death at the hands of Colossus, which started Colossus down a path away from his customary gentleness. Although seemingly dead, the Marauders' pact with Mr. Sinister (see Marauders) included sets of clones that were activated after their counterparts' deaths. His current whereabouts are unknown.

RICTOR

Julio Richter was originally captured by the anti-Mutant organization "the Right" to use his powers in a blackmail scheme. He was freed by X-Factor and has since been a major part of

the New Mutants and X-Force, fighting alongside the X-Men on several occasions. Although he has left the team at times in the past to take care of personal business, he is currently an active member. He has honed his formerly uncontrollable vibratory powers to precision to avoid accidents like those that devastated his hometown in Mexico.

ROCHE

The man called Roche was the most powerful crimelord in Madripoor until he clashed with Wolverine. Roche's power was threatened by the neophyte crimelord Tyger Tiger, so he attempted to have Tyger killed. Initially, Roche thought O'Donnel was Tyger, but he later learned that Tyger was in fact Jessan Hoan.

During that time, he had his underlings, Sapphire Styx and Razorfist, take Wolverine captive. Wolverine escaped and helped Tyger invade Roche's villa. Tyger decapitated Roche, believing he had killed Wolverine. When Tyger Tiger took over Roche's underworld empire, Wolverine vowed to destroy her if ever she became as evil as Roche. However, Tyger chose not to become involved in any of Madripoor's drug or slavery rings, leaving those areas to General Coy. As a result, Wolverine served as Tyger's protector and she is now one of his closest allies.

ROMA

As Guardian of the Multiverse and a powerful sorceress from Otherworld, Roma has used her power to keep order. She was a prime target of the entity called the Adversary when he attempted to return to this plane of reality. He captured Roma to prevent her meddling, but the X-Men intervened, sacrificing their lives to temporarily defeat the Adversary (*see Adversary*) and free Roma, who then secretly used her powers to resurrect them, however. As part of their new lives, she gave them guardianship over the Siege Perilous, an artifact that judged those who passed through it and gave them a new life.

ROSE

Rose Wu was an agent of Landau, Luckman, and Lake who at one point ran operations in Hong Kong. She was a metamorph, and as such, able to change her shape. The reason for these abilities has not yet been revealed, although it is likely she was from another dimension that is frequented by Landau, Luckman, and Lake. Rose took over the managerial position of the Princess Bar after Wolverine, then going by the alias Patch, left Madripoor. She was recently killed by General Coy and the Prince of Madripoor in an attempt to frame Logan for several murders.

ROGUE

The foster-daughter of Mystique *(see Mystique)* first entered the life of the X-Men as an opponent, crippling Carol Danvers *(see Binary)* and stealing her powers of flight, strength and invulnerability as Ms. Marvel. Rogue led a life of crime with the Brotherhood of Evil Mutants until she became unable to deal with the pressure of her ability to absorb powers and psyches. Rogue turned to Xavier for help. He accepted her, although none of the X-Men agreed with his decision. When the team was poisoned, Rogue and Wolverine were the only X-Men left unharmed. During the mission for an antidote, they formed a bond of trust that enabled them to save the rest of the team and began the process of Rogue's reformation and acceptance by the X-Men.

ROUGHOUSE

With Bloodscream *(see Bloodscream)*, Roughouse was a bodyguard for General Nguyen Ngoc Coy *(see Coy, General)* in Madripoor *(see Madripoor)*. After failing against "Patch" several times, Coy sold Roughouse to the Tierra Verden scientist and ex-Nazi scientist Geist. Experiments with a special designer drug increased his strength, but the side-effects were blind rage and pain. The healing touch of the nun Sister Salvation stopped the pain and took away all his violent tendencies. He remained in Tierra Verde to help protect her and her mission.

Roughouse has superhuman strength and stamina and cannot be killed by mortal-forged metal. Certain expressions he uses suggest he may have some link to the Asgardian race.

M·A·D·R·I·P·O·O·R

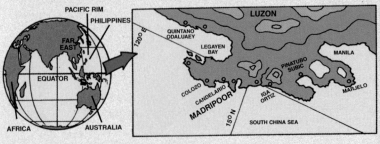

LOCATION: *Southern coast of Luzon Island, part of archipelago of the Philippines.*
TOTAL LAND AREA: *377 sq mi.*
COASTLINE: *259 mi.*
COMPARATIVE AREA: *About the size of Phoenix, Arizona.*
LAND USE: *12% arable land, 2% permanent crops, 8% forest and woodland, 78% other.*
POPULATION: *1,055,680 (est: 1992)*
ETHNIC GROUPS: *48% Filipino, 21% British, 11% Chinese, 4% American. 16% other.*
LANGUAGES: *Filipino (From Tagalog), English (both official)*
RELIGIONS: *81% Roman Catholic, 7% Protestant, 5% Muslim, 7% Buddhist and other.*
GOVERNMENT: *Colony of United Kingdom, scheduled to revert back to Republic of Philippines on May 1, 2000.*
STRUCTURE: *Governor assisted by advisory Executive Council.*
MONETARY UNIT: *Peso and Madripoor Dollar.*
BUDGET: *(1994) 2.65 Billion.*
MAJOR INDUSTRIES: *Textiles, Clothing, tourism, gambling, electronics and shipping.*

Madripoor, a colony of the United Kingdom, is noted for its vital dynamism and multicultural excitement. While a financial success it is considered a relatively moral failure. The traditional, positive attitudes toward luck and gambling have contributed to the proliferation of clubs, casinos and attendant subculture. The colony is run by a colonial government with direct ties to the United Kingdom. The 99-year lease will revert to the Filipino Republic on the first of May in the year 2000.

Noted for its permissive environment towards financial institutions, there is a major banking center in the central business district. The much anticipated reversion of the colony back to its mother country, in only a few years, has resulted in an explosion of cultural disunity, extreme financial experimentation and a new lawlessness

CITY OF MADRIPOOR

Illustration by Eliot Brown

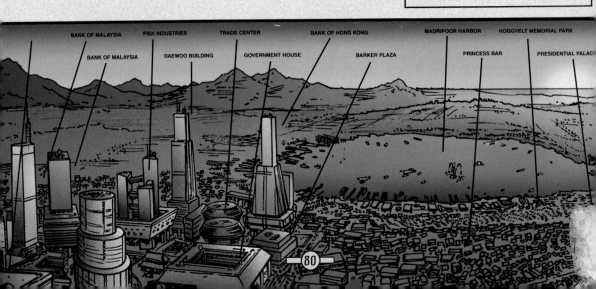

BANK OF MALAYSIA · FISK INDUSTRIES · TRADE CENTER · BANK OF HONG KONG · MADRIPOOR HARBOR · HOGGVELT MEMORIAL PARK

BANK OF MALAYSIA · DAEWOO BUILDING · GOVERNMENT HOUSE · BARKER PLAZA · PRINCESS BAR · PRESIDENTIAL PALACE

PRINCESS BAR

The Princess Bar has achieved a near-mythic status as a central point of perfidy and villainous treachery. While the bar and restaurant is situated in a Low Town enclave of gang activity, with the use of common sense, trouble can be avoided. Located in the Summit Church District, noted for its old world beauty and charming shops, the Princess Bar offers devoted service and attention to detail with the finest in Asian cooking with a Western flair. Master Chef Lo Chi can suggest the finest delicacies for the most jaded gourmet. For reservations, telephone Ho the Maitre D'Hotel at 54-1912 during any afternoon. Parties of 15 or more can be accommodated in the private rooms on the fabled second floor.

--Excerpted from MADRIPOOR on $20 and $40 per day.

◄ ∙∙∙∙∙∙∙∙∙∙∙∙∙∙∙∙∙∙∙∙∙∙∙∙∙∙∙∙∙∙∙∙∙∙∙ ►

The information on this map has been secured by the tireless efforts of the late Detective Chang and the officers of the Prefecture of Madripoor. The subterranean network of tunnels dates back to the early 1800s and has been constantly used by the criminal underworld. The Princess Bar has defied efforts to have its upper floors mapped completely, but the lower floor and tunnel connections are fairly certain. Their exits are less certain, but can extend several thousand yards in various directions. It is advised that under no circumstances is any officer to venture into the upper floors of the Princess Bar or the tunnels beneath alone or even in small numbers. Traps and/or ambushes are common.

--Excerpted from internal correspondence from the office of the Prefecture to the Provost Marshall Lionel Greenstreet, June 1991, in a report on the criminal conditions of Madripoor.

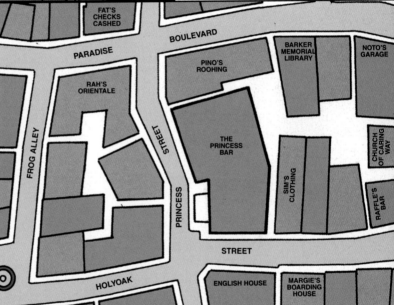

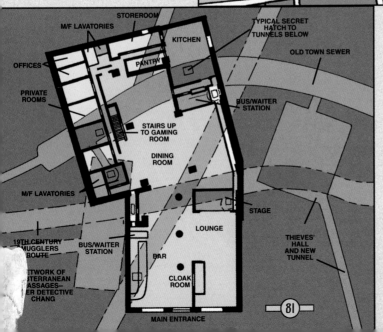

WOLVERINE
VS
OMEGA RED

CUMULATIVE
I • N • D • E • X

Volume two of the three part set that comprises the life and times, friends and foes, fights and follies of the X men's most volatile character... WOLVERINE!

BEAST

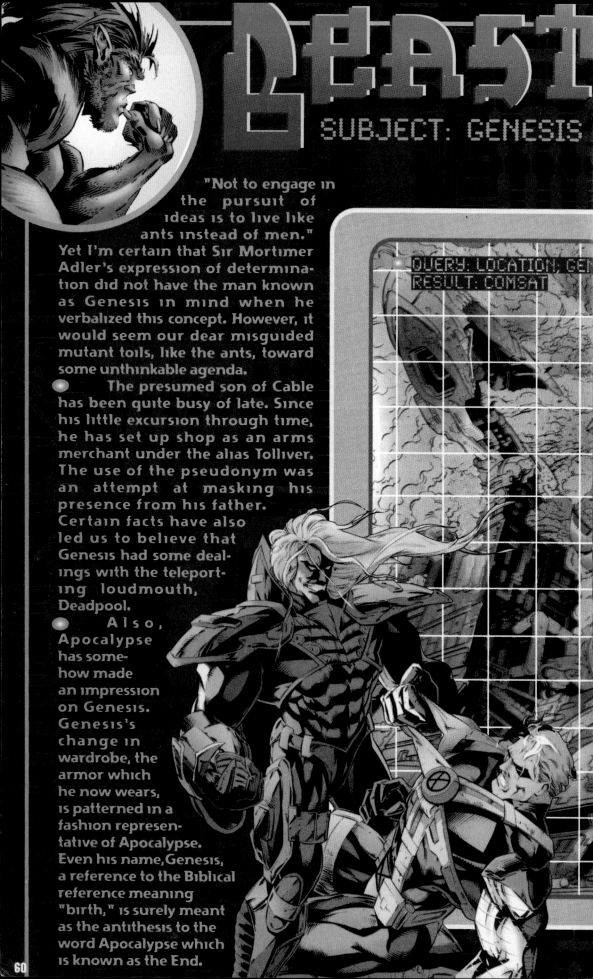

SUBJECT: GENESIS

"Not to engage in the pursuit of ideas is to live like ants instead of men." Yet I'm certain that Sir Mortimer Adler's expression of determination did not have the man known as Genesis in mind when he verbalized this concept. However, it would seem our dear misguided mutant toils, like the ants, toward some unthinkable agenda.

● The presumed son of Cable has been quite busy of late. Since his little excursion through time, he has set up shop as an arms merchant under the alias Tolliver. The use of the pseudonym was an attempt at masking his presence from his father. Certain facts have also led us to believe that Genesis had some dealings with the teleporting loudmouth, Deadpool.

● Also, Apocalypse has somehow made an impression on Genesis. Genesis's change in wardrobe, the armor which he now wears, is patterned in a fashion representative of Apocalypse. Even his name, Genesis, a reference to the Biblical reference meaning "birth," is surely meant as the antithesis to the word Apocalypse which is known as the End.

QUERY: LOCATION; GEN
RESULT: COMSAT

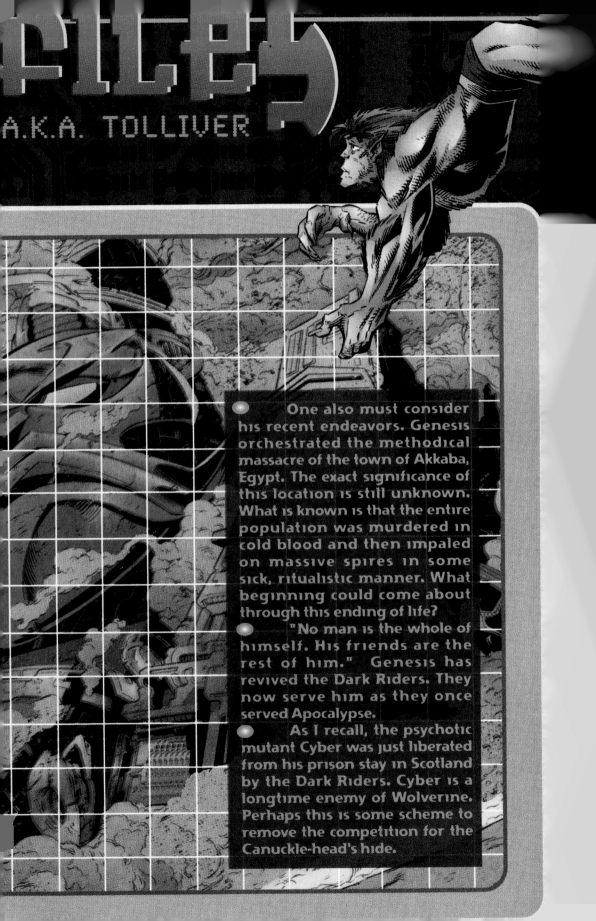

One also must consider his recent endeavors. Genesis orchestrated the methodical massacre of the town of Akkaba, Egypt. The exact significance of this location is still unknown. What is known is that the entire population was murdered in cold blood and then impaled on massive spires in some sick, ritualistic manner. What beginning could come about through this ending of life?

"No man is the whole of himself. His friends are the rest of him." Genesis has revived the Dark Riders. They now serve him as they once served Apocalypse.

As I recall, the psychotic mutant Cyber was just liberated from his prison stay in Scotland by the Dark Riders. Cyber is a longtime enemy of Wolverine. Perhaps this is some scheme to remove the competition for the Canuckle-head's hide.

BEAST

QUERY: SPECTRAL AN
RESULT: ON SCREEN

"The Holocaust is a central event in many people's lives, but it has also become a metaphor for our century. There cannot be an end to speaking and writing about it."
—Aharon Appelfeld, 1986

The first time I heard this quote, I recounted to myself that no truer statement could be made in regards to a creature this world had never encountered.

It all began in a parallel reality to this one. This reality diverged from the one I currently exist in due to a rift caused by a young mutant named Legion [See file: Legion / Sub-heading: Age of Apocalypse] who decided to carry out his father's [Charles Xavier: File: Prof X] work by using his immense powers to alter time itself. It was Legion's goal to travel back in time and eliminate Magneto [See file: Magneto] at a time before Magneto had ever made his presence known. It was Legion's belief that by killing Magneto, his father's work would be unhampered by the deeds of so-called evil mutants. A nice sentiment to say the least, but something went awry; Magneto survived and Charles Xavier died. The result on the time stream caused by Xavier's absence was phenomenal and a whole new world which would be the birthplace of Holocaust was created.

In the early years of this divergent universe, there were two extreme factions: the X-Men, under the tutelage of Magneto, and the other was Lord Apocalypse [See file: Apocalypse/Alternate]. In one of his earliest campaigns, Apocalypse sent a lone, young mutant who showed extreme promise to deal with the culling of the youngest members of the X-Men, as well as any stragglers who might be at the X-Men's base in Wundagore Mountain. The young mutant went by the name Nemesis.

Nemesis expected little or no resistance, certainly nothing that would be of any challenge to his powers, the ability to channel a form of biogenetic microwave blasts throughout his body. He was also blessed with a high degree of resistance to harm and a suit of armor which allowed him the ability to fly. Needless to say he was soon surprised to find a ready battle on his hands in the form of a young Rogue [See file: Rogue/Alternate] and the Scarlet Witch [See file: Scarlet Witch/Alternate], the daughter of Magneto himself. Although

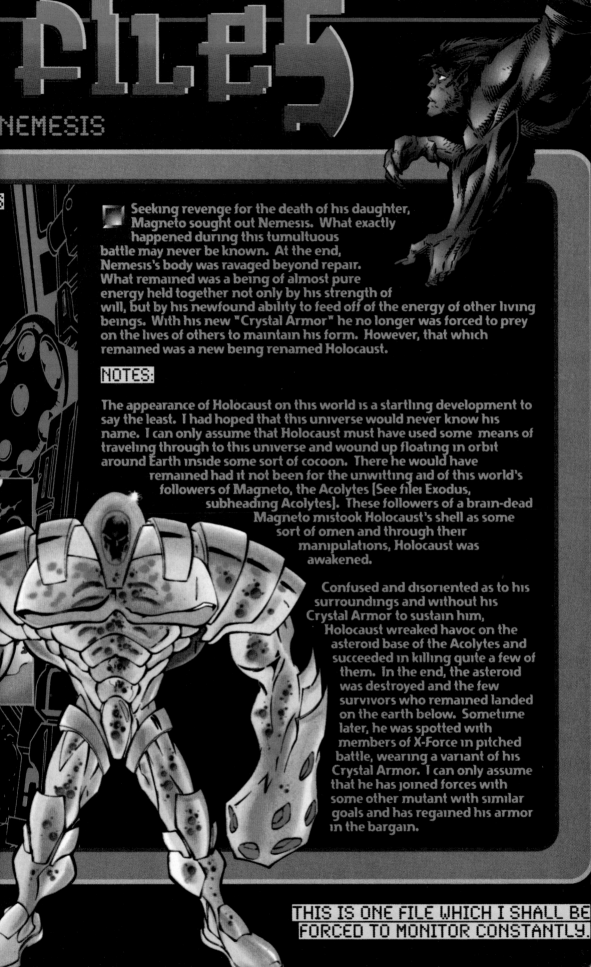

Seeking revenge for the death of his daughter, Magneto sought out Nemesis. What exactly happened during this tumultuous battle may never be known. At the end, Nemesis's body was ravaged beyond repair. What remained was a being of almost pure energy held together not only by his strength of will, but by his newfound ability to feed off of the energy of other living beings. With his new "Crystal Armor" he no longer was forced to prey on the lives of others to maintain his form. However, that which remained was a new being renamed Holocaust.

NOTES:

The appearance of Holocaust on this world is a startling development to say the least. I had hoped that this universe would never know his name. I can only assume that Holocaust must have used some means of traveling through to this universe and wound up floating in orbit around Earth inside some sort of cocoon. There he would have remained had it not been for the unwitting aid of this world's followers of Magneto, the Acolytes [See file: Exodus, subheading Acolytes]. These followers of a brain-dead Magneto mistook Holocaust's shell as some sort of omen and through their manipulations, Holocaust was awakened.

Confused and disoriented as to his surroundings and without his Crystal Armor to sustain him, Holocaust wreaked havoc on the asteroid base of the Acolytes and succeeded in killing quite a few of them. In the end, the asteroid was destroyed and the few survivors who remained landed on the earth below. Sometime later, he was spotted with members of X-Force in pitched battle, wearing a variant of his Crystal Armor. I can only assume that he has joined forces with some other mutant with similar goals and has regained his armor in the bargain.

THIS IS ONE FILE WHICH I SHALL BE FORCED TO MONITOR CONSTANTLY.

BEAST

He has gone by many names. The world, however, generally knows him as Magneto... the Master of Magnetism.

◉ Magneto was born Erik Magnus Lensherr. At a young age he, along with his family, was taken prisoner by Nazi Germany and sent to the Auschwitz concentration camp in Poland. He spent his early teen years in the camps and was the only member of his family to survive, eventually escaping with his future wife Magda.

The two lived happily together for a time and even sired a daughter. In a moment which was perhaps the defining.point of his life, the townsfolk decided to kill Magneto and his family because of his perceived "witchcraft." The town succeeded only in killing Magneto's daughter, causing him to unleash the full fury of his powers.

Magda fled from Magnus in terror. Sometime later it was learned that she died giving birth to twins, Magneto's children. [See file: Quicksilver/Scarlet Witch].

◉ As time progressed, Magneto, using his middle name first, wound up working as an orderly in a hospital in Israel. It was here that he first met Charles Xavier [See file: Professor X]. The two soon became fast friends; however, while Charles Xavier felt it was necessary to work towards a world where humans and mutants could coexist [See file: Xavier Manifesto], Magneto decided that the only way the two groups could live peacefully together would be if mutants ruled.

◉ Over .the years, Magneto and Charles Xavier would butt heads on numerous occasions. However, neither man would be alone. Charles Xavier founded his X-Men while Magneto would go on to form one group of followers after the other. As the years progressed, Magneto's attitudes seemed to change. He began to show signs that he had abandoned his dream. He stood trial in Paris, and even went so far as to assume the role as headmaster of Xavier's School,

under the guise of Michael Xavier, during Charles's medical absence.

⬤ However, this heroic stature would not last. Once again, he would become the "evil mutant" the world believed him to be. And in the last battle between Xavier and himself, the good Professor saw fit to destroy Magneto's mind... supposedly ending the threat of Magneto.

⬤ For a short period, Magneto sat catatonic in his asteroid base [See file: Asteroid M/Graymalkin] surrounded by his follow-ers, the Acolytes [See files: Exodus, Acolytes, Fabian Cortez, Colossus]. However, when Holocaust [See file: Holocaust] was brought aboard, he destroyed Asteroid M, sending its surviving inhabitants crashing to Earth.

⬤ Notes: Magneto can bend the forces of the electromagnetic spectrum with but a thought. Add to this: his indomitable will, strength of convictions, scientific genius, charismatic demeanor and complete mastery over his powers and you possess, quite possibly, one of the most powerful entities on the planet. I know far too much about this man to simply believe that we have seen the last of him. Unconfirmed rumors point to a young man matching Magneto's powers and description going by the name "Joseph." Magneto has reversed his aging process on at least one previous occasion [See file: Alpha Mutant]. It would not shock me to discover that we are facing a new, younger, Magneto.

SUBJECT: EMPLATE

Vampires. The stuff of legends and nightmares. Beings of indescribable power and ferocity who feed on the very life force of those around them.

Emplate is the mutant son of wealthy businessman Cartier St. Croix. Upon reaching puberty, Emplate discovered that he was a mutant. Not that this is unusual for mutants. (The onset of adolescence is normally the trigger for mutation manifestation.) What is unusual is what he mutated into. He was gifted not only with extraordinary powers, but also with the need to feed off of the genetic marrow of other mutants' bones. His every ability only seems to lend itself towards this end.

Emplate possesses the ability to feed on mutants via a mouth-like opening in his hands. When he feeds on a mutant, he gains the use of their powers as well as some of their body features and characteristics. Emplate is able to shunt himself inter-dimensionally, making him capable of approaching someone almost completely undetected. This inter-dimensional travel may even double as a form of teleportation. Then there is, perhaps, his most dangerous capability. With a glance he can not only know a body's

genetic potential but also gain instant knowledge of that person's memories.

Of late, it has come to my attention that Emplate possesses one more stagger-

ing capability. Not only can he feed on mutants himself, but he can also employ others towards this end. Through some as of yet unknown fashion he is able to imbue others with the same mouth-like opening on their palms that he has. It is my understanding that this process also grants him a measure of control over his "minions" as well as the benefit of their directly "feeding" him.

AM I THAT TRANSPARENT, SEAN?

SHAME ON ME.

While on the subject of minions, it might behoove me to add that he has been known to employ the services of four individuals for this purpose. [See File: Edgerton, Gayle; Bulwark; Murmur; Vincente.]

SHUT UP. YOU -- YOU NOTHING!

OPEN UP THE DOOR, QUICKLY!

FEEDING AGAIN -- SO SOON AFTER THE LAST SNACK?

IS THAT WISE?

KLAK

SIR.

Let us also not forget Emplate's diminutive driver, DOA. While it does not appear that DOA has any known powers, he does seem to serve some unknown purpose. This is one point which requires further investigation.

Notes: A very powerful loose cannon whose "taste" seems to lean towards the youngest generation of mutants. I must look into possible weaknesses to exploit. Perhaps there is something to be found in the recent revelation that the Generation X member M is his sister? Or maybe there is an avenue to be explored in his seeming need for a respirator? Then there is his weakest link of all... his NEED to feed. If only it were as simple as using a wooden stake...

SUBJECT:
THE ORIGINAL X-MEN

[Forward file to term:002181//banshee.xav.acad.com]

Cyclops, with his powerful optic blasts; Marvel Girl, the beautiful young woman who gave form to the expression, "Mind over matter"; Iceman, the human popsicle; Angel, the high-flying winged playboy; and the lovable, acrobatic, bouncing Beast. To say the least, these were strange names, strange abilities, and strange times to be alive. Collectively, however, these five mutants would forever be remembered as THE ORIGINAL X-MEN.

Scott Summers a.k.a. Cyclops, is quite often referred to as the FIRST X-MAN. While Cyclops was not the first mutant Professor Charles Xavier [See File: Professor X] ever instructed in the use of his powers, he was the first in several other categories. He was the first to wear the famous black and gold outfit. He was the first mutant Xavier ever rescued. And he was also the X-Men's first team leader. Since his earliest days at Xavier's School, Cyclops has remained the cornerstone upon which Xavier's foundation was built. Thankfully, he's lightened up considerably since then.

Jean Grey-Summers, a.k.a. Marvel Girl, is one woman who should always be loved for her mind. She was Xavier's first true pupil. At an early age, her psionic powers developed when a childhood friend of hers was struck and killed by an oncoming car. She was terrified when she suddenly found herself inside her dying friend's mind. Immediately sent to Xavier's, he helped her establish psionic blocks on her telepathy until such time as she was physically ready to use it. This didn't stop her one bit, however, from developing and using her other mental ability, telekinesis.

Robert "Bobby" Drake, a.k.a. Iceman, was the youngest member of the team. His ability to freeze water vapor in the air combined with his adolescent behavior made him the class clown. You could almost count on his using his powers to humiliate his opponents as well as

his teammates. When the chips were down, however, he would always prove to be a valued member of the team.

Warren Worthington III, a.k.a. The Angel, has always seemed to soar above the rest. Born into one of the nation's wealthiest families, Warren was never left wanting for anything. However, when he suddenly found two large feathered wings growing from his shoulders, his world was changed forever.

Henry "Hank" McCoy, a.k.a. The Beast, was not only the brains of the team but its brawn as well. Who says that the strong must be meek in mind as well? His mutant abilities were only part of what made up this peculiar package. He could lift nearly one ton, scale most surfaces with his bare hands and feet as easily as walking across the room, and was more agile than the most superbly trained Olympic athletes. His appearance was brutish and simian, with his arms, hands and feet being much larger than normal. His feet were as articulate as most people's hands. Add to this a genius-level intellect and scientific aptitude and you have the young man known as the BEAST. [The majority of the villains he faced are said to have preferred he simply pummel them rather than listen to his endless "jabbering." So it could be argued that it was his non-mutant abilities that truly struck fear into the hearts of his enemies.] [NOTE to Sean: you can leave that last part out if you want but if you do that, you obviously have no sense of vibrant verbiage.—Henry]

Through the years, the line-up of the X-Men has changed drastically; however, one thing will always remain the same. These five will always be the remembered as the first—and arguably the best—representatives of mutant-kind.

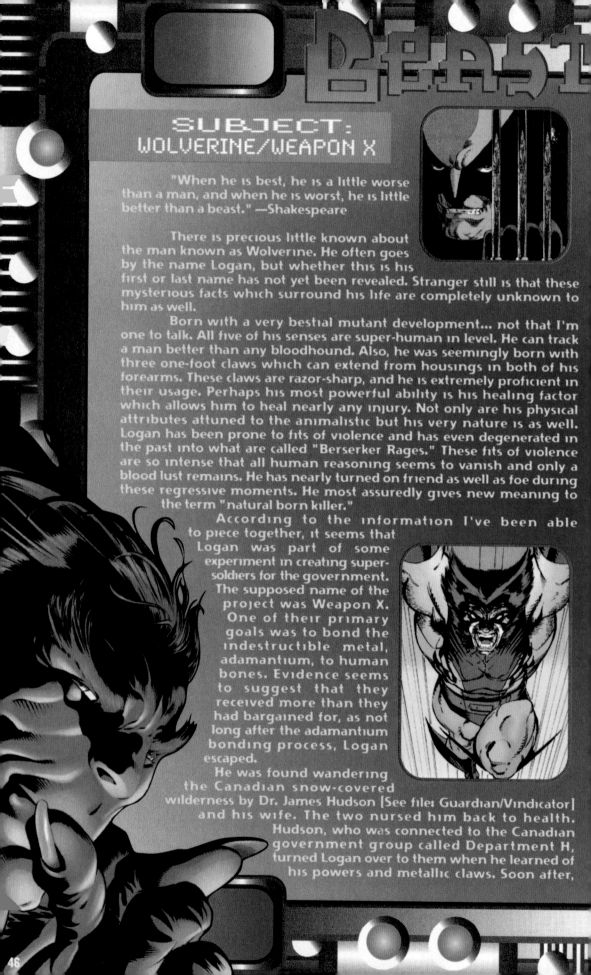

BEAST

SUBJECT: WOLVERINE/WEAPON X

"When he is best, he is a little worse than a man, and when he is worst, he is little better than a beast." —Shakespeare

There is precious little known about the man known as Wolverine. He often goes by the name Logan, but whether this is his first or last name has not yet been revealed. Stranger still is that these mysterious facts which surround his life are completely unknown to him as well.

Born with a very bestial mutant development... not that I'm one to talk. All five of his senses are super-human in level. He can track a man better than any bloodhound. Also, he was seemingly born with three one-foot claws which can extend from housings in both of his forearms. These claws are razor-sharp, and he is extremely proficient in their usage. Perhaps his most powerful ability is his healing factor which allows him to heal nearly any injury. Not only are his physical attributes attuned to the animalistic but his very nature is as well. Logan has been prone to fits of violence and has even degenerated in the past into what are called "Berserker Rages." These fits of violence are so intense that all human reasoning seems to vanish and only a blood lust remains. He has nearly turned on friend as well as foe during these regressive moments. He most assuredly gives new meaning to the term "natural born killer."

According to the information I've been able to piece together, it seems that Logan was part of some experiment in creating super-soldiers for the government. The supposed name of the project was Weapon X. One of their primary goals was to bond the indestructible metal, adamantium, to human bones. Evidence seems to suggest that they received more than they had bargained for, as not long after the adamantium bonding process, Logan escaped.

He was found wandering the Canadian snow-covered wilderness by Dr. James Hudson [See file: Guardian/Vindicator] and his wife. The two nursed him back to health. Hudson, who was connected to the Canadian government group called Department H, turned Logan over to them when he learned of his powers and metallic claws. Soon after,

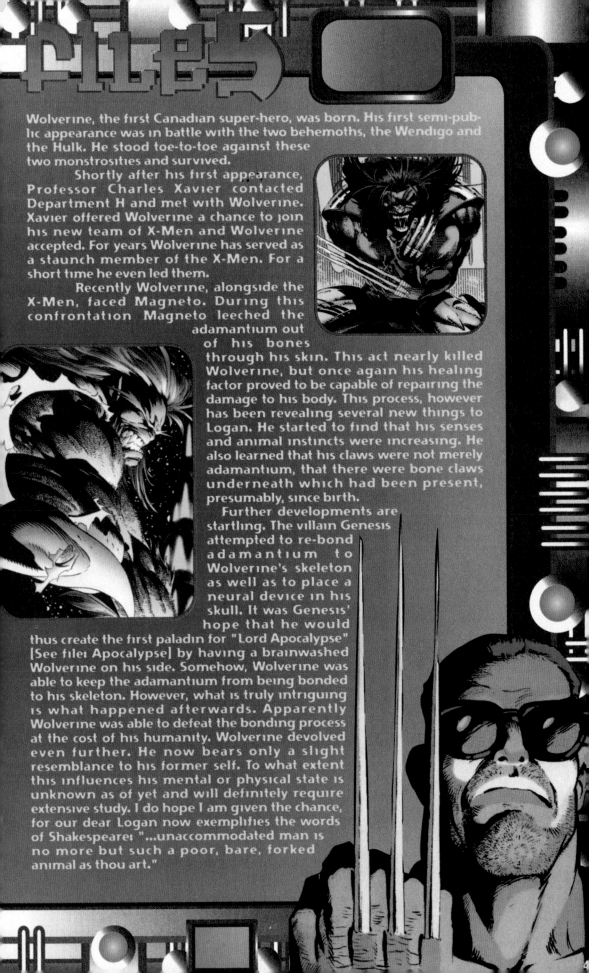

Wolverine, the first Canadian super-hero, was born. His first semi-public appearance was in battle with the two behemoths, the Wendigo and the Hulk. He stood toe-to-toe against these two monstrosities and survived.

Shortly after his first appearance, Professor Charles Xavier contacted Department H and met with Wolverine. Xavier offered Wolverine a chance to join his new team of X-Men and Wolverine accepted. For years Wolverine has served as a staunch member of the X-Men. For a short time he even led them.

Recently Wolverine, alongside the X-Men, faced Magneto. During this confrontation Magneto leeched the adamantium out of his bones through his skin. This act nearly killed Wolverine, but once again his healing factor proved to be capable of repairing the damage to his body. This process, however has been revealing several new things to Logan. He started to find that his senses and animal instincts were increasing. He also learned that his claws were not merely adamantium, that there were bone claws underneath which had been present, presumably, since birth.

Further developments are startling. The villain Genesis attempted to re-bond adamantium to Wolverine's skeleton as well as to place a neural device in his skull. It was Genesis' hope that he would thus create the first paladin for "Lord Apocalypse" [See file: Apocalypse] by having a brainwashed Wolverine on his side. Somehow, Wolverine was able to keep the adamantium from being bonded to his skeleton. However, what is truly intriguing is what happened afterwards. Apparently Wolverine was able to defeat the bonding process at the cost of his humanity. Wolverine devolved even further. He now bears only a slight resemblance to his former self. To what extent this influences his mental or physical state is unknown as of yet and will definitely require extensive study. I do hope I am given the chance, for our dear Logan now exemplifies the words of Shakespeare: "...unaccommodated man is no more but such a poor, bare, forked animal as thou art."

SUBJECT: PROFESSOR X/ONSLAUGHT

"The true teacher defends his pupils against his own personal influence. He inspires self-trust. He guides their eyes from himself to the spirit that quickens him. He will have no disciple." — Amos Bronson Alcott

Professor Charles Xavier failed. That is, at least, how some people may perceive his works. They might believe that because we still live in a world where humans and mutants cannot coexist peacefully, that his is a lost cause. Further still, they might believe that those who have taken up this dream are doomed to his same failure. That perception would be erroneous.

Xavier learned at a young age that he could read the minds of those around him. As he grew, he became aware of just how powerful he was, yet this increase in powers also resulted in the loss of his hair as well. Soon, he began to devote his life to the study of mutation and genetics. By the age of 20 he had completed a bachelor's degree in biology and two masters in biophysics and genetics. Immediately upon completion of his studies at Oxford, however, Charles found himself drafted and sent to fight in Asia.

After this, Xavier began traveling the globe, eventually finding himself in Cairo, Egypt. It was here that he met, battled and defeated his first "evil" mutant, the powerful telepath Amahl Farouk [See File: Shadow King]. It was this encounter which forged Xavier's path over the years. In an addendum to his dream,

Charles decided to devote his life to the protection of mankind from those mutants who would abuse their powers and humanity along with them.

From Egypt, Xavier traveled to Israel where he met two individuals who would become an important factor in his life. The first was Gabrielle Haller, who would years later bear Charles' only son, David Charles Haller [See File: Legion]. The second was one Erik Magnus Lensherr, who would later be known as Magneto, the master of Magnetism and arch-foe of Charles' X-Men [See File: Magneto]. Magneto and Charles were for a time the best of friends until they revealed to each other while battling Hydra that each possessed mutant powers. After their encounter they would part ways, each believing the other to be mistaken in his approach to the growing mutant populace and its role in the world.

A few years passed, and Xavier founded a school based in his

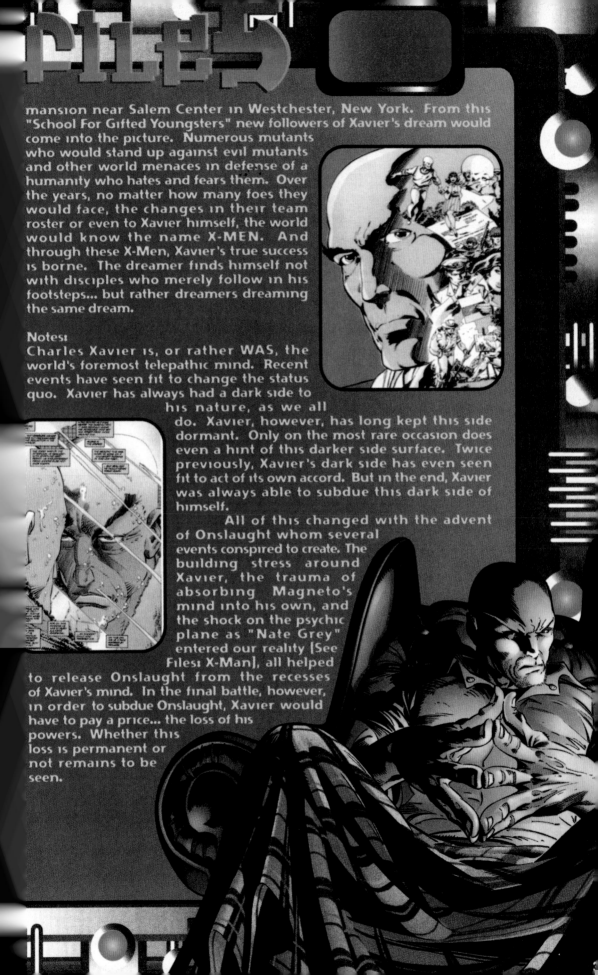

FILES

mansion near Salem Center in Westchester, New York. From this "School For Gifted Youngsters" new followers of Xavier's dream would come into the picture. Numerous mutants who would stand up against evil mutants and other world menaces in defense of a humanity who hates and fears them. Over the years, no matter how many foes they would face, the changes in their team roster or even to Xavier himself, the world would know the name X-MEN. And through these X-Men, Xavier's true success is borne. The dreamer finds himself not with disciples who merely follow in his footsteps... but rather dreamers dreaming the same dream.

Notes:
Charles Xavier is, or rather WAS, the world's foremost telepathic mind. Recent events have seen fit to change the status quo. Xavier has always had a dark side to his nature, as we all do. Xavier, however, has long kept this side dormant. Only on the most rare occasion does even a hint of this darker side surface. Twice previously, Xavier's dark side has even seen fit to act of its own accord. But in the end, Xavier was always able to subdue this dark side of himself.

All of this changed with the advent of Onslaught whom several events conspired to create. The building stress around Xavier, the trauma of absorbing Magneto's mind into his own, and the shock on the psychic plane as "Nate Grey" entered our reality [See Files: X-Man], all helped to release Onslaught from the recesses of Xavier's mind. In the final battle, however, in order to subdue Onslaught, Xavier would have to pay a price... the loss of his powers. Whether this loss is permanent or not remains to be seen.

> "Your bait of falsehood takes this carp of truth; and thus do we of wisdom and of reach, With windlasses and with assays of bias, By indirections find directions out."
> — Shakespeare: Hamlet

Masters of magnetism, maniacal mutant immortals, malevolent cosmic entities and invading alien forces. All of these and more, the X-Men have faced time and time again. And through it all, they have somehow managed to come out ahead of the game, somehow managing to turn the tide of the battle into a victory. Yet there is one foe the X-Men may never defeat... simple human prejudice.

Over the years, this prejudice has worn many faces and many names: Mutant Registration Act, Genoshan Extinction Agenda and now it goes by the name Operation: Zero Tolerance.

Operation: Zero Tolerance is, for the first time, a concerted effort being made by multiple global factions. With its international reach, we have only begun to scratch the surface as to the identity of the players.

⬤ HUMANITY'S LAST STAND/FRIENDS OF HUMANITY:

These two factions recently combined to form a larger, less openly militant group. This group's stated goal is simple: the eradication of the "mutant threat." Preying upon the fear, ignorance and insecurities of the American people, they continue to grow in popularity. It is through this organization that Graydon Creed has founded his platform for political power.

⬤ GRAYDON CREED:

Graydon Creed, while not a mutant himself, is the son of the mutants Mystique and Sabretooth. It is likely that this alone is reason enough for his hatred of all things mutant. Graydon first founded the Friends of Humanity and is currently the popular candidate for President of the United States. What his followers would do if they knew his lineage, however, is anyone's guess.

FILES

SENATOR ROBERT KELLY:

Senator Robert Kelly was foremost in breaking ground in the area of mutant regulations. Kelly was on the Council of Mutant Affairs and was instrumental in the creation of the Mutant Registration Act. Because of his stance on the "mutant problem," Kelly has himself become a target of numerous mutant attacks. However, even he sees the dangers presented by this new, growing movement. Thus, he has once again become a target of his "own kind."

TRASK:

The Trask name has long been associated with anti-mutant sentiments. Even as far back as the formation of the X-Men themselves, there was always a Trask to design a way to destroy mutant life. That legacy lives on. Whether it be through the use of human powered techno-armors or the ultimate Trask design—the Sentinels—mutants beware.

SENTINELS:

Mutant-hunting machines of immense size and power. Over the years, many makes and models have come and gone and with each passing, they only get stronger and deadlier. Their core programming? Simple and basic: destroy all mutant life and protect humanity. While they have yet to be completely successful, they are machines and they are legion.

BASTION:

This enigmatic player is the man behind the scenes pulling all the strings. With every question answered, more questions arise. Who he is, where he comes from, and why he does what he does may be known only to him. Perhaps time will tell us more about his motivations. Hopefully it won't be too late.

SUBJECT: COLOSSUS

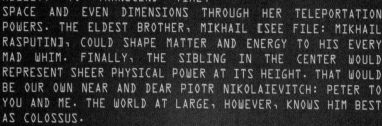

ON SCREEN:
DATA ANALYSIS

THE CHILDREN OF THE RASPUTIN FAMILY ARE A LESSON IN POWER. THE YOUNGEST, ILLYANA RASPUTIN [SEE FILE: MAGIK], HAD THE ABILITY TO TRANSCEND TIME, SPACE AND EVEN DIMENSIONS THROUGH HER TELEPORTATION POWERS. THE ELDEST BROTHER, MIKHAIL [SEE FILE: MIKHAIL RASPUTIN], COULD SHAPE MATTER AND ENERGY TO HIS EVERY MAD WHIM. FINALLY, THE SIBLING IN THE CENTER WOULD REPRESENT SHEER PHYSICAL POWER AT ITS HEIGHT. THAT WOULD BE OUR OWN NEAR AND DEAR PIOTR NIKOLAIEVITCH: PETER TO YOU AND ME. THE WORLD AT LARGE, HOWEVER, KNOWS HIM BEST AS COLOSSUS.

HAD PIOTR HAD HIS WAY, HE WOULD LIKELY STILL BE TENDING FARM WITH HIS FAMILY AT THE UST-ORDYNSKI COLLECTIVE IN HIS NATIVE RUSSIA. HE WOULD STILL BE SPENDING HIS FREE TIME PAINTING BEAUTIFUL WORKS OF ART. AND HE WOULD STILL HAVE ALL OF HIS FAMILY ALIVE AND WELL AROUND HIM. FATE WOULD NOT BE SO KIND. PIOTR HAD THE ABILITY TO CONVERT HIS ENTIRE PHYSIQUE INTO A FORM OF ORGANIC METAL. IN THE PROCESS, HIS ENDURANCE, RESISTANCE TO INJURY, SPEED AND STRENGTH ALL INCREASE EXPONENTIALLY.

COLOSSUS WAS ONE OF THE FIRST MUTANTS CONTACTED WHEN PROFESSOR XAVIER FOUND HIMSELF IN DIRE NEED OF A NEW TEAM OF X-MEN TO INVESTIGATE THE DISAPPEARANCE OF THE ORIGINAL TEAM [SEE FILE: KRAKOA]. HE JOINED THE X-MEN AND REMAINED A CORNERSTONE MEMBER FOR NUMEROUS YEARS. THERE WAS EVEN A BRIEF FLIRTATIOUS LOVE BETWEEN HIMSELF AND THE YOUNG KITTY PRYDE [SEE FILE: SHADOWCAT/SPRITE].

> "WHY, MAN, HE DOTH BESTRIDE THE NARROW WORLD,
> LIKE A COLOSSUS; AND WE PETTY MEN
> WALK UNDER HIS HUGE LEGS, AND PEEP ABOUT
> TO FIND OURSELVES DISHONORABLE GRAVES.
> MEN AT SOME TIME ARE MASTERS OF THEIR FATES. . . "
>
> --SHAKESPEARE: JULIUS CAESAR

ON SCREEN:
SUBJECT PROFILE

THEN TRAGEDY STRUCK. FIRST, COLOSSUS WAS FORCED TO KILL FOR THE FIRST TIME IN SELF-DEFENSE [SEE FILE: PROTEUS/ MOIRA MACTAGGERT]. THIS QUICKLY MARKED A TURNING POINT IN HIS OUTLOOK ON LIFE. YEARS PASSED. ON A MISSION WITH HIS FELLOW X-MEN, HE WAS REUNITED WITH HIS BROTHER MIKHAIL WHO HAD BEEN PRESUMED DEAD. SHORTLY AFTER THEIR REUNION, COLOSSUS LEARNED THAT HIS BROTHER, WHOM HE LOOKED UP TO, WAS COMPLETELY INSANE.

A SHORT TIME LATER, ILLYANA WOULD BE THE FIRST VICTIM TO DIE OF THE LEGACY VIRUS [SEE APPENDIX: LEGACY VIRUS; SEE FILE: STRYFE]. TO MAKE MATTERS WORSE, COLOSSUS WAS NOT THERE WHEN SHE DIED. IN FACT, HE SUSTAINED AN INJURY WHICH WOULD NOT ALLOW HIM TO TRANSFORM INTO HIS HUMAN FORM. PETER FELT AS IF HE HAD FAILED ILLYANA. NOT EVEN ILLYANA'S FUNERAL WOULD BE ALLOWED TO PROCEED IN PEACE. MIDWAY THROUGH THE SERVICE, MAGNETO [SEE FILE: MAGNETO] DROPPED IN. MAGNUS OFFERED THE X-MEN THE CHOICE TO JOIN HIM AND THE REST OF HIS ACOLYTES ON AVALON [SEE FILES: ASTEROID M/GRAYMALKIN/AVALON]. MUCH TO EVERYONE'S SURPRISE, COLOSSUS ACCEPTED HIS INVITATION. PETER BLAMED XAVIER FOR ILLYANA'S DEATH. HE FELT THAT IF XAVIER'S DREAM HAD FAILED HIM, PERHAPS MAGNETO'S WOULDN'T.

AFTER THE DESTRUCTION OF AVALON, COLOSSUS BEGAN WANDERING AGAIN. HE FELT AS IF HE WAS WITHOUT A HOME OR PURPOSE. IT APPEARS THAT OUR SHINING COMPANION HAS DECIDED ONCE AGAIN TO FIGHT ON THE SIDE OF THE ANGELS, AS HE HAS RECENTLY FOUND A HOME IN EXCALIBUR [SEE FILE: EXCALIBUR]. ALTHOUGH THE CURRENT QUESTION IS: HOW STABLE WILL HIS REACTIONS REMAIN TOWARDS KITTY AND HER NEW LOVE INTEREST, PETE WISDOM? [NOTE: CREATE FILE ON WISDOM.]

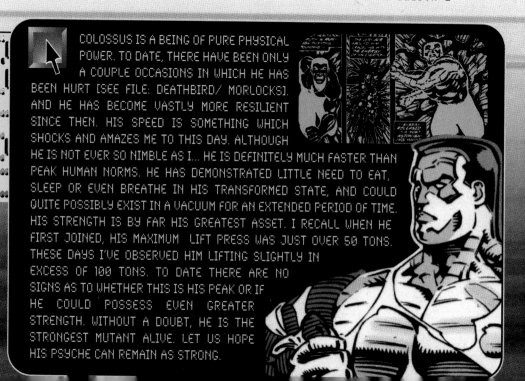

COLOSSUS IS A BEING OF PURE PHYSICAL POWER. TO DATE, THERE HAVE BEEN ONLY A COUPLE OCCASIONS IN WHICH HE HAS BEEN HURT [SEE FILE: DEATHBIRD/ MORLOCKS]. AND HE HAS BECOME VASTLY MORE RESILIENT SINCE THEN. HIS SPEED IS SOMETHING WHICH SHOCKS AND AMAZES ME TO THIS DAY. ALTHOUGH HE IS NOT EVER SO NIMBLE AS I... HE IS DEFINITELY MUCH FASTER THAN PEAK HUMAN NORMS. HE HAS DEMONSTRATED LITTLE NEED TO EAT, SLEEP OR EVEN BREATHE IN HIS TRANSFORMED STATE, AND COULD QUITE POSSIBLY EXIST IN A VACUUM FOR AN EXTENDED PERIOD OF TIME. HIS STRENGTH IS BY FAR HIS GREATEST ASSET. I RECALL WHEN HE FIRST JOINED, HIS MAXIMUM LIFT PRESS WAS JUST OVER 50 TONS. THESE DAYS I'VE OBSERVED HIM LIFTING SLIGHTLY IN EXCESS OF 100 TONS. TO DATE THERE ARE NO SIGNS AS TO WHETHER THIS IS HIS PEAK OR IF HE COULD POSSESS EVEN GREATER STRENGTH. WITHOUT A DOUBT, HE IS THE STRONGEST MUTANT ALIVE. LET US HOPE HIS PSYCHE CAN REMAIN AS STRONG.

BEAST FILES

No truer statement could be uttered in regards to this Beast. Nature has indeed taught me to know my friends... and in the X-Men I have found a family. But outside of them, I have known precious few. I had always considered the Avengers to be the closest I've ever come to good friends outside of the X-Men. Yet now with their recent departure, I'm left with a void in that department. A void which my mind can only fill with regards to one man... Spider-Man. Spider-Man is and may forever remain the friend I never quite know. It may just be part of his elusive nature, or perhaps for some darker reason. Whichever the case may be, I have chosen to leave him to his privacy. This does, however, make my task of preserving a catalog of our world a bit daunting in his particular file. I will, however, endeavor to do my best.

I am often amused that the first time Bobby [See File: Iceman] and I met Spidey, we actually believed him to be a mutant, and even invited him to join the X-Men. However, he quickly dismissed us and went on his merry way. I think it's safe to say that I liked him the moment I met him. Unfortunately, the second time we met it was over a misunderstanding and we devolved into fisticuffs. Over the years, however, he and the X-Men would grow to trust each other. And he and I would go on to join each other in many a worthwhile cause.

SPIDER-MAN

"NATURE TEACHES BEASTS TO KNOW THEIR FRIENDS." – SHAKESPEARE

Perhaps one of the most puzzling things about this paragon is his ever changing appearance and attitude. I've seen him go from a seemingly carefree spirit, laughing in the face of danger, to a deadly serious man, seemingly battling for life and limb. I've also seen him in enough costumes to give Janet Van Dyne [See File: The Wasp] a run for her money. Who can fathom the depth of changes wrought in his personal life which may account for these differences. Yet somehow, through it all, everyone's "friendly neighborhood" Spider-Man rises to the occasion. And despite what the Daily Bugle [See File: J.J. Jameson] may say, in picking friends, I believe I could do no better.

NOTES:

Spider-Man's powers seem to be a derivative of those of an actual spider. Exactly how he acquired them is anyone's guess, but he is definitely not a mutant. He seems to possess the proportionate strength and speed of a spider. These abilities alone would make him a very powerful adversary indeed. I have witnessed him pressing around ten tons, and moving with enough speed to easily dodge machine gun fire. Add to this his uncanny ability to adhere to seemingly any surface. Exactly how this is accomplished I'm not certain. Perhaps this is done through mechanical means such as Natasha [See File: Black Widow] uses, or it may simply be yet another manifestation of his powers. Next up are his web-shooters. I have ruled out the possibility that these are natural webs, as unlike a spider's web Spider-Man's webs dissolve in a little over an hour's time. However, if they are not natural, then this would tend to indicate the work of an advanced intellect. For it would take a genius level IQ to develop a propulsion system capable of deploying a web-line with as numerous capabilities as I've seen him use. Last but not least is a power I've long suspected our good ol' Spidey to possess. Only in the most rare of situations have I ever seen Spider-Man taken by surprise. It is my guess that he has some sort of clairvoyant sense that warns him of danger, thus allowing his agility and strength to carry him out of harm's way. If this is true, this may be the secret key to his consistent success.

BEAST FILES

SUBJECT

:MISTER SINISTER
:ESSEX

One man can make a difference. Every day we are reminded of this through the shining examples set before us. Where would our world be without people like Abraham Lincoln, Martin Luther King Jr., George Washington, Captain America or even our own Xavier? Yet for every action there is an equal and opposite reaction. This truth carries over in that for every positive influence on our world, there must be a negative. I can think of few more negative than the man known as Mister Sinister.

For the most part, Sinister has ever remained one of the elusive, unanswered riddles which has plagued the X-Men for years. Since Scott Summers' [See File: Cyclops] childhood, Sinister has been by his side, hiding in the shadows, manipulating him. Apparently, it turns out that Sinister found that the breeding of Scott Summers' and Jean Grey's [See File: Phoenix/Marvel Girl] DNA would create the ultimate mutant. So, like unto a puppet-master, Sinister has been ever the manipulator to see that this genetic stock is forged. When the Phoenix simulacrum [See Appendix: Phoenix Force] died, he got his wish. A long dormant clone of Jean was awakened. Seizing the opportunity, Sinister arranged for the Jean's clone which he dubbed Madelyne Pryor [See File: Goblin Queen/Pryor] to mate with Scott. The outcome would grow up to become Cable [See File: Christopher Summers/Cable/Askani'son]

Another machination which Sinister was revealed to have been behind was the so-called "Mutant Massacre." Sinister dispatched his Marauders [See File: Marauders] who swept a bloody path across the United States. They laid waste to hundreds of mutants, including a large portion of the Morlocks [See File: Morlocks]. It has remained a mystery as to why Sinister would commit such an act that seemed to be at cross-purposes with his stated goals. A large clue to this has now surfaced.

The time-traveling Askani recently dispatched Jean Grey and Cyclops into the industrial era of England. There, they confronted an obsessed scientist named Nathaniel Essex, who was on the brink of joining ranks with a mysterious benefactor. The strange benefactor who was none other than Apocalypse [See File: Apocalypse]. Despite Jean and Scott's best efforts to the contrary, they bore witness to the eventual birth of Mister Sinister... Thus the connection was revealed. The unholy union which would cause Sinister to enact a "culling" of the mutant populace for his "Survival of the Fittest" Darwinistic creator in years to follow. One can only hope that this duo's ties are severed.

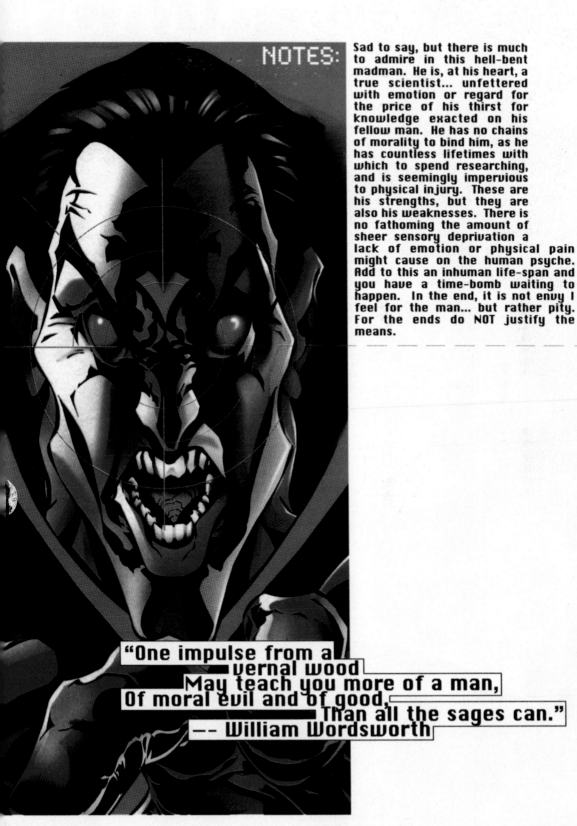

NOTES:

Sad to say, but there is much to admire in this hell-bent madman. He is, at his heart, a true scientist... unfettered with emotion or regard for the price of his thirst for knowledge exacted on his fellow man. He has no chains of morality to bind him, as he has countless lifetimes with which to spend researching, and is seemingly impervious to physical injury. These are his strengths, but they are also his weaknesses. There is no fathoming the amount of sheer sensory deprivation a lack of emotion or physical pain might cause on the human psyche. Add to this an inhuman life-span and you have a time-bomb waiting to happen. In the end, it is not envy I feel for the man... but rather pity. For the ends do NOT justify the means.

"One impulse from a vernal wood
May teach you more of a man,
Of moral evil and of good,
Than all the sages can."
-- William Wordsworth

"Mirrors should reflect a little before throwing back images.
--- *Jean Cocteau*

This is without a doubt the single most disturbing file I will ev
make. The proverb goes that if you travel long enough or far enoug
eventually you will meet yourself. Yet in all of my encounters with a
of the would-be world-conquerors or even destroyers... there can nev
be a more bone-chilling discovery than the man known as McCoy... th
Dark Beast.

It is not often that one gets a chance to literally meet one's se
One might think this would be a joyous occasion at best, or a
unsettling one at worst. When I first encountered this alternate versic
of myself however, I discovered much to my chagrin that I didn't lil
myself very much. Confusing, isn't it?

From what I could gather, this version of myself was apparent
spawned from the alternate reality which Bishop seems to have bee
alluding to since his return from the past. The general idea of sa
reality was that it was a world without Xavier. In this world, Apocalyp
reigned supreme in a veritable Apocalyptic Age to coin a phrase. O
good, or rather dark, McCoy was one of the chief scientists and w
quite instrumental in helping Apocalypse gain a large power-ba
through mutates.

SUBJECT:
DARK BEAST

DATA TRANSFER
COMPLETE

Needless to say, when that reality began to crumble, somehow McCoy gained entry to our own reality. Although chronal analysis seems to indicate that his arrival was displaced somehow and he arrived twenty some odd years in our past, his activities from his arrival till now are a mystery. Recent evidence, however, suggests he may have had a hand in the creation of the Genoshan mutates [See File: Genosha, See Appendix: X-Tinction Agenda] along with Sugar-Man [See File: Sugar-Man]. There also seems to be strong evidence of his influence in the Morlock [See Appendix: Morlock] community.

In a startling move, this darker version of myself recently lured me to one of his lairs. In that meeting, he not only defeated me in combat, but imprisoned me, bricked inside of a wall. He then proceeded to make his appearance out to resemble mine, then replace me within the X-Men. Apparently, his greatest fear was that Mister Sinister [See File: Mister Sinister] of our reality would press him into service as he had in his reality. So, as his logic went, he decided to hide in plain view... as me. Unfortunately for me, his ruse worked for quite some time. I can only hope that my teammates' lack of detection of this fraud was due to a brilliance that I and my counterpart share, or some influence Onslaught [See File: Professor X] had on the X-Men.

At the end of the Onslaught, I was freed, and my counterpart was incarcerated. This, I pray, will remain a permanent condition. There were, however, a couple of unexpected benefits from the arrival of my shattered reflection. One, I have been able to salvage some files he had been amassing in much the same fashion as myself. Second, I was able to gaze into the abyss that is possible within me. This alone is a very sobering opportunity, and is not wasted on me. Finally, my incarceration gave me time to contemplate my role and priorities in the world. Albeit a harsh way to learn, I have learned my lessons well. Mayhaps I'm better off because another me was worse.

BEAST

> **"O! What a rogue and peasant slave am I."** — Shakespeare: Haml[

☐ Stunning beauty, raw power, a sweet southern belle, and a fierce femme fatale. these things and more combine into the living paradox we know only as Rogue. There almost with her an aura of duplicity. One can only assume this stems from her less the humble beginnings, but I get ahead of myself. Perhaps I should simply start... at th beginning.

☐ From what has been gathered, Rogue's powers manifested themselves up puberty as do those of most mutants. However, Rogue's unique ability to trans the powers, abilities, and memories of nearly any being through physical conto could not have chosen a more awkward moment than her famous "first kiss." T results were devastating. A young lad by the name of Cody would nev recover from the shocking ignition of her powers and Rogue would have to spe the rest of her life knowing that she was to blame. A sad twist indeed on this you Romeo and Juliet was that a portion of his consciousness will always reside inside Rogue herself.

☐ Finding herself without a home... shunned by her natural family, t self-proclaimed Mississippi swamprat soon took refuge in the arms of a fellow mutc who would raise her as her own. Unfortunately or perhaps fortunately, this was no other than the infamous Mystique (See File: Mystique). Mystique's first use of h "daughter's talents" was also the first time I happened to have the "pleasure" of makir her acquaintance. With one fell swoop, Rogue took out the former Avenger, Ms. Marv (See File: Carol Danvers/Ms. Marvel/Binary) and using her intimate knowledge of the tea began systematically dismantling my then comrades in arms: The Avengers. With masterpiece of strategy she absorbed the powers of Captain America and Thor all in desperate bid to free her mother's team, the Brotherhood of Evil Mutants (See File: Brotherhood of Evil Mutants II) from Ryker's Island prison. This plan was narrowly thwarted by the remainir Avengers, myself included, and Rogue and Mystique quickly made their departure.

☐ During the course of this plan, however, a startling revolution occurred as Rogue four that she had accidentally made a permanent transfer of the psyche and powers of M Marvel. In a fit of shock and dismay, Rogue even attempted to murder the helpless bod of Carol Danvers by throwing her off the Golden Gate bridge. Perhaps this was in horr at what she had done, but whatever the motivation, it has yet to be explaine Furthermore, Rogue's mind has since become a mesh between that of Carol Danve and her own to such an extent that one can only guess where one begins and th other ends. There have even been times when the Carol Danvers side of her h taken dominance of their shared body.

ENTER DELETE E

FILES

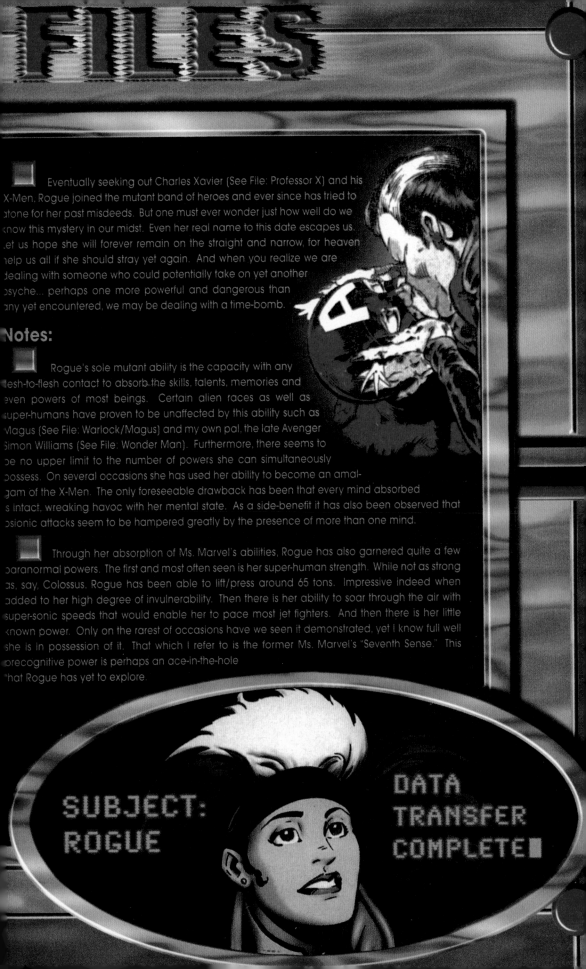

Eventually seeking out Charles Xavier (See File: Professor X) and his X-Men, Rogue joined the mutant band of heroes and ever since has tried to atone for her past misdeeds. But one must ever wonder just how well do we know this mystery in our midst. Even her real name to this date escapes us. Let us hope she will forever remain on the straight and narrow, for heaven help us all if she should stray yet again. And when you realize we are dealing with someone who could potentially take on yet another psyche... perhaps one more powerful and dangerous than any yet encountered, we may be dealing with a time-bomb.

Notes:

Rogue's sole mutant ability is the capacity with any flesh-to-flesh contact to absorb the skills, talents, memories and even powers of most beings. Certain alien races as well as super-humans have proven to be unaffected by this ability such as Magus (See File: Warlock/Magus) and my own pal, the late Avenger Simon Williams (See File: Wonder Man). Furthermore, there seems to be no upper limit to the number of powers she can simultaneously possess. On several occasions she has used her ability to become an amalgam of the X-Men. The only foreseeable drawback has been that every mind absorbed is intact, wreaking havoc with her mental state. As a side-benefit it has also been observed that psionic attacks seem to be hampered greatly by the presence of more than one mind.

Through her absorption of Ms. Marvel's abilities, Rogue has also garnered quite a few paranormal powers. The first and most often seen is her super-human strength. While not as strong as, say, Colossus, Rogue has been able to lift/press around 65 tons. Impressive indeed when added to her high degree of invulnerability. Then there is her ability to soar through the air with super-sonic speeds that would enable her to pace most jet fighters. And then there is her little known power. Only on the rarest of occasions have we seen it demonstrated, yet I know full well she is in possession of it. That which I refer to is the former Ms. Marvel's "Seventh Sense." This precognitive power is perhaps an ace-in-the-hole that Rogue has yet to explore.

SUBJECT: ROGUE

DATA TRANSFER COMPLETE

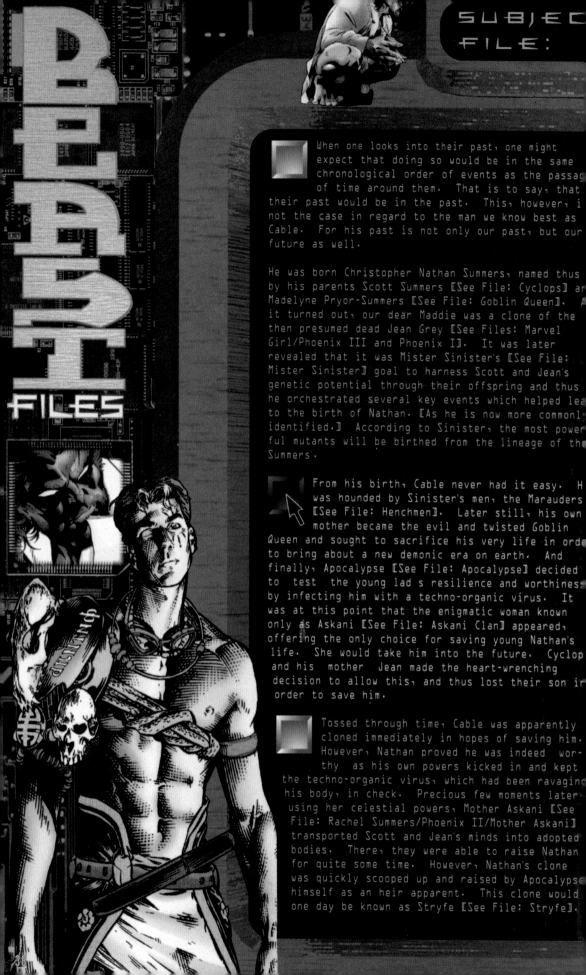

BEAST FILES

When one looks into their past, one might expect that doing so would be in the same chronological order of events as the passage of time around them. That is to say, that their past would be in the past. This, however, is not the case in regard to the man we know best as Cable. For his past is not only our past, but our future as well.

He was born Christopher Nathan Summers, named thus by his parents Scott Summers [See File: Cyclops] and Madelyne Pryor-Summers [See File: Goblin Queen]. As it turned out, our dear Maddie was a clone of the then presumed dead Jean Grey [See Files: Marvel Girl/Phoenix III and Phoenix I]. It was later revealed that it was Mister Sinister's [See File: Mister Sinister] goal to harness Scott and Jean's genetic potential through their offspring and thus he orchestrated several key events which helped lead to the birth of Nathan. [As he is now more commonly identified.] According to Sinister, the most powerful mutants will be birthed from the lineage of the Summers'.

From his birth, Cable never had it easy. He was hounded by Sinister's men, the Marauders [See File: Henchmen]. Later still, his own mother became the evil and twisted Goblin Queen and sought to sacrifice his very life in order to bring about a new demonic era on earth. And finally, Apocalypse [See File: Apocalypse] decided to test the young lad's resilience and worthiness by infecting him with a techno-organic virus. It was at this point that the enigmatic woman known only as Askani [See File: Askani Clan] appeared, offering the only choice for saving young Nathan's life. She would take him into the future. Cyclops and his mother Jean made the heart-wrenching decision to allow this, and thus lost their son in order to save him.

Tossed through time, Cable was apparently cloned immediately in hopes of saving him. However, Nathan proved he was indeed worthy as his own powers kicked in and kept the techno-organic virus, which had been ravaging his body, in check. Precious few moments later using her celestial powers, Mother Askani [See File: Rachel Summers/Phoenix II/Mother Askani] transported Scott and Jean's minds into adopted bodies. There, they were able to raise Nathan for quite some time. However, Nathan's clone was quickly scooped up and raised by Apocalypse himself as an heir apparent. This clone would one day be known as Stryfe [See File: Stryfe].

CABLE/NATHAN SUMMERS-DAYSPRING/ASKANI'SON

"WE SHOULD ALL BE CONCERNED ABOUT THE FUTURE BECAUSE WE WILL HAVE TO SPEND
THE REST OF OUR LIVES THERE." -- CHARLES FRANKLIN KETTERING

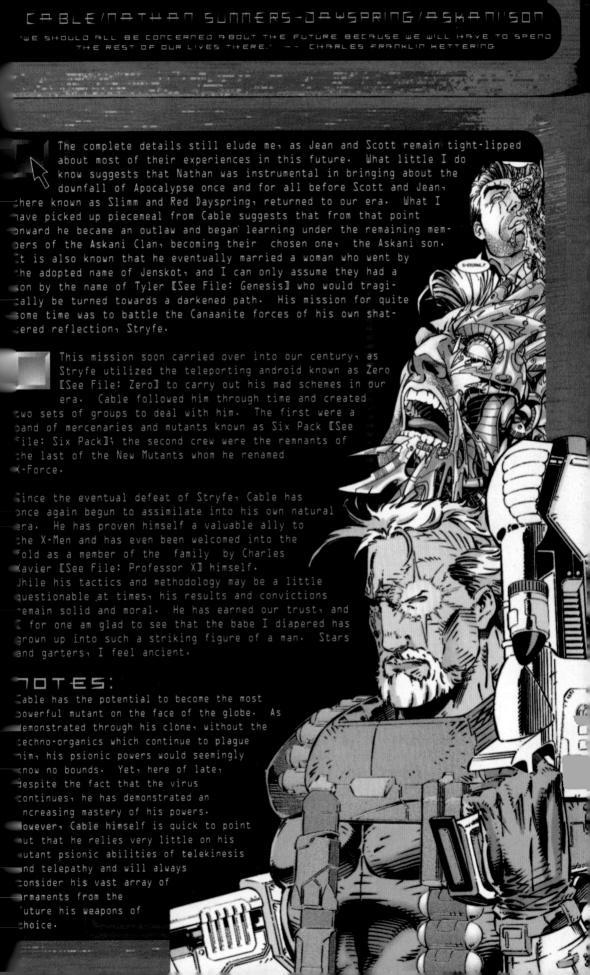

The complete details still elude me, as Jean and Scott remain tight-lipped about most of their experiences in this future. What little I do know suggests that Nathan was instrumental in bringing about the downfall of Apocalypse once and for all before Scott and Jean, there known as Slimm and Red Dayspring, returned to our era. What I have picked up piecemeal from Cable suggests that from that point onward he became an outlaw and began learning under the remaining members of the Askani Clan, becoming their chosen one, the Askani son. It is also known that he eventually married a woman who went by the adopted name of Jenskot, and I can only assume they had a son by the name of Tyler [See File: Genesis] who would tragically be turned towards a darkened path. His mission for quite some time was to battle the Canaanite forces of his own shattered reflection, Stryfe.

This mission soon carried over into our century, as Stryfe utilized the teleporting android known as Zero [See File: Zero] to carry out his mad schemes in our era. Cable followed him through time and created two sets of groups to deal with him. The first were a band of mercenaries and mutants known as Six Pack [See File: Six Pack]; the second crew were the remnants of the last of the New Mutants whom he renamed X-Force.

Since the eventual defeat of Stryfe, Cable has once again begun to assimilate into his own natural era. He has proven himself a valuable ally to the X-Men and has even been welcomed into the fold as a member of the family by Charles Xavier [See File: Professor X] himself. While his tactics and methodology may be a little questionable at times, his results and convictions remain solid and moral. He has earned our trust, and I for one am glad to see that the babe I diapered has grown up into such a striking figure of a man. Stars and garters, I feel ancient.

NOTES:
Cable has the potential to become the most powerful mutant on the face of the globe. As demonstrated through his clone, without the techno-organics which continue to plague him, his psionic powers would seemingly know no bounds. Yet, here of late, despite the fact that the virus continues, he has demonstrated an increasing mastery of his powers. However, Cable himself is quick to point out that he relies very little on his mutant psionic abilities of telekinesis and telepathy and will always consider his vast array of armaments from the future his weapons of choice.

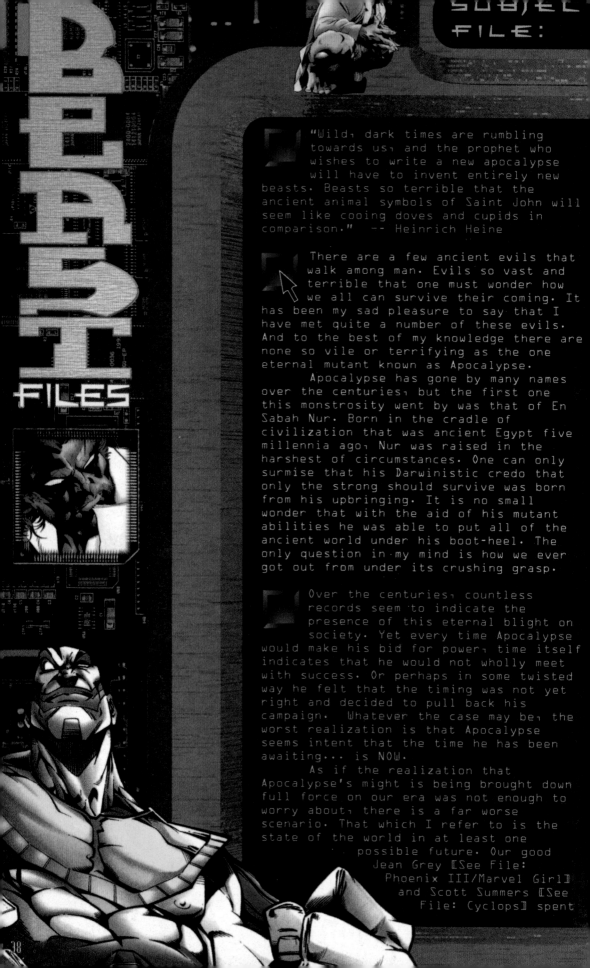

BEAST FILES

"Wild, dark times are rumbling towards us, and the prophet who wishes to write a new apocalypse will have to invent entirely new beasts. Beasts so terrible that the ancient animal symbols of Saint John will seem like cooing doves and cupids in comparison." -- Heinrich Heine

There are a few ancient evils that walk among man. Evils so vast and terrible that one must wonder how we all can survive their coming. It has been my sad pleasure to say that I have met quite a number of these evils. And to the best of my knowledge there are none so vile or terrifying as the one eternal mutant known as Apocalypse.

Apocalypse has gone by many names over the centuries, but the first one this monstrosity went by was that of En Sabah Nur. Born in the cradle of civilization that was ancient Egypt five millennia ago, Nur was raised in the harshest of circumstances. One can only surmise that his Darwinistic credo that only the strong should survive was born from his upbringing. It is no small wonder that with the aid of his mutant abilities he was able to put all of the ancient world under his boot-heel. The only question in my mind is how we ever got out from under its crushing grasp.

Over the centuries, countless records seem to indicate the presence of this eternal blight on society. Yet every time Apocalypse would make his bid for power, time itself indicates that he would not wholly meet with success. Or perhaps in some twisted way he felt that the timing was not yet right and decided to pull back his campaign. Whatever the case may be, the worst realization is that Apocalypse seems intent that the time he has been awaiting... is NOW.

As if the realization that Apocalypse's might is being brought down full force on our era was not enough to worry about, there is a far worse scenario. That which I refer to is the state of the world in at least one possible future. Our good Jean Grey [See File: Phoenix III/Marvel Girl] and Scott Summers [See File: Cyclops] spent

their honeymoon in this future world raising their son, Cable
[See File: Christopher Summers/Nathan Dayspring]. They are reluc-
tant at best to speak of that which they know, but from what
I've been able to gather...
Apocalypse wins.

«NOTES»

Apocalypse's mutant
ability is that of
complete molecular
control. Every cell of his
body responds to his every
desire. There seems to be
far more to him than that,
but extrapolating on this
alone we have a being who
may well be unstoppable.
Further add to this the
fact that he augments his
own natural mutant
abilities with technology
scavenged from the god-like
alien Celestials' craft
known as Ship [See File:
Ship]. If indeed there is a
way for us to stop him and all of the abilities in
his arsenal, I am at a loss for a suggestion. The
most we've been able to perform against him to date
is damage control and setbacks to his schemes of
utter world-wide ruin.

Unfortunately, he is not alone in his
mad dreams of carnage. Countless mutant
factions seem to bear some connection or
allegiance to Apocalypse. There are
the obvious groups: The Horsemen
[See Appendix: Horsemen of
Apocalypse], The Dark Riders
[See File: Henchmen], and the
Alliance of Evil [See
Appendix: Alliance of Evil].
But there seem to be ties
to Mister Sinister and by
extension those groups
in the employ of
Sinister. And the
newest revealed ally
in the form of the
blind precognitive
Ozymandius [Note: File
needed for Ozy]. There
may yet be more
undiscovered allies,
but only time will tell.
And time is definitely the most
powerful ally Apocalypse has.

«CASE FILE COMPLETE»

Like moths to a flame, somehow men of great charisma seem to attract the devotion of men around them. Not all of the groups the X-Men have faced over the years were teams. Quite frankly most of them were a collection of mutants who centered around a single individual. Thus, there is usually less to them as individuals than there is to them as a collective whole. That is why the creation of this file is necessary, as it will serve to house the collection of sheep aptly named: The Henchmen.

THE FOUR HORSEMEN OF APOCALYPSE:

While the roster of this quartet seems to change from time to time, Apocalypse's [See File: Apocalypse] reference to the Biblical four horsemen seems to be a fixation. Famine, Pestilence, War and Death will always be the names, though the players themselves may change. Usually these mutants seem to be those augmented in power by Apocalypse. The most glaring example would be that of the startling transformation our own Warren Worthington [See File: Angel/Archangel] underwent to become the Death horseman.

THE DARK RIDERS:

The Dark Riders are a group of fanatical mutants devoted wholly to the ideals represented by Apocalypse. However, unlike the Horsemen, they do not solely rely on their allegiance to Apocalypse himself. They have, in fact, shown that they are willing to follow anyone [See File: Genesis] who holds these same ideals and follow them through to the bitter end.

THE MARAUDERS:

The engine of destruction known collectively as the Marauders is a startling bunch indeed. While it is known that they all willingly follow the mastermind, Mister Sinister [See File: Mister Sinister], the group's true goal remains an unknown quantity.

INITIATE HOLOGRAM
THE DARK RIDERS

38

Furthermore is the startling realization that most of the group, if not all of them, are clones. As to the whereabouts of the originals, that remains to be seen. There is also the question as to why Sinister hasn't mass-produced a virtual army of Marauders; perhaps this is simply not an option. Let us hope so, as the Marauders were directly responsible for more mutant deaths than any other group to date.

THE NASTY BOYS:

This group of Sinister's seems to be his core strike force these days. As to group motivations, one can only guess they serve their master out of fear. Whether they too, like the Marauders, are clones or not remains to be seen. Whatever the case may be, they are a dangerous lot and should be treated as such.

MLF:

This group was created by Stryfe to further aid him in his mad schemes in our time period. Since Stryfe has shuffled off this mortal coil, they soon found a new master in Reignfire [See file: Sunspot]. However, soon after Reignfire's tenure as leader, they began to follow Dani [See File: Mirage]. Let us hope our former New Mutant can keep them in check.

PRESS GANG:

The island of Genosha may forever scar our memories as a shining example of racial inequality in its subjugation of their mutant populace as mutates. The saddest part, however, was that those mutants chose to use their powers to aid the state of Genosha in the subjugation of their mutant brethren. While the majority of the mutant populace suffered as near-mindless slaves, the select few members of the Press Gang lived the good life. Since the crumbling of the Genoshan hierarchy it is unknown at present where this group will pledge its allegiance.

UPSTARTS:

A group of rich mutants whose credo is merely the seeking of one thrill after another. They all fancy themselves to be leaders, but are instead nothing more than puppets on a string. And the man pulling their every movement is the enigmatic omnipath: Gamesmaster [See File: Gamesmaster.

ACOLYTES:

To my knowledge there exists no more fanatical a following than those found in the former Magneto's [See File: Magneto] Acolytes. This group believes that the master of magnetism is a god. Both Exodus [See File: Exodus] and Fabian Cortez [See File: Fabian Cortez] have stepped up to fill their "messiah's" shoes during his absence as self-proclaimed "prophets." Since the fall of Avalon to Earth and the revival of Magneto as the young Joseph, it is unknown exact-ly what the final fate of the Acolytes will be.

«INITIATE HOLOGRAM»
NASTY BOYS

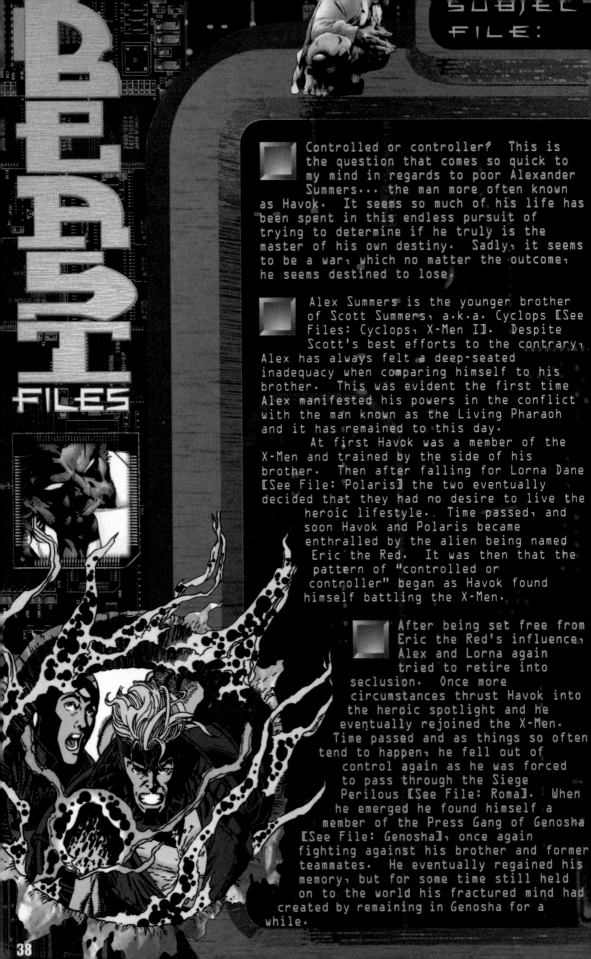

BEAST FILES

☐ Controlled or controller? This is the question that comes so quick to my mind in regards to poor Alexander Summers... the man more often known as Havok. It seems so much of his life has been spent in this endless pursuit of trying to determine if he truly is the master of his own destiny. Sadly, it seems to be a war, which no matter the outcome, he seems destined to lose.

☐ Alex Summers is the younger brother of Scott Summers, a.k.a. Cyclops [See Files: Cyclops, X-Men I]. Despite Scott's best efforts to the contrary, Alex has always felt a deep-seated inadequacy when comparing himself to his brother. This was evident the first time Alex manifested his powers in the conflict with the man known as the Living Pharaoh and it has remained to this day.

At first Havok was a member of the X-Men and trained by the side of his brother. Then after falling for Lorna Dane [See File: Polaris] the two eventually decided that they had no desire to live the heroic lifestyle. Time passed, and soon Havok and Polaris became enthralled by the alien being named Eric the Red. It was then that the pattern of "controlled or controller" began as Havok found himself battling the X-Men.

☐ After being set free from Eric the Red's influence, Alex and Lorna again tried to retire into seclusion. Once more circumstances thrust Havok into the heroic spotlight and he eventually rejoined the X-Men. Time passed and as things so often tend to happen, he fell out of control again as he was forced to pass through the Siege Perilous [See File: Roma]. When he emerged he found himself a member of the Press Gang of Genosha [See File: Genosha], once again fighting against his brother and former teammates. He eventually regained his memory, but for some time still held on to the world his fractured mind had created by remaining in Genosha for a while.

Eventually Havok once again returned to the fold, only this time as the team leader of a new government-sanctioned branch of X-Factor. For the first time, the mantle of leadership had been passed down from his brother to him, and the pressure produced a heavy weight.

Tragedy struck with the death of Jaime Madrox [See File: Multiple Man] from the Legacy Virus. Once again Havok found himself under the influence of someone other than himself, Malice. Oddly, Mister Sinister helped Polaris to eradicate this presence from Havok, and he was soon back with his team once more.

A short time ago, however, it appears my counterpart, the so-called Dark Beast [See File: Dark Beast, Age of Apocalypse] abducted poor Alex and performed some more personality alterations on him. Whatever my shadow self did to him, however, may this time be irreversible. Only time will tell the extent of the damage done, or if Alex will ever be back to his own true self. If indeed that is even a possibility, one can only hope that the end result would be a full and healthy mind. But I fear the worst.

‹NOTES››

Havok has the ability to channel and store massive amounts of ambient cosmic radiation and focus these into bolts of pure plasma through his hands. The sheer force and power which are his to command have been said to be enough to level a mountain. While this has not ever been fully tested, a close enough approximation was seen when he brought his immense powers to bear on the man-mountain known as the Hulk [See File: Hulk]. An interesting side benefit seems to be that his powers are ineffective against his brother Cyclops and vice versa. Small comfort indeed if we should happen to find ourselves crossing paths with him, but perhaps this advantage, no matter how slim, may be enough.

STORM

"She moves like a goddess, and she looks like a queen." --- Alexander Pope

We live in a world frequented by deities long thought myth. Hercules and Thor, two legendary gods of lore, have been seen to not only be real people... but I myself have fought alongside them on numerous occasions. In fact, many are the times I've even found myself at odds with the powers above and below. Yet through it all, never have I met someone more regal of bearing, more stunning of countenance, more worthy of the mantle of goddess than our own fair Ororo Munroe.

BEAST

Storm was born in America and named Ororo, which means beauty, by her loving parents. While she was still very young, she was taken with them on a diplomatic mission to Egypt where the cruel hand of fate would step in. While there, a terrorist air raid would cause a building to collapse on the Munroes including Ororo, killing her parents instantly and forever giving the young lady a severe case of claustrophobia.

After her rescue, Ororo found herself an orphan in a strange land and was quickly recruited into a band of children pickpockets and minor thieves just to stay alive. During one fateful day she happened to choose an American by the name of Charles Xavier [See File: Professor X] as a mark for her pickpocketing. Unknown to the young Ororo, he was a mutant, gifted with telepathic powers which froze her in her tracks as she tried to evade him. As Xavier probed her mind, he realized instantly she was, like him, a mutant. At that very moment, the use of Xavier's powers alerted him to the presence of the malevolent mutant telepath named Amahl Farouk [See File: Shadow King], and he was unable to further explore his find in Ororo.

However, he did make a note to keep tabs on her and he did just that.

Ororo was traveling through Kenya when her mutant powers first manifested themselves. The people marveled at her ability to control the weather and declared her a goddess. Realizing the folly in this, she herself declared that she was instead a servant of the Bright Lady and not a true goddess herself. From stories told me, however, this did not fully daunt her worshippers.

It was during her time as the "goddess" that Professor X came to her and recruited her as a member of his "new" X-Men, a team formed to save the original X-Men from the mutant island of Krakoa. From that moment onward, Storm has been a part of the X-Men, first serving dutifully as a member, and then later, during Cyclops' leave from the group, as team leader.

Over the years, many changes have occurred around her. She's been through a phase of outward coldness and rebellion. She's been

temperature changes was later found to be her body's ability to regulate its temperature from the standard 98.6 degrees Fahrenheit to match whatever weather conditions existed around her at any given moment. There does, however, seem to be a limit to the stress her body can withstand from such changes. Her eyes are most curious however, as they exhibit an almost feline look during normal time, and turn completely white and devoid of iris or pupil when she is actively utilizing her powers. I can only assume that her eyes have an inborn defense against flying debris which her winds may cause, thus protecting her eyes from damage. Truly an amazing and powerful example of genetic mutation at its zenith.

stripped of her powers. She's been reverted to childhood. Turned into a Genoshan mutate. Through it all there were many constants... iron will, inner strength, and tactical reasoning reign paramount in her nature.

NOTES:

Storm possesses the most startling mutation I have yet to see. Through some means she is capable of harnessing all of the varied forces of nature for various effects. She can hurl or summon lightning, create hurricane force winds, or even rain, sleet, or snow.

As a side benefit, Storm can not only utilize her powers in an offensive manner but in a defensive one as well. By utilizing her winds she can carry herself aloft in a form of simulated flight, and can also use them to deflect most physically based attacks.

Another couple of curious mutations are those concerning both her eyes and her skin. What once appeared to be an immunity to

NIGHTCRAWLER

"I have been one acquainted with the night." — Robert Frost

Nightcrawler, a word most oft associated with large earthworms which one digs for in the middle of the night. The term itself conjures up images of all of the creepy-crawly "things that go bump in the night." It is the stuff of horror. And when you find yourself gazing into the yellowy eyes of one Kurt Wagner, a man whose flesh is covered in a dark velvety fur, his canine teeth jutting out in a vampiric fashion, his ears coming to a devilish point, and his tail most certainly fitting with what one would expect from a demon, the term Nightcrawler does seem to fit. But that, of course, would only apply if one subscribed to the notion that appearances are the sole judge of a man.

Much of Kurt's early history had been a mystery... even to himself. The largest piece of information which had been previously missing was the identity of his parents. The maternal side of this question has recently been answered in the form of X-Factor's infamous blue-hued metamorph, Mystique

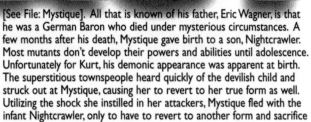

[See File: Mystique]. All that is known of his father, Eric Wagner, is that he was a German Baron who died under mysterious circumstances. A few months after his death, Mystique gave birth to a son, Nightcrawler. Most mutants don't develop their powers and abilities until adolescence. Unfortunately for Kurt, his demonic appearance was apparent at birth. The superstitious townspeople heard quickly of the devilish child and struck out at Mystique, causing her to revert to her true form as well. Utilizing the shock she instilled in her attackers, Mystique fled with the infant Nightcrawler, only to have to revert to another form and sacrifice him to save herself, by throwing him over a cliff into the raging waters below.

Miraculously, Nightcrawler survived the fall as well as certain drowning. Sometime later he was found by the Gypsy sorceress Margali Szardos. He was raised in the circus alongside Margali's own children, Jemain [See File: Daytripper/Amanda Sefton] and Stefan. Trained from his early childhood to be an aerial acrobat on the trapeze, Kurt's unnatural physical characteristics made him ideal for the rigors involved. Before long, he took his place as the star of the air, until one fateful day when Jemain suffered what would surely have been a fatal fall. In that instant Kurt's mutant power of teleportation activated, and using it, he saved her life.

This brought him to the attention of a Texas circus owner who wanted Kurt as a star in his freak show. Having no desire to play the freak for any man, Kurt struck out on his own. Disaster followed tragedy as he witnessed his "brother" Stefan killing multiple innocent children in an attempt to exorcise the demons from them. The two battled desperately, until Kurt accidentally crushed Stefan's skull, thus honoring a pact to kill his brother if Stefan's sanity should ever slip.

However, Kurt was quickly discovered by the townspeople who chased him through the streets, willing to destroy their own town in order to slay the demon they perceived as the cause of the carnage.

It was at this fateful point that Xavier [See File: Professor X] stepped into Kurt's life and forever changed it. Using his mental powers to stun the crowd, Xavier saved Nightcrawler from having a stake driven through his heart. Kurt was the first recruit of his "New" X-Men assembled to rescue the original team from the living island Krakoa.

From that day and years following, Nightcrawler was a cornerstone member of the X-Men, and fought unwaveringly alongside the team until he was badly injured in a battle with the Marauders [See Files: Henchmen, Mister Sinister] in the Morlock Tunnels [See Appendix: Morlocks]. Recovering from these injuries, Nightcrawler learned of the "death" of the X-Men in a battle in Dallas. Circumstances, however, quickly conspired to create the formation of a new team of superhumans built on the principles of the X-Men known as Excalibur. As one of the founding members, Nightcrawler has remained with the team to this day, serving through most of the team's existence as their leader.

If one judges the proverbial book by its cover, they would indeed be missing out on this treasure of a man. Sadly, that can be the case for most. But for those who dare to peer deeper into the heart of this swashbuckling

blue, almost indigo, fur not unlike myself. His fur, however, unlike mine, seems to radiate an aura which extends into the Darkforce dimension, thus causing him to become translucent while creeping through the shadows. Then there is the strange ability to adhere to practically any surface. In some manner, Nightcrawler is capable of walking along any surface similar to Spider-Man. It is my personal theory that he utilizes the energies from the Darkforce dimension to create a void surrounding his epidermal region, thus causing an attraction between the molecules to such an extent that he can travel along them easily.

His final and most used ability is his line-of-sight teleportation. By traveling through the Darkforce dimension, Kurt is able to seemingly traverse any distance instantaneously. The primary limitation to this seems to be that if he is unable to see where exactly he is teleporting to he runs the risk of teleporting inside solid matter, which would have a devastating and quite likely fatal reaction. Each teleportation is heralded by a loud sound affectionately referred to as a BAMF as well as the pungent odor of brimstone and smoke. The trip itself can be quite disconcerting as any matter traveling through the Darkforce dimension is slightly displaced. By taking a foe through a rapid succession of teleports, Kurt can easily stun them into unconsciousness.

<<END FILE>>

mutant acrobat, they will find a man of such depth, conviction, and warmth that they would see an angel where once a demon stood.

<<NOTES>>

Nightcrawler is a second generation mutant. As has been demonstrated by most mutants born of mutant parentage, his powers are much more diverse than the usual single-thread mutation. The first and most obvious example of his powers is that of his physical characteristics. He has on each of his hands only two fingers with an opposable thumb, while his feet have two forward toes and a thumb-like digit on the heel of each foot. His canine teeth are very prominent, almost vampiric in form, and he has a prehensile tail with a devilish point to it. This tail is a most astonishing formation as it has been seen to not only be capable of grasping items, but also capable of performing complex tasks such as the ability to duel an opponent effectively with a rapier. It has also proven strong enough and capable of gripping tight enough to support his weight or the weight of another.

The rest of his complex nature seems to revolve around darkness and has been shown to possess a link to the Darkforce dimension [See Files: Cloak, Darkstar. See Appendix: Dimensions]. His eyes are of a full yellow hue and devoid of a pupil. This has been proven to provide him with the capacity to see in near complete darkness. Mother Nature also saw fit to coat his entire body with a layer of

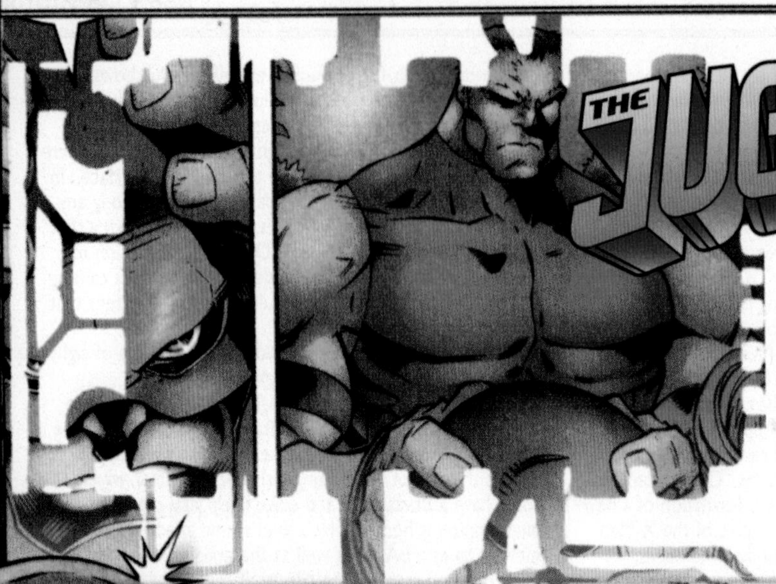

0 items

THE JUGGERNAUT

BEAST

"A great ball of fire about a mile in diameter, changing colors as it kept shooting upward, from deep purple to orange, expanding, growing bigger, rising as it was expanding, an elemental force freed from its bonds after being chained for billions of years."

—— William L. Lawrence

The description of the first atom bomb explosion is one wracked with horror, fear, confusion and awe. It is a force of nature which once unleashed, had a ripple effect throughout all of humanity for a while. Its power is unfathomable and frightening. These same emotions I know all too well. I experienced them the first time I met the man known to the world as the unstoppable Juggernaut.

The Juggernaut was born Cain Marko. Cain's father was a co-worker and partner with Charles Xavier's [See File: Professor X] father and a close friend of the family until one day Cain's father allowed an accident to occur which caused the death of Xavier's father. Eventually Charles' mother and the widowed Marko were married and Cain became his stepbrother.

Jealous of the high regard his father showed towards Charles, Cain began abusing the young boy both mentally and physically. The larger Cain used his brutality even further when he began to suspect Charles of possessing the mutant ability to read minds. Eventually another accident occurred with one of the older Marko's experiments when Cain accidentally caused a reaction to take place which spontaneously combusted. Acting quickly, the boys' father took them both to safety but himself perished from smoke inhalation.

The loss of a father who had never fully been close to him, coupled with his guilt at having caused the accident in the first place, only hastened the crumbling of Cain's fragile psyche. Irrationally Cain's mind chose to blame Xavier for the death of his father; he would continue to blame all things ill in his life on the young Charles, a pattern which continues to this day.

Not long after college both Xavier and Cain found themselves in the military. By a quirk of fate, the brothers were stationed in the same unit on their European tour. During a fire-fight, Cain became frightened and decided to try to go AWOL. In an attempt to save his brother from court-martial, Xavier tracked him down. By sheer accident Cain and Xavier found themselves in an ancient hidden temple of the great universal power known as Cyttorak. There on the altar, the impetuous Cain snatched up a large ruby red crystal which turned out to be the Crimson Crystal of Cyttorak. Reciting the inscription, power instantly began coursing through Cain, shaping and molding him into the being known as Juggernaut.

The power began feeding into him so rapidly that the walls and roof of the ancient cavern began closing in all around him. Realizing what was indeed happening and acting as quickly as he could, Xavier managed to make it to safety before the entire structure collapsed around him. . Knowing that a mystical change had happened to his brother and somehow using his psychic powers, Xavier prayed that the power of the Juggernaut had been contained forever.

Xavier's unspoken dreams were not to come true as years later the Juggernaut finally pummeled his way through his mountainous prison to freedom. Immediately, he made his way to America, moving ever forward with nothing standing in his way. It was by the narrowest of margins that the X-Men defeated him the first time with the aid of the Human Torch. And every subsequent defeat has been by ever narrowing margins. He truly lives up to his namesake, as he has gone toe-to-toe with such powerful beings as the Hulk [See File: Hulk] and Thor [See File: Thor], either triumphing or barely being beaten.

capacity in strength.

In addition, his body structure and mystical armor give him protection from conventional weaponry and are capable of withstanding the mountain-shattering blows of creatures such as the Hulk and Thor. Juggernaut is known to be able to generate a force field around himself that is completely impenetrable by any means, barring mental or magical attacks by a power higher than Cyttorak, which according to our good Dr. Strange [See File: Dr. Strange] does not exist. It is further said that once the Juggernaut begins moving, nothing can stop his forward progression. He is literally an unstoppable force. You can slow him, but nothing, not even the power of Thor's hammer Mjolnir, could halt him completely.

The Juggernaut's sole weakness is that of mental attacks. His armor, however, provides a complete psionic dampening field; thus to get to him you must first remove his helmet. In recent years, Juggernaut trimmed the size of his helmet and created a skullcap beneath it to further prevent this weakness from being exploited; thus it is not nearly the option it once had been.

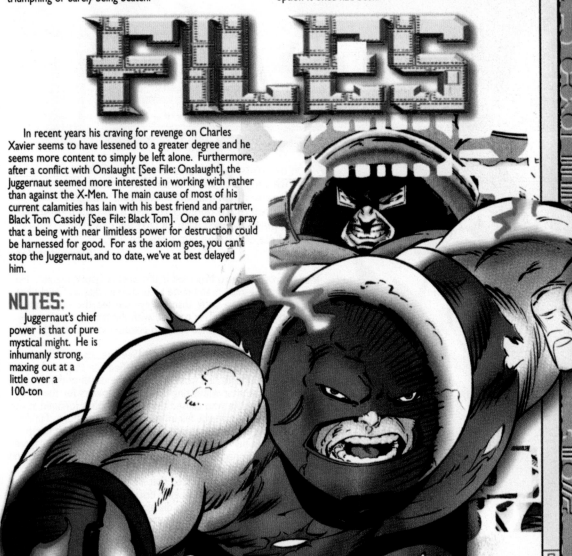

FILES

In recent years his craving for revenge on Charles Xavier seems to have lessened to a greater degree and he seems more content to simply be left alone. Furthermore, after a conflict with Onslaught [See File: Onslaught], the Juggernaut seemed more interested in working with rather than against the X-Men. The main cause of most of his current calamities has lain with his best friend and partner, Black Tom Cassidy [See File: Black Tom]. One can only pray that a being with near limitless power for destruction could be harnessed for good. For as the axiom goes, you can't stop the Juggernaut, and to date, we've at best delayed him.

NOTES:

Juggernaut's chief power is that of pure mystical might. He is inhumanly strong, maxing out at a little over a 100-ton

0 items

QUICKSILVER

BEAST

Wise wretch! With pleasures too refin'd to please;
With too much spirit to be e'er at ease;
With too much quickness ever to be taught;
With too much thinking to have a common thought.
You purchase pain with all that joy can give,
And die of nothing but a rage to live.

—Alexander Pope

Young, arrogant Pietro Maximoff is the world's fastest mutant. He is more commonly known, and quite accurately at that, as Quicksilver. With his ability to move faster than the eye can see, the world can seem a pretty slow place. This coupled with the factors surrounding the young man's very existence seem to create a virtual cascade of confusion and anger in his life.

Quicksilver and his twin sister Wanda [See File: Scarlet Witch] are both the offspring of Erik Magnus Lenscherr [See File: Magneto] and Magda Lenscherr. Magda fled from Erik after the death of their first-born daughter, after witnessing him use his powers for the first time in vengeance to slaughter the people who caused the child's death. Horrified at the brutality she witnessed, she felt that the man she fell in love with was no more. Further to her shock was the revelation that she was pregnant. Traveling alone through harsh weather and rough terrain, she made her way up the mountainous region of Wundagore. It was in the home of the High Evolutionary [See File: High Evolutionary] that Wanda and Pietro were born with the aid of the cow-woman Bova acting as midwife.

Shortly after the birth of the twins, Magda decided that life for them would be better off without her. Fearing for their lives if Erik should ever discover their existence, she made her way out into the harsh mountain winter, to die alone. Failing to place the children with his first choice for parentage, the retired super hero, the Whizzer [See File:

The Whizzer], the High Evolutionary eventually delivered the infants into the care of the Maximoffs, a pair of Gypsies who traveled the mountainous region surrounding Wundagore.

Early in their adolescence Pietro and Wanda learned of their mutant powers and soon after were forced to leave the Gypsies they had grown up with to make their way on their own. They were among the first mutants Professor Charles Xavier [See File: Professor X] approached about recruitment into what would prove to be the X-Men. They politely refused his offer and, had they not run afoul of a mob of angry villagers who witnessed the display of Wanda's powers, they may have never had anything to do with other mutants. At that moment, Magneto entered the picture, saving them from the mob and offering them a chance to join another mutant band. This time, they did not refuse and became founding members of the Brotherhood of Evil Mutants.

Quicksilver and his sister both soon tired of playing the role of villain. In a move as swift as his feet, the duo made headlines as the first mutant members to join the world-renowned Avengers. Only a couple of times since his joining has he strayed from the straight and narrow. Countless times he has proven himself as both an Avenger and later as a member of X-Factor.

Recently, with the events of Onslaught [See File: Onslaught], he along with the Black Widow were the only surviving members of the Avengers. Joining ranks with the X-Men for a short duration to keep an eye on the man known as Joseph [Note: A de-aged, amnesiac Magneto], he has since struck out on his own to find his own direction in life. What that choice will be, given the recent happenings in his life, remains to be seen.

FILES

NOTES:

Quicksilver's powers are all derived from beneficial mutations based around the concept of speed. His legs are superhumanly strong and quite capable of leg-pressing approximately 10 tons in weight. When using this strength in forward locomotion, he has been observed to move at speeds up to Mach 3. Presently, however, there is no known top speed, as it has never successfully been gauged. He has, however, been seen defying gravity by running straight up the sides of buildings and using the surface tension of water to run across its surface.

Further, his body has increased durability, metabolism, reflexes, and endurance which allow him to move at supersonic speeds for large time spans. The amount of his physical durability is unknown, but seemingly must be immense to withstand the air resistance and friction caused by moving at such high velocities. His metabolism and endurance are on a superhuman scale, allowing him to be immune to most fatigue poisons as well as heal himself far faster than normal if injured. His reflexes as well seem to stem from a difference in perceptions. The motor functions of his brain seem to work at an accelerated rate that is proportional to the speed of his body. Thus, to him the entire world is moving in slow motion, and he is the only one moving at proper speed.

0 items

THE PERFECT MAN!

THE SUPER-SOLDIER SERUM IS A SUCCESS! WITH STRENGTH, SPEED AND REFLEXES ENHANCED TO THE LIMIT OF HUMAN CAPACITY--

Captain America

"Then join hand in hand,
Brave Americans all!
By uniting we stand,
by dividing we fall."

— John Dickinson

We all need rallying points in our lives. A symbol to look towards and direct our efforts through. A place in our hearts where we can focus our efforts, and nothing can stand against us. Throughout history, there have been many shining examples, but none have been more enduring as

BEAST

those personified by one man.
A man known to all as Captain America.

Steve Rogers was born during the Depression in New York City, and spent much of his formative years there. He grew up a sickly, frail young man in a poor family. Despite the terrible circumstances surrounding him at such a tender age, his heart was forever thinking of others. When he saw newsreel footage of the Nazi activities in Europe, he was horrified and immediately attempted to enlist. Unfortunately, his frail stature made him unsuitable as an enlisted man, but his pleas to be allowed to join despite his shortcomings caused him to be noticed by a General who decided this young man's heart and physical form would make him the perfect specimen for a secret government experiment dubbed Operation: Rebirth.

Thus, that after weeks of testing, Steve Rogers became the initial recipient of the "Super-Soldier Serum." It immediately made his weak young body as perfect as a human body can be, in every way. The experiment's success, however, was short-lived as a Nazi spy immediately murdered Dr. Erskine. Erskine, who was wary of the dangers of spies, had not fully committed the process to paper, and thus the secret of the process died with him.

However, after outfitting and training Rogers, America had a new fighting symbol for her boys fighting in WWII. And through his exploits, countless lives were saved. For the duration of his WWII activities, Captain America teamed up with his teen-aged sidekick, Bucky. The duo were loved by all, until the fateful day when they tried to intercept a deadly radio-guided bomb in the final days of the war. Bucky and Cap climbed aboard the deadly plane and did their best to defuse the bomb. However, at the last moment, Rogers was thrown from the plane into the icy waters below, while the plane exploded shortly afterwards, killing Bucky.

Decades later Captain America was found by a group of Eskimos in a block of ice. The Eskimos worshipped the man trapped in the ice as a god, until The Sub-Mariner [See File: Namor] in one of his irrational fits of anger, attacked the Eskimos and hurled the block of ice into the sea. A few days later, his body was found floating in the water by the Avengers, completely thawed. To the newly formed Avengers' surprise, the strange man was indeed Captain America, and he turned out to be alive, saved from death by the complex nature of the serum working in his blood as he lay in suspended animation.

It was in his capacity as an Avenger that Captain America has most often been remembered. He is at his best when leading or working with "earth's mightiest heroes" and is without a doubt one of that team's greatest assets. His brilliant tactics, boundless combat experience, and battle prowess have served him well no matter what menace he has come to face. He is, indeed, an inspiration to us all.

NOTES:

Captain America is the peak of human perfection. The super-soldier serum coursing through his veins allows him great strength, endurance, agility, and reactions that far exceed the greatest Olympic athletes in any field. He can lift/press around 800 lbs, and run non-stop for extended periods of time. His body doesn't seem to produce fatigue poisons, and is therefore capable of working with very little rest. He has also displayed an accelerated healing ability that is attributed to his higher metabolism. Some theorize that he may be immune to aging; however, this remains to be seen.

Cap's skills are also very finely honed. He has proven himself to be a master of at least 12 distinctive martial arts as well as gymnastics; he combines them together with his vast experience to form a fighting style uniquely his. His indestructible shield is the only known synthesis of adamantium and vibranium. Adamantium is the hardest metal in the world, while vibranium is a metal capable of absorbing both force and sound completely. Thus through this synthesis, Cap does not experience any recoil from the impact of any projectile hitting his shield. Further, he has learned how to utilize the aerodynamic disc shape of his shield as a thrown weapon with such skill that he can cause it to impact any desired target and have it rebound back to any point he wishes.

His most powerful ability, however, is that of his mind. There is no greater tactical mind in all of my experiences than his. No one can compare with the analytical genius that Cap has displayed in countless battle situations. Captain America believes intensely that where there is a will there is a way. And where he is concerned, as long as there is an America to fight for and freedom to defend, there is always a will.

THE INCREDIBLE HULK

"It's not easy being green."
— Kermit the Frog

BEAST

What would go through your mind if you were caught in a nuclear explosion? The fraction of a second you had to live would scarcely be time enough to fully comprehend what was going on around you. The poetic among us would like to think that one's life would flash before his eyes shortly before he would becoming atomized by the intense heat and force generated by the blast's unrivaled power. Now, imagine being someone who no only was faced with this situation, but miraculously survived it. Further compound this quandary with the possibility that you now can change into the strongest being on Earth, but are cursed with the fact that you're hated, hunted, and hounded by nearly everyone else, all the while having to deal with the very problems characterized by the memories that flashed through your mind in that instant you thought you were going to die. Thus, in short, is the nature of the creature known as the Incredible Hulk.

Dr. Robert Bruce Banner was a nuclear physicist working specifically in the study of gamma radiation. He worked laboriously for the government, spearheading the development of new type of nuclear weapon, the Gamma Bomb. It was during the very first testing that Banner was faced with saving the life of a young Rick Jones who had inadvertently wandered into the testing facility on a dare. Bruce asked that the testing be stopped while he got the young man to safety, but because the man entrusted with stopping the testing was a foreign agent, the countdown was not halted. And so it was that Bruce hurled Rick Jones into the relative safety of a trench and the gamma bomb exploded, bathing his body with lethal amounts of the strange radiation.

Surprisingly, Banner not only survived, but soon found that he could transform into a superhumanly strong being. At first he only changed at night, retained his human intellect, and had a gray pigment to his skin. Also, his strength was not even half of what his current capacity is. But over time this was proven to be only a transitional stage, as his mind slowly regressed into a childlike state. Eventually his transformations were no longer triggered by the lack of daylight; instead they were initiated by the onset of severe emotional distress, while his skin became an emerald green. Most notably, anger drove this bestial form of his, and mass destruction was sure to follow in the creature's wake.

A large portion of the damage done around the Hulk, however, was not due to the direct actions of the Hulk, but instead to the fact that the Hulk himself was pursued at every turn by the military who wanted to destroy him, as well as other various agencies and other superhumans who wished to harness the Hulk's power

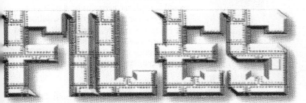

for their own benefit. During this time as well, Banner was able to maintain a relationship that would later blossom into a marriage with Elizabeth "Betty" Ross, the daughter of General Thaddeus E. "Thunderbolt" Ross. It was Thunderbolt Ross who most notably was responsible for much of the pursuit of the Hulk, while it was Betty who consistently responsible for calming the Hulk, triggering the transformation back into Banner.

Over the years, numerous transformations surrounding the creature have occurred. There were times when the Hulk's body was still governed by Banner's intellect. There was a time as well that Banner himself was separated somehow from the Hulk's body. Still later there was a gray-hued version, similar to the first incarnation, but he was much more cunning. In this incarnation, he retained much of Banner's intellect, but absolutely no morality. This form also was much weaker in strength than the green version of himself, and apparently available to him only at night and further affected by the phases of the moon.

Shortly after this development, Dr. Leonard Samson [See File: Doc Samson], a noted psychologist and superhumanly strong being also powered by gamma radiation, realized that he might in fact be dealing with a mental disorder rather than something physical, as had been previously explored. Upon investigation, Samson found that Bruce Banner had a severe case of MPD (Multiple Personality Disorder). Banner's MPD was caused when, as a child, his father systematically abused both him and his mother, which resulted in the murder of his mother. Fearing emotion, Banner decided that emotions as a whole were bad, and also lost his childhood in the process, thus explaining why the release of emotion triggered the change to a childlike or very emotional being.

Samson was, for a time, able to merge the various aspects of Bruce into one collective being. However, sometime later, other changes occurred which further

complicated the development of the Hulk. For a time, whenever the Hulk grew angry, he would turn into his very fragile, human form of Bruce Banner, who reacted the same as had the green, childlike Hulk of years prior. Then when the Onslaught incident occurred, Hulk inexplicably split into two forms, and the Bruce Banner aspect disappeared, leaving behind only the Hulk aspect. This creature carved a destructive path across America, including the capture, if one can call it that, of an entire island in the Florida Keys. Recently, the Hulk has apparently, once again, been reintegrated with Bruce Banner; however the effects of this reunion remain to be seen.

NOTES:

First and foremost, as the green-skinned goliath is fond of saying, "Hulk is strongest one there is." And as far as is ascertainable, this is quite an accurate phrase indeed. The Hulk is generally accepted as being able to easily lift/press over 100 tons. In years past, however, he has been observed to have a far greater strength, almost exponentially increased, exerted when Hulk becomes more angry. There were even reports of him lifting as much as 500 tons or more, as well as one account where he actually supported the weight of an entire mountain on his back. What exactly his current strength level is in his latest form remains to be seen, but it is highly unlikely that his strength will be matched easily.

In conjunction with his great strength, the Hulk possesses the capacity to make standing leaps up to 3 miles in distance in a single bound. Further, his skin is dense enough to easily repel most attacks on him, turning them into the slightest of inconveniences and nothing more than minor annoyances. Couple this with his healing factor which has proven effective enough to heal him nearly instantly when he was disemboweled, and you have a being that quite possibly may not be destroyed by anything short of his being ground zero during a nuclear blast.

As for my personal belief on the origin of his powers, I would surmise that we are in fact dealing with a metamorph of the highest order. He is a metamorph capable of changing his shape only by acts of his unconscious mind, however, with no seeming limit to the way in which he can harness the vast amounts of energy stored within his body. Where exactly he draws the extra mass from and where it is stored when not in use bears further investigation, but quite literally we may just have seen the tip of the iceberg as far as all things regarding this poor, living example of Jekyll and Hyde is concerned.

0 items

YOU FEEL SAFE HERE, ORORO? TRULY SAFE?

I TOLD YOU, CALLISTO. THE TIME FOR WORDS HAS PASSED!

ALL SURFACE-DWELLERS UNDERSTAND...

BEAST

"He knew the anguish
of the marrow
The ague of the skeletons;
No contact possible to flesh
Allayed the fever of the bone."
— T. S. Eliot

Over the years the X-Men has been the home for the reforming of those members of mutantkind who have used their powers on the "wrong side." Wolverine was the first among us who exhibited less than stalwart behavior, clearly displaying a propensity for violence. Yet through the years and the Professor's guiding hand he has proven an invaluable asset and cornerstone of all the X-Men represent. Rogue is yet another, who as a young teen raised by Mystique, had committed various acts of violence. Gambit would years later prove to be a part of one of the greatest mutant atrocities, dubbed the Mutant Massacre. And our visitor from the future, Bishop, made his debut into our time violently apprehending other time-lost mutant criminals from his future era. Yet none among us have yet been as troubled as the latest member in our ranks, the young woman known only as Marrow.

Marrow's story begins beneath the glimmer of the New York City skyline... far below in the catacombs known as the Morlock Tunnels [See file: Morlocks]. These tunnels, which were claimed as their home, are the unused portions of both the sewer and subway system of New York and once housed a large mutant populace, known as the Morlocks and led by the woman named Callisto [See File: Callisto]. The tunnels were a home to all of the deformed mutants who simply believed that they were better off living apart from humanity until humanity was ready to accept them. Among their number was a little girl known only as Sarah, who though she did not possess any seeming powers save a loss of hair on her head and strangely shaped eyes, was reportedly a rallying point around which all the Morlocks felt a sense of hope and love in the most dismal of environments.

One of the most important points in Morlock history occurred with the trial by combat between Storm and Callisto. This battle was fought without powers, only with their respective skill with knives. Storm surprisingly won the duel, stabbing Callisto without killing her. Thus Storm inherited the mantle of leadership to the Morlocks, and immediately offered the Morlocks a place at Xavier's School to live. This offer was turned down, and they elected to remain beneath the city streets. Young Sarah viewed Callisto as a being of darkness and in her youth saw Storm as a bright goddess who might lead their people to the surface. Her hopes were in vain.

A scant year later, the Morlock tunnels were besieged by the merciless Marauders.[See file: Henchmen] and a multitude of them were slaughtered. Sarah somehow survived this tragedy with the help of Gambit, and through it all, still kept her sense of hope. This hope was shattered a year later with the coming of Colossus' [See File: Colossus] brother

AS REPRESENTATIVES OF HOMO SUPERIOR EVERYWHERE --

-- WE HOLD YOU ACCOUNTABLE.

Mikhail. Mikhail went mad and used his reality and dimensional shifting powers to shunt almost the entire Morlock populace to another world. On this world where survival was next to impossible, the Darwinistic belief that the strongest should survive was paramount. Mikhail's castle was placed on the top of a mountain peak called "the hill" which could only be reached by those strong enough to survive the climb plus combat all others who wished to reach the top as well.

It was in this environment that hatred welled up inside of her. She blamed the "upworlders" and even Storm for the state of their lives. For in her mind, had Storm led her people to overthrow the humans above, they would have lived their lives in the sun where they truly belonged. Perhaps this is what drove her up "the hill" and caused her to become the leader of a group of mutants, who had similarly made the climb, called Gene Nation.

Time passed differently for those on this world of Morlocks, and while it may have only been months for our time, nearly a decade had progressed for them. However, when Gene Nation returned to Earth, they brought all of their hatred for humanity and the X-Men with them. In their first known act they committed mass murder at a New York nightclub. Later two of their members committed other acts of murder in New Orleans. Then finally on the eve of the anniversary of the Morlock Massacre, they set out to destroy a subway full of humans they kidnapped with

Perhaps through the examples set by the X-Men and Spider-Man, a change of heart, pardon the pun, had occurred within Sarah. As it now appeared, she was more willing to amend her ways and use her powers as a member of the X-Men. However, the moral dilemma remains for the rest of the X-Men. Do we admit a member among us who has so ruthlessly consented to the slaughter of so many innocent humans? Do we have the right to make such a judgment call? If so, where do we draw the line, and what price do we pay for such power and authority? More frightening still, what if our hopes and efforts are in vain, and we only succeed in strengthening the skills of a deranged psychopath?

NOTES:

Marrow is a peculiar mutant at best. Her body can seemingly continuously produce extra bone marrow at a rapid rate over which she has no control. These bones stick out of her body in various spots, and she can literally pull them out of herself without undue harm. Once out of her, the bones resemble large daggers and have a cutting edge on them which prove to be just as sharp as the bone claws of Wolverine. How many of these daggers she can produce and use at any given time is unknown. Further peculiarities are the strange configuration of her eyes and circulatory system. What the exact purposes of these mutations are is as of yet a mystery.

incendiary bombs strapped to their chained bodies.

Wolverine, Callisto, Colossus and Storm all responded to this threat, only to find that Sarah had wanted to make a point about Storm's weakness. The timing mechanism to the bombs was fused with Sarah's own heart. The only way to stop the bombs from detonating, she told Storm, would be to stop her heart. With this revelation, Marrow gave Storm two of her own bone daggers, and the two dueled in similar fashion to how Storm and Callisto had years prior. Once again, Storm proved her resolve the only way she could, by ripping out young Sarah's heart with the timing mechanism still attached.

Marrow survived due to an oddity of her body which seems to have been born with two hearts and other extra organs. However, her hatred seemingly was not diminished. She reappeared with Callisto in a nightclub where Lila Cheney [See File: Lila Cheney] was performing. Here she faced off against Cable and Thornn [See Files: Cable and Thornn] in yet another duel and succeeded in stopping her. A short while after this she faced off against Spider-Man [See File: Spider-Man] in her unsuccessful attempt to assassinate government agent Peter Henry Gyrich. Spider-Man allowed her to leave after a stern lecture and it was a short while later that she met up once again with the X-Men.

Fantastic Four

"Nobody who has not been in the interior of a family can say what the difficulties of any individu of that family may be."
— Jane Austen

Family. It is the foundation upon which society is based. In a family we all learn that we have roles, responsibilities, friendship, order and even a little chaos to shake things up from time to time. But most importantly, it is within a well-functioning family that we first learn compassion, understanding, reasoning, discipline and all of these things tempered with love. Is it any wonder that those of us who have

BEAST

chosen to take to our own small families of heroic groups can look upon the first family among us with such pride? Th family being none other than the Fantastic Four. It all started quite by accident. A scientist named Reed Richards was competir with the world in a race... a space race. Hi designs were brilliant, and all seemed wel until the U.S. government threatened to cut the project's funding. Desperate have his goals materialize, he recruited his best friend and project pilot Benjamin J. Grimm, his girlfriend Susan Storm, and h little brother Johnny. All four of them snuck into the experimental rocket and soon found themselves blasting off into the depths of space.

Shortly after their departu they passed through the Van Alle belt, and just as Grimm had earlier predicted, the spaceship was ill equippe to handle the lethal doses of cosmic radiation which penetrated the ship and their bodies. Wracked with pain, Grimm valiantly steered the craft back to Earth and into a successful landing. Upon exiting their ship, they quickly found themselves transformed into beings